EFFECTIVE
INTERCULTURAL
COMMUNICATION

A. Scott Moreau, *series editor*

Also in the series:

EFFECTIVE INTERCULTURAL COMMUNICATION

A Christian Perspective

A. SCOTT MOREAU
EVVY HAY CAMPBELL
SUSAN GREENER

Baker Academic
a division of Baker Publishing Group
Grand Rapids, Michigan

© 2014 by A. Scott Moreau, Evvy Hay Campbell, and Susan Greener

Published by Baker Academic
a division of Baker Publishing Group
P.O. Box 6287, Grand Rapids, MI 49516-6287
www.bakeracademic.com

Printed in the United States of America

Library of Congress Cataloging-in-Publication Data
Moreau, A. Scott, 1955–
   Effective intercultural communication : a Christian perspective / A. Scott Moreau, Evvy
 Hay Campbell, and Susan Greener.
      pages cm. — (Encountering mission)
   Includes bibliographical references and indexes.
   ISBN 978-0-8010-2663-8 (pbk.)
      1. Intercultural communication—Religious aspects—Christianity. 2. Missions.
   3. Communication—Religious aspects—Christianity. I. Title.
   BV2082.I57M67 2014
   266.001′4—dc23   2014024141

Contents

Introduction

Intercultural communication is a discipline that has come of age. Founded in the 1950s, maturing throughout the following decades, and now considered an independent discipline in hundreds of universities and colleges, its development parallels the development of instantaneous communication for people all over the world. Not surprisingly, Christians have been interested in learning how to understand culture and connect it with Christ's message for far longer than the discipline has existed. However, contemporary intercultural communication offers insights not often understood by Christians historically that will help us to communicate (both as learners and as ambassadors) and partner more effectively for the sake of Christ.

THEOLOGICAL FOUNDATIONS OF INTERCULTURAL COMMUNICATION

Intercultural communication for Christians rests on three primary theological foundations. First, since we are made in the image of the God who reveals himself to people and listens to their prayers, we are by nature communicating creatures. Second, we serve a Creator who has communicated himself to us by revealing himself to people who recorded the revelations they received. Finally, we are commanded to communicate the message of the good news with others.

Although we are made in God's image, there are realities that impact our ability to communicate. First, we are physical and therefore limited. We are creatures of our environment, but because we are made in God's image we can rise above the constraints our environment places on us. Second, our knowledge of ourselves and our own culture is finite, even more so our knowledge of the new cultures where following the evangelistic task and God's call may bring us. Thankfully, we are creatures created to grow and learn, so we always have the opportunity to reach a better understanding of what we face and to learn how to communicate Christ in more effective ways in those settings. Finally, we are categorizers. As humans, we see the world around us and want to make sense of it. Our families and societies offer us "maps" of the world that make sense to them, and we grow up learning how to see and read those particular maps. We use them to make sense of what happens around us, but each culture has unique approaches to this map-making and map-reading process, so there is an almost infinite flexibility in the ways we approach life, even though life is based on certain universals (such as the need for food and water, shelter, relationships with others, and social organization).

THE COMPLEXITY AND DISCIPLINES OF INTERCULTURAL COMMUNICATION

Another reality that must be considered is the sheer complexity of the communication process, which we tend to take for granted until we encounter people from cultures that differ from our own. We will explore the reality that communication is always a two-way street. We are always in the role of being *both* sender and receiver.

Further, we will explore how there are levels of interlocking and dynamically changing assumptions in everything we do. Communication—and the worldview on which we base our communication—is dynamic rather than static. We will see that the many factors involved in intercultural communication do not simply add up in a linear fashion; they blend together like ingredients in a cake. They are part of larger systems, which are themselves affected by the worldviews, the environments, and the dynamics of relationships that are always present. As individuals we will come to understand that we use different formulas of factors in different settings; we change depending on the context. Therefore, static models of intercultural communication by definition will never do justice to the complexity of the discipline. We will also see that, to some extent, the "cultures" we discuss are all the products of our own organizational frameworks and are really inventions that help us to understand the maps that people use to guide them through life.

The picture is further complicated by the many closely related disciplines— anthropology, linguistics, sociology, and psychology—that shed light on aspects of intercultural communication. For the Christian, of course, theology and missiology must also be included. It is not surprising that the resulting mix is so complex that most courses focus on teaching people *how* to communicate better in new cultural settings rather than laying a full theoretical foundation for the discipline.

As we wrote this book, the discipline of intercultural communication was constantly changing due to the increase of solid empirical research. The very complexity of the events involved in intercultural communication makes appropriate operationalization extremely difficult. There is no coherent, single intercultural communication model that is accepted across the board, though we will see in chapter 1 that the number of approaches is limited, as are the areas of contemporary inquiry.

OUTLINE FOR THE BOOK

Our task is to walk you through the critical elements that compose an introduction to intercultural communication for Christian workers of all types. To accomplish this goal, we have divided this book into four major parts with twenty-four chapters followed by a reference list of all cited sources. What follows is an overview of each part and a brief description of each chapter of the book.

Part 1: Introducing Intercultural Communication

For a long time Christians have struggled to communicate the "pure" gospel story across cultural boundaries. In more recent centuries, we have come to realize that the gospel is not naked; it is always enfleshed in culture if for no other reason than it is expressed in and constrained by human language. It is clear that we need to understand what intercultural communication has to offer in our increasingly multicultural world and church.

In part 1, therefore, we provide an overview of the historical development (both secular and Christian) of intercultural communication and deal with implications that are important for people who cross cultures to communicate Christ.

Chapter 1: What Is Intercultural Communication?: We lay some of the important foundations for the rest of the book by defining communication and culture, briefly surveying the development of the discipline, offering a model for the process of communication, and exploring the major approaches and themes found in the contemporary discipline.

Chapter 2: The Story Line of Intercultural Communication: We present two perspectives on the history of the discipline: the secular and the Christian. We also tell the stories of and draw lessons from three people who crossed cultures for Christ before the discipline of intercultural communication existed. Finally, we discuss how Christians currently handle the discipline.

Chapter 3: Perspectives on Intercultural Communication: We examine the differing perspectives on intercultural communication, including theoretical and methodological approaches to the discipline as well as core themes. Then we explore a Christian perspective on the purpose of communication, missiological implications of intercultural communication, and the more significant challenges that the secular discipline presents for Christians.

Part 2: Foundations of Intercultural Communication Patterns

In this section of the book we turn our attention to the foundations underlying patterns of intercultural communication.

Chapter 4: Worldview and Intercultural Communication: We look more closely at worldview, which has long been considered the cornerstone of what people believe, how they behave, and (more recently) how they communicate. No person's worldview is static; it changes as the person changes due to circumstances, environment, religious faith, or other factors.

Chapter 5: Verbal Intercultural Communication: We discuss the issues related to people's use of language as they communicate. Language gives humans a framework for understanding the world around them as well as the categories into which they organize what they observe and what happens to them.

Chapter 6: Societies and Social Institutions: All communication takes place in a social context. Understanding that context is just as important as understanding the ways in which communication takes place—without being able to place communication in its proper context, we will never be able to understand what is being communicated.

Chapter 7: Networks, In-Groups, and Social Change: We deal with the reality that within their social contexts, (1) people have roles and statuses that guide their behavior, (2) groups form, and (3) people network with others to accomplish their goals.

Part 3: Patterns of Intercultural Communication

In this section we focus on the cultural values reflected in the patterns of communication in cultures.

Chapter 8: Nonverbal Intercultural Communication: We explore the broad concept of nonverbal communication through three types of coding: paraverbal, stillness and silence, and nonverbal (including physical characteristics, environmental and artifactual communication, and kinesics). We then explore the functions of nonverbal communication.

Chapter 9: Contexting: We focus on the extent to which people rely on the context in which they communicate to be part of the message. In some societies, people live in an "ocean of information" that they glean from the events around them. They learn to value reading the message from that ocean rather than from actual words. In other societies, people are not expected to live in the same ocean of information and therefore rely more on words and what those words convey to grasp the meaning of what is being communicated. The former societies are called high context, the latter low context.

Chapter 10: Polychronic and Monochronic Time: We examine cultural understandings of time. Edward Hall divided cultures along a continuum at one end of which people conceive of time as a commodity that can be sliced into pieces and at the other end people see time as unitary and interwoven. The former societies he called monochronic (one-time) and the latter polychronic (multitime); people's use and understanding of time is radically different in each type of society—different enough to have an impact on how they communicate the things they value.

Chapter 11: Individualism and Collectivism: We address the way in which people define themselves, whether as independent individuals or as members belonging to a group. More than any other set of values, individualism-collectivism is central to understanding the ways that people in different societies communicate.

Chapter 12: Social Power in Intercultural Communication: Our discussion deals with the reality that all societies have ideals related to how they prefer to handle differences in social power. Do they want to level the playing field, or do they prefer to ensure that power differentials are maintained and supported? Geert Hofstede called the way we handle these differences in social power "power distance"; in this chapter we consider how power distance affects communication patterns.

Chapter 13: Gender Roles: We examine how differing societies understand the extent to which gender roles are intermingled or distinguished, and to what degree. We explain the various ideas as well as their impact on communication and ministry.

Chapter 14: Honor and Justice: What role does honor—and the idea of maintaining one's face—play in communication? How is it distinguished from the role of justice and a forensic approach to dealing with conflict? We will explore the impact of these orientations on how people prefer to communicate.

Part 4: Developing Intercultural Expertise

In the final part of the book we examine areas in which developing competency in communicating in a new cultural setting is important.

Chapter 15: Cultural Adaptation: We present what it takes to adjust to living in—and not just visiting—a new culture. This involves a four-step process from unconscious incompetence to unconscious competence that incorporates how to handle cultural incidents and differences when they occur.

Chapter 16: Intercultural Competence: We examine what is involved in not simply adapting but also developing a level of competence in the new culture. While it involves knowing the language, this competence goes beyond just language to include cultural learning as well.

Chapter 17: Intercultural Relationships: Christians cross cultures to develop relationships with people, and we explore what is involved in that process.

Chapter 18: Intercultural Evangelism: We give careful attention to the process of communicating Christ and inviting people to respond in ways that make sense in light of their communication patterns and values.

Chapter 19: Intercultural Discipleship: We present what is involved in helping people who have come to Christ better and more deeply connect to him and to his body in ways that are faithful to Scripture but understandable within their culture.

Chapter 20: Intercultural Church Planting: We introduce significant issues that are part of gathering new believers into vibrant and healthy fellowships for the purpose of building up one another in Christ.

Chapter 21: Cross-Cultural Teaching and Learning: Because so many Christians cross cultures as teachers or trainers, we examine what it takes to teach or train in ways that take into account how people in different cultural settings prefer to learn.

Chapter 22: Intercultural Ministry through Teams: We discuss the steps in building a strong team in which the gifts of its members are properly channeled into ministry for Christ—especially when that team is multicultural in composition.

Chapter 23: Conflict and Culture: Inevitably, conflict will be part of everyone's intercultural experience. Understanding how to engage in conflict in ways that are appropriate to Scripture and local culture is a challenging task, and we direct our attention to what that involves.

Chapter 24: The Future of Intercultural Communication: Finally, to close the book, we briefly address issues related to the future of intercultural communication, especially as it relates to Christian ministry.

A Note on the Case Studies

In most case studies in this book the actual names of the primary characters are fictitious to ensure minimal potential exposure for those who work in settings where being known as missionaries could be detrimental to their ministry. Unless otherwise noted, or if the name is historically well known (e.g., in chap. 2), the reader should assume that the names used in case studies and sidebars are not the actual names of the people involved. In many cases the circumstances described have been altered in ways that remain true to the issues faced but without giving so much detail that anyone could be identified.

Additional Resources for Students and Teachers

In addition to the reference list, we offer several sets of helpful resources. First, as we have done with the other books in the Encountering Mission series, we have included a case study at the end of each chapter. Most of them leave the reader with a dilemma for which a solution should be sought. For every case study, there are numerous good solutions as well as many bad ones. Having students wrestle with the dilemmas presented in a case study helps them learn to draw from theory in light of practical problems faced in intercultural life.

If you are a teacher, we encourage you to use the case studies in ways that fit your objectives for the class. Students might write an essay on possible solutions to a case study as a homework assignment. Class discussion of the case studies can also be used to determine student awareness of the issues raised. Students can be split into small groups to work together in developing possible solutions to prompt them to think more deeply about the issues involved. *Case Studies in Mission* (Hiebert and Hiebert 1987), from which some of the case studies in this book are drawn, also provides helpful ways to use case studies as teaching devices.

Finally, numerous helpful sidebars are scattered throughout the book. Most offer deeper consideration of a particular issue discussed in the text and include questions for reflection and discussion.

ENCOUNTERING MISSION SERIES

Effective Intercultural Communication is one of eight books in the award-winning Encountering Mission series. Each book focuses on mission from an evangelical perspective. For many years, J. Herbert Kane's textbooks, including *The Making of a Missionary* (1975), *Understanding Christian Missions* (1976), *Christian Missions in Biblical Perspective* (1976), *A Concise History of the Christian World Mission* (1978), *Life and Work on the Mission Field* (1980), and *The Christian World Mission: Today and Tomorrow* (1981), have been widely used in seminaries and Bible colleges as introductory texts. With the passing of time, however, his classic works have become dated, and Baker

7

Publishing Group recognized that the time had come to develop a series of books to replace Kane's gifts to the mission community. The *Encountering Mission* series, then, builds on the best of Kane's work but also extends the discussion in significant ways to meet the needs of those who are preparing for effective missional engagement in today's world.

ACKNOWLEDGMENTS

As authors, we offer our deepest gratitude to Baker Publishing Group not only for the opportunity to write this book but also for its ongoing commitment to mission as evidenced in its support for the entire series.

We also express our deepest appreciation to Michelle Asbill for her invaluable work in helping with a significant part of the initial research, and to Michelle, Lauren Moreau, and Kaylene Powell, who carefully read drafts of chapters and made numerous valuable suggestions. The book is certainly better because of their work with and for us.

PART 1

Introducing Intercultural Communication

At one time in mission history, it was thought that we simply needed to bring the "pure" gospel to the people whom God has called us to serve. Now, however, many—though not all—Christians recognize that our ideals of the "pure" gospel are always tainted by our own cultural viewpoints. The gospel is not naked; it is always enfleshed in culture if for no other reason than it is expressed in and constrained by human language. Evangelistic tools such as the Four Spiritual Laws, at one time considered the pure gospel, are increasingly regarded as culturally conditioned formulations of the gospel message that do not always communicate well in places where the culture differs from the one in which they were developed.

These realities, and others like them, clearly demonstrate the need for understanding and using principles of intercultural communication in our increasingly multicultural church. In our interconnected world, the ability to communicate well across cultural divides is more important than ever. From business people who travel internationally to short-term cross-cultural workers to long-term church planters, those skilled in understanding how to communicate well are more likely to succeed in the tasks they face.

To help you understand this principle, in chapter 1 we offer important definitions and a model of communication that sets the stage for all the discussion that follows. In chapter 2 we present two perspectives on the history of the discipline: the secular and the Christian. We consider three historical figures who crossed cultures for Christ before the discipline of intercultural communication even existed and present the ways in which Christians currently handle the discipline before examining the ways people approach intercultural communication in chapter 3. Finally, we explore selected issues from a Christian perspective, including the purpose of communication, the missiological implications of intercultural communication, and the more significant challenges that the secular discipline presents for Christians.

What Is Intercultural Communication?

In this chapter we lay some of the important foundations for the rest of the book by defining communication and culture, briefly surveying the development of the discipline, offering a model for the process of communication, and exploring the major approaches and themes found in the contemporary discipline.

DEFINING COMMUNICATION

One of the early problems facing the discipline involved the meaning of the two terms at its heart: culture and communication. Neither was clearly or even adequately defined (Saral 1978, 389–90; Kramsch 2002; Levine, Park, and Kim 2007). Although many definitions for each term have been proposed over the decades, there is still no single set on which everyone agrees.

With that in mind, how do we communicate? As early as 1970, almost one hundred definitions of communication had appeared in print (Mortensen 1972, 14). A very general definition is "communication occurs whenever persons attribute significance to message-related behavior."

This definition implies several postulates (Mortensen 1972, 14–21; compare with Porter and Samovar 1982, 30). First, communication is *dynamic*: it is not a static "thing" but a dynamic *process* that maintains stability and identity through all its fluctuations.

Second, communication is *irreversible*: the very fact that communication has occurred (or is occurring) means that the persons in communication have changed, however subtly. The fact that we have memories means that once we begin the process, there is no "reset" button; we cannot begin again as blank slates.

> *One foundational rule that people who are communicating across cultural divides must keep in mind [is this]:* ... people interpret your words and actions in ways that make sense to them. *Often, therefore, what you think you are communicating is not what they are receiving. If nothing else, knowing this may help you be more humble in attempting to convey the greatest message of all.*
>
> Moreau, Corwin, and McGee
> 2004, 267–68, emphasis in original

Third, communication is *proactive*: in communicating we are not merely passive respondents to external stimuli. When we communicate, we enter the process totally and are proactive, selecting, amplifying, and manipulating the signals that come to us.

Fourth, communication is *interactive* on two fronts: the intrapersonal, or what goes on inside each communicator; and the interpersonal, or what takes place between communicators. We must pay attention to both fronts to understand the communication process.

Finally, communication is *contextual*: it always happens in a larger context, be that the physical environment, the emotional mood of the communication event, or the purposes (which may be overt or hidden) behind the communication.

DEFINING CULTURE

As beings made in God's image and created with the need to learn, grow, and order our world, we learn the rules of the society in which we grow up. Those rules provide us with maps to understand the world around us. None of us escapes the fact that she or he is a cultural creature, and culture has a deep impact on communication.

At the same time, trying to understand any culture is like trying to hit a moving target. Your culture—like all cultures—is not rigid and static. It is dynamic. The rules you learned while growing up will not be identical to the rules you pass on to your own children, especially in technologically advanced settings. Scott still remembers learning how to use a mouse for a computer, while his children acquired the skill at such an early age that they have no memories of learning how to use one.

But what is this thing we all are immersed in that is called "culture"? In 1952, Alfred Kroeber and Clyde Kluckhohn (38–40, 149) compiled at least 164 definitions of culture for analysis and used close to 300 definitions in their book! One of the reasons culture is so difficult to define is simply because it is so deeply a part of each of us. Every interpretation we make—even every observation—is molded by culture.

One of the most commonly cited definitions is that of Clifford Geertz, who defines culture as a "historically transmitted pattern of meanings embedded and expressed in symbols that are used to communicate, perpetuate, and develop . . . knowledge about and attitudes toward life" (1973, 89). In this concise definition, Geertz indicates both the breadth and depth of culture, helping to frame its richness and complexity.

However we may choose to define culture, it is clear that it is a dynamic (Moreau 1995, 121) and interconnected (Hall 1976, 16–17) pattern that is learned (Hofstede 1991, 5) and transmitted from one generation to the next through symbols (Geertz 1973, 89) that are consciously and unconsciously framed (Hall 1983, 230) and shared by a group of people (Dahl 2004, 4); this pattern enables them to interpret the behaviors of others (Spencer-Oatey 2000, 4).

At the same time, culture is neither monolithic nor homogeneous. We can recognize at least four layers of culture (fig. 1.1; see also Hofstede 1991, 6–7; Hesselgrave 1978; Levine, Park, and Kim 2007, 211). The first layer encompasses the universals we all share as humans, including not only such things as language, institutions, values, and sociability, but also our bearing God's image, our need for relationships, our ability to learn and grow, and so on. We elaborate more on these universals later in the discussion of the common human core.

The second layer includes the specific values and worldview of the largest cultural (or national) unit that people identify as their own. They provide the rule book by which people from that culture operate in meeting their universal needs.

The third layer involves the reality that many of us are part of subcultures within the larger societal or national setting. Much intercultural communication research focuses on the second and third layers.

The fourth and final layer in the diagram reflects that people—even those of the most collective cultures—are still individuals and choose how they will live by cultural rules and regulations. It also reflects that as a genetically unique

FIGURE 1.1
THE LAYERS OF CULTURE

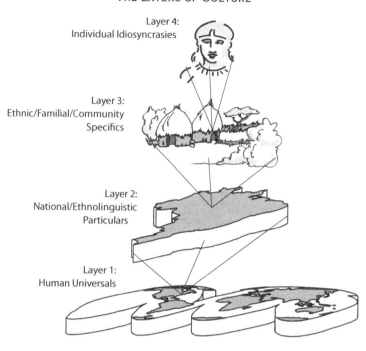

Layer 4:
Individual Idiosyncrasies

Layer 3:
Ethnic/Familial/Community
Specifics

Layer 2:
National/Ethnolinguistic
Particulars

Layer 1:
Human Universals

person who has a unique history, everyone has varying skills in applying his or her cultural rules to the situations of life. This is the layer at which individual idiosyncrasy emerges. Some cultures allow this layer to be valued, while others value less idiosyncrasy and greater harmony and conformity.

CHARACTERISTICS OF INTERCULTURAL COMMUNICATION

There are several realities that characterize all communication, whether intercultural or not. They are true of communication in every context (see Moreau, Corwin, and McGee 2004, 266–67). First, everything that we do "communicates"—it is *impossible* for us to stop communicating (Watzlawick, Beavin, and Jackson 1967).

Second, the goal of communication is always more than just to impart information—persuasion is behind everything we do. Even a simple "hello" is an act that requests a response or an acknowledgment of your existence and relationship with the person to whom you say, "Hello" (Berlo 1960, 12).

Third, the communication process is generally far more complex than most people realize. Because we have been communicating for so long, and because we do it all the time, we have the tendency to take it for granted (Hesselgrave and Rommen 1989, 180; Filbeck 1985, 2–3).

Fourth, we always communicate our messages through more than one channel, and we always communicate more than one message. At times, these "multiple" messages may contradict one another, causing our audience to respond negatively to our primary concern. At other times, they enhance and reinforce our message, helping to elicit a more positive response from our audience (Kraft 1983, 76).

Fifth, and finally, if we seek to communicate effectively across cultural barriers, the foundational consideration for all our communication should be, "What can I do to build trust on the part of the audience?" (see Mayers 1974, 30–79).

TERMINOLOGY

The discipline of intercultural communication has remained largely within communication studies, though its genesis came from anthropologists (Kitao 1985), and recently calls have been made for anthropology to add its voice to the ongoing discussion (e.g., Coertze 2000). Today the discipline of intercultural communication includes interracial communication, interethnic communication, cross-cultural communication, and international communication (Kitao 1985, 8–9; see table 1.1 for terminology).

WORKING MODEL OF THE COMMUNICATION PROCESS

In figure 1.2 we present a working model of the communication process (see also, e.g., Mortensen 1972; Applbaum et al. 1973; Hesselgrave 1991b, 51; Singer 1987, 70; Poyatos 1983; Dodd 1991, 5; Gudykunst and Kim 1992, 33; Eilers 1999, 242–43; Klopf 2001, 50; and Neuliep 2009, 25). In it we have Participant A, Participant B, and a whole host of communication issues within and between each. To make the following discussion easier to follow, we refer to Participant A as Megumi (from Japan) and Participant B as Jabulani (from Swaziland).

Communication Participant A (Source-Respondent)

The left side depicts Megumi, in this case the one who initiates communication and then responds to the feedback that comes from Jabulani. One of Megumi's purposes will be to convey some type of "meaning" to Jabulani such that they share understanding of what is being communicated.

15

TABLE 1.1
TERMINOLOGY

Term	Basic Concept
Intercultural communication	Communication between members from differing cultural backgrounds (Y. Y. Kim 1984, 16).
Cross-cultural communication	Comparison of the same communication phenomenon in two or more cultures (Gudykunst and Kim 1992, 14).
Interracial communication	Communication between members of differing racial groups (Rich 1974; see also Jackson and Garner 1998).
Interethnic communication	Communication between members of differing ethnic groups (Rich 1974; see also Jackson and Garner 1998).
International communication	Formal communication at national levels related to a political situation (Sitaram 1980, 91–92) or communication that flows between nation-states (Braman, Shah, and Fair 2001, 161; see also H. Schwartz 1969).
Intercommunication	Communication that crosses national or cultural boundaries (Prosser 1973).
Cultural communication	Communication within a particular culture or subculture (Y. Y. Kim 2001b, 147).
Intracultural communication	Communication between individuals of the same culture (Sitaram 1980, 93).
Minority communication	Communication between the people of two subcultures within a dominant culture (Sitaram 1980, 93).
Transracial communication	The understanding that persons from differing ethnic or racial backgrounds can achieve in verbal interaction (Arthur Smith 1971).
Transcultural communication	Communication that assumes there are universal constants (e.g., prohibitions against murder or incest; Christian doctrines about God, Christ, humanity, etc.) and relates them to communication (Küster 2005, 418).

Adapted in part from Saral 1978.

Our first dilemma is determining what is meant by the term "meaning" (on the different theories of how things "mean" and the steps we take to discover "meaning," see Hesselgrave 1978, 44–50). Ultimately, as David Hesselgrave points out:

> Meaning is in a sense contractual. Only by agreement in the area of semantics can we think about the same "thing." Only by agreement on the relationships that exist between linguistic symbols can we say anything significant about the "thing." And only as we agree on standards of right and wrong, truth and error, and good and bad can we make value judgments about any "thing." (1978, 40; note also Carson's discussion of this issue, 1985, 207–8)

MEANING SYSTEM

For Megumi to choose what signals to use to convey meaning, she will need to encode the message she wants to convey. A lifetime of sensory inputs

FIGURE 1.2
A SIMPLIFIED WORKING MODEL OF THE COMMUNICATION PROCESS

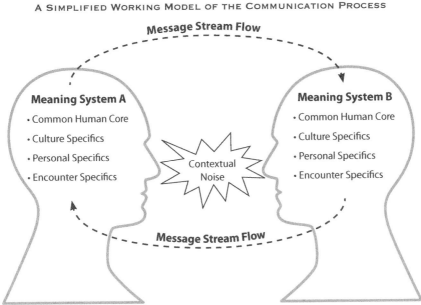

forms a reservoir of meaning in her. Past experiences and future expectations interact with the "now" to produce meanings. No two persons receive identical sensory impressions of a single event, nor do individuals respond in the same way that others respond. Each person develops a unique "meaning system" that is constantly changing. Each participant's meaning system is invisible to the other participant.

Four major components compose the total meaning system within each participant: (1) the common human core; (2) the specific culture of the individual; (3) the specific idiosyncratic nature of the person; and (4) the specifics of this particular communication event. All four components are woven together and enable Megumi to choose how to convey her message in a way that she assumes Jabulani will understand. We briefly touch on each of these components in turn.

THE COMMON HUMAN CORE

These are core aspects of our humanity that are common to all people. As noted by Scott Moreau:

> People of all races and ethnic identities share the fact and experiences of being human. Universals found in every culture include, among other things, language, thought, the process of enculturation, myth frameworks, authority structures,

and the many institutions necessary for survival of human societies (e.g., kinship, economics, education, politics, recreation, various types of association, health, transportation, etc.). (1995, 122)

However, these core aspects include not only those things that anthropologists see but also things appropriately discerned from biblical revelation (following Moreau 1995): we are all made in the image of God (Gen. 1:26–31); we have a purpose for our existence (Gen. 1:27; Isa. 43:7); we are all physical creatures with physical needs (food, water, shelter, etc.; Gen. 2:7); we are all thinking (psychological and cognitive) creatures (Gen. 2:16); we are social creatures who are not meant to stand alone (Gen. 2:18–25); we are all sinful creatures in need of redemption (Rom. 3:23; 6:23); we all have access to the general revelation about God (Rom. 1:20–21).

Cultural Specifics

In addition to the core shared by all people, each participant also has cultural specifics that frame the way he or she sees and understands the world. This component of the meaning system includes such things as worldview, religion, values, social structures and roles, and decision-making rules. At this juncture we must point out that some discussions have focused on issues of language and power and how the labels we choose will be those that tend to maintain the status quo for those who are in positions of power (see, e.g., discussions of how we define the "other" in Fabian 1983; Mudimbe 1988).

Personal Specifics

Not all people operate in congruence with their culture. To think that because a person is from a collective culture (see chap. 11) she will always act as we expect a collective person to act is to commit what is called the ecological fallacy. Further, even in the most collective of subcultures, people are not identical. Ways in which they are not identical include such things as cognitive style, God-given communication skills, knowledge, personality, total history of relationship with other(s), and life history and experiences. Each person has her own gifts, tendencies, and stories, and each brings those into communication acts. They provide an important part of the framing of how Megumi will choose to encode the messages she wishes to send.

Encounter Specifics

Finally, in addition to these three components, elements of the encounter itself partially determine how messages are encoded. These include the emotional/physical state or mood of Megumi at the time of the communication act; her degree of empathy, trust, and authenticity; her defensiveness; her understanding of the use of public and private cues in context; her motivations and the way she strategizes to accomplish her goals in this setting; and her current attitudes, feelings, and beliefs about Jabulani.

It is easy to see why understanding even a single communication event is such a complex process. Currently it is beyond our ability to devise some type of calculus by which we may compute the entire system; perhaps—due to such things as human choice and abilities—we may never devise such a calculus, even if we reached a stage at which we could agree on all the "inputs" into the system. After all, the reality of human choice in and of itself seems beyond human calculations.

THE CODING PROCESS

In any event, once Megumi chooses the message she wants to convey, on the basis of her meaning system she encodes the message into various channels in order to communicate with Jabulani. As Hesselgrave notes, "The word *communication* comes from the Latin word *communis* (common). We must establish a 'commonness' with someone to have communication. That 'commonness' is to be found in mutually shared codes" (1978, 31).

As with the meaning system, we can identify a set of components that are part of the coding and transmission process, such as preverbal coding and the actual physical coding (Applbaum et al. 1973, 36–38).

PREVERBAL CODING

Megumi experiences a need to communicate that comes from her own meaning systems. Much of this stage of preverbal coding involves feelings for which words are not attached. The meaning is private and frequently is not verbally expressed. Feedback loops operate within Megumi as she processes the preverbal encoding process in preparation for the next stage. For example, she may choose to use a particular word, and then, after she thinks about it and how that word might impact Jabulani, she may select a different word that seems more appropriate. This process occurs before and during the actual physical coding.

TRANSMISSION OF THE MESSAGE THROUGH PHYSICAL CODING

At this point Megumi "transmits" her message through signals (verbal and extraverbal) based on her preverbal coding. The actual encoding used depends on her needs in the situation and her experience with communication.

Verbal codes refer to language, whether written or oral. Though words (especially nouns) have external referents, the actual words we use do not "contain meaning" in and of themselves. Their meaning is an agreed-upon one chosen by the group using that code. "Friend" could mean anything an English-speaking culture (or audience) wants it to mean, but the meaning in common use today is a person who is on good terms with you. The meaning of "friend" is inherent not in the word but in the English-speaking world's agreement on its use.

Note that within the verbal codes, tonal stresses and emphases are also codes in the communication process. As with the words themselves, tonal emphases derive their meaning from the people who use them, not from an inherent quality.

Extraverbal codes come in a bewildering variety of forms. They include oral signals ("hmmmm"), hand gestures, posture, eye contact, smell, physical spacing (e.g., between source and respondent), position (placement of the head higher or lower than the head of the respondent), touch, leg position, and so on. Each form can carry many messages that intercultural communicators may miss or communicate improperly if they are not sensitive to their audience.

Media are the "vehicles" used in transmitting the message. The type of media chosen will have a definite impact on how the respondents will perceive the message. Each media channel has its own advantages and disadvantages, which should be understood if we are to communicate as effectively as possible.

Redundancy refers to how all messages have redundant elements, often simply because they are communicated along more than one channel simultaneously. Note this sentence:

SH PRFRS CRM ND SGR N HR T

The missing vowels are not even necessary for most people to understand the sentence. Today this is most easily seen in instant and text messaging, where a whole new code for commonly used terms has been developed. The extra letters (e.g., vowels in the above sentence) reinforce the message and help to ensure its clarity (that she prefers cream and sugar in her tea), but they are not necessary for the message to be understood.

Entropy refers to the reality that every message suffers from a certain degree of randomness or uncertainty. Whether this happens in transmission (due to deterioration in the encoding, the transmission itself, or in the decoding processes) or in distortion caused by noise and context, it affects all human communication to some extent. Note this string of letters from which you are asked to make a sentence:

GODISNOWHERE

We see the effects of entropy when a person has to decide whether to read "God is nowhere" or "God is now here."

Noise is any sensory data that is part of the context of communication but is not part of the actual communication event itself. It may either enhance or detract from the communication process. Do not confuse "noise" here with mere sounds; it also includes nonauditory "noise." This may be a headache from an argument with a close friend just prior to the communication event. It may be something taken for granted such as the weather, the time of day, or the season. It may include distractions from the competing agendas of each person participating in the event, and so on (see Larson 1966; Wendland 1995).

TOTAL MESSAGE STREAM

The verbal codes, extraverbal codes (including redundant elements), media, redundancy, entropy, and noise all combine to produce what we can call the "total message stream," which refers to all the sensory information that reaches Respondent B in the communication event.

Communication Participant B (Respondent-Source)

In our example, Jabulani serves in mirror fashion to Megumi. Based in part on the total message stream, Jabulani determines what he understands the message to be. This means not that there is no message in an absolute sense but only that the recipient of the communication is the one who decides what he understands the message to be.

RECEPTION OF THE TOTAL MESSAGE STREAM

All physical senses come into play in receiving the total data stream. Jabulani hears, sees, feels, (possibly) smells, and (possibly) tastes the data sent by Megumi, which is by now intermingled with the noise of the context and the entropy inherent in all messages.

As the message is received, Jabulani begins the process of decoding it so that he can understand what Megumi is communicating. He does so from within the context of his own meaning framework, not hers. If she wants to be understood, she has to take this into account in her encoding process. This is what it means to be receptor oriented in communication (Kraft 2005a; see sidebar 1.1).

To decode the total message stream, Jabulani must attend to the physical data that are part of the stream. Sound waves are turned into words, words are translated into the appropriate thoughts based on other things such as emphasis, tone of voice, hand or other bodily gestures, facial expression, the surrounding context, and what Jabulani knows of Megumi's communication patterns (e.g., she was taught to avoid saying no in a direct fashion).

SIDEBAR 1.1
IMPORTANT PRINCIPLES RELATED TO RECEPTORS

Kraft (2005a, 156–59, emphasis in original)

1. *Receptors are parts of reference groups.* Receptors (like all humans) are never alone, even when they are "by themselves." Whether one lives in an individualistic society, [as] Americans do, or in a strongly group-oriented society, like those of the [Majority] World, we always consider the reactions of others when we make decisions.

2. *Receptors are committed to their group and to the values of that group.* When approaches are made to people to make changes in their attitudes and/or behavior, it cannot be assumed that they are not already committed to competing attitudes and/or behavior.

3. If Christian appeals are to be attractive they need to be addressed to the *felt needs* of the receptors. An important thing to recognize, though, is that humans never seem to be fully satisfied with their state in life. And no sociocultural system seems to adequately provide for every need felt by the people within that system.

4. *Receptors are always interpreting.* And everything about the communicational situation gets interpreted.... Interpretation is clearly one of the most important, though least conscious, of the activities of receptors.

5. These interpretations feed directly into the most important of the receptors' activities, that of *constructing the meanings* that result from the communicational interaction.... It is messages, not meanings, that are transmitted from person to person.

6. Receptors, then, either *grant or withhold permission* for any given message to enter what might be termed the receptor's "communicational space." Receptors may be pictured as encased in a kind of bubble which only they can give permission to enter. When someone wants to transact or negotiate some form of communication, then, he/she needs to gain permission for the interaction from the one who can control access to that bubble.

7. Closely related to the activity of giving permission is that of *evaluating the message.* In any communicational interaction the participants evaluate each component of that experience.... From this evaluation the participants construct an overall impression of the situation, an impression that has much to do with how they interpret what goes on in that situation.

8. Another closely related kind of activity in which receptors are engaged is the matter of *selectivity.* People are selective in the kinds of things they allow themselves to be exposed to.... People tend to perceive messages in such a way that they confirm already held positions, whether or not the communicator intended them that way.

9. Receiving communication is a risky business. Receptors are, therefore, continually *seeking to maintain their equilibrium* in the face of such actual

or imagined risk. Whenever people expose themselves to communication they are risking the possibility that they might have to change some aspect of their lives. People ordinarily seek at all costs to maintain their present equilibrium, to protect themselves from assimilating anything that is perceived to possibly upset their psychological balance.

REFLECTION AND DISCUSSION

1. What are several implications or applications for evangelism in a new cultural setting for any one of these principles?

2. Using the same principle, what are several implications or applications for church planting in a new cultural setting?

The total data stream contains far more information than is needed for the communication event to take place. It is apparent that if Jabulani were to consciously attend to every detail of the total message stream, it would overwhelm him. Therefore, Jabulani both consciously and unconsciously filters out or ignores what he perceives to be irrelevant data (e.g., traffic outside the room, the hum of machinery, the smell of food from next door, the coolness of air blowing on skin, words that are verbal fillers). The selection of "relevancy" is determined by a variety of factors included in Jabulani's meaning system, which has been developed over the course of his life as he learned from parents, peers, and other people important to him how to decode messages that come to him. Hopefully his decoding system is the same as Megumi's coding system, or else they will misunderstand each other, possibly with severe consequences.

Interpreting the Decoded and Filtered Message Stream into a "Message"

Once the message, at least on the literal, denotative level, is understood, it is interpreted on the connotative level. For example, if Jabulani believes that Megumi cannot be trusted, even when properly understood, he may not believe her no matter how sincere she is. Again, the interpretation stems from the totality of factors in Jabulani's meaning system.

Responding to the Perceived Message through Feedback

As Megumi is communicating her message, Jabulani is giving her feedback. This may come through eye contact, gestures, touch, proximity, and/or paraverbal or verbal channels. In effect, they are both now operating simultaneously as sender and receiver, negotiating what they want to communicate and what they think was communicated in a type of dance in which conscious and unconscious signals are sent and received.

Once Jabulani has interpreted Megumi's message (whether rightly or wrongly), he decides how he will respond and follows roughly the same process that Megumi followed in trying to communicate with him.

The net effect is that Jabulani determines his understanding of the message Megumi sought to convey. Thus, her (and our) focus in intercultural communication must be on Jabulani (the audience) as much as on the message. Not only must we be sure we have perceived the message clearly; we must also seek to make that message clear to the audience in their terms. Moreover, Jabulani, as the receptor, makes the decision whether to grant, withhold, or even withdraw permission for Megumi to enter his "communicational space" (Kraft 1995, 97–105).

CONCLUSION

With the foundation set, you now have the background not only to understand the discussion that follows but also to see how it fits into the larger discipline. Before we can move in that direction, however, we need to integrate Christian insights into communication and consider the story lines of intercultural communication in light of the church's actions throughout history and the recent development of Christian thinking about the discipline. As you read through the case study at the end of this chapter, consider the type of advice you might give Muhia, bearing in mind that direct confrontation of Mark is something he would find exceedingly difficult to do.

CASE STUDY:
PUTTING THINGS INTO PRACTICE

A. SCOTT MOREAU

Muhia was dismayed as he listened to his friend Mark give a training seminar to an African group on how to communicate Christ. Mark had studied anthropology and had even written a brilliant paper under a local missionary's supervision on issues related to communication from an anthropological perspective. *If Mark could only see how they applied to what he was teaching,* thought Muhia, *Mark would make a great cross-cultural trainer!*

Muhia's frustration started during the seminar when Mark began to talk about eye contact. Mark noted that children who do not look you in the eye are hiding something, so he stressed the need to ensure that when you share your faith you look the person you are sharing with in the eyes and be sure that the person is looking directly at you. Otherwise, Mark related, you could not be certain that the person was really listening and you could not trust his or her response.

Muhia cringed as he listened to this part of the talk. He vividly remembered learning from his parents to never look an adult in the eye. For them (and for Muhia), direct eye contact from a younger person to an older or more respected person was an expression of rebellion, not of paying attention! He could never forget the day a classmate of his in grade 12 was caned by a teacher for looking that teacher in the eye. It was not that you could *never* look into the eyes of an older person; it was *holding* the eye contact that was bad.

Muhia knew that Mark meant well, and that Mark had put a lot of time into preparing for his training sessions. He also knew that Mark would feel humiliated if Muhia pointed out what he had done wrong, since Mark prided himself on his cultural sensitivity. Even worse, the very idea of telling someone to his face that he had just made such a big mistake completely violated Muhia's rules of being a good host, and Mark was, after all, a guest in Muhia's country.

REFLECTION AND DISCUSSION

1. What could Muhia do that would honor his own rules against direct confrontation but help Mark be a better trainer in the future?
2. What might you say to Mark to help him better understand the cultural values in his setting?

2

The Story Line of Intercultural Communication

Even though cross-cultural interactions have taken place for as long as cultures have existed (Bentley 1996, 756), intercultural communication is a relatively young discipline founded during the 1950s. The *need* for intercultural communication, however, is at least as old as the beginnings of human migration and the distribution of human societies and cultures, together with the development of differing languages (especially after the tower of Babel incident in Gen. 11) around the planet. Of all people, Christians in particular should be interested and involved in the discipline; after all, Christ commanded us to make disciples of every nation. That is best done by learning how to understand those who are different from us, which is the heart of intercultural communication.

In this brief overview of the story line of intercultural communication, we start with a survey of the history of the secular discipline, explore some of the Christian intercultural communication perspectives seen in missions history, and draw lessons for communicating across cultural boundaries today.

SIDEBAR 2.1
WHY EXAMINE THE HISTORY OF INTERCULTURAL COMMUNICATION?

Hart (2005, 176)

William B. Hart has noted these reasons for studying the history of intercultural communication:

> Why look back at the study of intercultural communication? Why read or write on the history of intercultural communication research? If simple curiosity alone is not enough, then there are other reasons. . . . We should study the history of intercultural communication to gain an appreciation of the work that has been completed in the past and to be humbled by the fact that many of the social problems that we currently study have been studied for nearly a century (e.g., ethnocentrism). Have we made progress? We should study the history of intercultural communication to gain a deeper understanding of why we study what we study. We should study the history of intercultural communication in order to recognize the fads and fashions of intercultural communication research. Why are certain topics considered important? We should study the history of intercultural communication to avoid repetition of past studies and past mistakes. We should study the history of intercultural communication to capitalize on a source of valuable ideas for further research. We should study the history of intercultural communication to show gratitude to prominent scholars of intercultural communication. We should study the history of intercultural communication to find role-models, especially for young scholars. We should study the history of intercultural communication to gain a sense of identity. Intellectually speaking, where do we come from and who are we?

REFLECTION AND DISCUSSION

What biblical or theological reasons can you add to Hart's for studying the history of intercultural communication?

THE STORY OF THE DISCIPLINE OF INTERCULTURAL COMMUNICATION

The foundations for intercultural communication were laid in Franz Boas's concept of cultural relativism (Hart 2005; and its parallel in the Sapir-Whorf hypothesis on linguistic relativism; Rogers, Hart, and Miike 2002, 19) and Freud's concept of the unconscious (see Gudykunst and Mody 2002, 2–3). Cultural relativism is the idea that the values of one culture should never be judged by the standards of another culture; it is one of the fundamental tenets of contemporary intercultural communication theory (see further discussion in chap. 3). The unconscious realm is outside one's awareness, and contemporary intercultural communication scholars, following Hall, hold that much of the communication process is not governed by conscious actions.

27

The discipline of intercultural communication actually originated in the felt need for better diplomatic (and business) training for Americans serving abroad, especially in Japan after World War II (Leeds-Hurwitz 1990; see table 2.1 for major events). The work to better train them was initiated with the founding of the Foreign Service Institute (FSI) in 1947. The FSI hired the best people it could find, and Edward Hall's focus in the FSI was to supplement the language training methods developed during World War II with parallel cultural awareness training.

The needs of the FSI trainees were not academic but rather applied and practical. They were dissatisfied with training that focused on theory or generalized ideas; rather than understand the entire culture, they wanted to know how they could better communicate in situations they would face in the field. As a result, the trainers were forced to make several important changes that shaped the FSI program into one that became the prototype for contemporary intercultural communication training (Leeds-Hurwitz 1990).

First, Hall saw that he had to focus on interaction between members of different cultures rather than on in-depth discussion of a single culture. Second, he narrowed the training focus to only those elements related to the task at hand in face-to-face communication (such as tone of voice, gestures, and time and space relationships) rather than to all events of a culture. Third, he incorporated anthropologically oriented communication insights (e.g., that communication in a culture has a systemic pattern that can be analyzed, understood, and learned) into the training. Fourth, he implemented more professionally oriented teaching methods, such as personal experiences to illustrate theory, simulations, workshops, and related assignments.

These changes were developed and implemented from 1950 to 1955, with Hall and linguist George L. Trager as the significant players. Table 2.1 presents the major events in the field of intercultural communication from 1950 to 1998. It is interesting to note that while Hall is recognized as the founder of the discipline, he appeared not to envision it as a new discipline, and until his death saw himself as an anthropologist rather than a communication scholar (Rogers, Hart, and Miike 2002, 13).

The term "intercultural communication" was apparently a refinement of "international communication," which had appeared in print since the 1930s (Ellingsworth 1978, 100). "Intercultural communication" can be found in the literature as early as 1955 (Allen 1955; see also Prosser 1969), "cross-cultural communication" in Christian literature in 1955 (Nida 1955) and in secular literature by 1964 (Chu 1964; Condon 1964).

Popularization of the term can be traced to the publication of *The Ugly American* (Lederer and Burdick 1958), which depicted American arrogance

TABLE 2.1

MAJOR EVENTS IN THE DEVELOPMENT OF THE FIELD
OF INTERCULTURAL COMMUNICATION

Date	Events
1950–55	Development of the original paradigm of training in intercultural communication by Edward T. Hall and others at the Foreign Service Institute in Washington, DC.
1955–59	First article on intercultural communication by Hall ("The Anthropology of Manners" 1959a); first article using the term "Intercultural Communication" in the title is published in *Journal of Communication* (Allen 1955). Publication of Hall's *The Silent Language* (1959b) in English (a Japanese edition appears in 1966).
1960s	Publication of Robert Oliver's *Culture and Communication* (1962) and Alfred Smith's *Communication and Culture* (1966). Development of the first intercultural communication courses at universities (e.g., University of Pittsburgh, Michigan State University).
1970	International Communication Association establishes a Division of Intercultural Communication.
1972	First publication of an edited book on intercultural communication, titled *Intercultural Communication: A Reader*, by Larry A. Samovar and Richard E. Porter. The first international conference on intercultural communication is held in July at International Christian University in Japan, with over two thousand attending (Kitao 1985, 12).
1973	*Intercultural Communication* by L. S. Harms at the University of Hawaii is published (the first textbook on intercultural communication). First PhD in intercultural communication is awarded (to William Starosta at Indiana University).
1974	First publication of International and Intercultural Communication Annuals. The Society of Intercultural Education, Training and Research (SIETAR) is founded.
1975	Publication of *An Introduction to Intercultural Communication* by John C. Condon and Fathi Yousef (the second textbook in intercultural communication). The Speech Communication Association establishes a Division of Intercultural Communication.
1977	*International Journal of Intercultural Relations* begins publication.
Late 1970s	Over two hundred universities offer at least one course in intercultural communication in widely diverse disciplines (from communication to nursing to social work), with roughly sixty offering graduate-level courses. The budding discipline is criticized for its lack of clear boundaries in relation to other disciplines; the "honorable retirement of the term" from course titles, publications, research designs, and organizations is considered a possibility (Ellingsworth 1978, 105).
1983–present	Theory development in intercultural communication is emphasized (e.g., three *International and Intercultural Communication Annual* volumes on intercultural communication theory are published).
1998	Founding of the International Academy of Intercultural Relations.

Adapted from Rogers, Hart, and Miike 2002; Kitao 1985; Gudykunst and Mody 2002.

and domination in a fictitious Asian setting. While the main character was ugly only in the physical sense, the physically beautiful bureaucrats who surrounded him acted in the ugly ways now associated with the term. This runaway best seller eventually resulted in a presidential reform of the US military aid system.

Following on the heels of *The Ugly American*, Hall's 1959 *The Silent Language* (still available in reprint) became a best-selling classic that introduced people to nonverbal communication and its relationship to culture. It also cemented Hall's founding role in the field and became the foundational means of disseminating the original model for intercultural communication (Rogers, Hart, and Miike 2002, 10–13). Later some scholars even described it as their "Bible of intercultural communication study" (Hart 2005, 179). One unintended outcome of Hall's contribution is that the field tended to be pragmatic rather than theory driven (at least until the early 1980s; Leeds-Hurwitz 1990, 269). As a result of this pragmatism, the new discipline was not readily accepted in anthropology, which otherwise would have been its natural disciplinary home.

SELECTED ISSUES IN THE STORY OF CHRISTIAN INTERCULTURAL COMMUNICATION

Modern critics have persistently accused missionaries of being insensitive to local cultural values, trampling on local religions and seeking to duplicate their culturally laden vision of what a church should be in the new settings where they serve. While there is certainly truth in many of these accusations, they do not tell the entire story.

Contemporary historical scholarship has been increasingly concerned with the ways in which characters in the past—as well as the historians themselves—constructed the objects of their focus (the other) through the images, stories, and historical incidents that they used to make their arguments. Intercultural communication is also fundamentally interested in how we understand others as we encounter them when we cross cultures.

Because intercultural communication and missions both focus on crossing cultural boundaries, it is not surprising that much of missions history—most notably the Crusades (e.g., Florean 2007), the colonial era (see discussion in Dunch 2002, 307–8; Wilson 2004; Jeyaraj 2005; for examples, see Stanley 1990; Comaroff and Comaroff 1991), and the contemporary era (see Coggins 1972; Tippett 1972)—has been under the reconstructive microscope over the past few decades. Also not unsurprisingly given the orientation of deconstructive methodology and ideology (especially the intimate connection between knowledge and power), the missionary encounter with others has not fared well when viewed through the ideological "lenses" currently employed (but see Dunch 2002).

However, the simple picture often portrayed in recent studies does not do justice to the whole enterprise of colonialism or missions. The very term "colonial" has become a rhetorical device for "denigrating, shaming, shunning"—a term of choice for "labeling, demonizing, or assigning collective guilt" (Frykenberg 2003b, 7). While it is certainly true that many missionaries of the colonial era were paternalistic, this does not mean that they were as successful in applying this paternalism as recent criticisms make them out to be. Ryan Dunch notes:

> Missionary paternalism is historically significant, but not because it was "cultural imperialism." Being on the receiving end of missionary condescension was often a galling experience for indigenous Christians or mission school students, and it is critically important for understanding the emergence of Christian nationalism, independent and indigenous church movements, and anti-Christian movements in the twentieth century in China and elsewhere. However, the attitudes of missionaries are beside the point when it comes to the crucial question of their *effects* on indigenous cultures. The distinction is not always kept as clear as it should be in literature criticizing the missionary impact on culture, in which the *intent* of missionaries to change a culture is frequently confused with the *actuality* of doing so. (2002, 310, emphasis in original; see also Frykenberg 2003b, 9)

To this we may add at least three further significant elements for analysis of missionary and colonialist relations (Jeyaraj 2005, 381–82). First, missionaries generally focused their attention on enabling the nationals to understand the gospel and what it meant for them. For example, the slave trade was still at its height during the mid-1800s, and missionaries across Africa fought it. By 1863 Roman Catholic missionaries had begun establishing farms for freed and runaway slaves in Kenya. The Church Missionary Society joined in the anti-slavery efforts in 1875 by establishing a colony it called Freetown, the largest refuge for escaped slaves in West Africa. The missionaries aimed to establish a Christian community as a model and begin to train future African leaders (Anderson 1977, 19). Peter Falk says of these former slaves:

> The freed slaves and the refugees worked, planted fields, and legally obtained their livelihood. They studied trades and learned how to use tools they had not known previously. New crops were introduced. Medical care was generally offered, even though in some cases it was rudimentary and limited. The settlements provided a sense of security, whereas the villages were frequently attacked and pillaged by the slave traders. Consequently the stations were respected by the people. (1979, 246)

Nevertheless, despite the differing sets of goals and focus, there was certainly an "inseparable link between the colonizers and the missionaries" (Jeyaraj 2005, 381), seen perhaps most strongly in Portuguese and Spanish efforts. In those cases, as for example in Latin America with such arrangements as the *ecomendero* system, the results were terrible and are rightly criticized today.

Finally, the ambiguities of the missionary-colonial relationship are reflected in how the various East India companies established by European governments from 1600 onward had at best a dubious relationship with missionaries. The simple reality that missionaries in India were not welcomed by the British East India Company and were marginalized where possible in India is a vivid reminder that the missionaries were hardly hand-in-glove with the colonial agenda. As Daniel Jeyaraj notes, "The relationship between West European colonialism and Protestant missionary activity is at best ambiguous. Post-colonial claims that Christian missions were the right hands of European colonialism cannot be always substantiated" (2005, 382).

The true story of the church in intercultural communication, however, extends back much further than colonialism or the Crusades. In fact, it goes all the way back to the book of Acts. Among the many cross-cultural workers we could choose, Paul the apostle stands out. Paul's one-year term serving with Barnabas at the church in Antioch certainly exposed him to people of multiple cultures. His three missionary journeys broadened that exposure, with incidents ranging from the miscommunication among the people of Lystra (Acts 14:8–20) to the oft-cited speech at the marketplace in Athens (Acts 17:16–33). A good lesson in intercultural communication can be learned from the Lystran encounter:

> The perils of intercultural communication are vividly captured in Luke's account. Paul went from being declared a god to being stoned and left for dead in a very short time! While Paul's treatment is extreme, the reality is that misunderstandings in communication due to culture are a regular part of the life of a missionary. Luke's story illustrates a fact that every missionary must face: *people "read" you in ways that make sense to them*. Further, their understanding of you and the message you bring can be radically different than what you intended. (Moreau, Corwin, and McGee 2004, 265, emphasis added)

That people understand the sojourner among them on their own terms rather than the sojourner's, while obvious, is one of the most often forgotten realities of missionary life. Paul went on to further encounters and never appeared to fixate on a particular method of communication (he ranged from quoting poets to engaging in power encounters). As noted previously, Paul

---

SIDEBAR 2.2
IMPLICATIONS FOR THE CULTURAL VALUES MISSIONARIES
HAVE INTRODUCED

Adapted from Comaroff and Comaroff (1991); see also Dench (2002, 312)

Here is a list of some of the cultural values that missionaries introduced among the Tswana of Botswana in southern Africa. As you look at the list, choose two or three of the items and consider how they have impacted the culture and communication patterns of the Tswana.

1. "Clock" time (time indicated by a clock rather than by seasons, sun, or moon)
2. The idea of private property
3. Individual labor
4. Wealth accumulation (whether on settled farms or in factories and mines)
5. New forms of architecture (buildings) and domestic arrangement (homes)
6. Medicine in relation to the body
7. The idea of the nation-state
8. Economic development
9. The desirability of literacy

---

demonstrated a clear "willingness to accommodate himself to whatever social setting he found himself in, so as 'to win as many as possible.' . . . Thus Paul's first concern in such matters is not whether he offends or does not offend—although that too is a concern ([1 Cor.] 10:32)—but whether the gospel itself will get its proper hearing (cf. 10:33)" (Fee 1987, 426–27).

This does not mean that Paul was *unconcerned* with offending people. Rather, he did not want to unnecessarily offend them with things that were not central to the Christian message (e.g., circumcision and even church polity). His flexibility, by some accounts, appears to be far greater than many more-contemporary missionaries, who are far more likely than Paul to implement a particular doctrinal orientation (e.g., Calvinism, Lutheranism, Pentecostalism) or denominational polity (e.g., pastor-focused, congregation-focused, presbytery-focused, or bishopric-focused) in cross-cultural settings.

Added to this lack of flexibility in the colonial era (and beyond) was the mythic imagery of the "white man's burden," framed in colonial terms of the three "Cs"—namely, commerce, civilization, and Christianity. To this we may also add the more secular image of the missionary as a bigoted destroyer of local cultures so focused on saving people from hell that he was of no genuine earthly good (e.g., James Michener's *Hawaii* [1959; the same year as *The Ugly American*] and Barbara Kingsolver's *The Poisonwood Bible* [1998]).

While we cannot deny that there were missionaries who exemplified these stereotyped attitudes, we must also recognize that missionaries who were successful had to navigate relationships over decades-long spans, and that complete dissatisfaction on the part of the indigenous populations would have negated the possibility of missionary success. Thus while some missionaries do illustrate the negative stereotype, it is unfair to assign these stereotypes to the average missionary. Dunch notes:

> By the nature of their work, even the most inflexible and churlish missionaries had to develop sustainable working relationships with people in their host society. As a practical matter, therefore, they could not afford to adopt a wholly negative attitude towards it. The popular image of the finger-wagging missionary condemning a host culture wholesale and seeking to replace it in its entirety is, to say the least, implausible as a general type; such a person would soon have proved useless as a missionary and been recalled. (2002, 322)

To help us more specifically focus on issues of intercultural communication, we now turn our attention to three figures from mission history who exemplify what we consider to be good intercultural communication practices, especially in light of the times in which they lived: Matteo Ricci, Bartholomäus Ziegenbalg, and Mary Slessor.

Matteo Ricci (1552–1610)

Matteo Ricci was born at Macerata, Italy, where he did his early studies before his concentration on law in Rome. He joined the Society of Jesus (the Jesuits) at the highly regarded Collegium Romanum, where he studied theology as well as mathematics and astronomy. Having requested to serve in missions in Asia, he left Europe in 1578 for Goa, the capital of the Portuguese Indies. There and at Cochin, he taught and ministered until 1582, when he was summoned by Alessandro Valignani to Macao, where he began to learn Chinese as preparation for ministry in China (Brucker 1912), which he entered in 1583.

Of all the missionary movements of the Catholic Church, the Jesuits are best known for adapting well to new contexts. That reputation was earned in part by their work in China, where their years of preparation learning Chinese philosophy, art, and literature enabled them to meet Chinese intellectuals on their own level. Thus, "instead of being rejected as foreign barbarians, they were accepted as intelligent and cultivated men"

> For a very long period, U.S. imperialism laid greater stress than other imperialist countries on activities in the sphere of spiritual aggression, extending from religious to "philanthropic" and cultural undertakings.
>
> Mao Tse-tung, in
> Dunch 2002, 314

SIDEBAR 2.3
RICCI'S APPRECIATION FOR CHINESE POLITICS AND CUSTOMS

Corradini (1990, 55)

Concerning the state, he showed a real admiration for it. . . . Here Ricci found a bureaucratic and meritocratic administration, in a unitarian state which was even larger than Europe. And this he admired. Moreover, coming from Europe, . . . Ricci was amazed at, and admired, the fact that in China rule and power were in the hands of the *literati* class.

Chinese family customs were in general well accepted by Ricci, who praised the Confucian virtue of *xiao*, filial piety, as the implementation of the Mosaic command to revere father and mother. But he could not accept, for obvious reasons, Chinese polygamy. . . . But his friendly and comprehensive approach to Chinese civilization does not remain a dream. He was a forerunner of our times, and the present dialogue between western and Chinese scholars is a clear demonstration that Ricci's approach to China was the correct one.

(Highet 1950, 222–23). Ricci was able to fill this role superbly (Bresner 1997, 108–10).

One of the many ways that Ricci distinguished himself was in finding appropriate places to connect Christian faith with Chinese culture. For example, once he realized that appropriating the role of a Buddhist monk would lead to his being despised by the elite, he quickly adapted to the role of a member of the literati, for which his training and temperament were perfectly suited (Chan 2003, 272–73). Mark White wonderfully summarizes Ricci's orientation to intercultural sensitivity and the reason that his impact is still felt in China four hundred years after his death:

> Ricci respected those he met so much that he wanted to know everything that they knew. He loved them enough to tell them that he knew something that was better than anything they had ever heard. Because he listened carefully to them, Ricci's friends paid attention to him as he told them of the Lord in their own language. There, I think, is where the Christian call to mission and the ideal of social justice come together and, in fact, become one: in a conversation between friends. "I do not call you servants, because I have revealed to you everything that the Father has revealed to me. I call you friends." Jesus teaches us this: If you listen to everything that someone wants to tell you, no matter how painful or jarring it may be to hear, then, when you say, "God loves you," perhaps that person will actually believe you. (1996, 21)

Bartholomäus Ziegenbalg (1682–1719)

Bartholomäus Ziegenbalg was born to a Pietist family in Saxony (Germany), and was introduced to the tenets of Lutheran Pietism early in life by his sisters. This interest was cemented when he studied at Halle under Augustus Franke. Jeyaraj notes a formative moment in Ziegenbalg's teen years: "When he was sixteen, he met a friend, who as a musician, told him about the importance of harmony in music, and drew a parallel harmony between God the Creator and God's creatures. Ziegenbalg concentrated his efforts on finding out ways to live in spiritual and moral harmony with God, as revealed by Jesus Christ in the Bible" (2005, 385).

This orientation toward harmony with God gave Ziegenbalg a great respect for people and the cultures in which they were embedded (Hille 2000) and served as a guiding orientation in his cross-cultural service. His call to missions came when the Danish king Frederick IV developed a desire to send missionaries to his overseas colonies. However, this missionary effort was done without formal state or church approval. Thus, while Ziegenbalg was appointed to serve at Tranquebar, neither the Danish Lutheran Church (displeased with his Pietism) nor the Danish East India Company (Frykenberg 2003a, 49) supported the appointment.

Once he arrived in Tranquebar on July 9, 1706, he immediately devoted himself to studying the Tamil language and culture. When his language skills had reached a sufficient level, he studied Tamil religious beliefs by reading Tamil texts and engaging in discussion with Tamil leaders, resulting in what could be called his own "conversion" to the richness of the Tamil culture, which he expressed this way:

> When finally I was completely able to read their own books, and became aware, that among them are taught, in an entirely regular manner, the very same philosophical disciplines as, for instance, are dealt with by scholars in Europe; and also that they have a regular written law from which all theological matters must be derived and demonstrated; then this astonished me greatly, and I developed a very great desire to be thoroughly instructed in their heathenism from their own writings. I therefore obtained for myself ever more books, one after the other, and spared neither effort nor expense until I have now—through diligent reading of their books and through constant debating with their Bramans or priests—reached the point where I have a sure knowledge of them, and am able to give an account. (cited in Sweetman 2004, 23)

As a result of his orientation and study, several themes related to an intercultural attitude can be seen in his life and work (Jeyaraj 2005). First, local people are equal partners, neither superior nor inferior to the people of the missionary's own country. Ziegenbalg was far more critical of the supposed Christian Europeans than of local Tamils (Sweetman 2004, 19) and was quick to recognize the help of his national workers in the works he translated (Liebau 2003, 89).

Second, the missionary's task is neither to destroy local culture nor to dislocate converts away from it, but rather to reorient all questions about culture and society toward Jesus Christ. This principle is evidenced in Ziegenbalg's translation of multiple Tamil religious and cultural texts as well as his work to secure a significant library of such works.

Third, lower-caste converts are not to be suppressed or subjugated but rather are to be liberated in Christ from their old ways of seeing the world to seeing it as Christ leads. This principle helps to explain Ziegenbalg's orientation toward fostering universal literacy (Frykenberg 2003a, 49).

> *The missionaries who are willing to acquire the language and learn from the culture of their hosts experience positive conversion experience, which they wish to communicate to their friends and patrons. Their intercultural life builds bridges and facilitates intercultural learning.*
>
> Jeyaraj 2005, 388

Mary (Mitchell) Slessor (1848–1915)

Born to a poor family with an alcoholic father in Aberdeen, Scotland, Mary Slessor received only a basic education and was employed for half days at the age of eleven in a textile mill. Once she came to Christ as a teenager, she became highly active in her church as a natural leader for the other teens there. Her strong determination was such that she developed a reputation of persevering whenever she had resolved to do something, which prepared her well for mission work: "A study of Slessor's life reveals certain factors leading to a missionary fervor, combined with a large measure of down-to-earth common sense. Through the trying circumstances of her youth, she learned to face and overcome difficult situations in ways that often challenged the mission methods and attitudes of her era" (Hardage 2002, 178).

As is so often the case, however, this strength also could work against her when carried too far. She had a well-deserved reputation for being a disciplinarian (Livingstone 1916), though this was not a significant cultural issue in the Nigerian culture where she worked.

On arrival in Nigeria, she was advised to make the study of Efik—a prominent local language—her highest priority, so she devoted herself to learning it. She was so gifted in languages that native speakers described her as "having an

Efik mouth." Once she was grounded in the language, she began more careful consideration of cultural practices. In keeping with her headstrong personality, she fought vigorously against such practices as twin murder and the killing of wives and slaves as part of the funeral for a chief (Livingstone 1916, 179), and demonstrated an orientation toward social action, adopting numerous orphans during her career, working to make life better for women, and taking a role in settling disputes (181). More than Ricci or Ziegenbalg, however, Slessor believed that the colonial enterprise and missionary work belonged together (Proctor 2000, 46). As noted in one biography, "Her life was an example of Christian inculturation, but regrettably it was trivialized by a romantic 'white queen of Okoyong' attitude toward her in Britain" (Ross 1998, 624).

LESSONS FROM HISTORY

What can we learn from these historical examples? First, the actual history of how well missionaries fared in intercultural communication is not as one-sided as some assume. Second, paying attention to cultural factors (language, customs, manners) is extremely important. Imitating others in one's new setting while still maintaining one's own identity is an important balance to seek. Third, when missionaries see those among whom they minister as people rather than objects ("targets," "receptors," etc.), it can keep them from abusing their power. We have seen that missionaries do have a significant amount of social power, which can be wielded well (e.g., gaining entry into places normally forbidden) or not so well (e.g., identifying themselves too closely with colonial administrations by using social connections to gain assistance to support their goals). Fourth, personality can be a driving factor—especially a strong personality—and it too can work either to the missionary's advantage (e.g., the ability to persevere) or disadvantage (e.g., when the missionary's personality stifles leadership development among the local population).

CONCLUSION

Understanding the history of intercultural communication—that it has always been part of the mission of the church, and the contemporary development of the more formal academic discipline—gives us perspective on the long-term realities as well as current approaches. Both set the stage for digging more deeply into what today's scholars and practitioners are saying, thinking, and doing—and in the process enriching our own understanding and practice of communicating well when we cross cultural boundaries. In light of that framing, the case study that follows is an excerpt from a letter written by Ziegenbalg illustrating some of the issues that we have explored and still face today. The letter, written more than three hundred years ago, offers the valuable insights of its author, whose perspectives were far ahead of his time.

CASE STUDY:
LETTER FROM BARTHOLOMÄUS ZIEGENBALG

The following excerpt comes from a letter written by Bartholomäus Ziegenbalg on August 22, 1708:

Most Christians in Europe are of such opinions that the South Indians are an extremely barbarous people without knowing anything about the one true God and that among them there are no academic disciplines, good customs, virtues or moral code of conduct. This opinion comes from the fact that some Europeans came to the South Indians not knowing their language or reading their books. They derived their conclusions from their external observations. I myself have to confess that, at the time of my first arrival among them, I thought that their language did not have reasonable grammatical rules and that they were living an unorganized life without any civil code of conduct. Basing my judgment on what they did and what they failed to do, I too had all kinds of wrong conceptions about them thinking that the South Indians possessed neither a civil nor moral code of conduct. For this reason I excuse those who have never known the South Indians, yet have such wrong preconceptions about them. Before I lived among the South Indians, I too had the same kind of prejudice.

After I learned to speak their language to some extent and discuss with them all kinds of things, I was freed gradually from such vain imaginations. I began to have a much better opinion about them. Finally, when I acquired the ability to read the literature, I realized the following: in their own orderly way they teach well-organized philosophical disciplines that are similar to the disciplines discussed only by experts in Europe. Moreover, they have religious scriptures that are written systematically. All theological subject matters should be derived from and based on these scriptures. (cited in Jeyaraj 2005, 390)

REFLECTION
AND DISCUSSION

1. If you were to receive a more contemporary language version of this as an email from a friend, how would you respond?
2. How do you identify prejudicial attitudes displayed by others (especially fellow cross-cultural workers), and how might you address them when you encounter them?

3

Perspectives on
Intercultural Communication

I n the first two chapters we introduced intercultural communication and surveyed the story line of communication from secular and Christian orientations. At this stage we are ready to examine facets of intercultural communication from these perspectives, including theoretical and methodological approaches and selected themes. Then we will have the necessary background to explore some of the issues from a Christian perspective, including the purpose of communication, missiological implications of intercultural communication, and the more significant challenges and tensions that the secular discipline presents for Christians.

GENERAL APPROACHES TO STUDYING INTERCULTURAL COMMUNICATION

Edward Hall not only developed the discipline in its early stages but also pioneered the approaches that shaped the discipline for several decades (see sidebar 3.1).

SIDEBAR 3.1
HALL'S PARADIGM FOR INTERCULTURAL COMMUNICATION

Rogers, Hart, and Miike (2002, 10–11, emphasis in original)

What were the main elements of the paradigm, defined as a conceptualization that provides exemplary problems and methods of research to a community of scholars (Kuhn, 1970), for intercultural communication?

1. The FSI scholars focused on intercultural communication, rather than on macro-level monocultural study, which Hall originally (and unsuccessfully) taught the FSI trainees. Although intercultural communication had roots in anthropology and linguistics, it became quite different from either in the decades following 1955.

2. *Nonverbal communication, defined (by Hall) as communication that does not involve the exchange of words.* Hall, Trager, and Birdwhistell created the empirical study of various types of nonverbal communication (proxemics, chronemics, and kinesics), setting forth the leads that were followed up by later generations of nonverbal communication scholars.

3. *The emphasis, especially in nonverbal communication, was on the out-of-awareness level of information-exchange.* Here Hall was influenced by Sigmund Freud, Erich Fromm, and Harry Stack Sullivan (Hall, 1993), and by Raymond Birdwhistell.

4. The approach to intercultural communication accepted cultural differences and was nonjudgmental, reflecting a perspective from anthropological research and training. Here, Hall followed in the footsteps of Franz Boas and Ruth Benedict in strongly supporting cultural relativism, the belief that a particular cultural element should only be judged in light of its context (Modell, 1983; Herskovits, 1973).

5. Participatory training methods were necessitated in part because intercultural communication was taught in all-day workshop sessions at the Foreign Service Institute to mid-career trainees who already had extensive experience in the field. Hall and his fellow trainers at the FSI used simulation games, exercises, and other participant-involving methods of experiential instruction.

6. Intercultural communication began as a highly applied type of training, intended to ameliorate the lack of skills of U.S. American diplomats and development technicians.

These six main elements of the paradigm worked out at the Foreign Service Institute generally characterize the field of intercultural communication today as it is taught at U.S. universities (Gudykunst and Kim, 1984).

Theoretical Approaches

Table 3.1 presents the various theoretical approaches to understanding how people communicate across cultural boundaries. Although it would be

TABLE 3.1
THEORETICAL APPROACHES TO INTERCULTURAL COMMUNICATION

Theory	Orientation of the Theory in Intercultural Communication
Uncertainty Reduction Theory	Because we want to reduce our own uncertainty in a new setting, we initiate change (in ourselves or in the culture) so that we may fit in more appropriately (see Gudykunst 1995).
Adaptation Theory	We gradually adapt our communication skills in the process of acquiring intercultural communication competency (see Y. Y. Kim 1995).
Rhetorical Theory	Based on rhetoric theory in communication; pays particular attention to context and event in communication (see Starosta and Chen 2005).
Expectancy Violations Theory	All cultures have expectations about communication behavior, and we can learn more about intercultural communication by focusing on people's adherence to and deviations from these culturally framed expectations (see Burgoon 1995).
Relational Models Theory	Communication takes place through four fundamental and innate forms of the ways all humans relate and interact socially: communal sharing, authority ranking, equality matching, and market pricing (Levine, Park, and Kim 2007, 217).

possible to devote a chapter to each of them, space limitations require that we constrain ourselves to the concise summary found in this table.

Methodological Approaches

Not all contemporary scholars follow the same methodology in studying intercultural communication (see table 3.2). It should be noted here that each of the methodological approaches listed in table 3.2 (except critical methodology, which is more limited) can be used within the theoretical approaches listed in table 3.1. We integrate insights from the various methodologies listed in table 3.2 throughout the text, so we limit our discussion here to the concise descriptions in the table. In this text we do not focus on providing testable hypotheses, looking at communication as a whole system, interpreting individual instances, or critiquing the social context of the discipline, although some of these issues surface throughout the text. Rather, following the early lead of the discipline, our approach is more pragmatic with the aim of better preparing you to cross into a new culture.

THEMES IN INTERCULTURAL COMMUNICATION STUDIES

Young Yun Kim, a systems theorist, noted that there are five overlapping themes in what researchers of intercultural communication are exploring (2001b, 142–43; see also Y. Y. Kim 2005, 556):

TABLE 3.2
CURRENT METHODOLOGICAL APPROACHES

Neopositivism	Based on the notion that it is possible to generalize hypotheses (or models) that are predictive and can be tested empirically for rules that govern intercultural communication.
Systems	Also looks for rules, but does so by exploring systems and noting the emergent and dynamic quality of the entire system, the structure and functions of its various parts, and the way the system interacts with its "environment."
Interpretive	Built on a phenomenological approach, uses qualitative research methods to better understand individual instances or case studies of communication events.
Critical	Questions the legitimacy of traditional approaches; engages in ideological critiques of issues of power and control.

Adapted from Y. Y. Kim 2001a; compare to Starosta and Chen 2005.

1. intrapersonal processes of intercultural communication,

2. intercultural communication competence,

3. cultural adaptation,

4. cultural identity in intercultural contexts, and

5. power inequality in intercultural relations.

A brief explanation of these themes will help to set the stage for discussion integrated throughout the rest of the book. The following discussion draws from Young Yum Kim (2001b, 142–47), with the addition of cultural intelligence as a more recently introduced theme.

Intrapersonal Processes

Intrapersonal (psychological) processes are those mental images and constructs we use to guide us in our communication acts. The scholarly focus has tended to be on those things that impede good communication such as stereotypes, prejudices, racism, intolerance, and other types of ethnocentrism. Studies enable researchers to better understand these negative attitudes and how they are developed and reinforced in people's minds, and to identify potential ways in which they may be countered.

Intercultural Communication Competence

Competence focuses on the skills, attitudes, and knowledge (depending on the model) needed to develop proficiency in intercultural communication. These range from language acquisition to general knowledge to cognitive complexity and social skills (e.g., negotiation) that demonstrate empathy and understanding of the new cultural setting. While no single model has yet been accepted by theoreticians, such a model has potentially huge implications for areas such as business, refugee resettlement, development work, politics, and, of course, ministry of all types.

Cultural Adaptation

Cultural adaptation studies focus on the process involved in adjusting to living in a new cultural setting. Related terms include "acculturation," "assimilation," "adjustment," and "integration" (Y. Y. Kim 2001b, 144). This adaptation process is not always successful, so research in this area includes studies of marginalization and exclusion as well as integration in the new setting. Again, various researchers propose different sets of variables that compose the adaptation process, typically ones that come from their own disciplinary background. For example, psychologists might look at the ways people understand their identity in relation to a new setting (Berry 1995, 2001; Zheng and Berry 1991), and communication researchers might explore an interdisciplinary approach (Y. Y. Kim 2001a).

Cultural Identity in Intercultural Contexts

Studies in cultural identity focus on how the identity of an individual is formed and maintained within her or his cultural setting. This is especially important in heterogeneous settings, where multiple minorities exist, each group ostensibly with its own identity. Initial studies conceptualized this identity to be relatively static, but recently researchers have noted that it is dynamic and must be analyzed as such. Among missionaries, perhaps the most widely used model for understanding identity is Paul Hiebert's centered and bounded sets (Corwin 2011; Moreau 2012, 156–59; and Yoder et al. 2009; for Hiebert's use and development over the decades, see 1979b, 1983, 1994, 107–36, and 2008a, 33–37, 308–10).

Power Inequality in Intercultural Relations

A new area of interest in intercultural studies is a postmodern critique that asserts that the prevailing attitudes in intercultural studies are focused on building and maintaining the power of the status quo rather than empowering disenfranchised groups (Y. Y. Kim 2005, 562–63; Chen and Starosta 2005, 11). Those who perpetually struggle are victims of those in power, and this branch of studies explores this phenomenon (e.g., Orbe 1997). It could be thought of as a parallel to certain types of liberation theologies or the New Hermeneutic in Christian circles (Achtemeier 1969).

Cultural Intelligence

Cultural intelligence is a relatively new idea found in psychological discussions of intercultural communication. It may be defined as "the ability to engage in a set of behaviors that uses skills (e.g., language or interpersonal skills) and qualities (e.g., tolerance for ambiguity, flexibility) that are tuned appropriately to the culture-based values and attitudes of the people with whom one interacts" (Brooks Peterson 2004, 89; see http://culturalq.com/researcharticles.html).

Cultural intelligence incorporates cognitive, motivational, and behavioral components (Earley and Ang 2003; see Livermore 2013 for application to short-term missions). Cognitive skills are critical to understanding the new culture and truly seeing it as new and different. The level of motivation is also important; without it, adaptation will be shallow at best. Finally, the behavioral component includes the ability to use the right actions at the right time and thereby engage in culturally appropriate behavior for any given setting. The more capable one is in these areas, the higher the level of cultural intelligence.

A CHRISTIAN PERSPECTIVE ON THE PURPOSE OF COMMUNICATION

Is there a Christian purpose to communication? We will start with a brief biblical consideration of perhaps the most commonly used verse in relation to communicating Christ in new settings, 1 Corinthians 9:19–23:

> Though I am free and belong to no one, I made myself a slave to everyone, to win as many as possible. To the Jews I became like a Jew, to win the Jews. To those under the law I became like one under the law (though I myself am not under the law), so as to win those under the law. To those not having the law I became like one not having the law (though I am not free from God's law but am under Christ's law), so as to win those not having the law. To the weak I became weak, to win the weak. I have become all things to all people so that by all possible means I might save some. I do all this for the sake of the gospel, that I may share in its blessings.

Paul makes the choice to live within his context freely and does so in light of the gospel. Though on the behavioral level his actions are inconsistent, they follow a higher priority (and integrity) than simple slavish behavioral observance.

In this context, he specifically deals with food bought in the open marketplace. He draws the line by saying that he remains under Christ's law (or legal obligation to Christ, Barrett 1987, 212) even when living like a gentile (e.g., he would hardly murder someone no matter how favorably the culture looked on it!). As Gordon Fee explains it:

> This passage has often been looked to for the idea of "accommodation" in evangelism, that is, of adapting the *message* to the language and perspective of the recipients. Unfortunately, despite the need for that discussion to be carried on, this passage does not speak directly to it. This has to do with how one *lives* or *behaves* among those whom one wishes to evangelize (not, it needs to be added in passing, with social taboos among Christians). What needs to be emphasized is the point expressed clearly by Bornkamm: "Paul could not modify the gospel itself according to the particular characteristics of his hearers. The whole of his concern is to make clear that the changeless gospel . . . empowers him to be free to change his stance." (1987, 432–33, emphasis in original)

CONTEMPORARY MISSIOLOGY AND INTERCULTURAL COMMUNICATION

Christians were involved in the earliest development of the discipline of intercultural communication. In 1955, four years before Edward Hall's *The Silent Language* (1959b), linguist Eugene Nida published an article titled "Cross-Cultural Communication of the Christian Message" in the missionary journal *Practical Anthropology* (a Christian journal for anthropologically minded missionaries). In 1954 his *Customs and Cultures* was initially published (see also Nida 1972, 1999, 2003; Nida and Wonderly 1963; Nida and Taber 1974; Nida and Reyburn 1981).

John C. Condon, coauthor of one of the earliest intercultural communication textbooks (Condon and Yousef 1975), taught at International Christian University in Tokyo. He and Mitsuko Saito, a faculty colleague, organized two important conferences on intercultural communication held at International Christian University with some two thousand attendees (Kitao 1985, 12). As a result of these conferences, they published two compiled books (Condon and Saito 1974, 1976). Clifford Clarke, a founder of the Summer Institute in Intercultural Communication at Stanford University (now held annually near Portland, Oregon), was raised by American missionary parents in Japan (Rogers, Hart, and Miike 2002, 15). However, apart from those mentioned, Christians (and the developing field of missiology) did not play overt roles in the development of the contemporary discipline of intercultural communication.

At the same time, it can be said that in the early phases Christian anthropologists and missionaries were paying close attention to what those in secular settings were saying. This is clearly demonstrated by the 1963 republication of an article by Edward T. Hall and William Foote Whyte in *Practical Anthropology*

> **SIDEBAR 3.2**
> **DIMENSIONS OF CROSS-CULTURAL COMMUNICATION**
>
> David Hesselgrave delineates seven dimensions that are foundational for cross-cultural communication and elaborates a model with them that has been used to train missionaries for several decades (1978, 1991b). As you consider each of these dimensions, note how they correlate to several of the chapters in this book.
>
> 1. Worldviews—ways of perceiving the world
> 2. Cognitive Processes—ways of thinking
> 3. Linguistic Forms—ways of expressing ideas
> 4. Behavioral Patterns—ways of acting
> 5. Social Structures—ways of interacting
> 6. Media Influence—ways of channeling the message
> 7. Motivational Resources—ways of deciding

(first published in 1960 in a secular journal), and with publications such as William Smalley's "Culture Shock, Language Shock, and the Shock of Self-Discovery" (1963) and Charles Kraft's "Christian Conversion or Cultural Conversion" (1963). It is also reflected in some of the early publications in *Evangelical Missions Quarterly* (founded in 1964), including Donald Larson's "Cultural Static and Religious Communication" (1966) and the first master's thesis on the topic in 1967, by a Pepperdine University student (Ships 1967).

Despite this strong beginning, however, as the years wore on articles that were explicitly Christian or missiological were almost completely ignored by those in the secular field. Additionally, a review of the literature from the 1960s through the 1980s reveals that explicitly missionary reflection largely did not keep up with the expanding secular field (there are a few exceptions, like D. K. Smith 1992).

During the past several decades, perhaps the best-known authors in Christian intercultural communication (largely called "cross-cultural communication" in Christian circles) have been Charles Kraft and David Hesselgrave. Kraft, a prolific and widely known author, has been one of the seminal thinkers in approaching cross-cultural communication from an anthropological perspective (e.g., 1973b, 1973c, 1974a, 1978a, 1978b, 1978c, 1979a, 1979c, 1989, 1991a, 1991b, 1994, 1996, 1999, 2005a, 2005b, 2005c) as well as contextualization and power encounter (Van Engen, Woodberry, and Whiteman 2008). With a background in rhetoric, Hesselgrave has perhaps been equally well known and respected in missionary cross-cultural communication (1965, 1972, 1973, 1976, 1978, 1980a, 1980b, 1982, 1983, 1985, 1986, 1987, 1990, 1991a, 1991b,

---

SIDEBAR 3.3
BASIC VALUES MODEL IN INTERCULTURAL COMMUNICATION

In 1974, Marvin Mayers presented a taxonomy of six categories of opposites in his "Basic Values Model" (*Christianity Confronts Culture*, 157–61). Mayers's model is intended to be framed in terms of cognitive styles and is built on the work of Herman Witkin (field-dependent vs. field-independent), Marshall McLuhan (hot and cool media), Edward DeBono (vertical vs. lateral thinking), and others. Sherwood Lingenfelter and Marvin Mayers focused on these values in *Ministering Cross-Culturally* (1986), which has remained in print and continues to be widely used in Christian circles to train people for serving in another culture. Mayers explains:

> The basic values model posits that there are certain values that are basic and present in all human beings. This model of human behavior bases itself

on the premise that once these values and their order of importance have been established for an individual or group, one can predict behavioral response in any given situation. When applying the generative principles of the model, human behavior becomes predictable at a very high level of accuracy. This in no way implies that human behavior is determined, rather that it is effectively controlled within a social context. Knowing the model and applying it in a variety of contexts frees one from the burden of such control and allows one to gain fresh insight into his own and another's behavior. Such insight releases a person from taking himself too seriously and assuming a personal affront due to another's actions or words. (1974, 156)

DICHOTOMIZING	HOLISTIC
People oriented this way polarize life in terms of black and white, here and there, themselves and the other, right and wrong. It is relatively easy for them to evaluate the other on the basis of such dichotomies. They must feel that they are right in order to be satisfied.	People oriented this way see that the parts will have a vital function within the whole. No consideration can be given any part unless it is also considered within the whole. They derive satisfaction through integration of thought and life, whether planned or natural, and feel insecure when placed in a category.

CRISIS OR DECLARATIVE	NONCRISIS OR INTERROGATIVE
People oriented this way emphasize planning and the ability to anticipate crises. They repeatedly follow a single authoritative or preplanned procedure and seek expert advice to deal with problems that arise.	People oriented this way downplay the possibility of crisis and focus on the moment. They may avoid taking action and delay decisions. When problems arise, they will tend to seek off-the-cuff solutions from multiple opinions and distrust expert advice.

1997, 1999, 2000a, 2000b). His paradigm of seven dimensions of cross-cultural communication (sidebar 3.2) has been used widely in missionary prefield training. Other major missiological voices in intercultural communication include

TIME-ORIENTED

People oriented this way are concerned with the timing and scheduling of an event and will have a well-defined "range of punctuality" at the beginning and the end of the session. They plan time periods for efficiency. They remember and try to reinforce certain times and dates.

EVENT-ORIENTED

People oriented this way are concerned about the details of the event, regardless of the time required; they are willing to give exhaustive consideration of a problem until resolved and have a "let come what may" outlook not tied to any precise schedule. They tend to emphasize present experience rather than the past or the future.

TASK ORIENTATION

People oriented this way focus on tasks and principles, finding satisfaction in the achievement of goals. They tend to seek friends with similar goals and accept loneliness and social deprivation for the sake of personal achievements.

PERSON ORIENTATION

People oriented this way focus on persons and relationships, finding satisfaction in interaction. They tend to seek friends who are group-oriented and sacrifice personal achievements for group interaction.

ACHIEVEMENT FOCUS

(Prestige-Achieved)

People oriented this way feel that prestige must be achieved, and must be achieved again and again. They give far less weight to formal credentials. Rather, they tend to strive constantly to achieve prestige and are less likely to seek to attain a particular status in society. They give as much consideration to statements made by those without formal credentials as to those with them.

STATUS FOCUS

(Prestige-Ascribed)

People oriented this way feel that prestige is ascribed and then confirmed by the social group. They show respect in keeping with the ascription of prestige determined by society. They expect others to respect their rank and play the role their status demands. They see formal credentials as important and sacrifice to maintain the rank and prestige they have.

CONCEALMENT OF VULNERABILITY

People oriented this way prefer to conceal vulnerability. They take every step possible to avoid making errors—they double-check everything and are methodical and organized. They enjoy arguing a point to the end and hate admitting mistakes. They tend to cover up errors and will not expose weaknesses or tell stories about their personal lives.

WILLINGNESS TO EXPOSE VULNERABILITY

People oriented this way are willing to expose vulnerability. They do not find it difficult to admit mistakes and are less concerned with making errors. They tend to tell stories about themselves that expose their weaknesses. They are willing to be involved in new experiments and are open to alternative views and criticism.

Marvin Mayers (1974), Sherwood Lingenfelter (Lingenfelter and Mayers 1986—see sidebar 3.3; Lingenfelter 1992, 1996), and Paul Hiebert (1978, 1979a, 1983, 1985, 1989, 1994, 1999, 2008a, 2008b), though all three have found their framing through anthropology rather than communication studies.

Other voices in the field (in order of first communication publication) include Donald Smith (1971, 1992), Jim Engel (Engel and Norton 1975; Engel and Dyrness 2000), Dean Gilliland (1979), Duane Elmer (1993, 2002, 2006), and R. Daniel Shaw and Charles Van Engen (2003). In addition to the more important figures, numerous authors have written articles or books that focus on intercultural communication issues in missions (e.g., Larson 1966; Loewen 1972; Gordon 1973; Fountain 1975; Hile 1977; Brewster and Brewster 1978; Kelly 1978; Conn 1979; Parshall 1979; Seamands 1981; Shank 1979; Whiteman 1981, 1984; Dierks 1983; Verryn 1983; Allison 1984; Stafford 1984; Filbeck 1985; Reed 1985; Hovey 1986; Søgard 1986; Eitel 1987; Virts 1990; Dearborn 1991; Francis 1992; Hunter 1992; Priest 1993, 1994; Lenchak 1994; Wendland 1995; Jordan and Tucker 2002; Schalück 2003; Brown 2004a, 2004b; Dickerson 2004b; Greenlee and Stück 2004; Hoefer 2005; Moreau and O'Rear 2006b; Reese 2006; Thelle 2006; Johnson and Tieszen 2007; Sheffield 2007; Daniels 2008; Dzubinski 2008; Plueddemann 2009; Lederleitner and Elmer 2010).

CHALLENGES FROM THE DISCIPLINE FOR CHRISTIANS

The secular field of intercultural communication presents several significant challenges for Christian intercultural communication. At the surface level are the stereotypes of missionaries as people who destroy or run roughshod over local cultures (e.g., Michener 1959; Kingsolver 1998)—the *Ugly American* writ large on civil conscience. When Scott realized he was going to serve in missions, he was told by several friends to be sure he "was not like the other missionaries," who, it was assumed, were "ugly" Americans.

Today the image is even worse, since so much of North American culture is offended by a message that claims to be the truth, especially when that message includes telling others that they need to forsake their deities and follow Christ. This illustrates a second challenge for Christian intercultural communicators—namely, the noninterference orientation found among anthropologists and intercultural communication scholars. The basic tenets of a noninterference orientation are (1) all cultures are tuned to their environment, (2) introducing cultural change inevitably destroys their balance, and (3) it is unethical to introduce such change, especially changes of religion.

More recently, however, scholars have come to realize that the very act of observing a society makes noninterference impossible, and that all intercultural communication is a form of interference involving power. This is a third challenge for Christians. Postcolonial discourse denigrates any form of belief in absolute truth and challenges us by claiming that the ways (especially the positivist ones) that we analyze other cultures are in reality little more than a disguised means of maintaining our own created hegemonic power over the "others." This is a particular challenge for missionary work, and the need to find work alongside rather than on behalf of other peoples is a standing call from missiological circles. With the recent explosion in short-term missions, this issue has the potential to become an even worse problem in the future (e.g., Ngaruiya 2008).

A fourth significant challenge is that of the position of cultural relativism taken by the secular field. While Christians serving cross-culturally should recognize that *some* form of relativism is appropriate—such as Paul Hiebert's critical realism (2008b) or Steve Davis's biblical cultural relativism (2008)—the more absolute form of cultural relativism is not congruent with biblical revelation. Discerning what should be relative (e.g., individualism versus collectivism) and what should be absolute (e.g., abolishing slavery) is not always as easy as it may seem to those who have never been exposed to other cultures. Bribery, for example, is an exceedingly difficult issue to judge. This is not because bribery is acceptable, but because distinguishing among gifts, tips, extortion, and bribes is not as easy as it may appear in the cocoon of our own culture (see B. Adeney 1995).

CONCLUSION

As ambassadors of Christ, Christians should be the first to be deeply concerned about the issues and challenges raised by intercultural communication. Many engaged in cross-cultural service, though sold on the general nature of the concepts and ideas, have a hard time knowing what it means to implement them while engaged in their daily lives and ministries of evangelism, relief, discipleship, community development, education, or church planting. Because of this challenge, in the rest of the book we ensure that we show how the ideas we discuss make a difference in real life, not just in theoretical discussion. Application of the principles involved, especially in more pragmatic issues, can be difficult. Bear in mind that growing up you learned your language far more quickly than you learned the nuances of your culture; it is no different for Christians serving cross-culturally. We can easily see that we do not know the language, but it is harder to realize that we do not know the culture. This reality makes it harder for those who cross cultural boundaries as adults to live in a new setting. Our case study for this chapter illustrates just how challenging that can be.

CASE STUDY:
IDENTITY—MISSIONARY
OR INTERNATIONAL WORKER?

ALAN SEAMAN WITH SCOTT MOREAU

Jeremy and Karen served as missionaries for several years in two countries in the Middle East, becoming fluent in Arabic and raising their family there. Following God's call for a next step, Jeremy came back to his home country to earn a master's degree in teaching English to speakers of other languages (TESOL). As an older student with significant experience, he was instrumental in mobilizing many students on his campus to pray for the Muslim world and consider long-term ministry in the Middle East. After Jeremy completed his degree, the couple returned to the Middle East as empty-nesters. Jeremy became the director of an intensive English program (IEP) in a border city of a country adjacent to Israel in which the careful handling of religious and political sensitivities was part and parcel of the daily navigation of life.

The IEP program focused on developing academic English in preparation for work or study abroad. Almost all the students were Muslim. Jeremy's long-term strategy was to become well established in his city of service and eventually move to an "unreached" city in the northern part of the country, where he would establish a new IEP staffed by Christian teachers from various agencies.

After being welcomed into his new position, Jeremy spent the first few weeks getting to know the teachers, students, and staff of the IEP. He chatted easily with them in English and Arabic and hosted a series of key people in his apartment for meals. During one such dinner in his apartment, two important government officials were present. The officials were responsible for approving the visas for foreign teachers in the program, and they had been very helpful to date.

During a pause in the conversation, one of the officials looked intently at Jeremy and asked in a warm tone, "You know our customs and language well, and you care about the students here. You seem to be very different from the previous directors. Are you a missionary?"

Even though Jeremy had been prepared for this type of question, the directness took his breath away. With a quick prayer for wisdom, Jeremy responded by saying . . .

REFLECTION
AND DISCUSSION

1. What might explain the official's question? The case indicates he asked in a "warm tone." What might that indicate?
2. What do you think Jeremy should say in response to the question? Explain your answer.

PART 2

Foundations of Intercultural Communication Patterns

Mention "communication" to missionaries and many first think of language and language-related issues. Almost everyone who has learned a second (or third) language has stories to tell of embarrassing mistakes he or she made in confusing words or ideas in learning new vocabulary and ways of talking about the world around us.

Intercultural communication experts have long observed that cultures follow patterns in how they communicate. Those patterns are not randomly developed as time goes by. Rather, they flow out of foundations not readily seen when observing behavior.

Worldview, a concept criticized in anthropological circles (Moreau 2009), might be considered the cornerstone. However, worldview is not static but changes as circumstances, environment, and other factors change. We explore this in chapter 4.

In chapter 5 we discuss issues related to how people use language as they communicate. Their language gives them a framework for understanding the world around them as well as the categories into which they can organize what they observe and what happens to them.

In chapter 6 we turn our attention to how all communication in every language always takes place in a social context. Understanding that context is just as important as understanding the ways in which communication takes place; without placing communication in its proper context, we will never be able to understand what is being communicated.

Finally, in chapter 7 we deal with the reality that within their social contexts, people have roles and statuses that guide their behavior, groups form, and people network with others to accomplish their goals.

Worldview and Intercultural Communication

Almost everyone agrees that worldview is an important concept. However, trying to define worldview is no easier than defining "culture." The difficulty of defining it—the definitions range from something that is unique to every person to something that is shared culture-wide—has led some to say that we must abandon the idea or clarify it (see Howell 2006 and Moreau 2009).

There is little doubt that in popular use worldview is widely recognized as a driving force in everything we do. Typically it is defined as a set of operative assumptions that undergird everything we think, say, and do. In this chapter we survey the basic ideas about worldview and explore selected insights that will help us to understand the role it plays in intercultural communication.

WORLDVIEW

Worldview is often broadly (and circularly) defined as the way in which we view and understand the world around us (e.g., Geisler and Watkins 1989, 11; Kraft 1983, 222). In more technical terms, it is the complex and interactive set of assumptions through which we arrange our ideas and images of the

> *The concept of worldview has emerged during the past two decades as an important concept in philosophy, philosophy of science, history, anthropology and Christian thought. It is one of those fascinating, frustrating words that catches our attention. Its ambiguity generates a great deal of study and insight, but also much confusion and misunderstanding. There is no single definition agreed upon by all.*
>
> Hiebert 2008b, 13

world we inhabit. However, these are not just cognitive assumptions; worldview also includes our feelings and moral assumptions (Hiebert 2008b, 15). It is essentially pretheoretical in character; it is the foundation on which theories and the methods of theorizing are built (Walsh 1992, 16). As such, it is a belief system (Dodd 1991, 75; Olthius 1985, 155) composed of the fundamental assumptions we make about reality (Hiebert 1985, 45).

Because it is pretheoretical, worldview is generally not found at the conscious level, and the assumptions that compose it are not necessarily coherently linked to one another; they may even be contradictory. These assumptions are established and conditioned through the experiences, ideas, and enculturation people receive while growing up. Further, each assumption is intertwined with the others and cannot be viewed in isolation from the total framework.

These assumptions, and how they are worked out, are seen in three primary dimensions: _cognitive_, the content of the assumptions; _affective_, our feelings related to the assumptions; and _evaluative_, the moral structure that we build

> *A worldview (or vision of life) is a framework or set of fundamental beliefs through which we view the world and our calling and future in it.... This vision is a channel for the ultimate beliefs which give direction and meaning to life. It is the integrative framework by which order and disorder are judged, the standard by which reality is managed and pursued. It is the set of hinges on which all our everyday thinking and doing turns.*
>
> *For each adherent, a worldview gives reasons and impetus for deciding what is true and what really matters in our experience. In other words, a worldview functions both descriptively and normatively.... A worldview is both a sketch of and a blueprint for reality; it both describes what we see and stipulates what we should see.*
>
> Olthius 1985, 155

from our assumptions. We will return to these three dimensions later in the chapter.

A Map of Life

Worldview defines the way we "lean into life"; it is both a map *of* life and a map *for* life (Walsh 1992, 18). As a map of life, it is a lens or window through which we view and make sense of the events we experience every day (Kraft 1983, 222). In discussing the domination system and how it controls us, theologian Walter Wink asserts, "Every observation is a directed observation, that is, an observation for or against a point of view" (1992, 54). Similarly, Hall tells us that culture (which is built on worldview) serves as a set of blinders determining what we see (1991a, 220). As a map through which we make sense of life, worldview is built on a faith system (Luzbetak 1988, 252) and is religious in character since it deals with "ultimate" concerns, "limit" questions (Toulmin 1961), and "control" beliefs (Wolterstorff 1976; noted by Walsh 1992, 19). The kinds of issues with which it is concerned include (the first three draw from Walsh 1992, 19; see also Redfield 1957, 85–86; Kraft 1989, 181–205):

> *A worldview may be likened to a window through which human beings look out on reality. . . . The worldview of our culture, like every other aspect of our culture, is taught to us from birth, and so convincingly that most of us never question that our view of reality is the only accurate one. Our deep-level worldview perspectives provide us with our understandings of both the personal and the nonpersonal universes around us.*
>
> Kraft 1979a, 222

1. Where am I? (What is the nature of reality; what is time and space?)
2. Who am I? (What does it mean to be human; what are "being" and "existence"?)
3. Why am I? (What is the purpose for people and human history?)
4. Who is in charge? (What powers control the reality I inhabit?)

Answers to these questions are found at two levels. The conscious and articulated level is usually expressed through the formal philosophies of life seen in a society. Although the unconscious and unstated level is reflected in the social patterns of a society, people rarely consciously think these elements through. Rather, people consider them so obvious that they need no explanations; they are simply "the way it is."

57

A Map for Life

In addition to being a map *of* life, worldview provides a map *for* life (Walsh 1992, 18–19). Worldview informs us about what ought to be, provides the foundation on which we build a plan for living, and gives us the grid on which to map every event in life (Hall 1991a, 16–17).

THE INTERACTION OF WORLDVIEW, FAITH, AND LIFEWAY

Worldview serves as one component of a circular loop in which faith, world-view, and lifeway (how we actually live our lives) interact (fig. 4.1, adapted from Walsh 1992). Together they enable us to maintain the perception that we understand reality, help us to make sense of everything we experience, and anchor meaning and purpose for the way we live.

Our assumptions are conditioned and established through the concepts and training we receive from our societies as well as everything we observe and integrate into our lives as we grow up. As Christians, we recognize that these assumptions at every level are in some way distorted because of our sinful nature. Further, each assumption is intertwined with the others and cannot be viewed in isolation from the total framework. As a result, our worldview is dynamic. It changes all the time as new events and circumstances

FIGURE 4.1
THE INTERACTION OF WORLDVIEW, FAITH, AND LIFEWAY

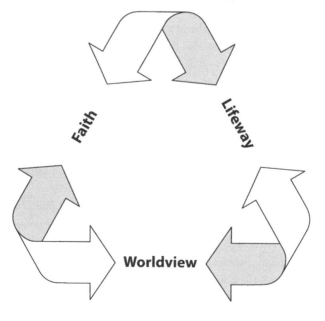

unfold around us. As Christians, our hope is that our assumptions—cognitive, evaluative, and moral—will be more and more conformed to the image of Christ.

By faith we refer to the beliefs, feelings, and evaluative orientations of people in regard to something beyond the level of the physical in the world. A change in a person's faith will generate a corresponding change in her or his worldview; likewise, a change in worldview will impact a person's faith. Christians believe that God created the universe, made people in his own image, loves each of us deeply, and interacts with the universe he created moment by moment. We also believe that the only way to be ultimately fulfilled is to be in relationship with our Creator through Jesus Christ. Faith provides a type of "sacred canopy" (Berger 1967) that helps us to understand life and concepts such as good and evil. However, a change in how we live can result in a change in our faith. A change in our faith—especially when a person comes to Christ and the Holy Spirit resides in that person—will result in a change of worldview.

By lifeway we simply mean how people choose to live on the day-to-day level. We are referring not to what they say are their ideals of how to live but to how they *actually choose* to live. It is obvious that choices made in life both come out of worldview and feed into it. A person choosing to join a cult or sect may have a radical change in worldview as a result, as may a Christian who chooses a particular path of sin and eventually changes faith as a result. Such choices may come out of a person's worldview, but they may also simply be made as opportunity arises and then have an impact on worldview.

CHANGE IN WORLDVIEW

This circular loop we have described shifts only when enough contradictory data has been admitted into the system to force a change. It is important that the data be understood and acknowledged as contradictory. For example, American-born professional baseball players, growing up in a society that professes a scientific and materialistic worldview, are infamous for using all types of magical practices and rituals to obtain the luck considered necessary to do well as individuals and win the game as a team.

George Gmelch, a professional player turned anthropologist, notes his own use of ritual: "In hopes of maintaining a batting streak, I once ate fried chicken every day at 4:00 p.m., kept my eyes closed during the national anthem and changed sweatshirts at the end of the fourth inning each night for seven consecutive nights until the streak ended" (1985, 232). He also points out the use of fetishes as producers of good luck: "The player during an exceptionally hot batting or pitching streak, especially one in which he has 'gotten all the breaks,' credits some unusual object, often a new possession, for his good fortune. For example, a player in a slump might find a coin or an odd stone just before he begins a hitting streak. Attributing the improvement in his performance to the new object, it becomes a fetish, embodied with supernatural power" (1985, 234).

Though professing materialism, the players live at a level of magic. They do not recognize this as self-contradictory because they focus on results rather than underlying systems. This is an example of American pragmatism (Hiebert 1985, 119), which is focused on results and often divorced from philosophical or theoretical consideration (Stewart and Bennett 1991, 140). As a result, they live in this state of contradiction, and their worldview is unaffected by it.

The church is not immune to its own sets of contradictions, especially in belief patterns. A 1991 survey reports that 52 percent of those who were born again indicated at least some agreement with the statement "There is no such thing as absolute truth; different people can define truth in conflicting ways and still be correct," even though 93 percent of the same respondents also felt that the Bible was the written word of God and totally accurate in all that it teaches (G. Barna 1991, 85, 294). While it is true that if you can change a people's worldview, you can change the world (Strauss and Steffen 2009), actually effecting that change is easier said than done. One of the reasons is the great degree to which our lives shape our worldview, a topic to which we next turn.

> *A worldview represents the deepest questions one might ask about the world and life, and about the corresponding orientation that one should take toward them. More concretely, the worldview provides answers to such basic questions as: Who or what am I? Why am I in the world? What is reality? How do humans differ from nonhumans (animals, objects, the invisible beings)? Who belongs to the invisible world and what are the invisible forces in the world? What is the proper orientation to time and space? What about life after death? What in life or the world is desirable or undesirable, and to what degree?*
>
> *The dozens of items that occur in most worldviews can be reduced to three or four categories, namely Supernature, Nature, Human Beings, and Time.*
>
> Luzbetak 1976, 252

THE CONSTRUCTION OF WORLDVIEWS

In developing an understanding of the ways in which worldview and intercultural communication are related, we must briefly consider how worldviews are constructed. What are the "raw materials" that provide limitations and definitive directions for worldviews? As illustrated in figure 4.2, we posit six foundational constraints true of all humans that provide the building blocks and the boundaries for worldview construction.

The figure avoids an overly mechanistic viewpoint, allows for an infinite diversity in the worldview sections, and provides room for changing worldviews throughout life. The danger of this metaphor is thinking of these areas as completely separated from one another. They are not separated but interwoven. The separation facilitates discussion of each factor and should not be taken as an indication that they are separated in actuality.

FIGURE 4.2
THE FOUNDATIONAL CONSTRAINTS
FOR WORLDVIEW CONSTRUCTION

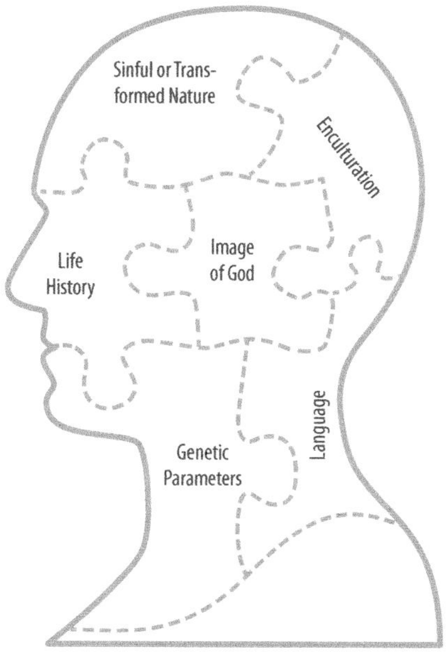

Genetic Parameters

Most generally we use this term to refer to our basic genetic parameters, including not only what we look like but also the predispositions and abilities encoded in our gene structure. None of us is purely a product of genes, but our genetic blueprint affects our neurochemistry, which in turn has been increasingly seen to have an impact on our traits and personality. Our genetic parameters also serve as a reminder that we are physical creatures with needs for food and shelter.

Life History

Every person has a unique life history, which includes family background and the personal choices made in life. It is important to note that we are not simply passive recipients of our family's influence. Rather, we are all in some sense both actors and playwrights in the drama we live.

Enculturation

Enculturation is the process by which our family (and our larger culture) molds and shapes us in both patterns of living and mores on which those patterns are built (Hesselgrave 1978, 124; Schusky and Culbert 1987, 4). It is intimately intertwined with our life's history.

Sinful or Transformed Nature

Our relationship with Christ has an impact on our worldview (Rom. 5–6). Unbelievers are dead in their sins and caught up in the world system (Eph. 2:1–3), while believers have been transformed (2 Cor. 5:17) and are being renewed in the image of Christ (Col. 3:10).

Language

Language is the foundation for thought expression. We use it to construct our perceptions of reality, but in significant ways it also bounds our construction because of its limitations. God chose to reveal himself to humankind using three languages, demonstrating that he is not bound to one language and that the Christian faith is translatable across all human languages. We discuss this in greater depth in chapter 5.

Image of God

Regardless of the hardware, all humans are made in the image of God. This is the single most significant factor for consideration in this discussion. It is the foundation of who we are as people and permeates every aspect of our existence. It also drives us to find religious significance in life. If Wink is correct in stating that our images of God create us (1992, 48), then this fact is at the very core of who we are and provides a central organizing force for our worldview.

FUNCTIONS OF WORLDVIEW

We have stated that worldview is a map and the set of map-reading rules. In more pragmatic terms, what does this mean? Several functions of worldview may be noted (see also Hiebert 2008b, 29–30).

First, it provides the set of benchmarks against which any new experience or idea is tested. Everything we see and observe is filtered through our worldview. When we are confronted with a new idea or teaching (whether religious, ethical, scientific, or philosophical) that contradicts what we believe, we test it against our benchmarks as part of our evaluative process. We may reject it out of hand, or we may explore it further, examining it cognitively, feeling out the consequences, and exploring the moral implications.

Second, worldview provides emotional and cognitive security against an uncertain and often hostile environment. When a friend falls sick and dies, when we experience failure in marriage, when the future looks bleak, or when tragedy or disaster strikes, we use our worldview as a source of security to face these trials. Christians can take comfort in knowing that God is in charge of all things. For some who are not Christians, the idea that God is in charge and yet allows bad things to happen provides a reason to deny either his existence or his goodness. Such people must find alternatives for comfort in times of trial that are within the scope of their own worldviews.

Worldview deals not only with the answers to ultimate questions but also with pragmatic issues that arise in daily life. What is fair in taking turns, how to fight, which activities to participate in and which to avoid, what we say and how we say it, are all framed—largely unconsciously—by our worldview.

There can be little doubt that for those who cross cultures to minister in the name of Christ, worldview is the primary area that must be addressed if they desire to see life-changing impact among those whom they serve. For far too long many missionaries have focused only on the cognitive component rather than recognizing that the affective and the moral components must also be considered. In order to have a more holistic approach, in each chapter of part 3 we explore all three areas.

UNCOVERING A WORLDVIEW

How do we unravel the worldview of another person or group of people? Because of the dynamic, ever-changing nature of worldviews as such, no analytic "paper report" of a worldview will ever be completely accurate. As indicated in figure 4.1, worldview also interacts with faith and lifeway. As either of these elements changes, there will be a corresponding change in worldview.

Although worldview is dynamic and impacted by faith and lifeway, selected analytic tools can help us to understand it in relation to intercultural communication. To do so, we briefly list the themes found in each of the three dimensions of worldview as proposed by Hiebert (2008b, 50–65).

63

Themes in the Cognitive Dimension

The cognitive assumptions of worldview include our ideas about the nature of the world we inhabit (time and space), the nature of the physical world (existence and being), the nature of the power(s) in our world and how they operate (e.g., Jacobs 1979), how we know, and the nature of causality (types of logic; see Hiebert 2008b, 39–46). Knowing the cognitive assumptions can make us aware of both barriers and bridges for more effective communication of the gospel in new cultural settings. We will trace assumptions about the nature of the powers as an example of the type of themes found in the cognitive dimension.

Because we are made in God's image, we have an innate need to connect with him. As a result of Adam and Eve's fall and their consequent expulsion from the garden (Gen. 3:1–24), our direct link was sundered. However, we retained the image of God (Gen. 9:6), and our search for intimate reconnection with the Creator continues, though it is now distorted and expressed as a deep concern with the powers that govern the world we inhabit (Jacobs 1979; Conn 1979; Wink 1992, 3–10). Thus our cognitive assumptions about the powers are at the core of our worldview.

This search for our image maker permeates every aspect of our existence and drives us to find religious significance in life and to attribute to the powers that govern our world a type of image significance. This concern has resulted in an almost infinite variety of postulated cosmic powers that serve as image replacements in every culture of the world. The different "geographies" of these powers in various cultural settings may be called *powerscapes* (i.e., landscapes of the powers).

The outlines of every culturally derived powerscape will be founded on the culture's identification of the power(s) dominating that culture's existence. People of every culture postulate a rich variety of power sources that impact their world (Jacobs 1979; Hiebert 1982; Burnett 1988, 2000; Van Rheenen 1991, 1993; Ritchie 1996; Hiebert, Shaw, and Tiénou 2000). Their understanding of these powers forms the religious landscape they inhabit, and their assumptions about them give people the range of answers to their questions of life and faith.

The types of powers accepted as real by the culture are deeply embedded in the cultural fabric and inform life not just in the religious arena but in every aspect of daily living. Each power within the worldview will have defined lines of authority, responsibility, and accessibility that can be thought of as spheres of operation.

Hiebert has convincingly demonstrated how this affects missionary work in explaining the "flaw of the excluded middle" (1982). By this he means that powers that have influence over life but are invisible (demons, angels) have been largely neglected by Western missionaries, who are products of increasingly secularized cultures.

The ascriptions to the powers are not limited to names and spheres of influence. Corresponding to the vocabulary and sphere of influence are emotional responses and attachments to each power. This in turn defines the types of scripting developed in the culture by which a person knows which power(s) to call on and how to do so (Jacobs 1979; Nuckolls 1991). Three classes of powers may be identified: impersonal, psychological/social, and personal (disembodied) powers.

Impersonal Powers

Impersonal powers are those that operate as laws of the universe. Knowledge of how the powers work ("science") and how they may be harnessed ("engineering") is important (see Hiebert 1982). This knowledge may require training (schooling or apprenticeship) and is usually guarded closely. Accessing these powers is exacting and may be dangerous (just like electricity), though there are relatively minor levels of access (e.g., the baseball magic described in Gmelch 1985). These powers may include fate, karma, astrology, and so on.

Until recently, the scientific worldview in the West has rested on the notion that the only powers of significance in our lives are the impersonal physical powers, which include gravity, electromagnetism, and the strong and weak nuclear forces. The resulting drive in the fields of the physical sciences has been the exploration of these forces and the desire to coalesce our understandings of them into a unified field theory that will potentially explain all the workings of the universe in mathematical terms. Though most in the physical science community continue to operate within this framework, the recent shifts in Western culture toward Eastern thinking have been felt even in the world of physics, in which a new approach in dialogue with Eastern philosophical (and spiritual) foundations has arisen.

Psychological/Social Powers

Bridging the gap between personal and impersonal powers are the types of forces in the domain of the "soft" sciences—namely, the _social_ powers. These range from the individual to the social levels, including the physical drives or motivations we have as humans (see McClelland's massive _Human Motivation_ [1990]) as well as the power that social systems (ideologies, bureaucracies, economic systems, etc.) exert in determining our existence. In one sense, these are personal powers in that they do not exist apart from people.

In another sense, however, they are impersonal powers because they do not have a separate ontological existence apart from the social structures found in human cultures.

PERSONAL DISEMBODIED POWERS

The vast majority of the world's cultures acknowledge powers endowed with personality that transcend the physical realm. In such cultures, the rules of relating among people in daily life are extended to relating to the powers that control the world.

Such powers require the same type of respect, means of initiation, and methods of supplication and petition used in approaching people in positions of social power. (For fascinating examples of how Africans address their ancestral spirits in terms that indicate the perception of the ancestors as still following the personality patterns they had while alive, see Mbiti 1975.)

The powers will be expected to respond within a context of culturally defined relational rules. Among many peoples in Majority World contexts, these powers are integrally involved in the daily events of life. Nothing takes place "naturally"; everything has a cause framed in spiritual terms and related to the personal spiritual powers recognized by the culture. This basic attitude toward the events of life has been called "animism," a term coined by E. B. Tylor in 1873 to refer to the belief in "a personalized supernatural power" (Van Rheenen 1991, 19).

Themes in the Affective Dimension

In every society people experience emotions ranging from joy to grief, from anticipation to anxiety. This capacity is a reflection of our being made in God's image. However, our worldview affects how we experience, exhibit, and value our emotions.

Rationalistic and mechanical approaches to the Christian faith found in Western cultures, for example, have characterized our emotions by likening them to the caboose (or last car) on the train. In other words, they are not truly relevant but just along for the ride. Pentecostals have been accused of making emotions the engine of the train, a metaphor indicating the scorn of those who use it. Theravada Buddhism teaches that all life is suffering, so even moments of joy are tempered by the fact that they will end. Forms of Hinduism teach that all of life is illusion, so emotions are something to leave behind so that people will not be distracted by them.

It should be clear, then, that all cultures value emotions in some way. Our ability to tap into those values, or possibly be agents of change when the values contradict Scripture, is predicated on knowing what role affect plays in religion and the larger worldview. These themes are typically embedded in the many stories, metaphors of life, myths, and proverbs that are valued by a society.

Themes in the Evaluative Dimension

As human beings we constantly face moral choices. They range from the mundane (speed limits) to the momentous (abortion, genocide), from what it means to be good (a hero) or evil (a villain). As we grow up, we are enculturated with a conscience that guides us in making moral decisions, even though we do not always follow it. Those in the United States hear stories about George Washington, Paul Revere, Betsy Ross, Abraham Lincoln, Susan B. Anthony, Martin Luther King Jr., Rosa Parks, or other heroes. Those in Kenya hear stories about people such as Jomo Kenyatta as well as those about traditional tribal heroes. As with the affective dimension, one of the important places where societies embed their moral values is their stories, metaphors of life, myths, and proverbs (see, e.g., Moon 2009; Moreau and O'Rear 2004, 2006a; and Unseth 2013).

This dimension, where cultures differ regarding moral prescriptions and understanding of sin, offers us opportunities to communicate the message of the gospel more clearly, provided we take the time to understand and communicate with the local conscience on its own terms rather than on our terms (Dye 1976; Priest 1993, 1994; B. Adeney 1995; T. Chuang 1996; Strand 2000).

Most simply put, for Christians crossing into new cultures, it is important to learn how to live out goodness through the practice of loving God and neighbor in a new cultural context (B. Adeney 1995). At least three questions must be answered: (1) How do we know ethical behavior? (2) How do we mediate cultural value clashes? (3) Can we account for human subjectivity? Of the three, question 2 is perhaps most central for intercultural communication.

CONCLUSION

We have set the stage for part 3 of the book by exploring worldview and briefly explaining the three dimensions that impact intercultural communication. From here we turn our attention to the visible expression of worldview—namely, culture. In the case study for this chapter, you will encounter not only a cross-cultural clash in worldviews but also a generational worldview clash in handling relationships with the opposite sex.

CASE STUDY:
THE LAW OF LIBERTY VERSUS
THE LAW OF LOVE

BOBBIE PENDELL

Reprinted with permission from Hiebert and Hiebert (1987, 49–52).

Kneeling numb and exhausted beside her bed in the back bedroom, Nancy knew it was more than the surprise of finding the two men, Mehmet and Zeki, in the house a moment ago that was filling her with such dread. (That meant an implied rule had been broken!) It was also her sore throat, and the weight of deciding whether to leave the House of Ruth under the care of twenty-six-year-old Reyhan, or to close it while she was on the year's furlough slated to begin in just two weeks.

Dismantling their lovely home was the last thing forty-five-year-old Nancy wanted to do. It was her dream-come-true for needy Muslim women in this unevangelized Middle East city, a peaceful base for single women to receive something in Christ's name—used clothing and a cup of hot tea for the "bag ladies" combing the trash outside, a tape library of Bible stories and tracts for cautious distribution, prayer and Bible study, and even live-in discipleship for three of the five single women who had been baptized.

"Lord, help!" she prayed. "I'm so mixed up and angry. Customs are changing, but how fast, Lord? Is what my friends advised only eight months ago already outdated? . . . You know I hate having to enforce on these young believers the taboos of their own culture; that seems so wrong. Lord, show me if their rebellion is your way of smashing a burdensome rule that shouldn't be. . . . But Lord, is it possible that you're showing me what will happen to your name after I leave if their defiance isn't dealt with?"

Everything had gone so well until now. Nancy had arrived four years before, wanting to establish a home for single women because she believed the gospel would spread quickly among independent and rejected women. The idea had come from her reading about Lydia, the woman at the well, the Magdalene, and the Macedonian slave girl. It was an unexplored concept. Her prayer partners at home caught her vision and had given financially so that she could open the first House of Ruth less than a year after her arrival in the Middle East.

That first year was grueling, but beautiful Mene, a twenty-six-year-old divorcée, committed her life to Christ and moved in with Nancy. She grew strong in the Lord and was thrilled to have a place for sharing Christ with their neighbors, many of whom, like Mene, felt rejected by society due to divorce or separation. All who visited the two learned something of Jesus, usually for the first time, and nobody left without prayers.

When Mene's brother pleaded for her help with his failing business in another city, she left for one year. Nancy moved into a large apartment in a less-conservative neighborhood and continued the House of Ruth. For the past ten months she had roomed with Selma and Reyhan, two recent converts who had taken the step of baptism. Neither of the two had ever lived in such comfortable surroundings, or with Christians, and both gloried in their newfound freedom to minister openly to their friends at work and school. The three women's "family prayer times" had created close ties between them. Nancy was pleased to think she could leave the home under Reyhan's supervision while she was on furlough, although Mene often warned her, "Reyhan can't manage it. She's too stubborn."

The "no-men-unless-accompanied-by-wives" rule for the House of Ruth was a long-standing one. Experienced missionaries had warned: "In this country, single girls should live with their parents if they are unmarried, so be absolutely certain you never entertain men or allow the women to do so." Mene had agreed. Although the residents of the House of Ruth had bent the rule occasionally for brief chats with Christian "brothers" (with the front door opened wide, as is the Muslim custom for such emergencies), so far as Nancy knew, no neighbor had ever criticized "the gavur" (non-Muslims/those who leave Islam) or "the foreign lady" ("everyone knows all Western women are immoral"). One neighbor had even told another that Nancy's companions were "pure girls." This delighted her, for Nancy wanted to win her neighbors to Christ.

Reyhan thought the rule forbidding male visitors was needless, but both she and Selma had agreed to it before moving in the previous September. When winter cold closed the city's outdoor cafés, however, and there seemed no place to gather after Sunday services, the women and several male converts, including Mehmet and Zeki, insisted that the rule was unnecessary. Mehmet had chided Nancy last fall, saying,

You misunderstand our people, Nancy. We are not such backward people as you think; this is a modern country. Your neighbors don't care what people do so long as they're polite. Besides, the women only want to entertain us Christian men, not Muslims. . . . Once we had to live under the harsh Muslim customs like this, but Jesus has set us free from the law. You urge us to love and trust one another, but you don't really trust us. How can we grow closer if we have no place to meet?

Nancy sympathized and hoped they were correct, but Mene insisted they were wrong. Not knowing what to believe or how to maintain unity without jeopardizing the House of Ruth's fine reputation, Nancy asked three non-Christian friends in the neighborhood how they would view the women's occasional entertaining of men. All three were in their early thirties and were considered "modern," having lived in America in recent years.

The first simply raised his eyebrows, a most emphatic way of saying, "No!"

"I say to hell with this sick society—let them do it, Nancy," fumed the second, a bachelor.

At that outburst, the third, an air-force major, bit his lip in the Muslim gesture that meant "Shame on you!" He added, "Why tell Nancy that? You know someone will call the police. Why, I probably would if they did it more than five times. I may be a modern man, but my wife and the neighbors are not. They'd call your ladies 'prostitutes.' No, Sister, never let those single women entertain men there."

When Nancy, Reyhan, and Selma could not agree on a policy, they agreed to abide by the decision of "the regulars." Since they were aware that, as "firstfruits," what each convert did very much affected the entire body, corporate decisions were encouraged. The decision of the five older members—four missionaries and Mene, who had recently returned from her brother's city—was a firm no. In the end, even

69

Reyhan and Selma joined in to make the vote unanimous.

Winter passed without further incidents, and Nancy assumed the issue was dead. The women matured as a body, thanks to one couple's increased willingness to host the singles and to the added availability of their meeting hall.

Now it was June, and Nancy was hoping to leave everything to Reyhan and Selma while she was on furlough. Then, last night, she was surprised to find Reyhan, Selma, Mehmet, and Zeki praying with an unfamiliar young woman in the living room with the door closed. All five had rushed to explain that the stranger had just confessed her faith in Christ. At this exciting news, Nancy had relaxed and enjoyed their brief visit.

But tonight was different. It began with an argument. "We've decided not to obey that silly rule, Nancy. We have been set free in Christ, and that means free to be ourselves," Reyhan had announced when she learned Nancy's sore throat would keep her at home that evening. "Jesus didn't worry about his neighbors, and neither should we. Besides, if we tell Selma's college friends about your rule, they'll mock Christianity and tell us it's as backward as Islam."

Nancy had pleaded: "But what about 1 Peter 2:12, where we're told to maintain good conduct among the Gentiles, so that when they spread stories about us as gavur, they will remember how honorably we live and someday give praise to God? We are warned never to give even the appearance of evil, Reyhan, so that we may win others to Christ." Reyhan had responded with well-chosen Scriptures

of her own. Nothing was resolved, and silence hung heavily over the usually cheery apartment until the doorbell rang several hours later.

Nancy went to the door, and much to her dismay, there stood Mehmet and Zeki. Reyhan and Selma had invited them as guests for dinner! Angry, hurt, and embarrassed, Nancy had reminded all four of the fellowship's decision last fall, but none of them could even remember voting.

Not knowing what to say or do, Nancy had escaped to her bedroom. She wanted to climb into bed and nurse her sore throat and hurt feelings until morning. But the issue about male guests had to be resolved immediately, for with that rested the fate of the House of Ruth. Nancy prayed once more, "Oh, Lord, give us love. Show us how to balance our liberty in you with your demands that we not cause others to stumble. And please, Lord, keep us from divisions between nationals and foreigners, young and old." She dried her eyes, opened her bedroom door, and walked down the hall toward the dining room where the four were seated.

REFLECTION AND DISCUSSION

1. Read the case carefully to identify elements of worldview as explained in the chapter. In what ways does this case illustrate the impact of globalization on cultural values?

2. How might you use the things you identify to help Nancy decide on a good way to address the issue?

Verbal Intercultural Communication

Some of the hardest issues to deal with are those of which we are least aware. As I was typing the previous sentence, I did not consciously pay attention to each word, making sure I had the order straight or wrestling with which word to use. I simply thought it and typed it. In our daily lives, most of us tend to take our native tongue for granted—at least until we start learning another language! Several things must be considered in the process of learning how to communicate well in another language. These are at the heart not just of linguistic theory but of such crucial missionary tasks as translating the Bible into another language and learning how to communicate important truths related to discipleship and obedience to Christ in ways that speak to the hearts of people among whom we minister.

ISSUES RELATED TO LANGUAGE AND INTERCULTURAL COMMUNICATION

A full discussion of issues related to language—and the roles languages play in communication—is well beyond the scope of this book. These issues in-clude such things as the ways language is used in particular social settings

> *Added to the difficulty of learning to speak the language was the greater difficulty of finding terms to express the ideas which the missionary had come halfway round the world to convey. . . . In many languages the most precious truths of Christianity had to force their way by bending stubborn words to new ideas, and filling old terms with a new content.*
>
> Montgomery 1910, 90

(sociolinguistics), how to learn a language (language acquisition), how we as humans learn language and the ways we are able to manipulate it to convey meanings (psycholinguistics), the ways signs (semiotics) and language are tied to the social processes that are part of every culture (anthropological linguistics), and solutions to language-related problems that are of importance for real life, such as translation and foreign-language teaching (applied linguistics). Here we will limit our considerations to several significant language issues—the importance of language, the relationship of language to message, and language as the vehicle of enculturation—as well as the necessity and process of becoming a language and culture learner.

What Is "Language"?

We use language all the time. "Language" once was used as a definition of what it meant to be human. Crossing cultures involves crossing language barriers; thus it is of critical importance in intercultural communication. What, then, is "language"?

> In the most basic sense, language is an organized, generally agreed upon, learned symbol-system used to represent the experiences within a geographic or cultural community. Language is the primary means by which a culture transmits its beliefs, values, and norms. It gives people a means of interacting with other members of the culture and a means of thinking. (Samovar, Porter, and Jain 1981, 49)

The Importance of Language

> *Since language itself is viewed as a gift from God, by implication all languages and all cultures have been, in a theological sense, potentially equal.*
>
> Frykenberg, 2003b, 3

Evangelical approaches to intercultural communication are built on the understanding that language is an appropriate vehicle for God's revelation to humankind. As Andrew Walls points out, it was God who first "translated himself" through the incarnation, and Bible translation parallels the incarnation: "As the Incarnation took place in the terms of a particular social context, so translation uses the terms and relations of a specific context"

(1990, 26). Thus the Bible and the Christian faith are "infinitely culturally translatable" (Bediako 1995, 173), and every language has the capacity to convey the message of the gospel adequately to those who speak it (Bediako 1998, 65; Escobar 2002, 173; Cortez 2005, 351).

Language and Messages

Without thinking about it, we use language to convey messages all the time. They may relate to our needs, our states, our desires for recognition, and our ideas. "More precisely for our purposes, since language is the principle medium for communicating messages, what is contained in language which in turn is transmitted and received? The answer is found in the way language is structured for transmitting messages" (Filbeck 1985, 13).

If language is used to convey messages, what do we mean by a "message"? Within a linguistics framework, a message consists of two parts. First is the content, or meaning, in its ordinary sense (formal linguistics). To date in missiological thinking, this has received the bulk of the attention. Equally important but more typically overlooked in missionary thinking are the details of social organizations that frame and shape the message (sociolinguistics) as well as issues of how culture and language shape each other (anthropological linguistics).

These areas have been neglected, which is unfortunate, "for while details of social organization may not be essential for salvation they are nonetheless essential for composing the message of the Gospel so it may be communicated in a social context" (Filbeck 1985, 14). As communication researcher Carley Dodd notes, "What

> *Experienced workers will not be surprised to learn that workers who are fluent in the local language consistently scored among the highest [in ministry effectiveness]. When applicable, workers who said they minister to people in their heart language scored better than those who ministered in the trade or national language.*
>
> Lai 2007, 173

> *Translation was a constant and inescapable requirement of the missionary endeavor, from mundane routines to the communication of the holiest mysteries, meaning that every "universal," from the term for God on down, entered an existing network of meanings that differed for every language. Moreover, the act of translation imparted value to each vernacular language, and by implication to the culture borne by each. The result could be more generous to variant cultures than the national state was prepared to be.*
>
> Dunch 2002, 324

73

SIDEBAR 5.1
MEANINGS AND MESSAGES

CHARLES KRAFT CONTENDS THAT MEANINGS LIE WITHIN PEOPLE WHO CONSTRUCT THEM FROM MESSAGES:

Contemporary understandings contend that a major difference between messages and meanings lies in the fact that messages can be transmitted in linguistic form while meanings exist only in the hearts and minds of people. Contemporary communiologists see communicators with meanings in their minds that they would like to transmit to receptors. Communicators take these meanings and formulate them, usually in linguistic form, into messages which they then transmit to receptors. Receptors then listen to the messages and construct within their minds sets of meanings that may or may not correspond with the meanings intended by the communicator.

Meanings, therefore, do not pass from me to you, only messages. The meanings exist only within me or within you. . . . The messages, then, serve as stimulators rather than as containers. Receptors, in response to the stimulus of messages, construct meanings that may or may not correspond to what the communicator intended. (1979a, 34–35)

. . . .

Communication does not consist of the transmission of meaning. Meaning does not inhere in linguistic and other cultural forms. Meanings are, rather, attached to those forms by the people who use them. For meanings are not contained in forms, though they are conveyed by them. Meanings are in people. It is people who attach meanings to the linguistic, religious, political, economic and other forms of culture they use. Meaning is,

therefore, a function of personal interpretation on the basis of social agreements rather than something inherent in the forms themselves.

Meanings are not transmittable, not transferable. Only messages are transmittable, and meanings are not in the message, they are in the message-users. Meaning is the result of interpretation. And interpretation is the subjective interaction of one or more persons with a situation. What that situation means to the person is what he/she comes away with from that situation. And persons attach their meanings independently of each other, though ordinarily in keeping with habits they have learned to share with other members of their community. (2005c, 163)

PAUL HIEBERT CONTENDS THAT THIS SEPARATION OF FORM AND MEANING HAS CONSEQUENCES THAT CANNOT BE IGNORED:

First, the separation of form and meaning is based on a too simple view of culture. In this view, language is the basis of culture, and all other areas of culture can be understood by analogy to linguistics. But culture is more than language. It is made up of many symbol systems, such as rituals, gestures, life styles, and technology. In these, . . . the relationships between form and meaning are often complex. Moreover, even in language the linkage between form and meaning is not always arbitrary. . . .

In the second place, a total separation of meaning and form tends to be asocial. It does not take seriously enough the fact that symbols are created and controlled by social groups and whole societies. As individuals and minority groups, we may create our own symbols and words to express our faith in our own circles. When we try to reinterpret symbols used by the dominant society, however, we are in danger of being misunderstood and ultimately of being captured by its definitions of reality. . . .

Third, to separate meaning and form is to ignore history. Words and other symbols have histories of previously established linkages between form and meaning. Without such historical continuity, it would be impossible for people to pass on their culture from one generation to the next or to preserve the gospel over time. We are not free to arbitrarily link mean-

ings and forms. To do so is to destroy people's history and culture. Moreover, it is to forget that people who become Christians gain a second history—the history of Christianity. Among their new spiritual ancestors are Abraham, Moses, Jesus, Paul, Aquinas, Calvin, Luther, and many others. (1989, 105–7)

REFLECTION AND DISCUSSION

1. What are the strengths and weaknesses of each perspective?
2. What are the implications for intercultural communication if Kraft is correct?

we say and how we say it comes directly from our perception of the cultural climate in which we find ourselves" (1991, 126–27).

In each context we place certain restrictions on our total linguistic abilities based on our perceptions of the context (e.g., we do not swear in "Christian" contexts, we may use special phrasing for public prayers). This aspect of linguistics becomes extremely important when we consider how many Christians carry the restricted codes they use in Christian contexts (i.e., "Christianese") into contexts where those codes are misunderstood or not understood (e.g., the office).

In many cases the sociolinguistic element weighs more heavily in determining the message being conveyed than the words themselves. To point to a campfire and say, "Fire," is radically different than to yell it out in a movie theater. It is the context that enables people to interpret the meaning of the message you intend to convey, together with the interpretive system they have developed.

Language, Culture Acquisition, and Thought Processes

How do children learn their culture? Not through some mysterious socialization process that is divorced from language acquisition. Rather, anthropological linguistics frames this process in terms of language socialization, which insists

One would be hard pressed to find a better way of communicating the incarnate love of the Living God than in learning the language of those people with whom one lives.

Roembke 2000, 120

that in becoming competent members of their social groups, children are socialized *through* language, and they are socialized *to use* language. Hence, language is not just one dimension of the socialization process; it is the most central and crucial dimension of that process. The language socialization paradigm makes the strong claim that any study of socialization that does not document the role of language in the acquisition of cultural practices is not only incomplete. It is fundamentally flawed. (Schieleffelin and Kulick 2003, 350, emphasis added)

This being true, then what is the relationship between language and thought? Does language determine the extent of thought? Over the course of the past century, linguists have been wrestling with this question, debating whether language determines thought or thought (and worldview) determines the basic frames that languages can take. On one side, theoreticians Edward Sapir and, later, Benjamin Whorf posited that "language is the *means by which we acquire a world view and logic*" (Hesselgrave 1991b, 368, emphasis in original). On the other side, Noam Chomsky and later Robert Longacre have proposed that the deep structural levels of languages are similar enough that language is limited in terms of the extent to which it can structure reality (see table 5.1).

TABLE 5.1
LANGUAGE AND WORLDVIEW

Sapir and Whorf	Chomsky and Longacre
"Language is the *means by which we acquire a world view and logic*" (Hesselgrave 1991a, 368; emphasis in original); it is not just a vehicle to report "reality" but shapes our perceptions of reality. In effect, language is the mediator between perception and reality, for by language we codify, categorize, and create shared cultural experiences that determine how we perceive reality.	The differences between languages are at the surface level; at the deep structural level languages tend to be comparable. Thus there is a basic similarity of languages that results in a basic and limited range of options of how language can structure reality. The range of possible worldviews, though theoretically infinite in number, is limited in scope.

Hesselgrave concludes that there is a basic similarity in the ways people see and think about the world around them and that all people are enculturated into a linguistic community, which will tend to shape their perceptions and how they conceive of reality.

Once we begin to understand the language of the people with whom we communicate, we begin to participate in the "linguistic worldview" of those people, enabling more effective communication with them (Hesselgrave 1991b, 369–72; see also Bensley 1982, 236–44 and 409).

LANGUAGE LEARNING

People who cross into a new linguistic setting as adults do not have the advantage of children who have learned the language as they grew up. Why, then, learn a language? At the outset we should note with Michael Lessard-Clouston that "language learning can be a redemptive activity which God uses to bless people" (2012, 173).

Further, as David Filbeck explains, language is the main medium through which enculturation takes place:

> Where a missionary does not learn the language of the group among whom he is working, he has little or no social interaction with them. By not learning to interact with members of the group through the language of the group (as any new member born into the group must learn to do), he cannot in reality learn the "network of values, meanings, interests, concerns, and labelings which are wrapped up in the elaborate form" of that language; by not learning their language the missionary cannot communicate the Gospel cross-culturally to members of the group.
>
> The language learning process may be termed resocialization. In it, the outsider is learning to be a member of the society, and he must be resocialized (a process which, like his initial socialization, should never end). (1985, 51)

Finally, "to the degree that a missionary can achieve resocialization, learning to become a member of a new society, the better able he will be in communicating cross-culturally" (Filbeck 1985, 51). Since socialization involves *both* language and culture, missionaries who focus on learning one without learning the other will always be missing elements of the culture that are important to know.

Language Learning for Cross-Cultural Ministry

Almost everyone involved in cross-cultural ministry agrees that learning the language is critical. However, in today's globalized world in which English is possibly becoming the first true world language, in which many countries have English as an official language, and in which increasing focus is given to shorter terms of cross-cultural service, some have advocated that learning the language is not as critical as it was a century ago or that the need is ministry dependent (e.g., a rural church planter will need the language; an urban TESOL teacher may not need it as much; see Chapman 1998).

Even so, there is still general agreement that it is difficult at best to learn the heartbeat of a culture and to truly feel the worldview of a people without speaking the language they consider their own. This is more complex for those in urban centers, where the trade language (e.g., Swahili, French, Mandarin) may not be the heart language of the intended audience, and learning both might be necessary for effective ministry (McKinney 1990; Mustol 2004).

Variations in Dialect

Dialect differences are also important. Imagine someone who intends to minister in Alabama learning that state's English dialect from a native Bostonian, or someone who will be working in Paris learning the French dialect in Niger! Dialects carry the attitudes and stereotypes of the people associated with them in such a way that people who hear the dialect assign stereotypical characteristics to the person using it (Dodd 1991, 128). For example, southerners in the United States typically make quick attributions when they hear a New York accent. Dodd draws two principles from this tendency: A speaker's accented speech and dialect influence our attitudes toward the speaker; and speech forms outside the linguistic norms of the listener usually are evaluated negatively. Although not always true (e.g., a British Cambridge accent will sound highly educated to Americans), typically it is viewed positively when the accented speech conveys the impression of experience with the topic or task at hand.

It should be obvious that the dialect we learn can have a significant impact on how well our communication is received. For example, many working in Francophone Africa choose to learn French in France rather than in their location of service so that their dialect will be more in line with international norms and they maintain greater flexibility in terms of country of service for the future.

Life as a Language and Culture Learner

How much time should you plan to spend learning a new language? This will vary with your language aptitude and diligence in study and practice as well as the ability to overcome distractions. However, to be able to carry on basic conversations, you should be prepared to devote a minimum of one year to focused language study. Generally, however, for even a language of average difficulty, it will take a solid four years before you will be comfortable in the new language in a wide variety of settings (Dickerson 2004a, 2).

It might help to keep several things in mind. First, everyone who can currently speak a language can also learn a new language (Todd 2001), though the older a person is the more difficult that may be for her or him.

Second, recognize that the process of learning the language *is* ministry (Brewster and Brewster 1982; Willis 1996). Through the language-learning process, you follow in the incarnational footsteps of Jesus (Todd 1999). You also demonstrate a learner's attitude toward your host culture and communicate to the people that their language is important not only to you but to God as well (since they will see you as representing him). As you practice using the language, you are also developing relationships that can result in deep friendships later on in ministry, and these close friendships give you access to people's lives and concerns.

Finally, on a more personal note, you can use the time and discipline of language learning to develop a framework of spiritual disciplines in your new language (Dearborn 1991). Even something as simple as having your devotions in a translation of your language (if available) can help in the process.

Thankfully today many resources are available to assist in the process (see, e.g.,

> *Learning a language and culture through relationships in a community requires a tremendous commitment to the people of the new language. . . .* If your goal is to live with people, to love and serve them, and to become a belonger in your new community, then learning the language will prove to be a great means to that goal. *And learning the language will probably become quite manageable!*
>
> Brewster and Brewster 1982, 4, emphasis in original

SIDEBAR 5.2
STEPS IN LANGUAGE LEARNING

Adapted from Dickerson (2008)

1. **SLA COURSE.** Perhaps the best financial and time-management investment you can make is to take a pre-field second-language acquisition (SLA) program, like the summer ICCT course. Those who arrive overseas with this type of preparation consistently report that pre-field SLA preparation saves far more, in both time and money, than they spend to take the course.

2. **FIND A NATIVE-SPEAKER HELPER** to work with for a minimum of two hours each week. Your helper may be a neighbor, a student, or any person who is willing to give you some time. It is usually better if this person is not a language teacher.

(Your pre-field course should teach you how to learn from ordinary native speakers and give you practice in doing this. This will allow you to make the most of your language-learning sessions because you will know what you need to learn and how to go about the learning process.)

First, work on learning "survival language"—the kind of language you'll need right away in your new country—and some basic "building blocks" such as the alphabet, numbers, and a few of the most basic sentence patterns.

Here are some suggestions to choose from, but you should add to this list items that will be immediately useful to you and delete items that you will not need right away.

a. alphabet
b. numbers: most common numbers (e.g., 0–100) and common numbers used in currency denominations
c. common food items (e.g., fruits, vegetables, meats): 15–20 common foods
d. names of stores, shops, and other place names: 10–15 most common place names
e. names from a few of the most common signs such as street signs (e.g., metro, exit, entrance)
f. names of common modes of transportation (e.g., train, bus, car, metro)
g. conversational management phrases/sentences: 6–10 phrases/sentences (e.g., Please speak more slowly. Can you repeat that? I don't understand. What is this? How do you say ____?)
h. basic greetings and leave-takings
i. basic self-introduction
j. basic sentence patterns (e.g., a few of the most simple types of sentences in which you can substitute new words to change the meaning of the sentence. Here are two basic sentence patterns in English: "I need_____." and "Where is _____?" However, basic sentence patterns in your new language may be very different from these.)

For some languages you can find some basic online language lessons to supplement what you do with your native-speaker helper. These materials are usually no more than some basic vocabulary, a few conversational management phrases, and perhaps simple greetings and leave-takings. Two sites for online lessons in multiple languages are Foreign Languages for Travelers and Transparent Language. At each of these sites you can see the word or phrase and also hear it spoken by a native speaker.

3. COLLECT RESOURCES that you can use before you go overseas and/or in on-field language learning. These include language textbooks and dictionaries as well as articles, books, websites, and other information to help you become a more effective learner.

4. CD-ROM PROGRAMS. If these are available for your target language, purchase one or two programs. Use the lessons primarily for listening comprehension. Rosetta Stone, for example, is a good program to use in this way. If you are also using the program to learn to speak a little of your new language, be sure to check what you are learning with your native-speaker helper.

5. TAKE A LANGUAGE COURSE. For the most popular foreign languages—and for many of the less commonly taught languages—many universities, colleges, and community colleges offer courses that run from a week to a semester in length. The methods and techniques used for most North American language courses are "communicative." This means that learners are involved in actual communication from the first day of class, thus providing a good foundation for continued learning in the on-field language program.

http://www2.wheaton.edu/bgc/ICCT/slares/SLAresources.html). Contemporary language-learning courses and methods offer more than just lists of words or declensions or conjugations to memorize; they also include a variety of approaches that let you take advantage of those that play to your personal strengths in the language-acquisition process.

Language learning always has a goal beyond fluency, and language learning in and of itself is not enough to understand the new culture or to communicate well across cultures. If it were, the entire focus of this book would be how to acquire a new language. We need to find appropriate ways to integrate our language learning with new insights into the culture. Just as we can always be learning new vocabulary and new nuances in expression, we can also always be learning new things about the culture and integrating how we use our language skills with those things we learn (see Steffen 1993, 103–12, for an example).

CONCLUSION

Learning a new language is a challenging but essential step in learning a new culture. Although we should not mistake learning the language for learning the culture, neither should we think that we can really learn the insider's perspective on the culture without learning the language. In our case study, consider the types of messages that are given through the flavor of the cake, the use of "old man" for God, and the author's perspective on enabling people to distinguish our lifestyle from the gospel message.

CASE STUDY:
OUR AMERICAN CAKE

REAPSOME (1998, 8)

The staff of a seminary in Africa threw a big graduation ceremony and party. Government ministers and foreign ambassadors came to the event. One of the American missionary wives baked a chocolate cake. An African who had been to the United States tasted her cake and said to her husband, "I tasted something American about it the very first mouthful."

Write that down as another new slant on cultural sensitivity. Apparently our missionaries even taste American. If our cakes have that unmistakable American taste, what about our gospel, our programs, our way of doing things? No matter how hard we may try, we cannot shed our Americanism like a snake sheds its skin.

However, we say that our gospel is transcultural. It's universally applicable. It fits any people, anywhere, any time. Jesus said people everywhere must hear his good news. He did not limit his mission to one people, language, religion, or culture.

Therefore, Christians continually fight to take America out of their cake. The fight rages not only in Africa but in the United States, where the gospel makes little sense because of the inroads of popular culture and biblical illiteracy. We cannot assume that anyone knows anything about simple Bible stories, let alone the reason why Jesus came, died, and rose again.

For example, I listened to a sermon that included repeated references to "the old man," without any explanatory comments. I began to think about the multitude of meanings "the old man" could possibly have in that audience. We have to make sure that our biblical and doctrinal terms really mean something in today's world.

Of course, we cannot remove basic Christian ideas from our language. We cannot risk stripping the gospel of its deep-seated theology about sin, salvation, and judgment. We face the difficult task of taking things that are hard to understand and making them understandable, whether in Africa or the United States. But before we try to do it in Africa, we should have some success doing it in America.

We can never take America out of our cake, but in our presence and in our proclamation we must bend over backwards to avoid even the smell of America. For one thing, America smells bad in many parts of the world because of the sensual, materialistic culture we have exported. It's even worse because this bad odor emanates from a country that is part of Christendom.

Therefore, as gospel messengers we live so that people can distinguish our lifestyles from what they see and read about. We are sorely tested to follow a different standard, one set by Jesus, not by our culture.

Jesus said that he lives in us so that people will get some idea of who he is and why he came. People want to see Jesus. They may not understand our theology at first, but if they see Jesus in us we will have ample opportunities to tell them why we love and serve him.

When I was a kid, growing up in Hershey, PA, I loved to tour the chocolate factory and watch those giant granite rollers smashing through huge vats of milk chocolate. Back and forth, back and forth, they relentlessly made sure Hershey's was the smoothest chocolate on the market. The presence of tiny bits of granite never inhibited my consumption of Hershey bars.

For sure, some of America will always be in our gospel cakes. That's okay. People will eat them if they taste our integrity, love, understanding, acceptance, and patience. Our job is to see that the taste overrules any foreign elements in our cakes.

REFLECTION AND DISCUSSION

1. What is your view of the missionary who made the cake?
2. What is your impression of the pastor who referred to God as "the old man"?
3. How do you feel about the view of the author of the essay?

Societies and Social Institutions

A s noted in the introduction to this part, all communication takes place in a social context. In this chapter we explore issues related to understanding the social context that cross-cultural communicators must know if they are to communicate well in their cultural settings.

Every person who engages with another society must sooner or later face issues such as what type of society it is and how social relationships work within it. The type of society will determine such things as the extent to which individual expression is encouraged or discouraged, how decisions are made, levels of stratification, and how to develop relationships within that society.

TYPES OF SOCIETIES

The institutional makeup of a society depends to some extent on the type of society. At the risk of reductionism, we can say that four major types of societies are found in the world today: (1) band, (2) tribal, (3) peasant, and (4) urban. In reality the categories are somewhat blurry, and societies are constantly shifting and changing. With those limitations in mind, we offer a brief description of each type (derived in part from discussion in Filbeck 1985; Hiebert and Meneses 1995; Hiebert 2008b) as well as cursory notes on some of the communicational patterns that relate to developing the types of deep relationships necessary for effective ministry.

Band Societies

DESCRIPTION

Band societies are small groups of people who live together as nomads on the peripheries of larger societies. They live close to nature and draw largely on the resources of the land they inhabit. Limited by what the local environment will support, they are often small independent family units that must migrate on a regular basis throughout the year in order to survive. In seasons of abundance or at locations where food is more plentiful, they join together with other bands in celebration. They are independent in that they must be able to survive off the land individually, but they are also part of a small collective that must work together if it is going to survive. They are so small that everyone knows everyone else intimately and individuals are recognized for their uniqueness rather than their socially defined positions. Because a band is so small, the development of separate institutions within the band is not necessary for its survival (Hiebert and Meneses 1995, 51–53).

> *For intercultural communication the knowledge of the structures and their workings are essential to be able to match and come to successful exchange and mutual understanding.*
>
> Eilers 1999, 240

COMMUNICATION PATTERNS IN BAND SOCIETIES

People who want to serve among band societies need to be aware of the following patterns of communication if they hope to develop significant relationships. Because individuals in band societies must be able to survive independently, there is a certain amount of individualism within the group. At the same time, however, the willful individual can jeopardize the entire group, so too much individualism is not tolerated, and people who are not part of the band may not be seen as important or even as people. Because bands are small and lack formal institutions, social power is typically vested in the hands of the adult males as a group rather than in a particular individual, and important decisions are often made by the group rather than by individuals. Gender roles within the group are clearly defined and delineated, with each playing its part in the group's survival. The group tends to live in the moment rather than planning or scheduling a day's events. However, people live with the reality that migrations must take place according to seasonal and environmental cues, for the seasons will not wait for the group. Thus there is a well-defined rhythm to their lives, and disruption of that rhythm is potentially threatening to them. Finally, they tend to see life as an integrated whole and respond better to communication that respects a holistic approach to life.

Tribal Societies

DESCRIPTION

The word "tribe" is typically avoided in academic circles today because of the negative connotations associated with the word (e.g., primitive, backward, undeveloped). However, and unfortunately, while alternatives (clan, ethnic group, people) can be and have been used as a label, no other term has been accepted as a general substitute for societies meeting the descriptions in this category. Thus we reluctantly use the term here but not in the pejorative sense (see also Hiebert and Meneses 1995, 31).

Tribal societies are groups that have a large enough agricultural base (in both plants and animals) to enable them to remain in one general location rather than moving with the seasons. Typically the people see themselves as having a common ethnic and linguistic identity and feel that they share a common heritage. As a result, they share a strong group orientation, though if the tribe is large enough there may be several subgroups, each with its own group identity. Typically tribal groups train their children to share mutual responsibility and participate in group decision making. Often social institutions are highly integrated and interrelated, and the functional load of maintaining society is distributed more or less equally throughout all five social institutions (association, kinship, education, economics, and law; see table 6.1), though the organization is based primarily on kinship ties. These ties extend to the ancestors (who are considered ongoing members of the society) and possibly to animals and/or plants in totemic systems.

COMMUNICATION PATTERNS IN TRIBAL SOCIETIES

People who want to serve among tribal societies need to be aware of the following patterns of communication if they hope to develop significant relationships. Tribal individuals have less need to survive individually than those in band societies and so are more interdependent. However, because the tribe can be large enough to support numerous subgroups, tribalists have a stronger allegiance to members of their particular in-group than to people outside it. Tribes are large enough to manifest the beginnings of institutional identities based on the subgroup (e.g., elders, diviners, royalty, age groups). Decisions are generally made by the appropriate institution (or block of people within

85

the institution). Gender roles may still be clearly defined, though this is not as important as it is in band societies. Traditionally, tribal peoples have tended to live in the moment, but because of the increasing influence of globalization, even in rural areas it is becoming increasingly necessary for people to develop more time-oriented skills in order to thrive. As with band societies, tribal people tend to see life as an integrated whole and respond better to communication that respects all of life rather than communication that separates life into categories.

Peasant or Multigroup Societies

DESCRIPTION

Peasant societies emerged as villages grew and industry began to develop. The specialized needs of those such as traders and travelers (for means of bringing in trade, for food and accommodation) as well as specialists (for training, education, and socioeconomic space to practice their specialty) resulted in increasingly greater divisions within the society. Typically peasant societies consist of at least two groups (e.g., ethnic, class, caste), with one dominant and the other (or others) dependent. Depending on the history of the groups, there may be overt or more covert rivalry between them. *Within* each group, communication may be horizontal (peer to peer) and two-way, though between groups it is usually vertical (top-down) and one-way. While individual members of any of the dominated groups may be self-sufficient, the group as a whole is not. Institutions are even more pronounced than in tribal societies. Religions develop into formal institutions with experts. Economic exchange becomes more exacting. Political institutions are more formalized, and people may feel no connection of heritage with their rulers; rule and order are maintained by specialized people loyal to political rulers.

COMMUNICATION PATTERNS IN PEASANT SOCIETIES

People who want to serve among peasant societies need to be aware of the following patterns of communication if they hope to develop significant relationships. Peasants are more self-sufficient than individuals in tribal societies and so may experience a larger degree of independence. However, they maintain loyalty to their larger group heritage and have smaller reference groups from which they derive their identity and to whom they owe the greatest loyalty. Decisions in peasant societies affecting the entire society are made from the leaders on down, and there is typically a sharper separation of social power than in band societies. Gender roles may remain very distinct or blur with time, depending on environment, religious values, and political events. The more developed the villages, the less people are able to live in the moment. However, when strong political power is valued and supported with religious teachings, a sense of fatalism may pervade the society such that its members do not think that individuals are the source of control. Rather, they think it is the larger group or the social setting that controls them. Peasants may still have a relatively holistic view of life, but the ongoing development of specializations (carpenter, scholar, warrior, healer, etc.) tends to allow greater compartmentalization than in band or tribal societies.

> *Though the receiver of the communication will always have to make some adjustment, the major responsibility for adjustment belongs to the one who seeks to communicate a message across a cultural barrier.*
>
> Kraft 1979b, 295

Urban and Individualistic Societies

DESCRIPTION

As villages continue to grow, life becomes more complex and compartmentalized. Cities often arise as either centers of power or centers of trade (or sometimes both), and today's urban settings are massive locales with highly specialized institutions that are often felt to be autonomous from one another. Each institution has its own specialists (politicians, priests, economists, doctors, educators, etc.) who can easily live within the confines of the institution. Although it requires politicians to regulate the life of the city, the businesses provide the economic foundation for the city to continue its existence. While religion may play only a peripheral role for the entire city (unless the values of the city cherish the integration of religion and government, such as in Islamic settings), it is still a significant force for many of the individuals who live there. There is more individual autonomy but fewer integrated safety nets for the individual who is unable to cope with city life. In most Western cities, values are considered personal choices, and the city embodies a multicultural environment where choice and relativism in values is highly prized. The city also has areas that can be mapped according to the inhabitants: ethnic enclaves, wealthy sectors, slums and shantytowns, industrial areas, business centers, and so forth. While each city may have its own unique flavor, globalization threatens to homogenize the large cities so that they all have a common feel, although they retain their individual idiosyncrasies.

Further, because cities have far more groups and layers, or strata, than other types of societies, it is important to explore the types of communication that occur within and between layers, as summarized in figure 6.1.

87

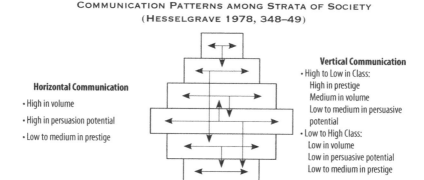

FIGURE 6.1
COMMUNICATION PATTERNS AMONG STRATA OF SOCIETY
(HESSELGRAVE 1978, 348–49)

Horizontal Communication

• High in volume

• High in persuasion potential

• Low to medium in prestige

Vertical Communication

• High to Low in Class:
High in prestige
Medium in volume
Low to medium in persuasive
potential

• Low to High Class:
Low in volume
Low in persuasive potential
Low to medium in prestige

COMMUNICATION PATTERNS IN URBAN SOCIETIES

People who want to serve among urban societies need to be aware of the following patterns of communication if they hope to develop significant relationships. While urbanization tends to lead toward individualism, time and goal orientations, and secularization, there is no single pattern for intercultural communication in all urban centers around the world. Generally, urban settings are more individualistic than their rural counterparts in the same country, but in some cities the collective mind-set is still part of daily life (e.g., Japan; see Yamazaki 2004). The more heterogeneous a city, the more direct communication patterns tend to be, since city dwellers have less common background information than their rural counterparts. City business and transportation systems, for example, tend to force people to develop clock and task skills, which may or may not spill over into personal relationships. Children who grow up in major cities of a multilingual country (e.g., Kenya) where a trade language is mainly spoken (Swahili or English) may very well not know the language of their grandparents (such as Kikuyu), resulting in diminished traditional values in future generations.

FACETS OF SOCIAL RELATIONSHIP SYSTEMS

Within each of these four types of societies, humans have developed institutions that give cohesiveness to the society and facilitate the functioning of all elements of life. These institutions—ranging from neighborhood associations to the military—provide the mechanisms by which a society regulates itself. More often than not, an institution within a society arises because someone or a small group of people see or feel a need that is not being met. They join together (the internet makes this easier than ever) to ensure that the need is met.

If others find their own interests aligning with this new group, they may also join the effort. Initially no formal organization is necessary; everyone simply knows who everyone else is and what each one does. However, as the group grows in size and complexity, more formal organization (or institutionalization) becomes necessary to keep the group focused.

An intercultural communicator who wants to plant a church, help a community develop holistically, or meet a particular need in the local setting, must understand how relationships are developed and regulated within these institutions. It is in the context of these social relationships that significant growth activities such as socialization, identity development, community development, and leadership development all take place.

There is a very wide range of what are called "institutions," especially in contemporary urban settings. At the highest formally organized level, they include such things as governmental organizations, industries such as banking and commerce, and religious groups. At the lowest level, they can include neighborhood clubs, dinner clubs, and small group Bible studies. They also can be abstract ideas with visible examples, such as the institutions of family and marriage, and different groups within the society may struggle over whose definitions are considered "normal" for them.

> *An institution is any structure or mechanism of social order and cooperation governing the behavior of a set of individuals within a given community. . . . Institutions are identified with a social purpose, transcending individuals and intentions by mediating the rules that govern cooperative living behavior.*
>
> "Institution," in Wikipedia, https://en.wikipedia.org /wiki/Institution

Scholars who study the institutions found across cultures have identified at least five facets of human social relationships that underlie all institutions. Each is focused on meeting a particular need of humans in society and has associated elements that signal its presence. Each can be the main driving force behind an institution, and typically all five will be found within any institution. They can also be thought of as institutions in and of themselves (in the abstract sense of the word mentioned above). The five facets are association, kinship, economics, education, and law (table 6.1; Hiebert and Meneses 1995; compare Dodd 1998, 38). In the rest of this chapter, we briefly introduce each in turn. The sidebar in each section is intended to give you a starting set of questions or things to observe to help you learn the system when you enter a new cultural setting.

TABLE 6.1
SOCIAL INSTITUTIONS

System	Need	Elements
Association	To connect people with similar purposes and/or objectives	Symbols or slogans, purpose (formal or informal), number of persons belonging
Kinship	To biologically reproduce new members	Descent, authority, residence, inheritance, marriage
Education	To provide new members with the knowledge, values, and skills of the society	Formal: schools, universities, trade schools Informal: books, television, newspaper, effective people Nonformal: kin, friends, peer groups
Economics	To distribute the goods and services that sustain the livelihood of its members	Types of enterprises, population of persons who work, ecology, systems of exchange, and means of payment
Law (Political)	To maintain internal order and to regulate relations with others	Government: courts, city hall, police Public utilities and services

Adapted in part from Harris and Moran 1982, 62–72.

Association

The associational system focuses on how people connect and how groups of people separate themselves from others. It is one of the more difficult categories to conceptualize because it is so broad and inclusive, involving institutions such as unions, clubs, societies, cooperatives, churches or other religious groups, political parties, hobby groups, and web groups (e.g., Facebook and other social networking apps). Many of these are embedded within

---

SIDEBAR 6.1
RELIGIOUS ASSOCIATION

Religious association involves how people connect religiously. The following questions are intended to give you leads on the types of things to study when you need to understand the associative functions of religion in a new culture. Discovering the answers to these questions will lead you to develop new ones that will help you to dig deeper into the culture.

1. What religious associations are found in the culture?
2. How are they governed?

3. How do religious adherents in the culture relate to outsiders?
4. How are barriers to and options for affiliation supported by religious beliefs?
5. What symbols are used to identify members of various associations?
6. How are new religious associations formed?
7. In what ways does the gospel condone or condemn indigenous religious associations?

SIDEBAR 6.2
RELIGIOUS KINSHIP

What role does lineage play in the way people connect religiously? The following questions are intended to give you leads on the types of things to study when you need to understand the kinship functions of religion in a new culture. Discovering the answers to these questions will lead you to develop new ones that will help you to dig deeper into the culture.

1. What spiritual roles can (or must) be inherited within lineage?

2. What are the religious rules for marriage and sexual relations (e.g., celibacy for priests, definitions of incest)?

3. Do relatives of religious leaders enjoy special status or access within the religion?

4. In what ways does the gospel condone or condemn indigenous religious kinship standards?

---

larger institutions (e.g., alumni associations are part of schools; city, county, or state political groups are part of national political parties; scout troops are part of the scouting organization).

In many secular societies, religious associations may be subgroups within larger nonreligious associations (e.g., Christian sociologists within a national sociological society).

Kinship

Every society must provide for the biological reproduction of new members and see that they are nourished and cared for during infancy and childhood. Almost universally, the family, whether nuclear or extended, provides the basic context for the performance of these activities. Most early training and socialization of children also takes place within the family. While kinship is actually a type of association, because so much anthropological work has focused on this area it has been treated as a separate institution.

Education

Education involves the methods used to enable people to develop into responsible adults within their society. It includes formal, nonformal, and informal educational modes. Formal education is ladder-structured and involves accreditation as seen in schools and universities. Nonformal education has a development orientation, as in scouting groups and community sports programs, but is not accredited. Informal learning, such as the language learning of children, is a form of socialization.

SIDEBAR 6.3
RELIGIOUS EDUCATION

How do people learn to become responsible followers of religion in their societies? The following questions are intended to give you leads on the types of things to study when you need to understand the educational functions of religion in a new culture. Discovering the answers to these questions will lead you to develop new ones that will help you to dig deeper into the culture.

1. How are each of the approaches to education (formal, nonformal, and informal) understood and lived out in the society?
2. How do they prepare the next generation for future religious challenges?

3. What roles do age, class, and gender play in religious education?
4. How does the use of social power affect religious educational processes?
5. In what ways does the gospel condone or condemn indigenous religious educational standards?
6. What is the society's understanding of
   a. the religious training of children,
   b. the religious instruction of every age group, and
   c. the educational methods (e.g., teaching, preaching, apprenticeship, discipleship) appropriate for religious instruction?

As an institutional term, education refers to all activities that in any way, directly or indirectly, contribute to providing new members, either by birth or by immigration, with the knowledge, values, and skills of the society. These are transmitted to the new member in order to prepare her or him to live and function within the society in a socially acceptable manner with some degree of independence.

Economics

Every culture must have some way to produce and distribute the goods and services that sustain the lives of its members. The set of institutions and roles organized around the performance of these activities constitutes the economic system of the culture.

Do not limit yourself to thinking about money for this institution. It encompasses money, as well as other forms of social exchange for material goods or services, but economics also includes the system of social capital and social power exchange.

Social capital refers essentially to the potential for exchange between persons and networks that are connected to one another and can mutually benefit from the exchange. You may have a friend whose father owns a business and

SIDEBAR 6.4
RELIGIOUS ECONOMICS

How do people learn to become responsible followers of religion in their societies? The following questions are intended to give you leads on the types of things to study when you need to understand the economic functions of religion in a new culture. Discovering the answers to these questions will enable you to develop new ones that will help you dig deeper into the culture.

1. What are the religious regulations for economic and social capital exchange?
2. What are economic religious obligations (e.g., rites of transition, funerals)?
3. How do these obligations affect economic status?
4. How is capital (goods, monetary, social) used
   a. internally (inside the religious community), and
   b. externally (outside the religious community)?
5. How do socioeconomic strata affect religious function?
6. In what ways does the gospel condone or condemn indigenous religious economic or social capital standards?

SIDEBAR 6.5
RELIGIOUS LAW AND POLITICS

How do people learn to become responsible followers of religion in their societies? The following questions are intended to give you leads on the types of things to study when you need to understand the legal and political functions of religion in a new culture. Discovering the answers to these questions will enable you to develop new ones that will help you dig deeper into the culture.

1. What are the normal leadership selection and installation processes?
2. What types of leadership roles exist?
3. What constraints exist on various leadership roles (gender, age, ethnicity, etc.)?
4. How do leaders exercise power?
5. How is discipline in the religious community carried out?
6. How is authority delegated and received?
7. In what ways does the gospel condone or condemn indigenous religious legal and political systems?
   a. Cultural leadership values/ preferences
   b. Culturally appropriate decision-making methods (e.g., divination)
   c. The cultural preference for the relationship between religious institutions and the state
   d. Local preferences for use of social power

93

who provides you with a job. You may teach people how to grow better crops (knowledge capital) or how to understand the Bible better (spiritual capital). These are examples of types of social capital that must be considered under the larger "economics" system.

Legal and Political Systems

All communities or cultures must have some means of maintaining internal order and, at the same time, regulating their relations with other communities or cultures. Internal threats to a culture's existence result from the competition for power, here defined as the control over human-made and natural resources. Since the availability of such resources has ultimate limits in any community or culture, conflict of visions and plans for the use of those resources is inevitable. The political system, therefore, is the network of institutions and social roles that exist to control the competition for power.

CONCLUSION

As you can see, social structures play foundational roles in intercultural communication patterns and styles. We have only skimmed the surface of important issues and not touched on some of the more significant topics that could be presented (such as networking, social change, status, and roles). We encourage you to pursue an understanding of the social structures of the area in which you minister so that you know how to best utilize the bridges that exist and anticipate the roadblocks before you come to them. Our case study for this chapter illustrates the reality of kinship as a significant factor in intercultural communication.

CASE STUDY:
FAMILY PROBLEMS IN ASIA

SUZANNE SCOTT

Mary had lived in the city only two years when she met Zhen Lien, who started attending Mary's Bible study and soon turned her life over to Christ. Now Mary and Zhen Lien were both spiritual sisters and such close friends that Mary became an "adopted" part of Zhen Lien's family. Over the years Mary reached out to all of Zhen Lien's siblings and her mother (her father had died twenty years earlier). As the years passed, the eldest sister, her husband, and "Mama" came to Christ. Zhen Lien's brother didn't have time for any religion, while the other three sisters clung to their traditional Buddhist religion and ancestor worship.

Mary was truly embraced as part of Zhen Lien's family and spent the most

---

important holidays with them. She also had her "adopted family" over every Christmas to celebrate with her. So it was not unusual that Zhen Lien began to confide in Mary when it came to family problems.

The only boy in the family, Zhen Lien's brother Ching Hwa, was not a very good businessman. He kept finding promising business deals, and since he was "head" of the family, he would get the entire clan involved in his projects. This had happened several times, and each time the family lost money. When Mary asked why the other family members didn't just refuse to give him money, Zhen Lien explained that they could not refuse since he was the only son and therefore head of the family.

Then one day Ching Hwa heard of a surefire deal and insisted that the family members not only use their money but also find friends to borrow money from so that they could invest in the plan. The business plan failed, and the family lost all their money and the money they had borrowed. Zhen Lien had to quit her job with a Christian organization and find a job that would pay more and give her more working hours so that she could repay her friends the money she had borrowed.

Zhen Lien was single and almost forty so the family assumed that Mama would live in her home and Zhen Lien would care for her. But the new job meant that she had to be on the road long hours. The family pressured her to be "a better daughter." Zhen Lien was becoming more and more frustrated with the family. After all, it was her brother who had caused this mess in the first place.

Then Ching Hwa did the unforgivable. He took three of the sisters' "chops." In this country people do not do business with signatures on contracts. Instead a chop, or stamp, is used. Each person has his or her own chop, which is the legal method of signing. Ching Hwa used the chops to borrow a large sum of money for a business deal. He mortgaged the sisters' homes. This included Zhen Lien's house. Since Zhen Lien was single she depended on her house for her future security. It would be where she would live when she was old, and since there is no form of social security in this country, it was important that she had the house. The two sisters' homes were lost to the bank (they were second homes for both sisters), and it looked as if Zhen Lien would lose her house too.

The entire family was furious with Ching Hwa. Time and again he had caused real problems for the clan. Zhen Lien told her family that she wanted to turn him over to the police, to tell the police and the bank that she had not authorized him to use her chop, but he had stolen it. This would mean that she would not be liable for the loan, and she would not lose her house.

The family was astonished that Zhen Lien would even think that way. Ching Hwa was, after all, family. How could she even consider bringing such disgrace on the family? The amount of anger and hurt was so extreme that Zhen Lien did not want even to talk to her mother and other siblings. She refused to go to church because Mama and her eldest sister attended the same church that she did.

REFLECTION AND DISCUSSION

1. Is there an equivalent in your own culture to this type of "adoption" by a family of an outsider? If so, what are the obligations for each person in such a relationship?

2. Because Mary is considered part of the family, Zhen Lien wants to know what Mary thinks the family should do. How would you advise her?

Networks, In-Groups, and Social Change

N o normal person in today's world is an isolated individual. She has
relatives, acquaintances, enemies, friends, work associates, and
neighbors. He has individual relationships, relationships because
of the groups he belongs to (work, neighborhood associations, and religious
associations), and relationships with the institutions of his culture (government, bank, school, city, and county). All these relationships exist because
God has made us relational creatures; the need to belong is part of our wiring as human beings. Thus, every person is networked to multiple layers of
individuals, groups, and institutions.

In the previous chapter we introduced social institutions. Here we drop
down to the bottom of the social organizational ladder and work our way
back up by starting with the individual.

Everyone who has a relationship with someone else has a particular role
and status within that relationship. They may be changeable (within a company through promotion) or fixed (as a daughter to her father). They may
follow a long set of regulations formally imposed by cultural values (e.g., in
caste relationships), but even so the nuances of how the two people in the

relationship work out their roles and statuses in light of those values will have been refined over the time they have related to each other.

The set of a person's total relationships is her network, which is the next level up. Each relationship within the person's network has its own set of rules. Depending on the stratification in the society, this variation may be quite large. To be networked to someone, you need only to know that person. You do not need to belong to the same group or be of the same gender, the same age, or the same socioeconomic status. However, understanding how the networks function within a society can open the door to quickly broadening (and deepening) the number of connections you have, which is an important skill for anyone ministering in a new society. The rapidly evolving way that the internet has changed what people think of as "connecting" (e.g., social networking and connecting sites and feeds) makes this issue far more complicated than it was a few decades ago. The ability to analyze those networks is a relatively new discipline in the intercultural communicator's toolkit, and a very helpful one.

Often, though not always, networked relationships come into existence because both people belong to the same group. When that is not true, and if the two find a common purpose that is broader than their own relationship, it might result in a new group being formed. Groups, in this sense, may be thought of as smaller, less organized, and more fluid than institutions. However, some groups are more important to us than others. It is toward these ideas of role and status, networks, and important groups that we turn our attention in this chapter.

STATUS AND ROLE

Status is the position assigned to an individual by his or her culture, subculture, and/or group within the social institutional setting. Everyone has a number of status situations within her social setting (e.g., mother, daughter, sister, aunt, niece, teacher). Status confers certain rights and protections but also places certain obligations and responsibilities on us. *Role* is the acting out of the status accorded a person by his culture, subculture, network, and/ or group within a social institutional setting. Abuse of one's role can result in either ostracism or popularity (depending on how the abuse is perceived by the society).

Implications of Status and Role

Even those who think they will not have to make a great adjustment in the new culture (pastors, mothers whose main responsibilities will be with the family, technicians, and so on) may still find themselves playing roles they never expected. Scott vividly remembers the visit he, together with all the expatriate teachers in Swaziland, made to the king of Swaziland just two weeks into Scott's sojourn in the country. That he had personally met the king opened doors for roles he had never expected prior to arriving in Swaziland. This small example illustrates that even those roles that we think will require less adjustment will still have different expectations attached to them by the new culture.

There are two major implications of role and status for cross-cultural workers. First, they must be aware of their status and seek to respond within it, especially during the early part of their term of service. Typically cross-cultural workers from industrialized nations are given higher status in many Majority World societies than they are used to having at home, and this can make them feel uncomfortable with the expectations that accompany their higher status. As a result, they may deny their new status. This denial can result in confusion on the part of the local population, which has expectations about how higher-status people should behave.

Second, cross-cultural workers need to be aware of the status of the respondents—what their position is in society and how their profession of faith will affect the community's response (Hesselgrave 1978, 336–43). On the one hand, the people with whom the missionary develops a relationship may be marginal persons in society, and their faith response may add a sociological barrier that prevents others who are "normal" within the society from even investigating faith. On the other hand, they could be influential individuals, who may bring many others along with them into the new faith. They may be formal leaders who possess prestige and influence by virtue of occupying key positions of prominence and power in the community and who may bring others to faith as well. They might be opinion leaders who exercise personal influence in the community by force of personality, competency, and communication ability. Or they may be considered good speakers or orators who will be able to persuasively communicate the new faith. They are potential patrons or sponsors who (especially in patron-client societies; see chap. 12) will lend social legitimacy to the new faith. Finally, some will be mediators who will be able to explain the new faith in a socially nonthreatening way.

With the exception of the marginals, all these types will help propagate the gospel more effectively. However, we cannot neglect or ignore the marginals. After all, Jesus came for them, and his good news is particularly good for them (Klaus 2000).

Implications of Status and Role for Christians

The Bible clearly indicates that God intends people to be socially situated. Husbands and wives, children and parents, church leaders and other Christians all have roles spelled out in the New Testament. Each person can see his or her uniqueness in light of status/role, and God provides people with special gifts for fulfilling role requirements. At the same time, however, a Christian's status should be founded on humility before God and in agreement with her or his God-given abilities, gifts, and stage of life; status definitions should not be based on social situations. Ultimately we are to accept a status for its responsibilities and not just for the rewards (Heddendorf 1982, 104–6).

NETWORKS

Every individual within a group (as well as the group as a whole) is connected with a limited number of group members (or other groups). However, they are also connected to people outside the group.

FIGURE 7.1
NETWORKS ILLUSTRATED

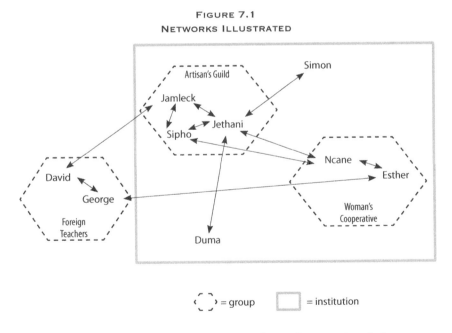

Figure 7.1 illustrates a small network of people. David and George are foreign teachers who have come to a rural village in Swaziland. David knows Jamleck, a member of a local artisan's guild, but does not yet know the other members. George knows Esther, who belongs to the women's cooperative.

99

As the diagram illustrates, networks are not confined to groups. David and Jamleck do not belong to the same group, but they are linked. The same is true of George and Esther.

The sum of these networked relationships forms the person's concept of the groups to which she is connected and her role in them. We can analyze these social networks by examining the individuals or groups (called *nodes*) and their connections to other individuals or groups (called *ties*). The connections can have multiple levels. Does George go to Esther for information? Whom does Simon go to for help?

This type of analysis can tell us about the *centrality* of a person or a group—how important that person or group is to the rest of the network in terms that we choose. For example, in the diagram Jethani is the one who knows the most people in the culture, yet neither David nor George have met him. It is this type of analysis that search engines such as Google use to determine the importance of websites for the search terms you type in. Just as it can find the most important websites for your search, good network analysis can help you to find the most important people to help you in a given task, whether that task is finding information, clearing an administrative logjam, making an important decision, or getting permission to register a church.

Network analysis can help us to understand how decisions are made. Whatever the formal structure of the group, network analysis can uncover the actual connections and the people who make decisions and whom they consult to make those decisions. Sophisticated network analysis requires appropriate software and field research (see, e.g., http://www.orgnet.com/cases.html for a variety of network analysis case studies, including http://www.orgnet.com/decisions.html, a network analysis with diagrams and brief explanations of how decisions are made within a particular company).

Popular social networking sites enable the development of virtual communities of people who are linked to one another individually and through groups that they join. The nodes and some elements of the ties of such groups are easier to analyze than real communities because the web programming on which they are based tracks all the connections automatically.

As churches go virtual in more highly connected countries, virtual connecting will play an increasingly important role in how people are tied together as growing numbers of them will no longer rely exclusively on face-to-face contact to form faith communities.

Although the term "social network" is relatively new, such networks have been effective bridges for the gospel that Christians have utilized since the church has been in existence. Evangelical missiological framing of social networks started with Donald McGavran's *Bridges of God* (1955), and such networks continue to be utilized today through tools such as network analysis to better understand social issues ranging from church networks (McConnell 1990) to racism (McConnell 1997). Social network analysis has been recognized as a vital component of fruitful strategic practice in Muslim settings (Daniels and Allen 2011), especially among those who advocate for insider movements (e.g., De Jong 2011; see chap. 20), and we anticipate that as Christians grow in understanding this concept, their use of it in strategic thinking will increase.

IN-GROUPS

Every society has groups. Even small nomadic peoples distinguish adults from children and men from women, resulting in subgroups within the society. At the other end of the spectrum, in urban settings there can be thousands—if not hundreds of thousands—of groups, including church groups, school groups, volunteer associations, business groups, political groups, hobby groups and clubs (from computer users to runners to stamp collectors), and so on.

Of the many groups to which a person belongs, some will be more important than others. That group may consist of family, peers, colleagues, and friends. The most significant group in a person's life is called her or his *in-group*, the "group of people about whose welfare one is concerned, with whom one is willing to cooperate without demanding equitable returns, and the separation from whom leads to discomfort or even pain" (Triandis 1992, 72).

However, that group does not give each member all its values. Another type of important group is called the *reference group*, which refers to a group that "possesses some quality to which we aspire and hence serves as a 'reference' to our decisions" (Neuliep 2006, 216). The groups we use for reference may vary from social setting to social setting as well as with age and stage of life. In-groups give people their sense of identity and demand their deepest loyalty; reference groups provide them with points of orientation.

Characteristics of Groups

There are several important considerations for understanding groups (the following discussion draws from Dodd 1991, 102–5). The first is *group size*. Typically, the smaller the group, the tighter the observations of each person by the whole group and thus the greater the pressure to conform.

A second consideration is *cohesiveness*, which is the degree of group attraction for group members. The more cohesive the group, the greater the pressure to conform and the fewer deviations allowed. When groups are more

---

SIDEBAR 7.1

GROUP STRUCTURES IN INTERCULTURAL COMMUNICATION

Adapted in part from Hesselgrave (1978, 377–78)

1. The more closely communication follows the patterns of the prevailing group network structures, the more effective it will be.

2. People communicate more to others of their own group; that is, interpersonal communication is usually horizontal.

3. Interpersonal, horizontal communication within groups lends itself best to effecting voluntary changes in attitude and behavior.

4. The more face-to-face the group, the more difficult it becomes for the outsider to establish effective communication (and, therefore, the more important it is that communication be based on personal friendship).

5. In all groups, the initial communication of the gospel should be to responsible, accepted members of the group who are, therefore, good potential channels of communication.

6. The more heterogeneous the group, the more flexible and variegated the communicative approach to its included networks must be.

7. In face-to-face groups, consideration should be given to communicating the gospel first to someone at the top (or someone near the top) who is more capable of making decisions and presenting the gospel to the larger group.

8. The more cohesive, homogeneous, and face-to-face the group, the more likely it is that communication will be along established network lines and that decisions will be collective.

9. The more cohesive, homogeneous, and face-to-face the society, the more aware of cultural values of time the communicator must be to effect lasting changes.

---

cohesive, there is greater loyalty to the group, and the group will offer more support and band together to deal with threats (for application in church planting, see Dunaetz 2008).

Another consideration is *group salience*, which is the importance of the group to the individuals who compose it. Resistance to changing group norms is directly related to the group's degree of salience. This is a very important consideration in understanding cult members and how to reach them.

A fourth consideration is the *clarity of group norms*. The greater the ambiguity of norms, the less control the group has over its members. When ambiguity is present, group interaction may increase to reduce the ambiguity (depending on the value placed on uncertainty reduction by the group).

An important consideration for Christians to keep in mind is that of *homogeneity*, which refers to the extent of similarity among group members. This idea is foundational for the so-called Homogeneous Unit Principle (HUP) in church growth, as formulated by Donald McGavran:

> People like to become Christians without crossing racial, linguistic, or class barriers. This principle states an undeniable fact. Human beings do build barriers around their societies. More exactly we may say that the ways in which each society lives and speaks, dresses and works, of necessity set it off from other societies. The world's population is a mosaic and each piece has a separate life of its own that seems strange and often unlovely to men and women of other places. (1990, 163)

Though called a principle, it is really an observation about an almost universal phenomenon (e.g., many have noted that the hour of church worship is the most segregated hour in the American week).

While many practitioners are not aware of it, the HUP forms the underlying presupposition behind such ideas as adopt-a-people and people-group thinking, strategies based on reaching a people within their own ethnolinguistic identity. A crucial question of this observation is the extent to which it fits what the Bible teaches about what the church should be (see sidebar 7.2). As a result, significant discussion and disagreement over the HUP was generated in American missiological circles from the 1970s until the end of the twentieth century (e.g., Kraft 1978a; Gration 1981; Wagner 1981; Padilla 1982; Cornett and Edwards 1984; Plaisted 1987; Moreau 2001).

Types of In-Groups

Perhaps the most prominent type of in-group is the *family*. In more-individualistic cultures, this in-group may include only the nuclear family and possibly the grandparents. In collective cultures, however, the family also includes aunts, uncles, cousins, nephews, and nieces. Proverbs such as "Blood is thicker than water" concretize the feeling that family is the group that deserves loyalty over other relationships (blood refers to genetic inheritance).

Another type of in-group is the *organization*, from which the members derive their identity and to which they give their loyalty (e.g., Rotary Club, Masons). For example, in Japan workers traditionally expect to spend their entire career with the same company. The social bonding that takes place during and after work is very time intensive. This fact has been a significant obstacle to evangelizing Japanese men, who are not ready to switch their in-group from occupation to church. It was also prevalent in the post–World War II US business sector, which at times expected employees (typically husbands and fathers) to put their careers ahead of family when a choice had to be made.

SIDEBAR 7.2
CONSIDERATIONS OF THE HUP

The Homogeneous Unit Principle (HUP) has been a hotly debated concept in missiological circles for decades. As you read through the following summary sections, consider whether you would be willing to implement an HUP-oriented strategy for church planting in a multicultural (and multilinguistic) setting, such as a large city. Why or why not?

1. The possible benefits of a homogeneous congregation or denomination include:
   a. Everyone within the group shares a common worldview (including common patterns of thinking, belief systems, behavioral ethics and norms, nonverbal communication signals, decision-making methodologies, etc.). Of all these, language is the "gatekeeper." If someone does not know the language of the church, she will not be interested in working through other issues.
   b. Everyone within the group shares a common language.
   c. Everyone within the group shares a common history.
   d. Everyone within the group shares a common identity (including family roots, music, traditions, geographic origin, etc.).
   e. Everyone within the group feels comfortable; the "climate" is understandable and culturally relevant.

2. Possible negative factors of a homogeneous congregation or denomination include:
   a. In-growth develops, which does not allow new members from other ethnic groups to join the group, possibly even preventing some from coming to Christ.
   b. The group members may lack maturity in learning how to relate to members of other cultures within God's family.
   c. The group suffers from "monocultural myopia": the short-sightedness that comes from having only one cultural perspective.
   d. Those from a minority group are forced to assimilate the values, culture, and identity of the dominant group.
3. Some pragmatic questions:
   a. Can a local church made up of one ethnic identity reach a community around it that is of a different ethnic identity?
   b. When do we seek to build homogeneity, and when do we need to fight ethnocentrism? How can we discern the difference between them?
   c. What importance should we give to the development of multicongregational churches that share a building (especially relevant in urban areas that have a high degree of heterogeneity)?

A third type of in-group is an *ideological* group, with common loyalty to an ideology or religious orientation. Cults are an extreme example of this type of group, and fundamentalist organizations in many religions around the world

---

SIDEBAR 7.3
QUESTIONS TO HELP YOU UNDERSTAND LOCAL GROUPS

An important task early in the sojourn of a cross-cultural worker is to understand how groups are formed and operate in the new culture. The rules the sojourner has used at home likely will not work in her new cultural setting. Thus the ability to ask—and answer—these questions and others like them will help her adjust more quickly than otherwise. The answers will vary from group to group, though common cultural values will mediate the driving forces underlying the answers. For any particular group being considered, the cross-cultural worker should ask the following questions:

1. What is the basis of the formation of the group?
2. How is the group regulated?
3. What are the group's norms? What values underlie these norms? What factors played roles in their development (ecology, group history, common human core, intergroup interaction, etc.)?
4. How is membership determined and regulated (individual/collective and power-distance factors such as fate, birth, choice, and active allegiance)?
5. How are role and status determined and regulated?

provide the in-group for their adherents. Jesus's call to follow God rather than family is an important Christian value (Matt. 10:34–39), and how this value works out in churches, small groups, and local parachurch organizations can be quite complex. This type of in-group can also have a political (e.g., Black Panthers, Marxists, socialists), philosophical (e.g., free thinkers), lifestyle (e.g., environmentalists; Dead Heads, i.e., followers of the rock group the Grateful Dead), or patriotic (e.g., AmVets) orientation.

SOCIAL CHANGE

Societies, because they are composed of people, all change over time. The major causes of social change are *borrowing* (from another culture) and *invention* (whether new ideas, products, or processes developed from within the culture). The way that social change spreads throughout a society is called *diffusion*. Since people crossing cultural boundaries who want to introduce Christ are coming as those who want to introduce social change, this is a critical topic for them.

Borrowing

Borrowing occurs when one society has something that appeals to members of another, and these people introduce change in their own society by borrowing from the other. An obvious example is the availability of ethnic foods in any urban center around the world. Another is the movies that come from Hollywood and Bollywood, which are seen in every corner of the globe. Yet another is the fashion industry and its worldwide impact. Technology has played a significant role in borrowing. Without knowing what is happening in other societies, borrowing is impossible. For example, for several years *Wired* magazine had a section titled "Japanese School Girl Watch." It described what was trendy among Japanese schoolgirls because the odds were high that the same thing would be trendy among American school children in the near future.

New ideas, values, and lifestyles that are already developed in one society are "discovered" and then borrowed by another. In our globalized world, the amount of borrowing across cultures is, for all intents and purposes, limitless. Some societies are seen as having the edge (in the case of technology, Japan), and others follow their lead (in this case, the United States).

This particular effect of globalization has not been all for the good. Scott has a friend who did not get his first pair of shoes until he was ten years old, and at that time he had only one set of clothes. He was poor, but he did not know it and was content. The difference between then and now is that people who are in the same situation today also have access to urban environments and methods of communication where they see and hear about worlds that they previously did not know existed. They are poor, and unlike Scott's friend, *they know it and are not content.* They would like to borrow but cannot. This leaves them angry and their anger constrains the ways they may choose to handle their frustrations.

Invention

Invention occurs when some new way of living, new religious teaching, new technology, or new thinking is created within a culture. It can range from something as simple as a toy to a new religion. The iPod is a classic example. Until its debut on October 1, 2001, handheld music players were not best sellers. They were expensive, there was no common format for the music, and there was no "buzz" factor. With its intuitive interface, ease of use, reliability, and "cool" factor, the iPod made it easy to download and play music for everyone who could afford it. The fact that a newer version was available on a regular basis made it even more enticing to those who always want to be on the cutting edge—not even considering the parallel evolution of iPhones and iPads.

Inventions may come about for several reasons. In the case of the iPod, the idea was to capture an existing anemic market and turn it into a big profit maker for the company, not to mention to help Apple gain market share outside the normal computer industry. Invention may also occur when there is a crisis in the culture (from invasion to hurricanes) or when there is an ecological change that makes former ways of living impossible to sustain.

Diffusion

Diffusion is a technical term used for the spread of gas from a more concentrated area to a less concentrated area. It was borrowed by social scientists as the term for the mechanism of the spread of technology (or ideas) in a society. Everett Rogers (1962, 2003) popularized the idea, noting that diffusion of technology through a society takes place through five levels of adopters:

1. *Innovators* (2.5 percent of the population): risk takers, venturesome people, more wealthy.
2. *Early adopters* (13.5 percent of the population): social leaders, respectable, popular, well respected, educated.
3. *Early majority* (34 percent of the population): thoughtful, deliberate, many informal social contacts, more open to social change than the rest of the population.

4. *Late majority* (34 percent of the population): skeptical, traditional, lower socioeconomic status, more willing to follow once the majority has changed.

5. *Laggards* (16 percent of the population): averse to risk, traditional, fear newness, will accept change once it has become the new "tradition."

Since missionaries come to enact not simply social change but social transformation (Hiebert and Meneses 1995, 373–75; see also Coffey 2011), knowing who the innovators and early adopters are can help in the church-planting process.

CONCLUSION

We have covered several significant topics as well as the idea of social change—each worthy of book-length discussion—in two brief chapters. To help you thoroughly grasp the ideas, read the case study, looking at the role and status of the individuals involved, their networks (and how that may or may not help them), and their groups—together with the obligations that come with group membership.

CASE STUDY:
THE TRIUMPH OF THE CHIEFMAKERS

WILSON AWASU

Reprinted with permission from Hiebert and Hiebert (1987, 100–102).

Dake had just returned to his home village in Africa. He had carefully avoided coming home for a number of years because of his Christian faith, but now he was sure there was nothing to worry about. It had not even occurred to him that this was Chiefmaking season.

After the usual exuberant reunion with uncles, aunts, nephews, nieces, and cousins, Dake decided to visit the old palace where he had grown up. His father had been the reigning chief of their royal line. Dake, however, was not allowed to daydream for long. He had barely seated himself in the palace when he heard the war cries at the gate. There was an onslaught of people surrounding the palace. Every outlet was blocked—there was no escape. The Chiefmakers were upon him!

Almost before he knew what hit him, Dake was smeared with white clay. A goat was slaughtered and the blood was sprinkled on him. The cries of triumph ascended and a stampede ensued.

The village had just installed him as its new chief. It was too late for Dake to regret coming home! It was all over. Dake was the new chief, and there was no way to undo what had been done.

The Council of Chiefmakers had not acted impetuously—they were carrying out a long-overdue assignment. As the youngest son of the reigning chief, Dake had been chosen for royal succession when he was only three years old. Until now, however, circumstances had prevented the council from carrying out their duties.

Dake's great-great-great-grandfather had won royal status for their lineage among these warlike people who lived in the mountains and had their own language. Dake's ancestor was made chief because of his bravery in battle against the dreaded Ashanti, whose forces were defeated and forced to retreat. He was made chief of a jurisdiction that included seventeen villages. Dake was the youngest son of the fourth chief of this royal line. He was carefully groomed in the intrigue and tradition necessary to carry out the duties of a chief.

Even when Dake was a boy, however, the royal succession was threatened. His mother was a Christian and had done everything she could to instill Christian principles in her son. Her great desire was that Dake would become a fine Christian man, educated and trained for Christian service. Her wishes began to be realized when Dake became a Christian during his high-school years.

Just a year after Dake's conversion, his father died. That was when the trouble started. Everyone expected that after the eight weeks of funeral ritual, Dake would be installed as the new chief. He would be expected to take part in all the rituals, beginning with the invocation of the ancestral spirits, through the veneration of his late father, the dances, the offerings, and the purifications. He would play his part by following, in shadow fashion, the movements of a senior elder, who traditionally replaces the old chief until a new one is installed.

Dake and his mother faced these proceedings with a great deal of consternation. How could he pour libations to the spirits and lead his people in the worship of ancestors now that he was a Christian?

A solution for them came with the help of Dake's mother's brother. This uncle was sympathetic and did not believe Dake should have to become chief against his will. At the dawn of the final day of the funeral, Dake's uncle whisked him away from the village.

Dake's absence became obvious immediately, and the funeral rites could not be completed satisfactorily. Dake's mother was blamed, and everyone expected that the ancestors would exact the normal penalty of death for the interruption of the traditional procedures. But that expectation decreased after two years passed without Dake or his mother being taken.

In the meantime, a regent occupied the throne. Dake, for his part, avoided the palace area during the special seasons when it is appropriate to enthrone a chief. He wondered if this would be the pattern for the rest of his life.

Dake went abroad for college and graduate school. He completed a master of divinity degree and then pressed on for a PhD in theology. When he returned home from abroad, Dake married a woman from a tribe that was a traditional enemy of his own. She was a medical doctor.

On the morning that Dake returned to his village, he felt quite safe from the Chiefmakers. It had been years since his father died. He was now a trained Christian theologian who had violated the "orders" and angered the ancestors. His wife was from an enemy tribe; she did not even come from a royal family. Surely his people would not want anyone like him for the throne! The ancestors would have to be pacified, and there was just too much against him in other ways as well.

Now, however, Dake's world had been completely shattered. He had been trapped and made chief. His people would expect him to pacify the ancestors as well as lead them in all aspects of the traditional religion. His marriage would be seriously threatened.

REFLECTION AND DISCUSSION

1. In what ways might this be an opportunity for Dake? For example, could he bring his people to Christ as chief?
2. How might you advise Dake?

PART 3

Patterns of Intercultural Communication

O ver the past decades, intercultural communication specialists have explored numerous dimensions that guide communication within societies (e.g., business; see Beamer 2000). We have previously mentioned how the nonverbal side of communication plays a significant role in our interpretation of what is meant by a communication event. In this section we explore that element of intercultural communication by starting with the broad concept of nonverbal communication in chapter 8.

As part of nonverbal communication, we use patterns for communication that in the discipline have been characterized as two ends of a scale of values. For example, Hall has proposed several sets of values that affect communication patterns, but two of them have been recognized as having particular importance: contexting and the approach to the concept of time. His differentiation along these two axes is widely used within the discipline of intercultural communication.

Every society is an ocean of information. On the one hand, more collective societies value taking their communication cues from their shared ability to "read the currents" of that ocean. Members anticipate that others in the society read the currents as they do, so that friends do not need to explain the current to each other. As a result, they value indirect verbal communication, anticipating that everyone will fill in the gaps based on their mutual reading of the current. On the other hand, in more individualistic societies members operate independently from each other and do not assume that even their friends read the current the way they do. They prefer direct communication that fills in the gaps to ensure they are understood.

In chapter 10, we take on cultural understandings of time. Hall divides cultures along a continuum: at one end are cultures that consider time a commodity that can be sliced into pieces in which people focus their attention on one thing (or person); at the other end are cultures that see all time as unitary and do not value slicing it into pieces (see Lindquist and Kaufman-Scarborough 2007). The former societies he calls monochronic (one-time) and the latter polychronic (multitime), and people's use and understanding of time is radically different in each type of society—different enough to have an impact on how they communicate what they value.

From 1967 to 1978, social psychologist Geert Hofstede collected data on the attitudes and values of employees of a large multinational organization and its subsidiaries. All employees of the organization, ranging from unskilled laborers to research scientists, were surveyed. The surveys were originally designed to help managers in the organization see how the employees felt about their work, their boss, and their company. In all, the responses of 116,000 questionnaires with over one hundred standardized questions each were collected. The surveys were statistically analyzed, and it was discovered that the most significant factor in understanding the difference in responses was nationality (second was occupation; Hofstede 1983b, 293–94). The analysis also indicated that four sets of values accounted for one-half of the variations in the patterns of answers (1983a, 78). Those four sets of values Hofstede labeled individualism-collectivism, power distance, masculinity-femininity, and uncertainty avoidance. Each represents a cluster of linked values, and in recent years studies have validated the three axes that we explore in this section (e.g., Merritt 2000).

The first, individualism-collectivism, is how people define themselves: either as independent individuals or as members belonging to a group. Harry Triandis, a social psychologist who taught at the University of Illinois, calls this "perhaps the most important dimension of cultural difference in social behavior" (1992, 71). More than any other axis it has been seen as central to understanding the ways people in different societies communicate. We work through these issues in chapter 11.

The second of Hofstede's dimensions relates to how people idealize differences in social power. In essence, do they want to level the playing field, or do they prefer to ensure that power differentials are maintained and supported? This is called power distance, and the implications of this axis for intercultural communication are examined in chapter 12.

Third among Hofstede's dimensions is the extent to which people idealize separating gender roles. Are they completely interchangeable (which Hofstede labels "femininity") or to be separated (which Hofstede labels "masculinity")? It is obvious that this will have a significant impact on communication and ministry, and we explain it and the implications in chapter 13.

Finally, because so much work has been done recently in biblical and cultural studies in terms of honor, face, and shame as opposed to justice and guilt, and because of its significance in many Majority World countries, we explore the impact of these orientations on communication patterns in chapter 14.

Nonverbal Intercultural Communication

One of Edward Hall's greatest contributions to intercultural communication is the recognition that we communicate not only verbally but nonverbally as well, and that we are often unaware of how (or at times even what) we communicate through nonverbal means. His best-selling book *The Silent Language* (1959b) paved the way for deeper exploration of this issue on the level of popular culture. Most simply stated, nonverbal communication is communication through means other than language (Martin and Nakayama 2005, 161). Because it is less consciously directed, it is harder to control. When given a mixed message in which the verbal and the nonverbal portions contradict each other, most people will believe the nonverbal portion (Dodd 1998, 134–35; Neuliep 2006, 287).

NONVERBAL COMMUNICATION TYPES

While all researchers agree that there are several types of nonverbal communication, they do not all agree on how to categorize them. We explore seven categories, including communication through (1) paraverbal methods (using our vocal apparatus), (2) stillness or silence, (3) physical characteristics,

> ## SIDEBAR 8.1
> ## HISTORICAL FACTORS IN NONVERBAL COMMUNICATION STUDIES
>
> *Rogers, Hart, and Miike (2002, 17)*
>
> Hall's work directed the attention of Japanese scholars and language educators to nonverbal aspects of Japanese interpersonal and intercultural communication. Stimulated by Hall's writings, they started to describe cultural characteristics of Japanese nonverbal communication . . . and to examine the influence of nonverbal communication on Japanese intercultural communication, primarily with English-speaking people. Such cross-cultural and intercultural nonverbal investigations had important implications for the study of intercultural communication in Japan, since the Japanese people were often said to rely less on verbal communication than English-speaking people (who often have difficulty in reading the Japanese mind). A number of relevant studies . . . cited Hall's work and/or used his theoretical framework to understand Japanese non-verbal behavior from both interpersonal and intercultural perspectives. . . .
>
> Intercultural communication investigations in Japan explored such varied topics as silence, facial expressions, hand gestures, bowing and hierarchical relationships, gazing, eye contact, touching, proxemics and personal space, and the sense of time. . . . Several of these topics for intercultural communication inquiry were suggested by Hall . . . , and were then advanced by research on American/Japanese differences, and which illustrated the uniqueness of Japanese culture and communication behavior. Hall . . . studied the role of *wa* (harmony) in Japanese culture. The study of nonverbal communication in Japan was directly influenced by Hall, particularly in its early years . . . , although in recent years, some Japanese scholars . . . criticized elements in Hall's paradigm for intercultural communication as they apply to Japan.

(4) proxemics (spacing), (5) chronemics (timing), (6) kinesics (body movement), and (7) artifacts and environmental factors.

Paraverbal Communication

Paraverbal coding (or *vocalics*) refers to "audible sounds that accompany oral language to augment its meaning" (Dodd 1991, 220). The same sentence can be made to carry a message of simple fact, demand, resignation, excitement, conspiracy, invitation, or question through variations in volume, intonation, accent, emphasis, rhythm, drawl, resonance, inflection, and timing. One problem in learning another language is the tendency to import paraverbal codes from one's first language into the second. For example, Zulu speakers utilize a different inflection for questions than English speakers. Thus native English speakers must stop using their native inflection as well as learn the proper inflection for questions when learning to speak Zulu.

Silence and Stillness

Silence and *stillness* can be communication events in themselves. When a Bible study leader in an individualistic society asks a question and no one answers, she or he makes assumptions about the participants. Perhaps they have not prepared. However, if the participants are from a different culture, they very well may be thinking that the leader should know the answer to the question and are simply waiting for it to come. International students sometimes complain that Americans always want to talk when they visit, giving the impression that silence is a vacuum that Americans abhor. Japanese (and other Asian groups) have a reputation in Western circles for communicating through silence and stillness (Morsbach 1988; Martin and Nakayama 2005, 173).

Physical Characteristics

Physical characteristics of nonverbal communication include such things as physique, body shape, general attractiveness, body and breath odors, height, weight, and skin color or tone. Some are either out of our direct control or more difficult to control (body shape) than others (hair color, breath or body odors). Generally we seek to control the latter in such a way as to gain advantages we consider important based on how we value these characteristics.

The Bible offers numerous illustrations for each type of nonverbal coding presented here (see sidebar 8.2 for a few examples). We encourage you to find your own examples and see if you can determine the significance of them as you read the Bible. To start your thinking, in the sidebars that follow in this chapter we offer a few examples of each of the areas being discussed. Here are several questions that should be considered in regard to physical characteristics in the cross-cultural setting:

1. What physical characteristics are admired or liked?
2. How will the source's physical characteristics be regarded?

SIDEBAR 8.2
COMMUNICATION THROUGH PHYSICAL CHARACTERISTICS IN THE BIBLE

Genesis 29:17: Leah had *weak eyes*, but Rachel had a *lovely figure and was beautiful*.

1 Samuel 9:2: Kish had a son named Saul, as handsome a young man as could be found anywhere in Israel, and he was *a head taller than anyone else*.

Isaiah 3:24: Instead of fragrance there will be a stench; instead of a sash, a rope; *instead of well-dressed hair, baldness*; instead of fine clothing, sackcloth; *instead of beauty, branding*.

3. What part does race play in interpersonal relationships?
4. What effects accrue to differences in the body sizes of source and respondent?

Proxemics

Proxemics refers to the use of space as a means of nonverbal communication. Areas where proxemics play a role include such things as seating arrangements; spatial arrangements related to leadership; crowding, size, and layout of an office or residence; conversational distance; and territoriality (see sidebar 8.3 for examples from the Bible).

It has been long known that different cultures use different spatial distances to communicate meaning. The closer two people stand to each other while talking, the greater the intimacy. Problems arise when what one party considers merely a social distance the other considers an intimate distance. The former will be read by the latter as being aggressive or pushy (or perhaps as making a sexual advance), while the latter will be seen by the former as evidence of being cold and distant. Practical questions the cross-cultural communicator should seek to answer as soon as possible in the new setting include:

1. What is a comfortable conversational distance?
2. At what distance can a person be before I must interact?
3. Can the local people feel comfortable in my house?

Chronemics

The nonverbal communication aspects of time include punctuality, duration of meetings, length of conversations, the part of the day or night, and special times and seasons (see sidebar 8.4). This is especially important for those with a high value on punctuality, for example, who then move to live in cultures with a different chronemic orientation.

SIDEBAR 8.3
PROXEMIC COMMUNICATION IN THE BIBLE

Psalm 103:12: As far as the east is from the west, so far has he removed our transgressions from us.

Zephaniah 3:2: She obeys no one, she accepts no correction. She does not trust in the LORD, she *does not draw near to her* God.

Ephesians 2:6: And God raised us up with Christ and *seated us with him* in the heavenly realms in Christ Jesus.

SIDEBAR 8.4
CHRONEMIC COMMUNICATION IN THE BIBLE

Genesis 29:20: So Jacob *served seven years* to get Rachel, but *they seemed like only a few days to him* because of his love for her.

1 Kings 18:21: Elijah went before the people and said, "*How long* will you waver between two opinions? If the LORD is God, follow him; but if Baal is God, follow him."

2 Peter 3:8: But do not forget this one thing, dear friends: With the Lord *a day is like a thousand years, and a thousand years are like a day.*

Because differing values of time are so important, sensitive, and often lead to conflict and problems, we later devote an entire chapter to it (chap. 10). For now, questions that can help the cross-cultural communicator include:

1. At what time would visits in the home be welcome?
2. How is "punctuality" understood?
3. What is an "interruption"? What rules govern our understanding and response to them?

Kinesics

Kinesics include such things as gestures, movements of the body or trunk (somatics), movements of the hands (dextrics), movements of the feet and legs (podiatrics), facial expressions (prognatics), eye behavior (oculesics), and posture (see sidebar 8.5). It includes the equivalents of basic gestures such as pointing, beckoning, refusing, and agreeing. Here we present four types of kinesics: posture, gesture, physical contact, and eye gaze.

POSTURE

Posture refers to such things as sitting properly (different in Japanese settings than in American, for example), acceptable postures for men and women in private and public settings, etiquette on standing or sitting when meeting someone, proper forms of bowing, and so forth. When Scott was in Swaziland, he and a group of American teachers met King Sobhuza II. Before the meeting, the visitors were told never to let their heads be above the king's, because this would communicate great disrespect for him. Thankfully they were all sitting on the ground when the king came out to speak to them, for he was a very short man!

Posture can be used to include people in a group (opening up and making space for them) or to exclude them (closing off a circle). It can be used to

119

SIDEBAR 8.5
COMMUNICATION THROUGH POSTURE IN THE BIBLE

Job 2:7–8: So Satan went out from the presence of the LORD and afflicted Job with painful sores from the soles of his feet to the crown of his head. Then Job took a piece of broken pottery and *scraped himself with it as he sat among the ashes.*

John 8:3–8: The teachers of the law and the Pharisees brought in a woman caught in adultery. *They made her stand before the group* and said to Jesus, "Teacher, this woman was caught in the act of adultery. In the

Law Moses commanded us to stone such women. Now what do you say?" They were using this question as a trap, in order to have a basis for accusing him.

But *Jesus bent down and started to write on the ground with his finger.* When they kept on questioning him, *he straightened up* and said to them, "Let any one of you who is without sin be the first to throw a stone at her." *Again he stooped down and wrote on the ground.*

---

indicate interest (leaning forward while listening to someone) or disagreement and distance (leaning back and crossing your arms). Questions sojourners newly arrived in an unfamiliar setting need to ask include:

1. What is the range of acceptable postures for my gender?
2. What should I do with my hands when I am talking with someone, and what should I avoid? (For example, in Uganda, putting your hand in your pocket means you have something to hide.)
3. What are appropriate postures for religious leaders, especially when they are performing religious duties such as preaching or leading a Bible study?

GESTURES

Gestures include a whole range of physical movements that support, contradict, emphasize, or explain the verbal component of the message. Every culture has gestures commonly understood among the people of the culture that may or may not be understood the same way in another culture. We can gesture with our arms and hands (demonstrating actions, putting them in ritual postures such as for prayer), with our trunks (shrugging our shoulders), with our faces (rolling our eyes), and with our feet (shaking the dust off, Luke 9:5; washing feet, Gen. 18:4).

Questions to ask as you learn your new environment include:

1. What is the etiquette for proper and improper gestures?
2. What gestures that I consider proper does my new culture consider improper (e.g., pointing, the OK signal)?

SIDEBAR 8.6
COMMUNICATION THROUGH GESTURES IN THE BIBLE

Exodus 9:29: Moses replied, "When I have gone out of the city, I will *spread out my hands* in prayer to the LORD. The thunder will stop and there will be no more hail, so you may know that the earth is the LORD's."

Esther 5:2: When he saw Queen Esther standing in the court, he was pleased with her and *held out to her the gold scepter* that was in his hand. So Esther approached and *touched the tip of the scepter.*

Isaiah 58:9–10: Then you will call, and the LORD will answer; you will cry for help, and he will say: "Here am I. If you do away with the yoke of oppression, with the *pointing finger* and malicious talk, and if you spend yourselves in behalf of the hungry and satisfy the needs of the oppressed, then your light will rise in the darkness, and your night will become like the noonday."

3. What gestures are appropriate across age boundaries (older to younger; younger to older)?
4. What gestures can help communicate love and acceptance as taught in the Bible?

PHYSICAL CONTACT

Nonverbal physical contact includes such things as stroking, hitting, greetings, farewells, holding, and guiding another's movements. We use these for affirmation, correction, discipline, and affection. Some societies are more touch-oriented than others; the former are called contact societies and the latter noncontact societies. This factor is especially important across gender lines. In Kenya, people typically shake hands with everyone when they come into a

---

SIDEBAR 8.7
COMMUNICATION THROUGH PHYSICAL CONTACT IN THE BIBLE

Genesis 48:14: But Israel *reached out his right hand and put it on Ephraim's head*, though he was the younger, and crossing his arms, *he put his left hand on Manasseh's head*, even though Manasseh was the firstborn.

1 Samuel 10:1: Then Samuel took a flask of oil and *poured it on Saul's head and kissed him*, saying, "Has not the LORD anointed you ruler over his inheritance?"

Luke 7:37–39: A woman in that town who lived a sinful life learned that Jesus was eating at the Pharisee's house, so she came there with an alabaster jar of perfume. As she stood behind him at his feet weeping, *she began to wet his feet with her tears.* Then *she wiped them with her hair, kissed them* and poured perfume on them.

SIDEBAR 8.8

COMMUNICATION THROUGH THE EYES IN THE BIBLE

Proverbs 16:30: Whoever *winks with their eye* is plotting perversity; whoever purses their lips is bent on evil.

Isaiah 3:16: The LORD says, "The women of Zion are haughty, walking along with outstretched necks, *flirting with their eyes*, strutting along with swaying hips, with ornaments jingling on their ankles.

Acts 13:8–10: But Elymas the sorcerer (for that is what his name means) opposed

them and tried to turn the proconsul from the faith. Then Saul, who was also called Paul, filled with the Holy Spirit, *looked straight at Elymas* and said, "You are a child of the devil and an enemy of everything that is right! You are full of all kinds of deceit and trickery. Will you never stop perverting the right ways of the Lord?"

---

group. However, when an Iranian came to visit Scott and his wife, Emily, in their Kenyan apartment, he adamantly refused to shake her hand, expressing shock at how inappropriate that would be.

Questions to ask as you learn your new environment include:

1. Is this a contact or a noncontact group?
2. How are greetings performed?
3. What are the rules for touch within gender and across gender?
4. Are certain parts of the body (e.g., the head or the face) taboo to touch, especially in public?

EYE CONTACT

Nonverbal signals with the eyes (including the eyebrows) can communicate surprise, doubt, conspiracy, anger, pity, challenge, humility, and more. Generally direct eye contact shortens the distance between two people, and indirect eye contact lengthens it (Martin and Nakayama 2005, 168). In Swaziland, it is rude for a younger person to look an older person directly in the eyes. In fact, Scott remembers that a teacher punished a high school senior for looking directly at him. As Scott observed Swazi eye contact, he also noted that typically people would look at an equal not in the eyes but off to the side of the head, with actual direct eye contact only a fraction of the time. Scott began practicing this, and it felt terribly awkward at first. Eventually he grew accustomed to it and discovered that it was easier this way to have a deep and genuine conversation with Swazis. Direct eye contact was too strong for the Swazi and made it hard for Swazis to speak openly when Scott looked them in the eyes.

Questions to ask as you learn your new environment include:

1. What is the preferred degree of eye contact between equals? Between superior and inferior?
2. On what occasions is direct eye contact important?
3. What is meant by various eye gestures (such as rolling of eyes, eyes looking away, and eyes looking down)?

Classifications of Kinesthetic Communication

At least five categories are used to classify nonverbal body movements that are intended to communicate (the following discussion draws from Lustig and Koester 2010; Neuliep 2009; Martin and Nakayama 2013). It should be noted that while all societies use these types of body movements, the actual movements used to indicate something are typically not universal (Axtell 1991; Ngai 2000). At the same time, however, children studied in four countries all increased the same types of nonverbal gestures (pointing at a person, object, or event; object exchange, such as offering or taking something; and agency gestures, in which the infant attempts to motivate another person to do something for or with him or her) and decreased the same types of nonverbal gestures (reaching as a request and emotive gestures such as bouncing and clapping hands) as they transitioned into language learning (Blake et al. 2005), indicating the possibility of some type of universal base for certain types of nonverbal communication.

In one country a senior missionary and his wife were in constant conflict with their understudies, all in their first term of service. On the surface the senior missionaries appeared extremely insensitive. More correctly, they were not reading the informal cues in the behavior of their associates. Most of the blame fell on the woman. She had the responsibility of scheduling and explaining daily assignments to the men. Men do not like to take orders from women. To make matters worse, she had a tendency to talk from a distance of between twelve and fifteen inches, so close it seemed difficult to focus one's eyes. Twelve inches is perfectly proper in Latin America, but not in the United States. I actually saw men lean backward or sideward attempting to adjust away from what they interpreted as an "intimate" or "confidential" distance, to an ordinary business conversation distance.

Gordon 1973, 232

EMBLEMS

Emblems are nonverbal bodily behaviors that have direct verbal counterparts (such as the peace sign in the United States and Europe and the victory symbol in much of the world). They are used as a substitute for the verbal channel, either by choice (to emphasize a message, to participate in a group effort) or when the verbal channel is blocked for some reason. Sign language is essentially emblematic nonverbal communication.

ILLUSTRATORS

Illustrators are nonverbal bodily behaviors that are directly tied to, or accompany, the verbal message. They are used to emphasize, explain, and support a word or phrase. They literally illustrate and provide a visual representation of the verbal message (e.g., spreading the hands to show how big something is; shrugging while saying, "I don't know" to indicate lack of knowledge concerning a question).

AFFECT DISPLAYS

Affect displays are facial and body movements that show feelings and emotions, such as facial expressions of surprise when describing a reaction to an unexpected event or news. Psychologists who study the face recognize that facial expressions are physically limited by the muscles present in the face, and they have used this knowledge to determine the range of facial affect displays, which in turn has helped them to better understand nonverbal communication (Gladwell 2005). It is thought that as many as seven emotional states may be universally recognized: anger, disgust, fear, happiness, sadness, surprise, and possibly contempt (Matsumoto, Wallbott, and Scherer 1992, 284; Gudykunst and Kim 1992, 186; Martin and Nakayama 2005, 166). Studies have indicated that with appropriate training people can become more adept at recognizing those emotions cross-culturally (Gladwell 2005; Nixon and Bull 2005; Elfenbein 2006).

REGULATORS

Regulators are bodily behaviors that help to synchronize the back-and-forth nature of conversations; they help to control the flow and sequencing of communication, helping people to synchronize and remain in sync when they converse. They can include such gestures as raising the hand (either to indicate the person wants to say something or to stop someone from jumping in, depending on how the hand is raised), leaning forward, and fidgeting, as well as paraverbal pauses.

ADAPTORS

Adaptors are body movements that occur as a reaction to an individual's physical or psychological state (e.g., scratching an itch, fidgeting, tapping a

124

pencil, rubbing the hands together, shivering, tearing up, trembling of lips, looking downcast). They may also include the largely unconscious signals we send during random, unfocused encounters such as choosing a seat in a crowded coffee shop or walking past another person on a sidewalk (see Patterson et al. 2007; Patterson and Montepare 2007).

Artifacts and Environmental Factors

Artifactual and environmental factors also communicate nonverbally. Massive buildings, closed offices, offices with windows, corner offices, and cubicles all communicate various levels of hierarchy in many business settings. Things such as architectural style, furniture, interior decorating, colors, clothes, cosmetics, adornment, and material symbols also communicate things such as power, cultural values related to decorum, and social constraints (e.g., designating places for special purposes or restricting their use; see sidebar 8.9).

This type of communication can be seen in the way the homes of cross-cultural workers are decorated. Often the decorating reflects tastes and styles found in their country of origin. This is not surprising, since "home" is usually considered a place where people can feel comfortable and relax. When local home decor does not meet that need, the person from another culture will naturally turn to her or his own set of sensibilities rather than new ones. Questions to ask as you learn about your new environment include:

SIDEBAR 8.9
ARCHITECTURAL AND ENVIRONMENTAL COMMUNICATION IN THE BIBLE

Leviticus 16:17: No one is to be in the tent of meeting from the time Aaron goes in to make atonement in the Most Holy Place until he comes out, having made atonement for himself, his household and the whole community of Israel.

Esther 8:15: When Mordecai left the king's presence, he was wearing *royal garments of blue and white*, a large crown of gold and a purple robe of fine linen. And the city of Susa held a joyous celebration.

Matthew 27:50–51: After Jesus cried out again in a loud voice, he gave up his spirit. At that moment the curtain of the temple was torn in two from top to bottom. The earth shook, the rocks split.

Acts 21:27–28: When the seven days were nearly over, some Jews from the province of Asia Minor saw Paul at the temple. They stirred up the whole crowd and seized him, shouting, "Fellow Israelites, help us! This is the man who teaches everyone everywhere against our people and our law and this place. And besides, *he has brought Greeks into the temple and defiled this holy place*."

1. What is the functional and symbolic significance of the indigenous architectural style?
2. What values can you discover through the layout of land, places of business, community spaces, and homes?
3. What do colors communicate? Which colors are used in homes, offices, and community spaces? Which colors are avoided?
4. What is appropriate in terms of clothing and jewelry?

FUNCTIONS OF NONVERBAL COMMUNICATION

What types of functions does nonverbal communication serve? At one level, and not surprisingly, gesturing as a means of nonverbal communication has been demonstrated to enhance the accuracy of the message, especially when what is being communicated is less amenable to verbal description (Graham and Argyle 1975). A variety of other functions may be noted (discussed below; see Samovar, Porter, and Jain 1981, 158–59; Argyle 1982). In each case, the message we send by nonverbal communication channels may be the same as or radically different from the message we send by the verbal channel.

First Impression

We develop our initial impression of others largely on the basis of nonverbal factors, and we convey impressions to others by the same means—often within the first few seconds of meeting them (Gladwell 2005). We can be aloof or warm, compliant or demanding—all without saying anything. When communication is cross-cultural, it is far more likely that the first impressions will be incorrect because they will be based on one person imposing her cultural interpretation on the other's nonverbal communication.

> *Non-verbal communication functions in several different ways: it (1) supports speech by supplying additional information about the content of utterances, providing feedback, and controlling synchronization; (2) communicates attitudes to others and negotiates interpersonal relations; (3) expresses emotions; (4) conveys information about personality, voluntarily and involuntarily; (5) is used in ceremony and ritual, persuasion and propaganda.*
>
> Graham and Argyle 1975, 57

Relational Messages

Nonverbal communication enables people to send and receive signals from each other about their relationship. They can indicate how they feel about each other, themselves, and the

126

relationship they share. Syncing—in American English we commonly use the term "clicking"—is almost always a signal of compatibility, especially when both people experience it.

Affect

Have you ever asked someone how he feels and heard him answer, "Great!" but realized that he felt far worse than his verbal message indicated? We use nonverbal signals to indicate how we feel, from euphoric to miserable. In the United States, women are considered better readers of this signal system than men. Most men will *hear* what someone says (and

> *At most only about 30% of what is communicated in a conversation is verbal.*
>
> Raymond L. Birdwhistell,
> in Eilers 1999, 239

later even remind the person, "But you said . . ."), while most women will *observe* what someone says and *the way she says it.*

Self-Presentation

People use nonverbal cues to present themselves to others (to influence other people's thinking about them). For instance, they use nonverbal cues to convey messages of social power in the relationship. The more powerful person will use direct eye contact, while the less powerful will keep his eyes downcast or look away. The more powerful might assume a posture conveying confidence and being in charge, while the less powerful might assume a posture intended to communicate submission.

CONCLUSION

Understanding the nonverbal signals in a new culture is critical for successful adaptation. No one knows with certainty, but most (estimates range from 70

SIDEBAR 8.10
SELECTED WEB RESOURCES ON NONVERBAL COMMUNICATION

Exploring Nonverbal Communication (http://nonverbal.ucsc.edu)
Nonverbal Library (http://www.lin guaggiodelcorpo.it/sezione -internazionale/)

Wikipedia (http://en.wikipedia.org/wiki /Nonverbal_communication) to 93 percent) communication is nonverbal. In other words, learning how to read nonverbal cues and signals is nonnegotiable in cross-cultural settings. As you read the short case study, try to imagine what things you might have looked for in the nonverbal channels of the store clerk.

CASE STUDY:
FIXING THE CAMERA

CHIP NOONAN

A man walked into a camera shop hoping to have his expensive camera fixed. He showed it to the shopkeeper. "I love this camera a lot. I would really hate to lose it. Is there any way it can be fixed?" he asked somewhat insistently.

"There's a good possibility," the shopkeeper hesitantly replied.

The man looked the shopkeeper in the eyes and pleaded, "I really, really need this fixed by Tuesday because I'm flying back home. Can you have it fixed by then?"

The shopkeeper paused and then slowly nodded his head and said, "Yes."

"Great," said the man as he turned and left.

However, when he returned he found not only that his camera had not been fixed but also that the shopkeeper could not fix it and never had any intention of trying. The man stormed out of the shop. He felt deceived and was angry.

As he talked with me about it he shared his anger and frustration and noted:

"But I will tell you what will happen to people who tell lies. They will be thrown into that lake of fire and burning sulfur. The Bible is crystal clear in its condemnation of lying. Accordingly, if I ask a person to do something, and he replies, 'Yes'— although he has no intention of fulfilling that request—then this would be a good example of a lie. Obviously, his yes did not mean yes as our Lord commands, 'But let your "Yes" be "Yes" and your "No," "No." For whatever is more than these is from the evil one.' Thus the person who says yes but really means no would be telling a lie."

But is the picture as clear as the man thought it was? Does it matter that this scenario took place in a different country? Or that the shopkeeper is from a culture where people communicate indirectly? Perhaps many would say no. One might appeal to the absoluteness of the biblical morals, which are binding on every individual regardless of tribe or tongue, including the shopkeeper. Perhaps some would even say that this cultural practice reflects humankind's fallen nature and Satan's hold on a people group. However, though I hold to the infallibility of Scripture and the absolute truth contained within its pages, I trust that serious consideration of what a lie is and what communication and indirect communication entail will reveal that indirectness is not necessarily lying, even saying yes but meaning no.

REFLECTION AND DISCUSSION

1. What did the man with the camera communicate nonverbally to the shopkeeper?
2. How might you advise him to approach similar situations in the future?

9

Contexting

How do we understand the meaning of what someone is trying to communicate when the person speaks to us? More specifically, to what extent do we listen to the words, and to what extent do we look behind the words to see what she is actually trying to say? The extent to which we are enculturated to pay attention to the "ocean of information" mentioned previously results in two different patterns of communicating called high context and low context, which we explore in greater depth in this chapter.

WHAT IS CONTEXTING?

Contexting refers to a strategy of choosing the appropriate mix of verbal and extraverbal communication to get a message across (Hall 1991a, 85–116; Hall and Hall 1990, 6–10; see also Kraft 1983, 183–84; Gudykunst and Nashida 1986; Chua and Gudykunst 1987; Ting-Toomey 1989; Elgstrom 1994; Dsilva and Whyte 1998). Certain cultures and situations within cultures (e.g., negotiations) demand that more attention be paid to the context, while other cultures (and situations) require more attention to the actual words rather than their context (e.g., computer programs).

As can be seen in figure 9.1, a low-context communication is one in which the meaning of what is being communicated lies in the explicit words used in the communication process. This style of communication, according to

Edward Hall, is more commonly found in places such as Germany, Switzerland, Scandinavia, generally among northern European peoples, and in the United States (Hall 1991a, 59–77). When a low-context communicator asks people how they are doing, she will typically not pay any attention to things such as state of dress, facial expression, or other contextual issues; she will only listen to the verbal response. Computer programming is a perfect example of low-context communication, since a computer will perform the instructions *exactly* as given, no matter what the programmer intended for it to do.

FIGURE 9.1
HIGH- AND LOW-CONTEXT COMMUNICATION ILLUSTRATED

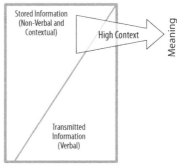

Low Context
Meaning derived from
verbal information

High Context
Meaning derived from non-verbal
and contextual information

As figure 9.1 also shows, a high-context communication or message is one in which most of the meaning is either in the physical context or internalized in the persons, while very little is in the coded, explicit, verbal part of the message. This style of communication, according to Hall, is more commonly found in places such as China, Japan, Vietnam, Korea, southern Europe, and Arab and African countries (Hall 1991a, 59–77). It can be seen as a type of "mind reading" because the words are not used to convey what is being communicated, and both sender and receiver must be on the same page mentally for the communication to be understood.

While Hall's basic idea has been criticized (e.g., R. Chuang 2003), studies that have attempted to validate the high- and low-context paradigm have produced generally persuasive results (e.g., Kim, Pan, and Park 1998; Kim et al. 2001; Yamazaki 2004).

In low-context cultures, direct, verbal skills are valued, for the ability to give detailed, exacting information is important. By contrast, in high-context cultures, indirect, nonverbal skills are valued; direct verbal skills may even be regarded with suspicion. Hall recognizes that there are variations within every culture. For example, the more intimate the relationship, the higher the context of communication. Conversely, computer programming is low in context, whatever the culture, since computers are unable to context communication (unless they are programmed to do so in a low-context way).

It is also important to note the relative position on the contexting scale for people as individuals. Even within a single culture, some people will be higher-context communicators than the average person in that culture and some will be lower-context communicators. For example, we must be careful not to think of all Japanese as high-context communicators. On average, they will be much higher than Germans. However, this is a statistical average that will not apply in every individual case.

CONTEXTING: THE WAY WE SEE THE WORLD

Contexting is not limited to verbal communication. People context through two entirely different but related processes. The first is the *internal*, which takes place inside the brain and is a function of either past experience (programmed, internalized contexting) or the structure of the nervous system (innate contexting) or both. The second is the *external*, which comprises the situation and/or setting in which an event occurs (situational and/or environmental contexting).

We context internally through each of our senses. Optical illusions take advantage of our desire to context information from two-dimensional drawings of three-dimensional objects. The object portrayed in figure 9.2 is physically impossible, even though it can be drawn, so the picture does not make sense to our brains because we cannot context it properly.

FIGURE 9.2
OPTICAL ILLUSION

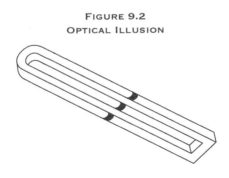

We context the sounds we hear. Hall notes experiments in which people were able to "hear" excised portions (in this case, up to a full syllable of a word) of a doctored tape recording without even recognizing that it was doctored

(1991a, 118–19). In terms of touch, hot and very cold water feel alike, a fact used in torture by making the victim think hot water will be poured on him and then using very cold water instead. Our olfactory contexting is used by perfume makers to help the women who wear their perfumes send messages to the people around them. Our sense of taste is connected to our sense of smell such that it is very difficult to eat good-tasting foods when we are in an environment with bad smells.

We also context externally, reading the setting in which an event occurs in a variety of ways (using, of course, our sensory abilities). Table 9.1 shows several of the external ways we context messages.

TABLE 9.1

ENVIRONMENTAL-INTERPRETIVE CONTEXTING

Type	Example
Spatial (Proxemic)	Each of us has a certain "intrusion distance"; if someone comes within that distance, we will read more than just physical proximity into the situation.
Temporal	Definitions of "promptness" vary from culture to culture, and our definition will determine how we interpret an arrival that is before or after an explicitly stated time.
Architectural	Buildings are not an end in and of themselves—they are for the people who will inhabit them. For example, office space (size, private, public, etc.) communicates different things in different cultures.
Behavioral	We constantly "read" our perceptions of the behavior of people in light of the context. "Actions speak louder than words" exemplifies this idea.
Websites	Studies done on the amount of contexting on websites have found what might be expected for people of the culture in which the website was created (Würtz 2005).

No matter where the society is on the scale, within that particular culture communication events are also relatively higher and lower in context. Through the socialization process, people learn the contextual rules for their culture and apply them "automatically." This automatic process is short-circuited in the intercultural setting, when our normal modes of operating are likely to lead us to misinterpretations of what we see going on around us until we have learned the new set of rules.

A BIBLICAL EXAMPLE

A clear example of the contexting of communication is seen in Abraham's negotiation for a burial site for Sarah in Genesis 23. Abraham approaches the Hittite men of Hebron and announces that he would like to buy a suitable burial site for Sarah. They give him permission, and he indicates the site that he would like and its owner, Ephron.

It is then that the text mentions that Ephron was present among them, and Ephron responds to Abraham. Notice that Abraham does not go to Ephron privately or ask him face-to-face in front of the rest of the people. He simply indicates the plot he wants to purchase. If Ephron is willing to sell it, he can respond publicly. If Ephron does not want to sell it, all he has to do is remain silent, and no one will lose face. It is likely that Abraham knew Ephron was present, and that is why he came. He also knew not to ask Ephron directly but rather to ask the leaders of the town on his behalf.

Ephron not only responds but also offers to give the plot to Abraham in front of the witnesses. However, this is not a case of Middle Eastern hospitality and generosity. Ephron is not actually expecting Abraham to accept the land as a gift; he is simply informing Abraham that he is willing to sell the land. Abraham understands the message and informs Ephron that he will pay the full price. Again, Ephron tells him that he will give him the land, but he now mentions that it happens to be worth four hundred pieces of silver. However, what is that among friends? Again Ephron invites Abraham to simply accept the land as a gift.

At this stage in the biblical narrative, it is noted that "Abraham agreed to Ephron's terms" (v. 16), and they sealed the deal when Abraham paid Ephron four hundred pieces of silver in front of everyone. Abraham was not obstinately refusing a free gift, because he knew that Ephron was not really offering one. Instead, he was following formal bargaining protocol, understanding what the meaning of the message was despite the words that seemed to contradict what was being communicated. Ephron was not being deceptive; he was following the rules of negotiating for his time and people. Abraham was likewise adept in playing the same game, and they came to mutually agreeable terms. Both knew the words to say, which words to ignore, and which ones had particular meaning and how to understand them. It is a clear example of high-context communication.

CONTEXTING AS A SIGNALING SYSTEM IN RELATIONSHIPS

Relationships in all cultures are subject to contexting. We are constantly reading and receiving signals that we need to interpret well if we are to successfully navigate the development of relationships within our own culture and especially across cultures.

For example, the longer a group is together, the higher in context its internal communication. This can be seen in teenage cliques, which use "in" vocabulary, dress, cosmetics, hairstyles, products, and so on. Someone who wears the wrong thing or acts the wrong way will soon get the message—even if it is not a verbal one. This phenomenon is also found in churches, clubs, offices (the "corporate culture"), and the like.

Because there is little or no shared background, all cross-cultural relationships will by definition start as lower-context relationships. However, this does not mean that both parties will automatically shift into a higher-context way of communicating. Unfortunately, they often act as they would with people of their own culture and are frustrated when their actions or words are misread as a result. By noting that they must start their relationship in a lower context fashion than they might otherwise prefer, we mean that the ability of each to "read" the other will be limited until they have enough in common to know what the other is like and how to understand him or her better.

> *The American seems very explicit; he wants a "Yes" or "No"—if someone tries to speak figuratively, the American is confused.*
>
> visitor to the United States
> from Ethiopia, Kohls 1981, 8

One common reality of friendships in all cultural settings is that the closer the friendship, the higher context the communication will be. Close friends, having shared many experiences and enjoying common ways of thinking, have much to draw on when they communicate with one another. One of the ways we demonstrate closeness to another person is to leave out verbal information as a sign that we know she will understand us. Relationships that are not developing higher-context communication are not growing in closeness. We can also show displeasure by lowering the context of our communication, giving too much verbal information as a type of insult or expression of frustration with the other. We return to this discussion on intercultural relationships in chapter 17.

CONTEXTING EMBEDDED IN WORLDVIEW

As we noted in chapter 4, all worldviews have three primary components: the cognitive, the affective, and the evaluative (Hiebert 2008b). In this section we explore each in turn.

Worldview: Cognitive

The *cognitive* component of worldview includes what people know about contexting. They may not even know the term *high context*, but they have learned early in life—by watching parents, siblings, and other relatives as well as friends and other people—that speaking in certain ways or saying

SIDEBAR 9.1
SIXTEEN WAYS THE JAPANESE AVOID SAYING NO

Adapted from Ueda (1974)

In Japan, it is difficult to say "no" simply and directly. A higher value is placed on maintaining the relationship than on clearly expressing one's own feelings. Thus it is often considered best to accept a request, though one does not want to or seems unable to accept. While this is different when people are on intimate terms, outside the family directly declining requests is very difficult. Directly refusing a request may hurt the other person's feelings and may give the impression that one is selfish and unfriendly for declining. For this reason, the Japanese equivalent of "no," *lie*, sounds rather formal and too straightforward to Japanese, and they seem to unconsciously avoid using it. Foreigners wanting to communicate appropriately must develop competence in sending and receiving "no" messages. Particularly important in a hierarchical society like Japan is knowing when and to whom a particular form of "no" is appropriate. The means of refusing requests from employers or superiors will be different from those used for requests from peers.

1. Vague no: Japanese like to use a vague response. Although the answer is negative, it is felt the listener will not be embarrassed if the speaker uses this "soft expression."
2. Vague and ambiguous yes or no: This is used when a person cannot make up his mind, or to create an atmosphere in which the person is dependent on the listener, who can then decide the answer she likes.
3. Silence: Silence can be used in two senses. First, silence can indicate that two can understand each other

without words. Or silence can indicate blocked communication between the two, where one does not want to express or cannot find the proper way to express his intention. Silence is sometimes used to decline requests to persons with whom one is not acquainted. However, since silence does not clearly express one's feelings, when used between persons in different positions, a superior can interpret it any way she likes, as a yes or a no.

4. Counterquestions: Sometimes when a person has to answer in the negative, she puts the focus back on the question, such as by saying, "Why do you ask?"
5. Tangential responses: To start talking about a different topic suggests a negative answer. Usually the questioner understands the meaning of this reply to be negative and does not press the issue further, accepting this as a no.
6. Exiting (leaving): Occasionally, the person questioned may simply leave without further explanation or comment.
7. Lying (equivocation or making an excuse—sickness, previous obligation, etc.): If someone wants to refuse with no specific conventional reasons, such as illness, previous obligation, or work, she may lie to make the refusal seem reasonable. Lying sometimes is taken as truth, which might, in some ways, be effective. Sometimes, the lies are more transparent, but they are

accepted since they are used to spare the hearer's feelings. Research suggests this is the most frequently used form of negation.

8. Criticizing the question itself: Criticizing the question itself, saying it is not worth answering, is used only by someone of superior status to the questioner.

9. Refusing the question: If a person is in an awkward situation, he may say he must refuse to answer and then go away.

10. Conditional no: If someone does not want to accept but is in a "delicate position," she may say that she will be able to do so conditionally. Or she can say she will do her best, but that if she cannot accomplish the task, she hopes that the other person will understand and appreciate her trying. According to research, this method is not favored because it maintains the expectation of the listener.

11. "Yes, but . . .": The person seems to accept the request but then expresses doubts whether he can fulfill it. The use of "but" expresses the real state of mind, which is that he hesitates or fears to accept the request. This is commonly recognized as meaning no.

12. Delaying answers (e.g., "We will write you a letter."): "I'll think about it" is commonly used, and can be taken as a negation or for its literal meaning. Its meaning depends on atmosphere, facial expression, tone of voice, and situation.

13. Internally yes, externally no: If someone really wants to accept but also has something else to do, she will decline without giving a direct no, using an expression of both apology and regret. While the regret may be sincere, the hearer may

merely perceive this as an indirect no and not recognize the speaker's sincere regret.

14. Internally no, externally yes: Even if a person must decline, he sometimes cannot answer directly and may even be forced to accept. This happens when one is asked by a superior. The person asked is pressed to accept but will likely add an excuse as a warning to the listener that he likely will fail to carry out the request.

15. Apology: An apology is often used instead of negative words. The apology can be a very humble response suggesting that the speaker is in an inferior position since she cannot meet the other's expectations. Thus a simple apology can be an effective negative answer.

16. *Lie* (the Japanese equivalent of the English no): This word is primarily used in filling out forms, not in conversation. Japanese speakers avoid using it, as it might disturb the other person immediately on hearing the word before an explanation can be given.

REFLECTION AND DISCUSSION

1. People from cultures who prefer direct communication methods often think that indirect communication methods are deceitful. Consider how you would respond to a colleague who asks, "Why don't they just come out and tell the truth?"

2. Brainstorm in small groups and develop a list of situations in low-context societies where it is considered acceptable to be indirect (such as a noncommittal response to a friend's new outfit or silence when a boss proposes a new idea that you have mixed feelings about).

certain things is correct or incorrect. They no longer think about how they communicate, but they do know "correct" communication and "incorrect" communication when they experience it. In sidebar 9.1, we present many of the ways that Japanese learn to say no without actually using the word. They know these options and expect not only to use them themselves but for others to use them as well. They will always read responses from others in terms of these ways of saying no and expect others to read them in the same way.

Worldview: Affective

The *affective* component involves people's emotional attachment and stability in relation to contexting their messages and the impact of raising or lowering the contexting. It is how they feel about contexting as a means of framing communication.

The affective dynamic in a worldview is typically played out in myths and stories found in the culture. As you watch an anime video (a Japanese style of animation; e.g., *Princess Mononoke*) or read a manga graphic novel (a Japanese style of comic book; e.g., Siku 2007), you may note that pieces seem to be missing—information that would help you to understand what is happening. You might also be surprised when things are not stated or are said in the opposite way they are intended.

The proverbs listed in sidebar 9.2 all either indicate a positive expectation toward high contexting or are themselves examples of high-context communication. The Vietnamese, for example, say, "When you eat, check the pots and pans." By that they mean that when you visit someone who prepares a meal for you, you should not speak about your favorite foods before you see what is being cooked, or you may make your host lose face by saying that you do not like the very type of food that is being prepared.

SIDEBAR 9.2
PROVERBS OF HIGH CONTEXT

A wise person is one who hears one word and understands two. (Yiddish)

An elder is like a bathtub. (Akan)

A horse released can be caught, a word released never. (Mongolian)

He who does not understand a look cannot understand long explanations. (North African)

Listen a hundred times; ponder a thousand times; speak once. (Kurdish)

SIDEBAR 9.3
SELECTED WEB RESOURCES ON CONTEXTING

Beyond Intractability article: Communication Tools for Understanding Cultural Differences (http://www.beyondintractability.org/essay/communication_tools)

High and Low Context (http://www.culture-at-work.com/highlow.html)

"High/Low Context Communication: The Malaysian Malay Style" (http://www.businesscommunication.org/conventions/Proceedings/2005/PDFs/09ABC05.pdf)

Kwintessential video: High and Low Context Cultures (http://www.kwintessential.co.uk/intercultural/highcontext-lowcontext-cultures.html)

Network for Strategic Mission Knowledge Base articles: High/Low Context (http://www.strategicnetwork.org/index.php?loc=kb&view=b&fto=1776&sf=Y)

Wikipedia article: High-Context Culture (http://en.wikipedia.org/wiki/High_context_culture)

Worldview: Evaluative

The *evaluative* component involves the moral decision-making rules for evaluating actions and attitudes that lead to contexted behavior, such as what are considered appropriate and inappropriate ways to disagree with someone or to engage in conflict. A Chinese student once said that Americans made her say no. When asked to explain, she told the story of being invited to eat dinner at an American's apartment shortly after arriving in the United States to study. The host put food on her plate, and when she had finished it, the host asked if she wanted more, to which she replied, "Yes." So her host gave her more, to her surprise! This was repeated until she was so full she was forced to say no to her host, which she felt would be seen by the host as bad manners. At this stage an American student in class asked her, "But why did you lie?" Both were evaluating the Chinese student's response to her host, but they were using different means of evaluation. The Chinese student had learned early in life not to say no directly to a host. She could communicate that she was full by leaving a little on her plate, and a good host would read that message and not have to ask her directly if she wanted more. The American, however, had learned that when you do not want more, you simply say so. Thus for the American the Chinese student's yes was a lie.

This is just one small example of how we evaluate the contexting behavior of others and how we can incorrectly judge them based on our own frame of reference.

CONCLUSION

For those who have grown up in a higher-context culture, learning how to be direct can feel like learning how to insult people and not feel guilty about it. For those who have grown up in a lower-context culture, learning how to be indirect can feel like learning how to lie. Each will struggle, and each will be tempted to judge the other culture as wrong. Each will have passages from the Bible to justify his or her position and will use them to justify his or her attitudes. Both will need to learn how to listen and how to read each other if they are to get beyond simply imposing on each other their own image of what a Christian should be.

As you read through the case study, see if you can read between the lines and understand what Pastor Yusufu communicates and what John Greenwood understands.

CASE STUDY:
WEST AFRICAN CHURCH

DEAN S. GILLILAND

Reprinted with permission from Hiebert and Hiebert (1987, 202–4).

The general council of the Benue Valley Church of Northern Nigeria was in a special session. It was a meeting called by the field secretary of the mission, John Greenwood. The African chairman of the church, Pastor Yusufu Bawo, said before the meeting began, "If the white people call a meeting, it will be *their* meeting, not ours."

For weeks the missionaries had been saying that if relations between the mission and the church did not improve, they would seriously consider returning to their homes in South Africa. Finally, Yusufu Bawo looked directly at the five missionaries present, shrugged his shoulders, and said, "We believe Peter Ewing was right. He said we have been controlled and impoverished by the mission. And we believe, further, that you, Reverend Greenwood, were influenced by your mission board in South Africa to terminate him because he

spoke the truth. Now whether you go or whether you stay makes no difference to us. Do as you please."

The Benue Valley Church. The Benue Valley Church was known as the South African Mission until the missionaries renamed it in 1962. The first missionaries came in 1926 from several denominations, including Baptist, Methodist, and Anglican. Little had been done in medical and educational work due to the high cost factor. As the spirit of nationalism grew in the 1950s and political independence came in the early 1960s, such missions generally began to transfer administration of the churches to African leaders.

The Benue Valley Church felt it lagged behind other denominations in being granted positions of leadership in their church. After forty years of missionary control, in 1966 Pastor Yusufu became the first

139

African to hold the office of chairman. His first two years, thus far, had been turbulent ones for mission-church relationships. At every meeting where missionaries were present, the same questions were being asked:

"Why are there no funds, even for church buildings?"

"Have you purposely not built us a high school in order to control us?"

"Do you want us to feel shame when we compare ourselves to the other churches around us?"

"Is it not true that even in South Africa, the black man is a mission field for the whites?"

Attitudes toward South African influence. Benue Valley Church was a poor church, even by Nigerian standards. Unlike neighboring churches, Benue Valley had received no subsidies or grants from its home mission board located in South Africa. The missionaries of Benue Valley had taught a strict rule of self-financing for the church from the beginning of its existence. However, while the Methodist and Lutheran missionaries had a comfortable life financially, the white staff at Benue Valley lived almost at poverty level. They and their sponsoring board had nothing to give, except what John Greenwood called "gifts of love and service."

Pastor Yusufu had been calling for a change in mission policies both in administration and finance. He also demanded African autonomy at every level and pressed the missionaries to build a high school and enlarge the medical work. In this he reflected the changing attitude of the Nigerian government, which had recently taken a hard line against all white South Africans. One example was that the prestigious Dutch Reformed Church Mission of South Africa had been evicted from the country six years before because their mission was regarded as an extension of the apartheid state church. Further, a nationwide daily paper described the D.R.C.M. in headlines as "the mission we do not want."

The arrival of Peter Ewing. The long-standing problems of slow growth in membership, poverty, and mission domination sparked a new crisis when Peter Ewing arrived from Johannesburg. He had been assigned to train the laity for evangelism and to do continuing education for pastors. Though he used as his base the leadership-training school in which he taught during the rainy season, Ewing moved about frequently. He was an impressive person, tall, with a strong physical build. His commanding presence was further strengthened by a gift for the Nigerian language.

Within a month after his arrival, he warned John Greenwood while visiting him in his home that unless a change of attitude and corresponding new programs came from the mission, there was little hope the mission would survive.

John admonished Peter that "to raise false hopes is immoral. We have a long history, which has been built on trust and service. Our board has no funds and we have no funds, and to act as though we do is courting disaster. Moreover, we have always encouraged self-support."

To this Peter replied, "How can you say this to any African, when he has been told over and over again by his own government that white South Africa is the richest nation in the world?"

John answered with obvious impatience. "Be reasonable, Peter. Look who we are. You are a part of us and belong to our history. The leaders of the church, especially Pastor Yusufu, must not be misled by promises that we know we cannot keep."

The termination of Ewing. After two years of service, Peter Ewing returned to Johannesburg for furlough. Almost immediately, the Benue Valley Church was informed by the South African headquarters of the mission that his services had been terminated. Embittered and angry, Peter Ewing's African following believed and circulated the word that John Greenwood and the other missionaries had requested the board to terminate Peter's service in Nigeria. Greenwood denied the charge.

In desperation the missionaries felt their presence may have now become a hindrance to the church. They decided to call together the general council of the church to seek a solution.

"Greenwood's Meeting." As the special council opened, Pastor Yusufu stepped out from behind the chairman's table and stated that this was "Greenwood's meeting." Following several hours of charges and sharp exchanges, John Greenwood stood to ask his final question: "In the light of all you believe we have said and done, and because our only reason for being here is for the good of the Benue Valley Church, shall we missionaries remain with you or should we leave the country?"

Pastor Yusufu replied that whether the missionaries chose to stay or to return to South Africa was of little interest to him or the church members.

John Greenwood was still standing when Yusufu, motioning with both hands in the direction of his African colleagues, said flatly, "We are waiting now for your decision. Do you go or stay?"

REFLECTION AND DISCUSSION

1. How would you advise Pastor Yusufu in light of what you have learned in this chapter?
2. What would you suggest to John Greenwood?

141

10

Polychronic and Monochronic Time

One of Edward Hall's earliest propositions was that "time talks" (1959b). By that he meant that we use time as a means to communicate with others. We can indicate their relative value to us, our status in relation to them, anger or pleasure, disdain or respect—all without actually saying anything.

Time is a curious item in the dominant North American culture. Over the years, our (mostly North American) students have brainstormed verbs and sayings related to time, and the vocabulary is rich (see a sample of the verbs in table 10.1). For them, time is an active, physical commodity that they think they can control in some way. While it is true that they cannot actually control it, they nonetheless use vocabulary that indicates that somehow they can "tame" it for their purposes.

Time is far more than just the movement of hands on a watch. It is integrated into everything we do, from how we hold conversations to scheduling of events such as appointments, meetings, or parties.

TABLE 10.1
ENGLISH VERBS ASSOCIATED WITH TIME

We can _____ time.				
allot	fill	lose	multiply	squander
arrange	find	make	organize	start on
begrudge	generate	manage	plan	steal
borrow	give	mark	redeem	take
buy	have	maximize	save	use
divide	invest	measure	schedule	value
do	keep	minimize	spare	waste
expand	kill	misuse	spend	while away

SOCIAL TIME

Social time, as opposed to pure clock time, has been called the "heartbeat of culture" (Levine and Wolff 1985). More than simply regulating seasons and days, social time is an integral part of every interaction in life, from the microlevel (interpersonal synchronicity) to the macrolevel (institutional time). While physical time marches on in discrete and homogeneous units, social time progresses through various rhythms (Lewis and Weigert 1981, 433).

With few exceptions, however, social time has not been studied systematically or integrated into the social sciences concerned with human behavior (Hall 1983). David Lewis and Andrew Weigert propose: "If social time received the attention it deserved in sociological considerations, no study of human organization and interaction would be considered reasonably complete unless it examined their temporal organization" (1981, 432). Social time may be seen as operating in three levels: individual time, group time, and cultural or institutional time (Lewis and Weigert 1981). Within each of those levels, there are at least five sets of cycles: daily, weekly, monthly, annually, and whole life.

Individual or Self Time

Self time is our experience of the flow of time and our memory of the past or imagination of the future. While time itself flows continuously and at the same rate for all people (ignoring relativistic effects for this discussion), we do not experience it as flowing homogeneously. On one hand, the more engrossed we are in an activity, the less time we perceive to have passed, so we say, "Time flies when you're having fun." On the other hand, all of us have experienced the apparent slowing down of time because we anticipate something exciting, such as a holiday, a special outing, or seeing a person who is important to us. Time in those situations can seem to drag along at a much slower pace than normal and so we might say, "A watched pot never boils."

143

Further, people can also remember the past and imagine the future. Thus, our experience of the flow of physical time is not limited to its physical nature; we develop mental constructs that help us to make sense of time as we experience and imagine it.

Group or Interaction Time

All social acts are "fit" inside other social contexts (e.g., we greet someone on the street when we are late for an appointment). This social component is called "time-embeddedness" (Lewis and Weigert 1981, 437). The tighter time embeddedness is perceived to be, the more important it is to know what is being embedded in order to know its relative priority. Monochronic cultures are more tightly time embedded. The less tight time embeddedness is perceived to be, the less important the surrounding events, and the more central the immediate circumstances. Polychronic cultures are looser in their sense of time embeddedness than are monochronic cultures.

> *If man does not keep pace with his companions, perhaps it is because he hears a different drummer. Let him step to the music which he hears, however measured or far away.*
>
> Thoreau 1854, 85

We can use the embeddedness of time to communicate connection or intimacy (e.g., by giving one person or group more of our interaction time than others) as well as distance or displeasure (e.g., by cutting someone from our interaction time). Perceptions of how this happens are culturally governed, and knowing the local rules of distancing and connection are critical for the intercultural communicator.

Cultural or Institutional Time

Institutions such as schools and businesses within a society set their own standards of time. Definitions of being on time, the differences between break and work time, when we are "off the clock" or "on the clock" are institutionally established in ways that make sense in the culture. This affects such things as when church starts, how long it goes, and the timing of committee meetings, Sunday school, and Bible studies. Some institutions within societies must follow the ebb and flow of seasons (e.g., agricultural institutions), while others may establish their own calendar in ways that make sense to them (e.g., fiscal years, school years in various countries around the world, review and promotion schedules, labor laws dealing with retirement or employment of children).

SYNC TIME

Important within the level of interaction is the concept of sync time. The original idea of synchronizing came when early moviemakers had to learn how to synchronize the sound of the movie with the pictures. Hall has pointed out that, without conscious effort, we synchronize all our daily transactions of life (1983). This includes synchronizing our own internal communication patterns (from the timing of our hand gestures to blinking our eyes) as well as synchronizing our communication with others (our ability to read hesitations in conversation, knowing who should speak when, and when it is appropriate to interrupt and when it is not).

It can now be said with assurance that individuals are dominated in their behavior by complex hierarchies of interlocking rhythms. Furthermore, these same interlocking rhythms are comparable to fundamental themes in a symphonic score, a keystone in the interpersonal processes between mates, co-workers, and organizations of all types on the interpersonal level within as well as across cultural boundaries.

Hall 1983, 153

We often see people who do not obey the conventions we are accustomed to using as socially maladapted. Syncing may be one of the most difficult things to do in another culture, since we have not grown up enmeshed in the syncing patterns considered normal there.

On a practical level, and following the work of sociolinguist Deborah Tannen (1986), we may note the simple act of syncing in a conversation (see fig. 10.1). Perhaps you have experienced conversations when you felt you could not "get a word in edgewise." Or perhaps you have talked with someone who never really seemed to get into the flow of the discussion.

Some people grow up thinking that they should wait until they are certain a person has finished a point or statement before they speak. A conversation takes place one person or voice at a time, in what can be called a "monovocalic" approach. Someone else, perhaps socialized in a different subset of the same culture, grows up hearing many voices speaking simultaneously and expects to interrupt and be interrupted on a regular basis (a "polyvocalic" approach).

When people from these two orientations get together, the monovocalic person may wait a long time to get a word in and feel that the other is pushy. The polyvocalic person may wonder why the first does not join in the discussion and see him as distant or uninvolved. We should note that each person fits somewhere within a range on the scale, and that culture, family, personality, and life history contribute to where one fits. Further, everyone has a sort

145

FIGURE 10.1
TURN TAKING IN CONVERSATIONS (ADAPTED IN PART FROM TANNEN 1986)

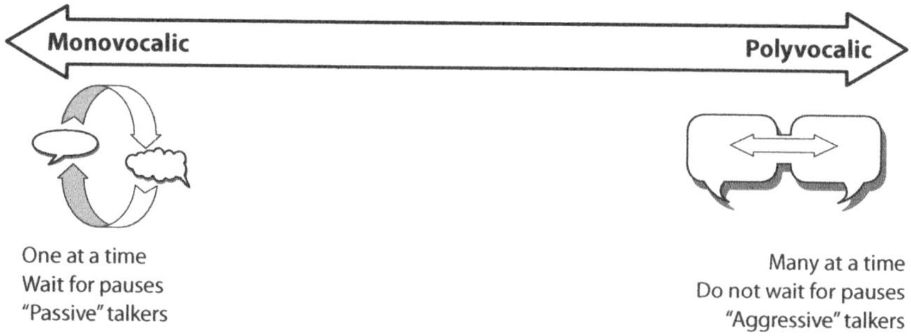

Monovocalic	Polyvocalic
One at a time	Many at a time
Wait for pauses	Do not wait for pauses
"Passive" talkers	"Aggressive" talkers

of conversation "toleration zone" of the amount of interruption anticipated and allowed.

Knowing this, we can expand our range of conversational turn taking through practice and learn how to operate in both spheres. It may be more difficult for the monovocalic person to learn to interrupt, since he typically considers it to be impolite. The polyvocalic person, however, has to learn patience in the conversation, being sure to give verbal pauses that are long enough for the monovocalic to join in the discussion.

POLYCHRONIC VERSUS MONOCHRONIC TIME

Hall has distinguished two approaches to time that are at what he calls the primary level of culture (the implicit or hidden level of culture in which the rules are known by all, obeyed by all, but seldom, if ever, stated): polychronic time and monochronic time (1983; 1990, 13–16; 1991a, 44–58; 1991b; see fig. 10.2).

For people who view time in a monochronic fashion (US and northern European cultures in particular), time is similar to a single ribbon or road. All people are thought to move along the road at the same pace, and each exists only during a certain "stretch" of the total road. History is linear, moving toward whatever end will happen. Like pearls on an unclasped necklace, each person has a limited amount of "time," and he is to make the most of it. For the individual, this road can be divided into segments and then scheduled and compartmentalized, which makes it possible for a person to concentrate on one thing at a time.

Scheduling in monochronic societies is more likely to conform to actual time on the clock. Time serves as a classification system for ordering life and setting priorities in relation to the job ("I don't have time to see her"). The important things are scheduled in; the unimportant are scheduled out. People with this orientation plan for the future, anticipating how long it will take to complete certain tasks. Throughout their lives, time has been sliced up, with each "pearl" being seen as a discrete segment. Unplanned events in life, from a simple knock on the door to a major calamity, are "interruptions" and typically not appreciated (note the negative connotations of the term "interruption").

FIGURE 10.2
MONOCHRONIC AND POLYCHRONIC TIME (CONTENT SOURCES:
HALL 1983; HALL AND HALL 1990, 13–16; DAHL 2004, 11)

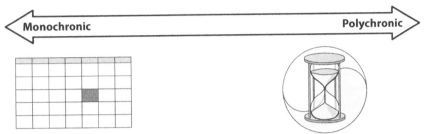

Monochronic　　　　　　　　　　　　　　　　　　**Polychronic**

Time as a ribbon or road	Time as a point
Attention to one thing	Multilevel simultaneous involvement
Time almost tangible	Time intangible
Interruptions unwelcome	No problem with interruptions
Scheduling	No scheduling
Clock-promptness	Relational-promptness
Privacy valued	Privacy not valued

In monochronic societies people are taught not to "mix" times—they should not play during work time, eat during nap time, or talk during a lecture. Events (movies, weddings, religious services, sporting events, plays, performances, parties) are generally expected to start at or very close to the stated time, and more-important events are tracked for their "on-time" record (e.g., air flights, train and bus schedules).

People in monochronic societies slice each day into smaller segments—an afternoon or evening, an hour, ten minutes—depending on their responsibilities and the nature of an event. They schedule appointments, including meals, "making time" for people who are important to them. Because of this, they tend to feel as though they "own" these segments of time, and they can be "wasted" if another person does not respect the schedule.

Since time is a limited commodity and each "pearl" of it is valuable, people who are monochronic demonstrate respect for one another by valuing one another's time. They do not take up someone's time without asking permission (even saying, "I was just in the neighborhood and thought I'd stop by" is a request to spend time with a person). They are not expected to simply

147

"show up" at someone's house without some reason, and they have the right to be too busy to see a person who drops by without planning it in advance.

Christians from monochronic cultures value church starting at the stated time and scheduling time for friends and acquaintances. People who cannot adhere to a time schedule may be seen as unreliable and not qualified for leadership in the local community. It is interesting to question whether the contemporary idea of a "short-term" missions trip could have arisen from a polychronic society, and if so, how it would differ from what is currently practiced. Notice how a veteran missionary explains how the gap between monochronic and polychronic approaches worked in his own experience on a short-term mission trip:

> As I escorted groups to remote villages where we had helped plant churches, I found that our experiences were different in each village. Preparing for the most remote village, I mailed the village pastor a letter to let him know what day we expected to arrive. Because I knew the mail service was poor, I mailed the letter six months in advance. As we approached the village, the pastor (who was also an old friend of mine) was standing on the side of the main road waiting for us. On the basis of a letter mailed six months earlier, he had walked five miles from his home to meet us and was prepared to wait all day if necessary! Our group was amazed and impressed, partly because it appeared the pastor was incredibly efficient (meaning, he valued the economy of time). Actually, we were the efficient ones, as the pastor knew, to be able to keep the appointment that day; the pastor, however, was effective (meaning, he was able to use time in a way that values quality of relationships). He valued our relationship and the event of hosting the group so much that he was willing to come and wait for us. This was one of the few times that American efficiency and African effectiveness synchronized into harmony. (Reese 2006, 474)

The African pastor in this case valued what Hall calls a polychronic approach to life (more typical of Latin America, Africa, Asia, the Middle East, and southern Europe). In this approach, time is viewed as an immediate point in which life takes place rather than a ribbon or a road on which we travel. Alternately, it may be thought of as a river on which we are all carried along, and it is wiser to simply experience the things we come across on the river rather than trying to fight against it or control it.

Additionally, rather than seeing things happening one at a time, people in polychronic cultures value seeing all things happening together and simply taking life as it comes rather than trying to plan it. This does not mean that polychronic people do not plan. However, their planning takes place on the macrolevel (planting, weeding, harvesting) rather than the microlevel (let's meet at 10:00 a.m.), and plans are seen as fluid and flexible rather than rigid and fixed.

For polychronic people, time alone with someone is not viewed in the same way as it is for monochronic people, and life is recognized as being full of "interruptions" that are normal and not considered negative. It is always easy to agree to meet at a certain day and/or time, but who knows what might happen between now and then to make one person miss the appointment? A friend might stop by, a relative might call, or another event might come up. These are not "interruptions" but simply part of the normal rhythm of life.

> *Americans seem to be in a perpetual hurry. Just watch the way they walk down the street. They never allow themselves the leisure to enjoy life; there are too many things to do.*
>
> visitor to the United States
> from India, Kohls 1981, 7

In polychronic societies people, and one's relationships with them, are not measured by blocks of time. Time is a community possession rather than something privately "owned" in some way. There are standards of promptness in polychronic societies, but they are more fluid and relationally based rather than rigid and clock based. One way to communicate distancing in a relationship is to live it out by the clock, an indication that it is really more of a business than a genuine friendship.

Christians in polychronic cultures are more relaxed with scheduling. Weddings, funerals, church services, and Bible studies all begin when enough people are present, and they end when the event is finished. Faithfulness is measured not by the ability to follow a clocked schedule but by maturity in handling the flow of life as it comes.

Understanding this notion is important in intercultural communication because polychronic people can conclude that monochronic people do not value relationships because they cut things off abruptly if they have another appointment. Monochronic people can conclude that polychronic people do not value relationships because they do not come when promised, and they outstay their welcome. Each reads the other in ways that make sense in light of his own values. Since by and large most missionaries in recent history have gone from more monochronic societies to more polychronic ones, the result has been that church events follow not local considerations but missionary considerations. Monochronic missionaries tend to elevate to leadership indigenous people who can adhere to monochronic schedules, and as a result the church feels foreign to the rest of the local population.

Understanding the difference between monochronic time and polychronic time is essential to success in international ministry. The suburban American

SIDEBAR 10.1
IN ANOTHER ZONE: TIME AND CULTURE

Sarah Behm (email, July 6, 2001)

Any pastor can tell you that weddings rarely start on time. Inevitably the groomsmen are not all together, or someone's hair just is not right! Maybe the flower girl decides to throw a tantrum or the photographer is a little tardy, throwing the schedule out the window. Guests expect this for the most part, and it is OK because, after all, this is someone's *big* day.

The bride has never looked so beautiful, and probably never will again. The groom is quite a sight and dresses, colors, flowers, and music are enough to keep anyone busy for forty-five minutes. A nice afternoon wedding was on our agenda for December 30.

Two friends from college decided to squeeze in a wedding during Christmas Break. For Michigan, you could not have asked for a better winter day. It was the first African-American wedding that I had ever attended.

My husband and I, together with another friend and his family, were the only whites present. The friend had his three sons along because babysitters were in short supply. The time of the ceremony was 3:00 p.m. We lived about 25 minutes from the church and we would have been running behind if we had been going to any other function. But a wedding, and especially an African-American wedding, would surely start late. One of the bridesmaids had warned me of that anyway.

People were milling around in the narthex, putting flowers on and greeting each other when we walked in. I wanted to get a good seat so that I could be sure to take in as much of the ceremony as I could. I had seen the groom pacing nervously down the hall, so we were right on time. At 3:30, there was still no prelude being played. We had pretty much exhausted all the small talk at this point and the mints from my purse were gone. My husband was getting annoyed. I was just hoping that the bride was OK. I could only imagine what might have happened to delay her so long. We waited a little longer.

Someone put a CD on; maybe that was the prelude music. Nope, the organist started warming up ten minutes later. The bride ended up coming down the aisle no earlier than 4:30 p.m.

Later, I asked the maid-of-honor about the delay, wondering what awful thing had happened to keep them so long. She just smiled at me and replied, "We told you it wouldn't start on time." She was right.

I learned a lesson about time that day. Some people do not order their lives by the clock. Some allow time to swallow them up. Some people are not slaves to the mechanism spinning on the wall. This would prove to be my first lesson in time and culture, where people and relationships, not the schedule, dictate the day. I hope next time I will not act so surprised.

ministering in a foreign country must immediately determine whether the people follow monochronic or polychronic time, because this will affect *everything* (Hall and Hall 1990, 179), from how ministry is organized, to the way scheduling takes place and whether schedules are adhered to, to how much lead time is needed, down to the basic orientation of the culture—past, present, or future.

TIME ORIENTATION EMBEDDED IN WORLDVIEW

How might we see time in relation to the three primary components of worldview—the cognitive, the affective, and the evaluative (Hiebert 2008b)?

Worldview: Cognitive

The *cognitive* component of worldview includes what people know about time, especially the rules and regulations for observing time-related protocols. They know what it means to come "on time"; they learn early in life how their parents, friends, and siblings value such things as schedules, appointments, seasons, and cycles of life. They know how to interact with others, and the perspectives they should have on the past, the current moment, and the future.

Worldview: Affective

The *affective* component involves people's emotional attachment and stability in relation to social time. It is how they feel about time as a component of life and how they experience loss of face or other negative emotions in relation to time. The affective dynamic in a worldview is typically played out in myths and stories found in the culture. Heroes follow prescribed approaches to time (or time in a linear sense may not be important in their hero stories at all). Saving the victim in "the nick of time," being too late to help, or not paying attention to the time may all be given prominence or lack it in the stories people tell one another. As you read or hear stories in your new cultural setting, consider what you learn about time from the perspective of the author or storyteller. The observations you make will help you to learn how the people among whom you sojourn feel about time, as do the proverbs found in sidebar 10.2.

SIDEBAR 10.2
PROVERBS OF TIME

Time waits for no man. (American)
Patience; in time the grass becomes milk. (Chinese)
Youths look at the future, the elderly at the past, our ancestors live in the present. (African)

He who takes his time to choose gets the worst one. (European)
The rich man thinks of next year, the poor man of the present moment. (Japanese)

Worldview: Evaluative

Finally, the *evaluative* component involves people's moral decision-making rules about how to evaluate actions and attitudes related to time, such as what are appropriate and inappropriate ways to use time as a strategic communications device. The evaluative dynamic is framed in terms of how actions and beliefs are assessed as good or bad. On the one hand, among monochronic people it is considered rude to arrive anywhere more than ten minutes late without some type of apology. To be consistently late is to be considered undependable—even with apologies. On the other hand, to refuse to see a visitor because you are busy or have something coming up that you must prepare for (such as a presentation or a major project) is considered rude by polychronic people.

When Scott was discussing time and intercultural communication in a class of African students, an older Ugandan man began to speak. He passionately stated, "There is nothing I would like more than for you to come to my house someday. Don't make an appointment, just come by. When you arrive, do not tell me why you came. Spend several hours with me without ever talking about business. Ask permission to leave, and when it has been given simply leave without ever explaining why you came. Then I know that you are my friend."

This is what it means to evaluate messages communicated by use of time. Before this comment, Scott could hardly imagine just dropping by; it would be rude. After the conversation, he began simply dropping by his students' houses to visit, being careful never to say why he had come. Student evaluations began to state, "He did not just say he was my friend. He showed it."

SIDEBAR 10.3
SELECTED WEB RESOURCES ON POLYCHRONIC AND MONOCHRONIC TIME

Carol Kaufman-Scarborough and Jay D. Lindquist. 1999. "Time Management and Polychronicity: Comparisons, Contrasts, and Insights for the Workplace," *Journal of Managerial Psychology*, special issue on polychronicity, 14 (3/4): 288–312. (http://www.crab.rutgers.edu/~ckaufman/polychronic.html)

Network for Strategic Mission Knowledge Base articles: Time (http://www.strategicnetwork.org/index.php?loc=kb&view=b&fto=632&sf=Y)

Time-Sense: Polychronicity and Monochronicity (http://www.harley.com/writing/time-sense.html)

Why Time Is a Social Construct (http://www.smithsonianmag.com/science/nature/why-time-is-a-social-construct-164139110/?no-ist)

Wikipedia article: Polychronicity (http://en.wikipedia.org/wiki/Polychronicity)

CONCLUSION

It is true that "time talks." Unfortunately, it talks in different ways in different societies around the world. It is critical for the cross-cultural sojourner to learn the language of time in the new setting and begin to speak it as soon as possible. Doing so will take adjustment and will feel artificial (or even rude) initially, but with enough practice it will begin to feel comfortable. Ultimately, it will pay dividends for the kingdom of God. As the exercise for this chapter, take a moment to reflect on the following rewrite of Psalm 23 in light of the ever-increasing pace of life today.

SIDEBAR 10.4
PSALM 23 FOR BUSY PEOPLE

Toki Miyashina (1998)

As you read the following adaptation of Psalm 23, consider your reaction to it. How well does the author capture the sense of David's psalm?

> The Lord is my pace-setter, I shall
> not rush;
> He makes me stop and rest for quiet
> intervals,
> He provides me with images of
> stillness,
> which restore my serenity.
> He leads me in the way of efficiency,
> through calmness of mind;
> and His guidance is peace.
> Even though I have a great many
> things to accomplish each day
> I will not fret, for His presence is
> here.

> His timelessness, His all-importance will keep me in balance.
> He prepares refreshment and renewal in the midst of activity,
> by anointing my mind with His
> oils of tranquility;
> my cup of joyous energy
> overflows.
> Surely harmony and effectiveness
> shall be the fruits of my hours
> and I shall walk in the pace of my
> Lord
> and dwell in His house for ever.

REFLECTION AND DISCUSSION

1. In what ways does this speak to you in your present situation?
2. How might you integrate these ideas into your new cultural setting?

Individualism and Collectivism

In this chapter we explore the way in which people define themselves, whether that be as independent individuals or as members of a group. Understanding individualism-collectivism is central to understanding the way in which people in different societies communicate with one another.

DEFINING THE SELF: INDIVIDUALISM AND COLLECTIVISM

In collectivist societies, the interests of the group are more important than those of the individual. The family of any child is its first group, but in collectivist societies the family is an extended one, including grandparents, aunts, uncles, cousins, and others who commonly live in proximity. This extended family becomes the in-group of an individual, and loyalty to this group is expected throughout life.

In contrast to collectivist societies, individualistic societies give priority to the interests of the individual. "Family" refers only to the nuclear family, consisting of parents and children. While those in collectivist societies are born into an in-group, in individualist societies in-groups need to be cultivated. It is expected that children will grow up to be independent and move away from their parental home. Significantly, individualist countries tend to have more wealth and lower power distance.

A majority of people in the world live in collectivist societies, but it is important to keep in mind that the types of individualism and collectivism vary, as shown in table 11.1 (e.g., the different collectivisms in Japan [Yamawaki 2012] and differences in collectivism as seen in East Asia versus Mexico [Ruby et al. 2012] or China versus Korea [Choi and Han 2009]). Rarely is a society a simple collectivist setting; this is almost impossible except in isolated settings. At the same time, the *truly* independent individualist is rarely totally free from group relationships that shape him or her in a more collectivist direction.

TABLE 11.1
SPECTRUM OF DEFINITIONS OF SELF IN INDIVIDUALIST
AND COLLECTIVE SOCIETIES

Simple Collectivism	Contextual Collectivism	Consultative Individualism	Independent Individualism
One in-group dominates and determines many of the behaviors.	One or more in-groups exert substantial influence on one or more behaviors.	Two or more in-groups influence behaviors.	No in-group determines the behaviors.

A key difference is related to self-construal or an individual's self-perception and self-evaluation. Thus in the most individualistic countries, there is an interest in "self-image, self-reliance, self-awareness, self-actualization, and self-determination," while collectivists see themselves as members of a group and share its goals (Klopf 2001, 80–81; Fujino 2009).

The proverbs in table 11.2 further illustrate how this set of values works out in the way people idealize behavior.

TABLE 11.2
PROVERBS OF INDIVIDUALISM AND COLLECTIVISM

Collectivistic Proverbs	Individualistic Proverbs
A single banana does not grow bigger than the stalk. (African)	Live and let live.
	To each his own.
The bird that stands out will be shot first. (Asian)	Look out for number one.
	Be true to yourself.
The chicken is never ashamed of its coop. (African)	The customer is always right.
	The squeaky wheel gets the grease.
Brothers and sisters are as close as hands and feet. (Asian)	If you want something done right, do it yourself.
One piece of wood will not make a fire. (Asian)	God helps those who help themselves.

CONTRASTS IN INDIVIDUALISM AND COLLECTIVISM

Harry Triandis, raised in the traditional Greek collectivist culture, has contributed significantly through his research and in the writing of *Individualism and*

Individualism pertains to societies in which the ties between individuals are loose: everyone is expected to look after him- or herself and his or her immediate family. Collectivism as its opposite pertains to societies in which people from birth onward are integrated into strong, cohesive in-groups, which throughout people's lifetime continue to protect them in exchange for unquestioning loyalty.

Hofstede, Hofstede, and Minkov 2010, 92

Collectivism (1995) to an understanding of the dimensions of these values. He describes collectivist cultures as the most stable, with people's conduct being in accord with the obligations and duties of their collective. Individualists, however, give precedence to personal goals and drop relationships when goals change.

Triandis notes that all people manifest elements of both individualism and collectivism (see fig. 11.1). For example, among individualists, politics, race, and religion often create in-groups in which individualists act as collectivists. Thus, within all cultures there are individualists who act like collectivists and the converse. Additionally, in many countries women are more collectivist than men. Further, younger, upper-class, and urban people tend to be more individualistic (Triandis 1995, 17).

FIGURE 11.1

DISTRIBUTION OF INDIVIDUALISTIC AND COLLECTIVISTIC TENDENCIES WITHIN COUNTRIES (ADAPTED FROM WALKER 2013, 162)

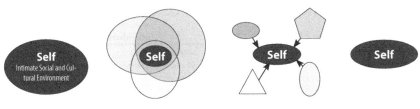

Collectivism	Individualism
Concrete	Abstract
Close/Touch	Distant
Non-Verbal Skills	Verbal Skills
Real Events	Principles
Shame	Guilt
Face	Self Respect

Work

In collectivist cultures it is customary to hire members of an in-group, and sons more often take on the occupation of their fathers (Hofstede, Hofstede, and Minkov 2010, 119). Individualists, who stress independence and individual achievement, are likely to simply change employers when it suits them to do so (Samovar and Porter 2001, 66).

While individualists expect clear boundary distinctions between their own work and that of a coworker, this is not true in collectivist Japan, much of Latin America, and in some countries in southern Europe. In those countries employees are more likely to assist one another, and supervisors may encourage subordinates to fill in for one another. Supervisors themselves work to maintain group harmony (Martin and Nakayama 2005, 268).

> *The motivation for work in collectivist countries is related to what Frederick Herzberg described as* extrinsic *motivators, that is, the conditions in which the work takes place—a pleasant place and favorable hours—and the material rewards such as pay and other benefits. Herzberg termed these* hygienic factors *and contrasted them with* intrinsic *motivators such as satisfaction with the work itself, which is more common in individualist cultures.*
>
> Hofstede, Hofstede, and Minkov 2010, 106

In terms of performance, individualists tend to do better when there is low accountability, while collectivists perform better with their in-group than they do either with out-group members or on their own (Jandt 2004, 14). Candid negative performance feedback from an individualist supervisor can create a sense of shame for a collectivist employee. Individualists perceive preferential treatment of in-group members as nepotism (Hofstede, Hofstede, and Minkov 2010, 122).

When introducing himself, a Japanese person will commonly first give the name of his employer before giving his family name and then finally his personal name. Thus if working for the Takashimaya Department Store in Tokyo, he would say, "Takashimaya no Motoyama Hirosi," or "Takashimaya's Motoyama Hiroshi" (Hesselgrave 1991b, 457). In marked contrast, young people from North America often introduce themselves using only a first or given name.

Community

In collectivist societies a person is part of an in-group and is seldom alone, even at night. It was not uncommon where Evvy lived in rural West Africa for family members to all sleep side by side on mats in one room. She was touched, when ill, that visitors would simply come to sit with her. Conversely,

SIDEBAR 11.1
THE IN-GROUP ADVANTAGE: GETTING A VISA IN INDIA FOR TANZANIA

Sheri Skinner

On Monday my husband and I went to the Tanzanian High Commission to apply for a visa. When we walked in, we were greeted by a rather formal, middle-aged Indian receptionist who promptly demanded, "Who are you?" It's really a hard question to answer when you think about it, but we settled on, "He's Indian. She's American. We'd like a visa."

After some discussion, she demanded proof of our marriage and was dissatisfied with the document we gave her. She gave it back to us, and her posture and silence seemed to indicate that we should go away.

We asked if it was really necessary to prove we were married in order to be allowed into Tanzania. The receptionist leaned back in her chair, folded her arms, and looked down her glasses at us in a half-annoyed, half-amused manner. "In this life nothing is necessary, my dear, but many things are customary. You must provide the customary documents, or we cannot let you in."

We just stood there a while longer and tried to look pleasant and visa-worthy. Finally she said she'd have to call her supervisor and explain the situation. She told us to sit down.

After a few moments, we were told to follow someone to a back office. We found ourselves at the door of the deputy high commissioner, and the scene instantly changed. The man welcomed us in joyfully, smiling and laughing the whole time. It turned out that our friend who had sent the required invitation letter for us to visit Tanzania was a friend of the deputy high commissioner. Their families went way back; small world! We had a very pleasant conversation that ended with the man picking up the phone and telling his receptionist, "Give them the visa." We hadn't even filled out the form yet!

When we returned to the front office, the receptionist's frost had thawed. She even let us borrow her pen to fill out the application form and started making jokes with us about how marrying an Indian had turned me into an Indian myself. From there we headed over to the travel agent's office and got our tickets . . . no problem!

REFLECTION AND DISCUSSION

1. In what ways was the receptionist acting appropriately in the opening paragraphs?
2. Beyond knowing the person who wrote the letter of invitation, what was the fundamental reason that the deputy high commissioner authorized the visa to Tanzania?

an African church leader who was an exceptional student when studying at Wheaton College spoke with distress of eating meals alone in the dining hall or of not interacting with anyone from Friday after classes until Sunday morning.

With such closeness in collectivist societies, a high value is placed on harmony and avoiding confrontation or of saying no to a request. Indirect ways of saying no can be conveyed by hesitation in a reply or by not showing enthusiasm. The use of yes may simply mean "I heard you" as opposed to conveying agreement or approval (Hofstede, Hofstede, and Minkov 2010, 107). Opinions and perspectives are derived from one's in-group. Collectivism also involves providing for one's in-group. An employee in maintenance at the West Africa hospital where Evvy worked was particularly entrepreneurial, but the more he prospered, the more people came to stay at his home, until finally he was providing meals and shelter for eighteen people.

Individualists feel a need to talk when together, while collectivists are comfortable simply being together. In his seminal work on the context of messages, Edward Hall (1983) discusses the diminished need for verbal communication when messages are conveyed in a commonly experienced culture.

Technology

Of interest is the way in which an entity can be used very differently in individualistic or collectivistic societies. For example, in the individualistic United States, being online is not commonly a group experience. In collectivist South Korea, however, it is customary for young people to gather in an online game room known as a "PC baang" (of which there are more than 20,000 in the country) to play games like LAN-based Starcraft. In 2002 the game Lineage had more than 3 million players and as many as 150,000 playing online simultaneously. Players will even assemble at a specific PC baang to destroy a castle while shouting at one another across the room (Herz 2002, 96).

In Europe, however, people in less individualist countries said that not using the internet provided more personal and family time, as well as additional time for friends (Hofstede, Hofstede, and Minkov 2010, 124).

Educational Settings

From the first years of school, individualism and collectivism are evident not only in the students but in the curriculum itself. In the Dick and Jane primer used from the 1930s until the 1960s in the United States, the characters Dick, Jane, and their dog, Spot, were active individualists. "See Dick run. See Dick play. See Dick run and play." In contrast, a Chinese primer of similar vintage depicted a small boy sitting on the shoulders of an older boy with the text, "Big brother takes care of little brother. Big brother loves little brother. Little brother loves big brother" (Nisbett 2009, 134–35).

In collectivist societies a diploma provides an opportunity to affiliate with higher-status groups, while in individualist societies the focus is on learning how to learn (Hofstede, Hofstede, and Minkov 2010, 118–19). Individualist

> No matter how stout, one beam cannot support a house.
>
> Chinese proverb, in Samovar, Porter, and McDaniel 2010, 201

students expect impartial treatment, while collectivists will both treat in-group class members more generously and anticipate preferential treatment from teachers with whom they have a close relationship.

Small group discussion tends to work better for collectivist students, while individualists are more comfortable speaking out in large group situations. Indirect communication and saving face for students in the classroom needs to be a priority for teachers with collectivist students.

Family and Children

Marriage in collectivist countries is an agreement between families and thus is often arranged, while marriage-partner selection based on love is more normative in individualistic countries. Where kinship ties are weak, romantic love is emphasized, while companionship is emphasized more where kinship ties are strong (Triandis 1995, 119). Additionally, divorce is more common in individualist societies and in marriages with greater diversity, whether the diversity be that of age, level of education, ethnicity, national origin, or religion (Triandis 1995, 141).

In collectivist societies parent-child dependence is expected, and parents provide a great deal of guidance and interaction in seeking to assure that the child will be a good in-group member. Individualistic societies, however, value independence and leaving the parental home. In collectivist Russian society, it is common for an adult other than the parent to admonish or correct a child in a social setting (Triandis 1995, 65).

Collectivist societies commonly have a more dominating government, but as they grow economically there is a concomitant shift toward individualism. One indicator of this would be less care for the elderly provided by the family (Hofstede, Hofstede, and Minkov 2010, 134).

Biblical Examples of Collectivism and Individualism

As in the preceding chapter, we can ask whether it is possible to define or defend one of the orientations toward understanding the self as more biblical than the other. As noted, our own cultural tendencies will predispose us to favor a particular position. Therefore, we present evidence in sidebar 11.2 for both a collective and an individualistic orientation in the biblical data. As you read through these passages, consider whether there is enough evidence to make a biblical case *against* the position your own culture and life history have predisposed you to favor.

SIDEBAR 11.2
BIBLICAL TEXTS ON INDIVIDUALISM AND COLLECTIVISM

COLLECTIVISM

Joshua 24:15: Choose for yourselves this day whom you will serve. . . . But as for me and my household, we will serve the LORD.

Nehemiah 7:1–2: After the wall had been rebuilt and I had set the doors in place, the gatekeepers, the musicians and the Levites were appointed. I put in charge of Jerusalem my brother Hanani, along with Hananiah the commander of the citadel, because he was a man of integrity and feared God more than most people do.

John 4:53: Then the father realized that this was the exact time at which Jesus had said to him, "Your son will live." So he and all his household believed.

Acts 10:2: He and all his family were devout and God-fearing; he gave generously to those in need and prayed to God regularly.

Acts 16:31–34: They replied, "Believe in the Lord Jesus, and you will be saved—you and your household." Then they spoke the word of the Lord to him and to all the others in his house. At that hour of the night the jailer took them and washed their wounds; then immediately he and all his household were baptized. The jailer brought them into his house and set a meal before them; he was filled with joy because he had come to believe in God— he and his whole household.

Acts 18:8: Crispus, the synagogue leader, and his entire household believed in the Lord; and many of the Corinthians who heard Paul believed and were baptized.

Romans 12:4–5: Just as each of us has one body with many members, and these members do not all have the same function, so in Christ we, though many, form one body, and each member belongs to all the others.

Romans 12:10: Be devoted to one another in love. Honor one another above yourselves.

1 Corinthians 12:7: Now to each one the manifestation of the Spirit is given for the common good.

1 Corinthians 12:12, 24b–27: Just as a body, though one, has many parts, but all its parts form one body, so it is with Christ.

But God has put the body together, giving greater honor to the parts that lacked it, so that there should be no division in the body, but that its parts should have equal concern for each other. If one part suffers, every part suffers with it; if one part is honored, every part rejoices with it. Now you are the body of Christ, and each one of you is a part of it.

Philippians 2:1–4: If you have any encouragement from being united with Christ, if any comfort from his love, if any common sharing with the Spirit, if any tenderness and compassion, then make my joy complete by being like-minded, having the same love, being one in spirit and of one mind. Do nothing out of selfish ambition or vain conceit. Rather, in humility value others above yourselves, not looking to your own interests but each of you to the interests of the others.

INDIVIDUALISM

Acts 17:27: God did this so that they would seek him and perhaps reach out for him and find him, though he is not far from any one of us.

Romans 12:1–2: Therefore, I urge you, brothers and sisters, in view of God's mercy, to offer your bodies as a living sacrifice, holy and pleasing to God—this is your true and proper worship. Do not conform to the pattern of this world, but be transformed by the renewing of your mind. Then you will be able to test and approve what

God's will is—his good, pleasing and perfect will.

Romans 14:5: One person considers one day more sacred than another; another considers every day alike. Each one of them should be fully convinced in their own mind.

1 Corinthians 7:24: Brothers and sisters, each person, as responsible to God, should remain in the situation they were in when God called them.

1 Corinthians 12:7: Now to each one the manifestation of the Spirit is given for the common good.

1 Corinthians 12:27: Now you are the body of Christ, and each one of you is a part of it.

1 Corinthians 16:2: On the first day of every week, each one of you should set aside a sum of money in keeping with your income, saving it up, so that when I come no collections will have to be made.

2 Corinthians 5:10: For we must all appear before the judgment seat of Christ, so that each of us may receive what is due us for the things done while in the body, whether good or bad.

2 Corinthians 9:7: Each of you should give what you have decided in your heart to give, not reluctantly or under compulsion, for God loves a cheerful giver.

Galatians 6:4–5: Each one should test their own actions. Then they can take pride in themselves alone, without comparing themselves to someone else, for each one should carry their own load.

Ephesians 4:7: But to each one of us grace has been given as Christ apportioned it.

Ephesians 5:33: However, each one of you also must love his wife as he loves himself, and the wife must respect her husband.

James 1:14: But each person is tempted when they are dragged away by their own evil desire and enticed.

1 Peter 4:10: Each of you should use whatever gift you have received to serve others, as faithful stewards of God's grace in its various forms.

Revelation 20:12: And I saw the dead, great and small, standing before the throne, and books were opened. Another book was opened, which is the book of life. The dead were judged according to what they had done as recorded in the books.

Revelation 20:15: Anyone whose name was not found written in the book of life was thrown into the lake of fire.

Revelation 21:27: Nothing impure will ever enter it, nor will anyone who does what is shameful or deceitful, but only those whose names are written in the Lamb's book of life.

REFLECTION AND DISCUSSION

1. What does the diverse array of Scriptures related to individualism and collectivism suggest when considering these two cultural values?
2. In what ways and at what times in Scripture does God deal with individuals or collective groups?

CONCLUSION

In discussing both the theoretical and the practical implications of individualism and collectivism as we have done in this chapter, it becomes quite clear that these values permeate virtually all aspects of daily life. Understanding both the source and the manifestations of the differences is vital in helping us to avoid misunderstandings and subsequent tensions. Understanding helps us to move from unreflective conformity to our existing values and resistance to change toward redefining our own identity and becoming competent in understanding cultural diversity (Hogan 2007, 23–24). We are then better able to relate with sympathetic acceptance and warmly embrace these valid but differing cultural values when we encounter them in others. Instead of experiencing conflict, we can move in small steps toward celebrating our differences.

Our case study for this chapter illustrates differences between how collectivists and individualists approach the crises that life brings. The individualists are challenged to understand why someone would simply decide to give up, while the collectivists wonder why someone would want to fight on if it meant risking dying apart from family and village. Just what is a "good death"? As you read it, try to identify salient features about the two contrasting perspectives on health and death—and ask which elements of each fit Scripture as well as which elements go against Scripture.

CASE STUDY:
NEMON'S DEATH

JOANNE A. WAGNER

Reprinted with permission from Hiebert and Hiebert (1987, 115–16).

Peter stepped out of the hut of his friend Besi, his heart heavy and confused. Besi was ill and convinced he was dying. Peter felt a trip to the coastal hospital, a two-hour drive away, would restore his health. However, because of what had happened earlier, he did not know whether he dared suggest the trip and what the effect would be on his attempts to plant a church in the village if his advice failed again. As he stood looking out across the valley bathed in morning sun, Peter's thoughts went back several months to the time when he was leaving the hut of Nemon, his co-translator and dear friend, who had just died.

Peter and Lillian had come to Kwili village in Papua New Guinea to translate the Bible and plant a church. There they came to love Nemon, a national co-translator who helped them with their work. Then, on one occasion when they returned after an absence of a few weeks, Nemon was not at the door with his usual warm welcome. The villagers told the missionaries that Nemon was suffering from much pain and that he had been ill for two weeks. Lillian and Peter were shocked and saddened to see Nemon with a swollen jaw, a high fever, and in obvious pain. When they talked to his wife, Swenge, she told them that Nemon, a fine Christian leader in the village, was convinced that this sickness was going to kill him, and he had resigned himself to death.

Ruth, a nurse who had accompanied Lillian and Peter to the village, examined Nemon and diagnosed the case as an abscessed tooth. She recommended strongly that he be taken to the coastal hospital where he could see a dentist and receive medical care. When Peter relayed her recommendation to Nemon's family and reinforced it with his own, their reaction was negative. Nemon's kin felt that if he was taken to the *haus sik*, he would surely die. Moreover, he had already announced to them that he was going to die, and they did not want the death to take place away from the village, which would bring it a bad reputation. Among their people it was important for the mental well-being of the kinsmen and the person involved that he or she be at home when death came.

Nemon remained in his home, and his condition continued to deteriorate. Peter persevered in his attempt to convince the family that hospitalization was necessary for Nemon's survival. Finally they consented. Peter, Lillian, Swenge, and Nemon hastily departed on the two-hour drive to the coast.

It was Friday afternoon when they arrived, and Lillian felt a profound sense of relief when they admitted their friend to the hospital. Now, she felt, he was in good hands and would be cured. With confident hearts she and Peter drove back to the village, leaving Swenge to remain at the hospital with Nemon.

However, it was a weekend, and few of the medical staff were on duty at the hospital. Consequently the care Nemon received was minimal. He did not see a dentist, but an appointment was made for Tuesday morning. In the meantime the nurses tried to keep him comfortable. However, on Sunday evening, the abscess in Nemon's jaw burst, sending toxins to his brain, and he died.

When his body was brought back to the village, Lillian and Peter were shocked and grieved. Nemon's family was angry at them, claiming that Nemon died because they took him away to the hospital. Only when an influential relative of Swenge's rebuked the people for blaming the missionaries for the death did the accusations stop. Moreover, when the family observed the genuine grief experienced by the translators as they shared in the burial ceremonies in the village, they concluded that Peter and Lillian were not to blame for their relative's death. Later the family placed the blame on Jeremiah, a member of an enemy clan who had been a close friend of the deceased. Jeremiah, already stricken with grief at the death of his companion, was finally forced to leave the area and seek residence elsewhere because of the pressures placed on him by Nemon's embittered clan.

Peter's thoughts returned to the present as he heard Besi moan with pain. "No," he thought, "it is not a clear-cut matter. Should I try to influence Besi to go to the hospital—or should I step back and not interfere in this case?"

REFLECTION AND DISCUSSION

1. In some instances, dying a "good death" is more important than always fighting for life. From the case, what factors seem to be part of a "good death" for those in the Kwili village?

2. In what ways did the perspectives and values of Peter and Lilian differ from those of the Kwili villagers when it came to understanding and managing a serious illness such as Nemon had?

3. As a result of the insights gained from Nemon's death several months earlier, what specific steps could Peter take in interacting with Besi and his relatives that might result in Besi getting helpful care?

12

Social Power in
Intercultural Communication

One day, as we were celebrating the birthday of our department administrator in her office, an African student who needed to see Scott came by. We invited her to share some cake with us, but she replied, "I could never stand and eat with teachers." To Americans this was a strange reason, but to our student it made perfect sense. What gave rise to her reasoning, and how were we to understand it?

In every society social power is distributed unevenly among its members. Those who are physically stronger (e.g., adults) may exercise power over those who are physically weaker (e.g., children). The wealthy have greater social power than the poor. Those in positions of leadership exercise power over those in subordinate positions. One issue that must be addressed is the way in which the distribution of social power is idealized, referred to by Geert Hofstede as "power distance" (1991). A second issue to consider is where the power for making decisions lies, and we explore the idealization of the location of power, the "locus of control," and implications for intercultural communication. Finally, we touch on the implications of understanding social power (and its distribution) in terms of economics, especially in societies that favor patron-client systems.

165

POWER DISTANCE

As noted, power distance indicates the culture's value orientation regarding the inequalities in real life, "the extent to which the less powerful members of institutions and organizations within a community expect and accept that power is distributed unequally" (Hofstede 1991, 46).

On the individual level, Hofstede defines power distance as the difference between the extent to which a boss can determine the behavior of the subordinate and the extent to which the subordinate can determine the behavior of the boss. That difference is programmed in a culture, and every culture has power-distance "lengths" that it considers appropriate in various settings (e.g., on the job, at home, in religious affairs, at school).

> *Children in the United States are very forward in their way of speaking, even to their parents and elders. Children here show a lack of respect for old age.*
>
> visitor to the United States
> from the Philippines,
> in Kohls 1981, 10

Hofstede proposes that the cluster value of power distance may be thought of as a spectrum, with the two extremes being "small power distance" and "large power distance." Broadly speaking, people of cultures of large power distance believe in a social order in which each person has a rightful and protected place, in a hierarchy presuming existential inequalities, and that the legitimacy of the purposes desired by the power holder is irrelevant. Examples of countries that have been evaluated as operating in large power-distance ways include the Philippines, Mexico, Venezuela, India, Slovakia, and Russia (for a more extensive list, see http://culturevalues.wordpress.com/).

Large power-distance cultures idealize maintenance of power and clear distinctions even among those close to each other in social power (see fig. 12.1). People in power are to be respected because they are the authorities. Therefore it is important to use titles to indicate power (such as pastor, reverend, or doctor), and to speak respectfully (e.g., not too loudly, not contradicting them). Those below people in power want to develop a dependence relationship with them and look for the personal wisdom they bring to situations. Those in power manage by decree, and those under them prefer to be taught by lecture. People in middle management in large power-distance cultures will not be able to make decisions about exceptions to rules and will generally not show great initiative (which could be perceived as a threat by those above them). The higher the power distance, the more limited the interaction (especially tactile) among people of different levels of power (Andersen 1991).

Figure 12.1
Large and Small Power Distance

Small Power Distance   Large Power Distance

Equality	Respect/Authority
Independence	Dependence
(Impersonal) Truth	(Personal) Wisdom
Negotiation	Decree
Discussion	Lecture

Again, broadly speaking, cultures with small power distance believe in minimizing social or class inequalities, reducing hierarchical organizational structures, and using power only for legitimate purposes. Examples of countries that value small power distance include Austria, Israel, Denmark, New Zealand, and Ireland. They value showing respect for the boss, but they also insist that the boss show respect for subordinates. The type of respect that each is to show the other is based on ideals of equality rather than titles or social distance.

Rather than dependence on those higher in power, subordinates who value small power distance prefer to maintain their independence, which allows them to pursue (and utilize) truth that applies to all rather than blindly following the personal wisdom of the boss, as valued in large power-distance settings. They arrive at decisions through negotiation rather than decree, and they prefer to learn through discussion rather than lecture.

Power distance is reflected in the cultural values such as whether the individual has a say in everything that concerns him or her, whether and what type of status is appropriate, whether the rules apply to all or only to those without power, and what type of leadership is appropriate for life (Hofstede 1984, 394–95). It is also reflected in the amount and type of display of affective emotions between superior and subordinate, in the extent of fear in new situations, and the extent of sadness after death or birth (Gudykunst and Ting-Toomey 1988). These attitudes and ways of acting can affect several important areas of life in a society, including such things as employment, religious life, and education.

Employment

Power distance is reflected in occupations (which would apply in church or mission settings; see, e.g., Jones 2009) in several ways. It affects, among other things, the amount of supervision expected by managers and employees, the freedom of subordinates to challenge decisions made by management, the amount of trust and cooperativeness among employees, the level of consideration shown to employees by managers, the view of the importance of conformity within the organization, the type of organizational chart, the rate at which change may occur and how that change is implemented, the proportion of wage differentials among various levels in the organization, and the degree to which employees may participate with management in any decisions.

Religious Life

Power distance is reflected in the types of equality and/or stratification in national religions, the valuing of truth as opposed to wisdom in the religions, the types of power ideologies expressed (e.g., oligarchy versus monarchy), and the presence or absence of elitist theories of society. Only recently have missionaries, with the help of anthropological insights, begun to look at the impact of power on missionary life and ministry (Howell and Zehner 2009).

Education

Power distance is reflected in educational settings in the relationship of teacher and student, the amount of nonconformity allowed students, the orientation of curriculum (teacher oriented or student oriented), the stress on either impersonal principles or personal wisdom given by an enlightened teacher, whether the students may interact in class and the type of interaction, the type and amount of criticism of the teacher that is allowed, whether teachers are respected only in the class or outside the class as well, and whether the parents are expected to side with the teacher or the students in teacher-student conflicts (Hofstede 1986).

Biblical Examples of Power Distance

Is it possible to define or defend one of the orientations toward power as more biblical than the other? At the outset of any discussion, it should be noted that our own cultural tendencies predispose us to favor a particular position. Therefore, we seek in this section to present evidence for both a large and a small power-distance orientation in the biblical data. Table 12.1 lists representative samples of the types of passages that may be used to justify the relative positions on the power-distance spectrum. As you look over these passages and others you may find, consider whether there is a single biblical position that Christians should take in relation to power distance in leadership.

TABLE 12.1
BIBLICAL PASSAGES RELATED TO POWER DISTANCE

Large Power Distance	Mixed	Small Power Distance
Romans 13:1–7: We are to submit to governing authorities. *Ephesians 6:1–3*: Children are to obey their parents in the Lord. *Ephesians 6:5*: Slaves are to obey their earthly masters with respect and fear, and with sincerity of heart, just as they would obey Christ. *Hebrews 13:17*: People are to obey their leaders and submit to their authority.	*1 Corinthians* 12:14–13:4: We are all members of one body, and we are all equipped with gifts. Some are equipped with gifts suitable for leadership offices in the church. Though they serve according to God's gifting, they are to do so in love. *1 Peter 5:1–5*: Elders are to serve as shepherds over the body of Christ, not lording it over those they lead. At the same time, the young men are commanded to submit to the elders.	*Matthew 20:25–28; Mark 9:35*: Leaders must be servants. *Galatians 3:26–29*: In Christ, there is no male or female, slave or free . . . *Philippians 2:3–11*: Humbly consider the needs of others first by having the attitude of Christ.

LOCUS OF CONTROL

In Swaziland, Scott's mission agency had a policy of dating in odd numbers. Two or four people on a date was inappropriate; three, five, or seven was allowed. As it was explained to Scott by Swazi friends, the Swazis believe that whenever two people who are old enough and of the opposite sex are together in an unsupervised situation, they will not be able to restrain themselves from sexual impropriety. The Swazis have ensured that this will not happen by insisting that external observers—or at least a third party—are always present when a man and a woman are together. The idea of an unchaperoned "date" made no sense to them because they believed that people would not be able to control themselves unless supervision was provided.

This illustrates the idea of a locus of control, which is the society's perception of where the power to make choice resides (see Shiraev and Levy 2004). Does it reside within the individual? If so, then people of that society value an *internal* locus of control, and public campaigns such as the "just say no" to drugs campaign, which require the individual to have the ability to say no, are culturally possible. In those societies, people are expected to develop a more individual locus of control as they grow and mature (see Neill 2006); it is seen as a significant part of their well-being (Fiori et al. 2006; though note Wong-McDonald and Gorsuch 2004).

If, however, the locus of control does not reside within the individual, then the people of that society believe in an *external* locus of control. In those settings, regardless of where the power of control lies (God, fate, luck), society as a whole is responsible for ensuring that people are not put in compromising situations where they would not be expected to control themselves.

It should be obvious from the first example that, on the one hand, dating as practiced in the West can happen only if the participants (and their parents) believe in an internal locus of control. Swazis, on the other hand, value an external locus of control and believe that people should not be allowed to get into a potentially compromising setting.

This belief eventually raised problems for Scott. He and his roommate were part of a team of four people, two men and two women. The men taught at one school and the women at another. As part of their mission responsibilities, they met together weekly at the women's apartment for Bible study, prayer, and planning. The women's apartment was in teachers' housing on the campus of their school, next door to a boys' dormitory. The dormitory had the lights turned out at nine o'clock every night. Often when Scott and his roommate would visit the women either for business or socializing, the men would stay past the lights-out time in the dorm.

Not until two years later did Scott and his roommate learn from some of the students at the women's school that the boys in the dorm assumed that the missionary team members were sleeping together. It was a natural assumption for the boys, since there was no supervision of the four people, and there were two men and two women. Scott and his teammates were not even aware that such an assumption was being made, because it would not have been made in their own culture.

It should be apparent that in societies that value an external locus of control, the cross-cultural worker must avoid even the appearance of sin from the local perspective, which in this case would have meant either having an extra member of the team on hand or leaving before the lights were turned off in the boys' dorm.

ECONOMIC APPROACH TO SOCIAL POWER

An economic approach to social power considers power a type of capital that is used as an exchange mechanism within a society. The idea that social power is distributed among members of a society is no different from the idea that monetary capital will be distributed in a society. Just as people are attracted to money and seek to accumulate it, they are also attracted to social power and try to accumulate it. People who have social power and can control distribution of it in some way (granting favors, naming people to positions of social power) are important in the social economy of a society. They are referred to as patrons (or power brokers). Those who come under their power are called clients, resulting in what is called a patron-client system.

Patron-Client Systems

The patron-client system is typically seen in large power-distance cultures. They are organized by the people in power and are used to maintain the status quo of the system as well as build the prestige of the patron and the loyalty of the client. Both acknowledge that the bond uniting them can take priority over family, though the patron-client system may be voluntary (except in situations such as those of slavery or bonded labor).

The Dance of Patron-Client

To become a client, unless one is born into this relationship, a series of discrete steps are usually followed (Chinchen 1995; Tino 2008). First, the potential client asks for an appointment or simply visits the patron to establish the opportunity to become a client. The patron may refuse, and the dance goes no further. Next, the potential client brings a small gift to the patron to indicate interest in a relationship. Again, the patron may refuse for a variety of reasons, which will be accepted by the potential client (the patron has the power in these exchanges). Third, the patron accepts the gift and eventually gives back a bigger gift. This can be a title or position of status, some type of insider or secret knowledge, money, an item needed by the client, and so on. When the client receives the patron's gift, the relationship is established. However, this relationship is always negotiable, and either may pull away or seek to revise the relationship.

> *Both patrons and clients regard the link between them as a personal attachment similar to the bond of affection holding members of a family or kin group together.*
>
> "Patron-Client Systems" 2006

Each side has certain responsibilities in this mutually beneficial "friendship with strings" (Tino 2008, 322) in which both parties win (DeSilva 2000, 97; P. Shaw 2013). The patron offers protection; access to resources or information; group identity; opportunities for social, political, or other advancement; and gifts or other favors. The client brings labor, income (monetary or other), public acclaim (which increases the patron's status), votes and other political allegiance, and support against the patron's enemies.

There are many examples of patron-client relationships in the Bible. For example, Paul was a bond servant (client) of Christ (Rom. 1:1; 1 Cor. 4:1; Phil. 1:1) who did not need to win the approval of people (Gal. 1:10). However, Jesus's inauguration of the kingdom of God and the concept of the leader who serves turns the patron-client system upside down. We see this in

But I won't do anything unless you agree to it first. I want your act of kindness to come from your heart, and not be something you feel forced to do.

Perhaps Onesimus was taken from you for a little while so that you could have him back for good, but not as a slave. Onesimus is much more than a slave. To me he is a dear friend, but to you he is even more, both as a person and as a follower of the Lord.

If you consider me a friend because of Christ, then welcome Onesimus as you would welcome me. If he has cheated you or owes you anything, charge it to my account. With my own hand I write: I, PAUL, WILL PAY YOU BACK. But don't forget that you owe me your life. My dear friend and follower of Christ our Lord, please cheer me up by doing this for me.

I am sure you will do all I have asked, and even more. Please get a room ready for me. I hope your prayers will be answered, and I can visit you.

Epaphras is also here in jail for being a follower of Christ Jesus. He sends his greetings, and so do Mark, Aristarchus, Demas, and Luke, who work together with me.

I pray that the Lord Jesus Christ will be kind to you! (CEV)

REFLECTION AND DISCUSSION

1. What impact does this type of language have on Philemon as he reads the letter?
2. Does this letter feel strange to you? If so, what can you identify in it that does not fit your expectations?
3. What does that say about your understanding of a patron-client system?
4. How can this help you be better prepared to cross into a new culture with greater sensitivity?

statements such as the description of Christ as a servant of the Jews on God's behalf (Rom. 15:8) and that of Paul as a servant of God's people for Christ's sake (2 Cor. 4:5).

Foreign Experts in Patron-Client Cultures

Often foreign experts—including missionaries—have significant social power in the cultures where they serve. Though they may not think of themselves as rich, in comparison to local populations they generally are very rich. Even when that is not the case, they often have access to economic capital that is inaccessible to the local population. They also are wealthy in social capital, including spiritual capital (their theological background and awareness as well as their relationship with Christ) and linking capital (they can connect with powerful people in the culture to whom locals may not have access).

Unfortunately, all too often they are unaware of the social-power ideals in the culture where they work. Further, they may be unaware of or uncomfortable with the realities of their own social power and of being possible patrons; this situation is especially complicated when concerns about dependency are added to the mix (Rickett 2012a, 2012b). People in the culture, however, will see them as potential patrons and engage in ritualized behavior if they choose to explore a patron-client relationship with them. Knowing this can help the foreign experts better interpret the actions of those people (including inquiries, visits, gift giving, requests, and so forth).

Social Power Embedded in Worldview

In this section, we consider the three components of worldview—the cognitive, the affective, and the evaluative (Hiebert 2008b)—in relation to social power.

Worldview: Cognitive

The *cognitive* component of worldview includes what people know about social power, especially the rules and regulations for maintaining, increasing, or losing it. It is framed in terms of the ideas of power distance, locus of control, and patron-client.

Worldview: Affective

The *affective* component concerns people's emotional attachment and stability in relation to social power. It is how they feel about it and how they experience the loss of social power or other negative experiences as well as the gain of social power and other positive experiences. The affective dynamic in

---

SIDEBAR 12.3
PATRON-CLIENT RELATIONSHIPS IN CHRISTIAN PERSPECTIVE

Stress is placed on personal "wisdom," which is transferred in the relationship with a particular discipler (a "guru").

A spiritual leader merits the respect and support of his or her followers.

The spiritual leader has the responsibility of disciplining his or her disciples.

Disciples are related to in a hierarchy (a "pecking order").

Disciples want the spiritual leader to initiate communication and outline paths to follow.

Disciples speak up only when invited by the leader.

The leader is never contradicted or publicly criticized.

Effectiveness of learning is related to the excellence of the spiritual leader.

Older spiritual leaders are more respected than younger disciplers.

Sidebar 12.4
Proverbs of Social Power

When walking under the sun, make sure it is at your back; when going near the fire, approach from your front; when going near your boss, use the appropriate channels; you may go to heaven by refuting feelings of anger. (Cambodian)

What is joke for a cat will be death for a mouse. (Mongolian)

When a cat steals a piece of meat, we chase it. But when a tiger takes a pig we stare wide-eyed and say nothing. (Vietnamese)

Before you beat a dog, find out who its master is. (Chinese)

The egg cannot fight the stone. (Chinese)

To him who is larger than you, say, "I am a dwarf." (African)

---

a worldview is typically played out in myths and stories found in the culture. How do heroes handle their social power in traditional literature? Do they embrace it and use it wisely or disdain it and recast it in terms of equality? Do heroes play by their own rules built into the roles they play or live by an independent set of rules that should apply to everyone? Superman, for example, is a person with ultimate social power, yet he eschews using it for his own ends and instead promotes "truth, justice, and the American way." As you look at the proverbs of social power listed in sidebar 12.4, consider the values they express in relation to power distance, locus of control, and patron-client relations.

Sidebar 12.5
Selected Web Resources on Social Power

Beyond Intractability article: Power (http://www.beyondintractability.org/essay/Power)

Clearly Cultural Power Distance Index (http://www.clearlycultural.com/geert-hofstede-cultural-dimensions/power-distance-index)

Hofstede Power Distance Rankings (http://lavidaprofunda.com/cultures/pdi/culture.html)

Kwintessential article: Power Distance (http://www.kwintessential.co.uk/intercultural/power-distance-index.html)

What Is Locus of Control? (http://wilderdom.com/psychology/loc/LocusOfControlWhatIs.html)

Wikipedia: Geert Hofstede (http://en.wikipedia.org/wiki/Hofstede); Locus of Control (http://en.wikipedia.org/wiki/Locus_of_control); Patronage (en.wikipedia.org/wiki/Patron); Power (http://en.wikipedia.org/wiki/Power_(sociology))

Worldview: Evaluative

Finally, the *evaluative* component involves moral decision-making rules about how to evaluate actions and attitudes that lead to an increase or decrease of social power, such as what are appropriate and inappropriate ways to defend one's social power when it is threatened.

The evaluative dynamic is framed in terms of how actions and beliefs are evaluated as good or bad. What is the right use of power by leaders? What perks are acceptable for those in power? Do we idealize those who claim the perks or those who deny them (e.g., Phil. 3:7–11)?

CONCLUSION

Missionaries going out from Western countries tend to have far more social power than they realize. In terms of their own culture, they are near the bottom of the economic scale. Yet, depending on where they serve, they are at least near the middle if not at the top of the economic scale in that country. They will do well to understand issues of power in their new home: how much people value disparity in power, where control resides, and what types of social power relationship are considered normal. In our case study, we present a case in which several players are fighting for power, with a missionary caught in the middle.

CASE STUDY:
THE AUTHORITY DILEMMA

MARK DANIELSON

Reprinted with permission from Hiebert and Hiebert (1987, 199–201).

Eileen Thompson, a North American missionary in the San Isabel Valley of Mexico, was committed to working within the structures of local church authority. It was important to her that the church be an indigenous expression of God's kingdom, so she was glad to submit to national leadership. The problem was that there were competing indigenous authorities who laid claim to her ministry. Eileen had just completed her furlough and was getting ready to return to Mexico. First, however, she and her mission board would have to decide where she would next be assigned to work.

Several different local groups had great plans for Eileen's life. She could not choose any of the options without offending people who wanted her to serve elsewhere, and her decision carried the potential for long-term consequences. Eileen had been put in the position of either defying the authority of the local Mexican church, to the possible detriment

---

of its future growth, or dropping a fruitful ministry among some 15,000 migrant farm workers. To complicate things further, the hospital where she had worked during her first term as nurse-anesthetist and evangelist also had designs on Eileen. According to the doctor in charge, the zeal for evangelistic outreach at the hospital had diminished considerably while she was away on furlough.

During her first years of ministry, Eileen had been assigned to the hospital, but she also began to evangelize the valley's migrant farm workers, whose ethnic identity was Indian rather than Mexican. Just before her furlough, after ten years of work among the Indians, she had begun to reap the fruit of her ministry. Several small congregations sprang up in a number of the Indian villages.

Eileen had carried out this ministry to the farm workers under the authority of the local national Baptist church. At the time she left, the infant Indian congregations still depended entirely on the Mexican church for leadership, support and nurture. Eileen trusted that the relationship would continue in the same way without her.

Soon after Eileen went on furlough, something else happened that seriously affected the Indian work. The pastor of the Baptist church left, and his successor gave very low priority to the Indian work. Pastor Gonzalez believed that attention should be focused instead on the Mexicans.

A group of national nurses from the mission hospital had tried to preserve the ministry to the Indians by teaching classes at the various camps throughout the week and arranging transportation to the Mexican church on Sundays. Because of the hospital's isolated location, however, it was difficult to keep their staff. So, within four months of Eileen's departure, two of the three nurses working with the Indians left the valley. The third nurse complained that her zeal for the Indian ministry had waned considerably for lack of support. She had tried to get incoming hospital staff interested in helping her, but it became harder and harder. The ministry to the Indians gradually slipped downhill.

When the Indian ministry went into decline, the leaders of the Indian villages took unprecedented action. They met together and drafted a letter to the mission board that sponsored Eileen, asking them to send her back to the valley to renew the ministry she had begun among them. Eileen was certainly willing to do that, because she had come to love the migrant Indian workers. Her mission board was also sympathetic to their appeal.

The problem was with the pastor of the local Baptist church. Pastor Gonzalez insisted that if a woman missionary were to be in the area, she would have to be under his authority. He would assign Eileen to playing the piano for church services and teaching a women's Sunday school class in the Mexican church. He gave two reasons for not allowing her to work with the migrant Indians. First, he believed it was wrong for a woman to teach men; and second, he emphasized the fact that his own ministry was to the Mexicans and not to the Indians of the valley.

Members of the Mexican church expressed a desire for a missionary to come and work with them because they felt the church was dying and in need of rejuvenation. The pastor, on the other hand, was cold to the idea of any missionary coming to work with the church, citing some bad experiences with North American missionaries in the border town from where he had come. He complained that the missionaries "always came in and did things their way" without heeding his authority.

Some church members who were close to the pastor expressed the fear that if

Eileen came to the valley and carried on her own ministry outside the authority of the pastor, it would reinforce his negative feelings about missionaries in general. This would further diminish their chances of ever getting a missionary to work with their church again.

Eileen now faced one final meeting with her mission board, during which they would have to make a decision regarding her assignment. She still could not see a way to resolve the conflict of other people's agendas for her ministry. It was still her deep desire to work within the national church structure. But now the Indian work also represented the "national church." Which national church had priority—Mexican or Indian? She hoped and prayed that her mission board would be able to help her make the right decision.

REFLECTION AND DISCUSSION

1. Why do you think everyone wants Eileen to work for them?
2. The action of drafting a letter to the board by the Indian village leaders is noted as "unprecedented"; is this good or bad (explain your answer)?
3. If you were a board member what would you advise Eileen to do?

13

Gender Roles

In this chapter we examine how differing societies understand the extent to which roles and positions between the genders are to be intermingled or distinguished, and if the latter, the degree to which they are distinguished. We explain the ideas as well as the impact on communication and ministry.

GENDER, GENDER ROLES, AND CULTURAL MANIFESTATIONS

Definitions

The terms used for describing the biological differences between men and women, or their gender, are *male* and *female*. Biological distinctions can be absolute, for example, when referring to the separate role of the sexes in procreation. But biological distinctions can also be statistical, such as "men are *on average* taller and stronger" or "women *on average* have greater finger dexterity" (Hofstede, Hofstede, and Minkov 2010, 137). When the social roles of men and women that differ across societies are being considered, however, terms such as *gender roles* are commonly used. Table 13.1 and figure 13.1 depict ways in which the social roles of the sexes are distinguished in societies.

These distinctions are *relative* rather than absolute. For example, typists in Pakistan are primarily men, and female managers are "virtually nonexistent"

TABLE 13.1
GENDER-ROLE SEPARATION VALUES DESCRIBED

Large Gender-Role Separation	Small Gender-Role Separation
Cultures with a masculine orientation make a strong separation in the social sex roles. Typically the masculine values permeate society: they believe in performance, achievement, ambition, the acquisition of material goods, and ostentatious manliness ("big is beautiful").	Cultures with a feminine orientation do not separate the social sex roles as strongly. They believe in the quality of life, not showing off, service to others, equality between the sexes, nurturing roles, and sympathy for the unfortunate ("small is beautiful").

Reprinted from Hofstede 1980, 176–77.

in Japan but common in both Thailand and the Philippines. Some gender roles tend to be consistent across both time and cultures. An illustration would be the role of men as external to the home, providing in some way for it. Women, however, have consistently had greater responsibility for both children and the home (Hofstede, Hofstede, and Minkov 2010, 137–38).

FIGURE 13.1
SPECTRUM OF GENDER-ROLE SEPARATION

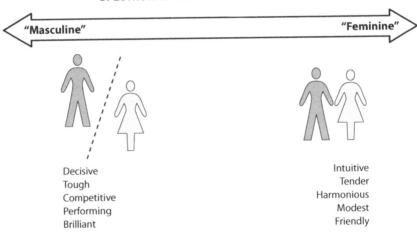

"Masculine"　　　　　　　　　　　　　　　　　　　　　"Feminine"

Decisive	Intuitive
Tough	Tender
Competitive	Harmonious
Performing	Modest
Brilliant	Friendly

Intermingling and Distinguishing Gender Roles

We describe societies in which the roles of men and women significantly overlap as having "small gender-role separation." Examples include the Scandinavian countries, the Netherlands, and Costa Rica. Conversely, we describe societies in which there is relatively little overlap in the roles of men and women as having "large gender-role separation." They include such countries as Japan, Austria, Venezuela, and Italy.

These differing values are manifested in many spheres of society. Of key importance is the fact that gender roles include both social aspects, which can be externally imposed, and emotional factors, which are internal. According to Hofstede and his colleagues,

> A society is called *masculine* when emotional gender roles are clearly distinct: men are supposed to be assertive, tough, and focused on material success, whereas women are supposed to be more modest, tender, and concerned with the quality of life. A society is called *feminine* when emotional gender roles overlap: both men and women are supposed to be modest, tender, and concerned with the quality of life. (Hofstede, Hofstede, and Minkov 2010, 140, emphasis in original)

These separate roles are manifested in different behaviors in virtually all aspects of life, from family and education to the workplace, religion, government, and interpersonal relationships.

The malleable rather than static nature of culture means that gender roles change over time. For example, women in the 1900 Olympics were permitted to compete only in lawn tennis, croquet, and golf. A sharp contrast, however, was evident by the time of the London 2012 Olympics, where there were thirty-four sports in which both men and women competed. As International Olympic Committee president Jacques Rogge said at the opening ceremony, "For the first time in Olympic history, all the participating teams will have female athletes. This is a major boost for gender equality" (Saporito 2012a, 44).

Women outnumbered men 268 to 261 on the US team and also won more medals. Significantly, 2012 marked forty years since the United States enacted Title IX, the legislation that prohibits sexual discrimination in education and has provided more funded sports opportunities for young women. The Chinese similarly had a larger pool of female athletes to draw from due to their intentional "focus on women, whose athletic efforts are underfunded in most countries" (Saporito 2012b). The effect of this focus was clear. Chinese women won 55 percent of their country's total number of medals.

The complexities of gender roles were nevertheless evident in the eight-hundred-meter heat of Sarah Attar, a nineteen-year-old dual Saudi and American citizen. When competing for Pepperdine University, she had worn characteristic track attire, but as a Saudi in the Olympics she finished last, but to warm applause, while running with long sleeves, leggings, and a head covering (Saporito 2012a).

SIDEBAR 13.1
SELECTED WEB RESOURCES ON GENDER ROLES

Clearly Cultural Masculinity Index
(http://www.clearlycultural
.com/geert-hofstede-cultural
-dimensions/masculinity)
Kwintessential article: Masculinity
(http://www.kwintessential.co.uk
/intercultural/masculinity/.html)

YouTube video: Gender Roles—
Male and Female (http://www
.youtube.com/watch?v=YIw
WS2atEmc)

The Impact of Gender-Role Differences on Communication

Deborah Tannen, a linguist with a PhD from the University of California–
Berkeley and author of eighteen books, is a professor at Georgetown University,
where she has taught since 1979. Tannen is widely known for her work on
gender communication and discourse. Her book *You Just Don't Understand:
Women and Men in Conversation* (1991) has been translated into twenty-nine
languages and was on the *New York Times* best-seller list almost four years.

Tannen initially became intrigued with gender communication when watching videos of girls and women talking to close friends. Consistently, they sat
face-to-face and looked at each other. In contrast, boys and men looked around
the room and either sat parallel or at angles. She thus interpreted cross-gender
communication as cross-cultural communication (2003, 5). Tannen also observed that girls spent significant time in talking to a best friend and sharing
secrets, downplaying their status, and offering suggestions rather than issuing
commands. In contrast, boys actively played in large groups, had high- and
low-status ranks, and used language and conversational patterns such as interruptions to maintain status. These patterns continue in adulthood and are
summarized in table 13.2.

TABLE 13.2
COMMUNICATION STYLES AND VALUES BY GENDER

Male	Female
Asymmetrical	Symmetrical
Status	Harmony
Competitive	Cooperative
Respect	Intimacy
Independence	Interdependence
Power	Connection
Information and Opinion	Supporting Others
Report	Rapport

Tannen's key point is that understanding these patterns is vital to learning to communicate clearly (2003, 7–8, 10). Considering genders as particular cultures in addition to ethnic-group culture indeed adds a further level of complication to communicating cross-culturally.

SUGGESTIONS FOR BETTER CROSS-GENDER COMMUNICATION

The following are suggestions for understanding patterns of cross-gender communication.

The first is to be an observer and student of the gender values of the culture you are in. For example, the feminist Nordic countries have a long history of valuing equal rights for women, including suffrage (women won the right to vote in Finland in 1906; in Norway in 1913; in Denmark in 1915; and in Sweden in 1921; see Pylkkänen 1997). It is not surprising, then, that in 2013 in Nordic countries 42 percent of lower house members of Parliament were female, compared to 15.7 percent in masculine Arab states ("Women in National Parliaments" 2013). Research both the history and the current affairs of a country to understand what you are experiencing.

Second, gain skills in interpreting style differences in communication and then learn to function with them. A case in point: in European and American contexts women bosses tend to use a consultative and consensus style of leadership, while male bosses are more likely to be directive. Be flexible and become comfortable working with differing styles of leadership and interaction.

Third, be attentive to nonverbal communication, such as more direct eye contact among women or occupying more physical space by men. While a woman may nod to say, "I hear you," a man may interpret that as "She said yes" (Lieberman n.d.). Build a knowledge base of nonverbal forms of communication.

Finally, enjoy and celebrate positive aspects of cross-gender communication. Determine to be both a person who communicates clearly, with tact and integrity, and also one who enables such communication in others.

A GLOBAL SNAPSHOT OF GENDER DISPARITY

Cultures and Organizations describes masculinity-femininity as "the most controversial of the five dimensions of national cultures," in part because cultures dramatically differ on the associated values (Hofstede, Hofstede, and Minkov 2010, 144). Profound contrasts exist globally in gender roles for women today. While men continue to dominate as CEOs of major corporations and heads of state, in this decade Fortune 500 companies such as PepsiCo, Kraft Foods, and Hewlett Packard have had female CEOs. Additionally, Argentina, Liberia, Switzerland, Lithuania, Costa Rica, Brazil, Kosovo, and Malawi have had female heads of state. Of particular note is Dr. Ellen Johnson Sirleaf of Liberia, elected in 2005 and reelected in 2011. Sirleaf was the first elected female head of state in Africa, and in 2011 she was jointly awarded the Nobel Prize for nonviolently promoting the safety of women and women's rights for full participation in peace-building work ("The Nobel Peace Prize 2011").

Yet simultaneously women and girls remain marginalized in many countries. In Sierra Leone, for example, Elizabeth Simbiwa Sogbo-Tortu, who sought to run for election as paramount chief in her district, was "denied the right to stand, despite being the eldest and coming from a ruling house," even though she had the support of women's rights campaigners and the protection of UN officials and armed police ("Sierra Leone Woman Barred from Becoming Chief" 2009). Such examples are hardly isolated.

> *You educate a boy, and you're educating an individual. You educate a girl, and you're educating an entire village.*
>
> African proverb, in Kristof and WuDunn 2009, 161

Half the Sky: Turning Oppression into Opportunity for Women Worldwide (2009), a national best seller by the Pulitzer Prize–winning couple Nicholas Kristof and Sheryl WuDunn, focuses significant attention on sex trafficking, female genital mutilation, HIV/AIDS, honor killings, female mortality, and gender-based violence through compelling vignettes of women ensnared in these situations. In recounting the grim death of Prudence, lying neglected in childbirth at a backwater Cameroonian hospital, and the plight of teenage Cambodian Rath, trapped by gangsters into sex slavery in Kuala Lumpur, it offers representative examples of the gender-related neglect and oppression that millions of women and girls face.

In a more concise manner but with a similarly sobering perspective, Ron Sider, the founder of Evangelicals for Social Action, summarizes key data on injustices against women worldwide in a *Prism* article. As described by Nobel laureate Amartya Sen, selective abortions of female fetuses and neglect of infant female babies have resulted in an estimated one hundred million "missing women." Unequal education has left 31 percent of young women illiterate compared with 19 percent of male youth in low-income countries. Economist Michael Todaro notes that girls in India are four times more likely than boys to suffer acute malnutrition, while boys are forty times more likely to be taken to the hospital. Property ownership favors men (73 percent) to women (22 percent) in Mexico in 2003, and women on average work longer days. Perhaps most grievous of all, a World Health Organization study of 24,097 women in eleven countries reports that an alarming number of them have suffered physical violence by intimate partners at least once: "40 percent in Bangladesh, 30 percent in Brazil, 49 percent in Ethiopia, 49 percent in Peru's cities and 61 percent in its rural areas" (Sider 2007). Also as reported by the World Health Organization, gender violence perpetrated against girls and women ages 14–44 creates more disability and death than war, malaria, and car accidents combined (Morgan 2014, 58).

Significantly, in the "What You Can Do" chapter at the close of *Half the Sky*, Kristof and WuDunn advocate for a concerted international response to gender disparities that cause so many evils, but they also urge that the response not be framed as a "women's issue," a characterization that routinely results in marginalization of the issue: "Sex trafficking and mass rape should no more be seen as women's issues than slavery was a black issue or the Holocaust was a Jewish issue" (2009, 234). Rather, all are transcendent humanitarian concerns. As a model, Kristof and WuDunn highlight the collaborative effort needed to end entrenched slavery in British colonies, which involved both significant personal sacrifice and economic cost to Britain. On ethical grounds alone, it was the right thing to do.

How much more, then, are Christians compelled by Old and New Testament calls for justice and care for the poor, aliens, widows, and orphans? Indeed, vibrant cooperative responses are under way through such groups as Accord (http://www.accordnetwork.org), Integral (http://www.integralalliance.org), and the Micah Network (http://www.micahnetwork .org). Child sponsorships are a helpful way to estab- lish personal connections, and well-structured church- based partnerships can also be effective. Supporting educational opportunities through indigenous institu- tions such as Forman Christian College in Pakistan also makes a difference (http://www.fccollege.edu.pk/). Busi- ness as mission initiatives (http://conversation.lausanne .org/en/resources/detail/12291), including both micro- economic development programs and large-scale busi-

> *It is time for Christian men around the world to say "Enough injustice and violence against our sisters!"*
>
> Sider 2007

ness endeavors, can lift whole communities out of poverty. The International Justice Mission (http://www.ijm.org) is the largest global human rights agency with a focus on protecting the poor from violence. Gary Haugen, IJM's founder and president, argues in his searing book *The Locus Effect* (2014) that the virtual absence of basic public justice systems in the Majority World is the scourge that undercuts development and fuels the cycle of poverty. Through teams of local lawyers, community activists, investigators, and social workers,

SIDEBAR 13.2
RIZPAH

Julain Smythe, Christian Service Organization Volunteer, Papua

Note: All names, including the author's, have been changed.

There is a young woman of eighteen. Her name is Rizpah. She is an orphan and has lived with various relatives and caretakers throughout her life. About a year ago, while her caretakers were away, she was raped by a policeman. Not long afterward, she became ill and made her way back to her home village, where her condition worsened. With bright, tear-filled eyes, she shared with me a story of miracles and prayer that gave her and a young friend strength to make their way on foot over the mountains of Papua to the capital city of her region so that she could find health care and finish high school.

She said to me, "There was a mountain and a road that was made by a bulldozer. I knelt down on the road at the bottom of the mountain and I prayed. There was no way I could make it up. I heard a sound. It was four motorcycles! I cried, 'O God, I have nothing but please let them take me to Mulia.'" And they did.

Rizpah arrived in Mulia and was able to finish her high school exam. It was in Mulia—and the name of the city means "glory"—where she met a nurse named Maria who was visiting outlying regions to find and help people living with AIDS. Rizpah tested positive for AIDS and discovered that she was pregnant. She was broken and afraid, but somehow God gave her strength. She gambled her way into enough money to fly to Jayapura,

where she was taken in by a Christian support group. Rizpah was very thin, desperately ill, and quite pregnant when she arrived, but her physical condition slowly became transformed. She now has a lovely nine-month-old son named Tono, who recently tested negative for HIV. Rizpah's eyes laugh as she holds her son.

Rizpah lives in a shelter with a number of other young women and takes antiretroviral drugs daily. She now sees it as her mission to tell her people about HIV/AIDS. In a time when discrimination remains rampant and many living with AIDS are afraid to share their stories, Rizpah puts aside her fear.

"God has guarded me," she says. "God has given me life. I'm going to take care of my son until he goes to school and finishes. I want to share my story with anyone so we can come together and learn about this disease."

REFLECTION AND DISCUSSION

1. Identify a biblical story of a marginalized person for whom God provided. What parallels do you see in the biblical story with Rizpah's story?
2. If Rizpah were your friend, what would you consider a response to the policeman's brutality against her that is congruent with God's justice as embodied in kingdom of God principles?

IJM works to rescue victims, ensure justice, and provide appropriate aftercare services (2014, 242). There is a place for a response to disparities at virtually all levels and from all people (see, e.g., Wood 2011).

GENDER ROLES AND MINISTRY

A chapter on gender roles in a missions- and ministry-related text like this one could quite naturally include a discussion of theological perspectives on gender roles, their impact on ministry, and the differing complexities facing married and single women who work cross-culturally. While some of these issues are touched on here, it is important to note that other books in the Encountering Mission series deal with them in greater depth. For example, Lois McKinney Douglas's "Women in Missions" chapter in *Encountering Missionary Life and Work* (Steffen and McKinney Douglas 2008, 253–75) provides an excellent historical overview of women in missions, an evenhanded discussion of associated theological debates, a consideration of relationships with sending churches and agencies as well as field teams, and a helpful overview of the roles of both single and married missionaries. Similarly, in *Introducing World Missions: A Biblical, Historical, and Practical Survey* (Moreau, Corwin, and McGee 2004) a variety of topics that relate to gender roles are addressed, including cross-cultural marriages (214–16), the advent of women's missionary societies (128–29), differing perspectives on women in organizational leadership (192, 200–201), and helpful steps toward resolving gender-related tensions (229–32).

Creating a Place for Women

In the oft-repeated Luke 10 story in which Mary sits at the Lord's feet listening while Martha is distracted by household preparations, two interesting gender-role elements are often overlooked. The first is that Mary crossed a boundary into a place belonging by custom to men. In the words of N. T. Wright, "Mary has shamelessly gone across the short but steep gulf that separates male and female space" (1997, 86).

The second gender-role element is that by sitting at Jesus's feet, Mary was taking the posture of a disciple before a rabbi, which men took in order to one day be a rabbi themselves. In approving Mary as having "chosen what is better" (Luke 10:42), Jesus "quietly and calmly dismantles a major social taboo and leaves the onlookers open-mouthed in amazement" (N. T. Wright 1997, 86). Jesus created a place for Mary.

The touching story in Luke 13 of the woman crippled for eighteen years whom Jesus healed contains a similar challenge of gender roles for that era. While evidence for synagogue practice at that time is limited (Cohick 2009, 218), as a woman with a "spirit of infirmity" this woman would have been considered unclean. Thus the combination of Jesus calling her to come forward, speaking to her publicly, putting his hands on her, and healing her on the Sabbath evoked an indignant response from the synagogue ruler (Pearson 1988).

187

SIDEBAR 13.3
MEN AND WOMEN IN PARTNERSHIP

THE CAPE TOWN COMMITMENT, PART II F: PARTNERING IN THE BODY OF CHRIST FOR UNITY IN MISSION

Scripture affirms that God created men and women in his image and gave them dominion over the earth together. Sin entered human life and history through man and woman acting together in rebellion against God. Through the cross of Christ, God brought salvation, acceptance and unity to men and women equally. At Pentecost God poured out his Spirit of prophecy on all flesh, sons and daughters alike. Women and men are thus equal in creation, in sin, in salvation, and in the Spirit.

All of us, women and men, married and single, are responsible to employ God's gifts for the benefit of others, as stewards of God's grace, and for the praise and glory of Christ. All of us, therefore, are also responsible to enable all God's people to exercise all the gifts that God has given for all the areas of service to which God calls the Church. We should not quench the Spirit by despising the ministry of any. Further, we are determined to see ministry within the body of Christ as a gifting and responsibility in which we are called to *serve*, and not as a status and right that we demand.

(A) We uphold Lausanne's historic position: "We affirm that the gifts of the Spirit are distributed to all God's people, women and men, and that their partnership in evangelization must be welcomed for the common good." (Manila Manifesto) We acknowledge the enormous and sacrificial contribution that women have made to world mission, ministering to both men and women, from biblical times to the present.

(B) We recognize that there are different views sincerely held by those who seek to be faithful and obedient to Scripture. Some interpret apostolic teaching to imply that women should not teach or preach, or that they may do so but not in sole authority over men. Others interpret the spiritual equality of women, the exercise of the edifying gift of prophecy by women in the New Testament church, and their hosting of churches in their homes, as implying that the spiritual gifts of leading and teaching may be received and exercised in ministry by both women and men. We call upon those on different sides of the argument to:

1. Accept one another without condemnation in relation to matters of dispute, for while we may disagree, we have no grounds for division, destructive speaking, or ungodly hostility towards one another;
2. Study Scripture carefully together, with due regard for the context and culture of the original authors and contemporary readers;
3. Recognize that where there is genuine pain we must show compassion; where there is injustice and lack of integrity we must stand against them; and where there is resistance to the manifest work of the Holy Spirit in any sister or brother we must repent;
4. Commit ourselves to a pattern of ministry, male and female, that reflects the servanthood of Jesus Christ, not worldly striving for power and status.

(C) We encourage churches to acknowledge godly women who teach and
model what is good, as Paul commanded,
and to open wider doors of opportunity
for women in education, service, and
leadership, particularly in contexts
where the gospel challenges unjust cultural traditions. We long that women
should not be hindered from exercising
God's gifts or following God's call on
their lives. ("Men and Women in Partnership" 2011)

REFLECTION AND DISCUSSION

1. Describe a situation of gender-
related tension that could have
been (or could be) resolved through
applying principles in the Men and
Women in Partnership statement.
2. Identify a partnership area that has
been of some difficulty for you. In
light of the statement, how might
you address that particular personal
difficulty?

Further, when rebuking the synagogue leader for his hypocrisy, Jesus called her "a daughter of Abraham" (Luke 13:16). There is no other place in rabbinical teaching where this name is given to an individual woman (Cunningham and Hamilton 2000, 116). Yet once again Jesus created a place of welcome.

In contemporary evangelical circles, there have been tense exchanges between complementarians and egalitarians on the issue of women's roles in the church and ministry. A helpful step forward has been the "Men and Women in Partnership" section of the Lausanne Movement's Cape Town Commitment (see sidebar 13.3). Irenic in tone, it is theologically grounded, respectful of differing views, and urges that all believers fully use their gifts for the praise and glory of Christ. Through a focus on partnership, it provides both a place and a mandate for service that welcomes all men and women.

Opportunities, Barriers, and a "Good Fit"

At the onset of the nineteenth-century modern missionary movement, a missionary was considered an ordained male engaged in preaching and church planting. Thus women figured little in historical documentation (Shenk 1996, xi–xii). Drawn nevertheless by the vision of missions, they served in humanitarian work and in establishing schools, training nationals, preaching, and evangelizing "far out of reach of critics back home." Others formed vibrant missionary societies, with over three million women participating in some forty societies by 1915 (Tucker and Liefeld 1987, 291). Cross-cultural service, from then until now, has offered extraordinary opportunities for women.

After serving two terms at Kamakwie Wesleyan Hospital in Sierra Leone, Evvy completed nine additional years with a Christian relief and development agency. From being enriched by West African women utterly immersed

> *We who lived in concentration camps can remember the men who walked through the huts comforting others, giving away their last piece of bread. They may have been few in number, but they offer sufficient proof that everything can be taken from a man but one thing: the last of the human freedoms—to choose one's attitude in any given set of circumstances, to choose one's own way.*
>
> Frankl 1984, 86

in domestic and farm work to engaging in health training for women following the collapse of Communism in Romania, she has been ever grateful for the privileged vocation that has been hers, what Frederick Buechner described in *Wishful Thinking* as "the kind of work that you need most to do and the world most needs to have done," "the place where your deep gladness and the world's deep hunger meet" (1973, 95).

But barriers exist as well. In *Living Overseas* Ted Ward makes clear that women are "under stricter constraints and will pay more severely for violating norms and expectations" in other cultures (1984, 315; see also Dzubinski 2011). Retrospectively, that was true in Evvy's experience only in relatively small ways. In those situations it was sufficient to exercise "the last human freedom" articulated by Viktor Frankl (1984) of choosing one's own attitude of response and thus choosing one's own way.

In cross-cultural work it is often quite necessary to know how to negotiate gender-role differences. In some cases, there is wisdom in not getting into a problem. For example, "an ardent advocate of women's rights would find an assignment in an Arab country almost unbearable," as she might well feel compelled to continue her efforts in her new culture (Ward 1984, 316). But when differences can't be avoided, they can often be navigated with humility, courtesy, and openness. When a situation can't be changed, then gracious acceptance and offering the problem on open palms back to the Lord may bring peace. It is a sacrifice that he will know how to receive.

Sidebar 13.4 contains a letter Evvy received from a former student, a young woman who had recently married and was en route to the mission field with her husband.

But as discussed earlier, gender differences can and often do result in painful gender disparities. Evvy grieves greatly for her sisters trapped by abject poverty, forced prostitution, illiteracy, and lack of health care, a grief that has been a driving force in her teaching in the field of transformational development. For them she seeks to be an advocate. With them, she seeks to celebrate their strength, achievements, and victories.

In sidebar 13.5, a former student of Evvy's serving in Papua relates the strengths of a neighborhood "mama."

SIDEBAR 13.4
NEGOTIATING DIFFERENCES

Personal communication; used with permission.

Hi, Evvy!

Mark and I had a great trip and think we know where God is calling us, but we've asked the elders of the church to confirm God's call through prayer and we're still waiting on that. We're excited and looking forward to serving the Lord!

We've been attending the church Mark grew up in and it's very strong not only on women not teaching men but also strong on women's silence in the church meeting. Well, since you know me, this has been an area of disagreement. Recently, something came up which brought all of this to the forefront again, and although I've studied the Scripture and Greek study helps for hours, I think I need some input from others I respect.

Some sort of agreement needs to happen between both Mark and myself and the elders of the church before we go on the mission field. So since you were a missionary and are also a professor of missions, how do you interpret the Bible passages on women's role and silence? Any insights you could give would be very helpful!

God bless you,

Margaret

REFLECTION AND DISCUSSION

1. What advice would you give or what insights might you share with Margaret to help her work through this difference of perspective with her husband?

2. Consider situations from your own experience or that of others in which such differences have not been addressed or resolved. What has been the outcome?

SIDEBAR 13.5
MAMA

Julain Smythe, Christian Service Organization Volunteer, Papua

I had a Mama who lived next door. She was the widow of the former seminary president and presided over her brood of children and grandchildren from a plastic lawn chair on her terrace. There were two plastic chairs and one wooden table that appeared at times on the terrace and then were brought inside. Aside from beds and closets, these were the only furniture in the house. Other furniture has been destroyed by her youngest son, a man with no economic recourse, in drunken rages.

There were times when we heard his hollering, and we heard crashing. Once, his daughter Martha came running in the direction of our house for protection.

It was in the middle of this brokenness that Mama lived. In the worst of times I could hear her singing hymns at the top of her lungs. And they were mighty lungs! When things were peaceful, she sat on the porch on her teal plastic throne, head held high, her chin strong, her face holding the grief that her land and nation and family

191

lived. She sat like a queen in the faltering light of an oil wick stuffed in a sardine can, facing the palm tree and the road with its motorcycles and horns and water spinach vendors.

Her dignity and fortitude in the midst of suffering touched and humbled my easy life and I longed to reach out to her, but instead it was she who reached out to me. When I collapsed in tears after encountering a persistent drunk in my yard, it was Mama who I found next to me, surrounded by daughters and granddaughters. It was her regal self that humbled itself to sit on the cement floor at my side, and it was her work-hardened fingers that wiped my tears and stroked my hair. She was a treasure I was unworthy to hold in my soft hands, and yet there she was.

REFLECTION AND DISCUSSION

1. To what extent does the posture of an observer and learner facilitate cross-cultural communication and understanding?
2. In what ways are "the gift of presence" and appreciation of great importance in situations where there seems to be only limited opportunity for change?

CONCLUSION

A missionary colleague once commented on the need for "the wisdom of Solomon, the dedication of Saint Paul, and the cunning of a second-hand car dealer" in working through cultural complexities. The same may be said for the joys and difficulties that come in understanding gender roles, communicating across them, knowing when and how to effect change, the art of insightful compromise, and gracious acceptance of differences when needed. The concluding case study portrays the tension we often feel in discerning how to respond in situations with multiple complex layers, in which gender-role difficulties are only one element. But, as advocated in this chapter, through understanding the values underlying the roles and with a commitment to work through disparities for the common good, there are indeed ways forward.

CASE STUDY:
ONIONS AND WIVES

ROGER DAVID HEEREN

Reprinted with permission from Hiebert and Hiebert (1987, 202–4).

Beth Jones downshifted her Honda 125XL dirt bike into first gear as she wearily climbed the last hill into Kabala, a village in the northern mountains of Sierra Leone, West Africa. At three o'clock there would be a meeting of the Kabala Women's Agricultural Cooperative—KWAC—and Beth knew there would be trouble. The village chief (and husband of the president of KWAC) had used his wife's onion money to buy two more wives. Should she take the wife's side and save her friendship with the women, who were already angry at her? Or should she save her job as agriculture extension agent and side with the chief?

Beth thought back to the cross-cultural training she had received one year ago during her first month as a volunteer in a Christian development agency for work in Sierra Leone. They had never warned her about a situation like this. Before joining the agency, she had campaigned for the Equal Rights Amendment in her New England college. Now a man had actually used the money she had helped the women earn in order to buy more wives to be used for work, almost as slaves!

Beth had arrived in Kabala one year earlier at the end of the dry season, determined to get her agricultural cooperative program off the ground within the first year. The relief agencies had declared this "the year of the woman," so she had no trouble in getting money, tools, seeds, and even surplus bulgur and oil from the United States. She organized the women of the village and helped them develop programs that would improve their conditions. These included maternity and child care, health, nutrition, basic education, and kitchen gardening. Beth had a particular interest in the last of these, for it enabled the women to earn a little money on their own, money they could use to purchase clothing, toiletries, magazines, and other personal and family items. It also gave them a sense of dignity and independence.

Under Beth's guidance, many of the women that first year planted onion patches in unused land around the village. The project went along well through the rainy season. Meetings with chiefs and meetings with the women to distribute the food, money, tools, and seeds had about drained her of all her strength, but Beth saw the onions sprouting on time, at the end of the rains!

Beth slowly learned the Koronko language during those first months by staying in the village for two and three days at a time, living in the house of Abu, the village chief, and his wife, Isatu. Beth ran weekly meetings with the women of the village, discussing baby formula problems and lack of medical facilities as well as local gossip. Isatu had spoken many times with the women about how they should use their cooperative earnings for a health center for a midwife. All the women agreed.

Beth learned to respect and love these people, especially the way that the women worked so hard without complaining. Isatu showed her many women's secrets, such as how to cook meals with oil, salt, leaves, and rice over a fire. Despite their cultural differences, the two became fast friends. Abu even joked that Beth was one of his wives.

Throughout the year, the chief was friendly and even contributed his own male laborers for the heaviest of the work, even if it was only for three days. Beth thought that it was a good token of his interest in the progress of women's rights in the village. Chief Abu Bakar was not one to be taken lightly. He was not pleased with a previous rice project sponsored by a development agency, and he had had enough political power to have the agency thrown out of the chiefdom.

Beth had been away from the village for only two weeks to attend a conference on "Women in Development" when she had received a barely legible letter from Isatu. In it Isatu stated that Abu had hired laborers to harvest the onion crop before it was even fully grown and had sold the crop. He had taken the money and arranged to buy two new wives. Isatu was furious, suspecting that Beth was tricking her and the other women by having planned the whole scheme for Abu's benefit. Beth had written that she would be back early to help work on the problem. Now she was returning to the village.

The meeting was scheduled for three o'clock. Beth pondered her circumstances. What should she do? With whom should she identify? If she refuted the charges of her consorting with the chief and sided with the women, she would not be able to continue the project, because the chief determined all work assignments in his chiefdom. If she chose to side with the chief, then the women would not cooperate with her anymore. Possibly she could be a diplomat and not take sides, trying to facilitate change, but then she might infuriate both sides. As Beth pulled into town, the sweat poured down her forehead, partly from the hundred-degree heat and partly because of the situation she was about to face.

REFLECTION AND DISCUSSION

1. How might Beth best begin her conversations with Isatu and Abu?
2. What experiences have you encountered in which, like Beth, you are seeking to ameliorate a contentious situation fraught with underlying gender-role differences?

Honor and Justice

W hy did the Pharisees and the Sadducees become so angry with Jesus that they eventually plotted to kill him? Many people from Western settings read the Bible and see that in the verbal contests Jesus always won. They can, perhaps, feel the embarrassment of the religious leaders of his day. But why would that become a motivation for killing him? In much of the West, we have lost perspective on an important component of how people relate in other parts of the world.

To understand the anger of the religious leaders of Jesus's day as well as how people negotiate life today in many parts of the world, we need to understand the social "game" that a large majority of the world's peoples play: the game of honor and face. Contemporary biblical scholarship in the last several decades has emphasized the importance of honor in understanding the Bible (e.g., Corrigan 1986; May 1987, 1997; Moxnes 1988, 1993; Bowen 1991; DeSilva 1994, 1996, 1998a, 1998b; Matthews and Benjamin 1994; McVann 1994; Elliott 1995; Pilch 1995; Neyrey 1996; Olyan 1996; Batten 1997; Hellerman 2000, 2003; Landry and May 2000; Gosnell 2006), and we will do well to follow their lead in seeking to better communicate Christian truths, especially in societies that are honor oriented.

In this chapter we focus on three areas. Note that because so much of the world is honor oriented, and we anticipate that those reading this book will tend to be more justice oriented, once we have explained the two orientations we focus on issues of honor orientation for the rest of the chapter. First, we explain the difference between an honor and a justice orientation. Next, we explore the concepts of honor and face by mapping out their meaning, how they are played out, and how people relate to shame and loss of face; we also consider examples from Acts of how these concepts were lived out in New Testament times. Finally, we explore how the concepts of honor and face are embedded in worldview and draw some implications for intercultural communicators who cross from a justice-oriented society to an honor-oriented one.

HONOR AND JUSTICE ORIENTATIONS

In *The Chrysanthemum and the Sword*, Ruth Benedict (1946) notes the difference between cultures that focus on shame and those that focus on guilt. Others, including missiologists, have followed up on this distinction and discuss the major differences between these two orientations (e.g., Hiebert 1985, 212–13; Hesselgrave 1991b, 590–96; Francis 1992).

However, Ruth Lienhard (2001), a missionary with over twenty years of experience in Africa, correctly points out that guilt and shame are but the surface-level behavior of the underlying orientations, which are honor (for shame) and justice (for guilt). She notes the difference between honor and shame: "Honor is a basic cultural value. Shame is a mechanism for punishment and keeping individuals in line" (133). In similar fashion, justice should be understood as a basic cultural value, with guilt as the corresponding mechanism for social conformity.

Honor Orientation

Honor or face (the "social impression that a person wants others to have of him or her"; Lustig and Koester 1996, 253) has two components: (1) a claim to positive worth along with (2) the social acknowledgment of that worth (Crook 2009). Honor is something that the individual recognizes as having. This claim can be made (or acknowledged) only in culturally appropriate ways, and one's claim to honor does not stand alone.

For a person's claim to be acknowledged, his or her in-group must have a positive appreciation (or esteem) of that person (which is more important in collective cultures than in individualistic cultures) (Malina and Neyrey 1991, 45). This element is seen most clearly when people honor their in-group by doing and saying what the in-group members expect of them (they fulfill their in-group obligations) rather than what they may want to do and say. This type

196

of behavior—placing the in-group obligations above personal desires—is a mark of honor societies (see Hiebert 1985, 212–13).

At its core, the concept of honor is a statement of *who a person is*. A person of honor is a worthwhile person; a person who has no honor has no worth in the eyes of his or her culture. Honor is framed in light of the person's in-group (or patron in a patron-client system). It does not matter as much what others think of someone if they are not part of that person's in-group. As mentioned earlier, people in an honor culture are *expected* to favor their in-group members over other people, for it is the in-group that establishes their honor. Therefore, the ideals of conformity are centered on relationships and behaving in ways acceptable to the in-group in concrete settings rather than on some type of absolute and abstract set of rules or standards, and an external locus of control is valued (see chap. 12).

> *Honor is what makes life worthwhile; shame a living death, not to be endured, requiring that it be avenged. What otherwise seems self-destructive in Arab society is explained by the anxiety to be honored and respected at all costs, and by whatever means.*
>
> Pryce-Jones 2002, 35

When a person brings dishonor (or shame) to the in-group, the only way to restore purity or expunge shame is through some type of ritual that will erase the impurity and restore the relationship. What is required depends on the extent of the dishonor involved and may include death (whether at one's own hands or the hands of a member of one's in-group). Christians who live

FIGURE 14.1
HONOR AND JUSTICE ORIENTATIONS

Honor ← → Justice

- Core idea: **what you are**
- In-Group (or patron) is primary focus
- Favor in-group members
- Shame (of self or in-group) controls behavior
- Conformity centered on relationships/behaving in ways acceptable to the in-group
- Restoration to purity comes through ritual to erase defilement or restore relationship

- Core idea: **what you have done**
- Individual is center of focus
- Treat all equally; no favoritism
- Guilt (of self) controls behavior
- Conformity to rules that apply to everyone
- Restoration of guilt comes about through punishment/forgiveness

197

in honor societies will tend to search for ways to be restored to a pure state through cleansing (Heb. 9:14) and restoration of relationship (John 1:12–13) (Francis 1992). They will look for rituals to do this rather than rely on simple declarations of innocence.

Justice Orientation

In contrast to honor, justice does not see the world in terms of personal credit ratings with the in-group. At its core the basic focus in justice-oriented societies is *what a person has done* rather than *who a person is*.

Justice-oriented societies tend to be individualistic rather than collective, so the individual (and his or her deeds) is the focus. As a result, the group has less sway in the life of the individual. What replaces the influence of in-group mores in individualistic cultures is a "blind" system of rules and regulations that applies to everyone in the same way (Hsu 1977). In this blind system, guilty offenders are punished while the shamed are innocent as long as they have not violated the law themselves. As Lienhard notes, "This kind of conformity is centered on rules, not on people or relationships. Keeping the rules is essential for justice to reign. The rules also must be fair; each person must have the same possibilities" (2001, 133).

Thus, in a justice-oriented society people are expected to be treated the same as everyone else, and they value treating others in the same way. Similarly, the established rules are expected to apply to everyone regardless of her or his position in the society. This, of course, is the ideal. The real-life realities of such things as prejudice and economic disparities intrude into this idealistic picture. In the United States, for example, we proclaim, "Liberty and justice for all," but for many minorities the reality is that things are more free and just (and equal) for some than they are for others. Even so, the concept of equal justice for all is idealized in justice-oriented societies such that people believe that the potential for guilt within the individual will act to regulate behavior; thus the development of an internal locus of control is a valued part of the enculturation process for children in these societies.

> *Lying and cheating in much of the Middle Eastern world are not primarily moral matters but ways of safeguarding honor and status, ways of avoiding shame.*
>
> Musk 1996, 75

Once a person has become guilty by breaking a rule or a law, he or she can be restored through acknowledgment of guilt, appropriate punishment, and forgiveness. The goal of those who are guilty—and who experience their guilt—is to find a way to pay the penalty and correct the

198

wrong through justification (Rom. 5:18). This may be accomplished through such things as paying a fine, doing community service, or incarceration. If the crime is deemed significant enough, the individual may be incarcerated for life or even put to death at the hands of the state.

THE HONOR/FACE GAME

We can map out the way in which the "honor/face game" plays out in cultures that rely on the honor code as seen in figure 14.2. At the core is the theme of honor (or face) as a central value in the culture.

Figure 14.2 illustrates three layers that apply in understanding the honor-and-face game. In these societies the idea of honor is a core value at the heart of their worldview. Honor in this sense is a type of social rating that entitles a person to interact in specified ways with equals, superiors, and subordinates, according to the honor rules of the society. It parallels in some respects credit ratings in the United States. Honor ties the in-group together; it creates and maintains unity.

FIGURE 14.2
MAP OF THE HONOR GAME

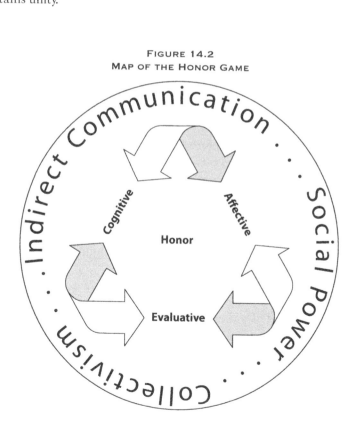

Surrounding the core value of honor are the three dimensions of worldview that we explained in chapter 4 (cognitive, affective, and evaluative). These components are all framed in terms of honor and face. How people think about honor and face, how they feel about them, and how they judge actions or attitudes in light of them are all reflected in their worldview. We will explore this later in the chapter.

Finally, people act out their values of honor and face through the communication means that they value. Though not universally true, the social patterns most often valued by honor cultures are typically collectivism, large power distance, and high-context communication. All three are utilized to build and protect the honor of the in-group. Members may also use these strategies to make people outside their in-group lose face or honor, especially when they consider honor a zero-sum game in which the only way for one to gain honor is to take it from someone else (e.g., see Dzubinski 2008).

How Is Honor Gained or Lost?

ASCRIBED HONOR

A person may have or gain honor in two major ways. First, it may be *ascribed*. Honor can be ascribed because a person is born with a certain family status. Someone may also receive honor as a gift or a grant from a more powerful person. Biblical examples of ascribed honor are seen in the honor that comes through birthright (e.g., Ps. 89:27; Jer. 31:9; Col. 1:15) and the honor that is given by God as a gift to all believers in Christ (Rom. 8:29; Eph. 2:8–9).

Alternatively, a person may have honor taken away—or less honor given— by a more powerful person. In this case it might be because of deception or even simply because of the whim of the more powerful one, for ascribed honor is not gained or lost on the basis of performance. This happened to Joseph when Potiphar was deceived after his wife unsuccessfully tried to seduce Joseph (Gen. 39:6–20); it also appears to have been David's lot in relation to Saul once David had a good reputation among the people of Israel (1 Sam. 18:5–12).

ACHIEVED HONOR

The second means of gaining honor is through *achievement*. A person (and that person's in-group) can achieve honor—or lose it (shame)—through success or failure in accomplishments and/or public challenges by individuals or the in-group. For example, the American who angrily blames a Chinese host makes the host lose face—and this is never forgotten by the host (e.g., Cardon 2006, 441).

In the Bible we see people achieving honor through diligence (Prov. 12:24; 22:29), by obeying God rather than people (Acts 4:18–22), by dying an honorable death (Acts 7:54–60), by acknowledging shame over sin (2 Cor. 2:5–11), and by winning public challenges (Matt. 12:1–14).

It is this last method of achieving honor (or shame) that played such a crucial role in Jesus's relationship with the religious leaders. Public challenges to honor are acted out using social rules that the players know and follow, having learned them in the enculturation process. Typically, there are three main components of this struggle to gain or retain honor: action, perception, and reaction.

The *action* is usually in the form of a challenge: positive, such as a gift, a word of praise, or a request for help; or negative, such as an insult, a threat, or a physical affront. The religious leaders issued these types of challenges to Jesus on a regular basis. They publicly challenged his source of power (saying it was the prince of demons; Matt. 9:34; 12:24), his actions (eating with tax collectors and sinners; Matt. 9:11), his disciples' actions (picking grain on the Sabbath; Matt. 12:1–2; and eating with unwashed hands; Mark 7:1–3), and tried to trap him with vexing questions: "Is it right to divorce for any and every reason?" (Matt 19:3); and "Is it right to pay taxes to Caesar or not?" (Matt. 22:15–17).

How a challenge is *perceived*, both by the individual challenged and the witnessing public, is also important. If no one even knows it is a challenge, it can be ignored. However, when everyone recognizes it as a public challenge, then it cannot be ignored without the one being challenged losing face in public. Jesus's response to the accusations directed at the woman caught in adultery is a powerful example of initial silence and refusal to respond to the challenge until those who brought her to him were in a position of greatest exposure and thus most vulnerable to shaming. While this built her up publicly (or at least did not bring her down any further), Jesus also dealt with her needs by confronting her privately once her accusers had all lost face and left (John 8:1–11).

Last, based on the perception comes the *reaction* to the challenge. There are three types of reactions to a challenge of honor (May 1997).

The first possible reaction is a *positive rejection* of the challenge, usually found in the form of disdain or contempt for the challenge or the one offering it. When the Pharisees asked Jesus to give them a sign, he simply refused, noting that nothing would be given to this generation (Mark 8:11–13).

A second type of response is the *acceptance* of the challenge, which brings about a counterchallenge. When challenged that his disciples ate with hands that had not been ceremonially washed, Jesus turned the language around on his accusers, as noted in Mark's Gospel: "'You have let go of the commands of God and are holding on to human traditions.' And he continued, 'You have a fine way of setting aside the commands of God in order to observe your own traditions!'" (Mark 7:8–9).

A third type of response is a *negative refusal*, which is no response to the challenge. Amounting to a tacit admission of shame, it is typically considered shameful for the one challenged to ignore the challenge. This is why it is so important in honor cultures for the one challenged to respond. We see this type of response when Jesus stood at his trial before Pilate (Mark 15:3–5) and refused to answer the charges laid against him. His lack of response exasperated Pilate and ultimately led to Jesus's condemnation.

Shame: Honor's Contrast and Protector

Shame—loss of face—accrues when one has behaved in ways that run contrary to the values of the group. For example, John Mark abandoned Paul and Barnabas on their missionary journey and was deemed by Paul not fit to go again. Barnabas—related to John Mark—had to defend his honor (Acts 13:13; 15:36–40). However, shame can also be a positive reinforcer when it is built on sensitivity to the opinion of the group such that one avoids actions that bring disgrace. For example, the Corinthians would have been ashamed that one of their own was sleeping with his father's wife (1 Cor. 5:2) had their sense of shame been working appropriately.

> *Muslims live in this biblical world of a shame/honor dialectic. The word* sharif *(honor) is a common name for males throughout the Muslim world. The word for shame (*ayb*) is a dirty garment to be cast off by every effort. Women must acquire and maintain honor for the whole family; otherwise, they bring disgrace, which only their deaths may erase.*
>
> Blincoe 2001, 19

Shame can accrue to a person by someone noting a negative birthright (e.g., when Jesus tells the Pharisees "You belong to your father, the devil"; John 8:44). It can also be declared by Jesus (Mark 8:38) or the church (1 Cor. 5:1–5) over erring individuals. People can also incur shame through shameful actions (Acts 5:1–11; 1 Cor. 5:9–11; Phil. 3:19) or by a loss of face in a public challenge (a typical method to gain face over an opponent; Mark 7:1–16).

What happens when someone loses too much face? Hiebert notes:

> Those who fail will often turn their aggression against themselves instead of using violence against others. By punishing themselves they maintain their self-respect

before others, for shame cannot be relieved, as guilt can be, by confession and atonement. Shame is removed and honor restored only when a person does what the society expects of him or her in the situation, including committing suicide if necessary. (1985, 212)

This is not universally true, however. In many Middle Eastern cultures when a person and that person's in-group have been shamed, members of the in-group may be obligated to use violence against those who brought the shame (Blincoe 2001). For example, women who have been sexually unfaithful are subject to what are called "honor" killings by their own family members as a means of restoring honor to the family (see sidebar 14.1 for another example of this type of response to shame).

The biblical vocabulary of honor and face includes terms such as "glory" (1 Tim. 1:17), "reputation" (1 Tim. 3:7), "honor" (Exod. 20:12), and "praise" and "fame" (Deut. 26:19). Biblical vocabulary for shame includes terms such as "dishonor" (Lev. 18:7), "contempt" (Ps. 79:4), "ridicule" (Deut. 28:37), "shame" (Deut. 32:5), and "slander" (Jer. 6:28).

SIDEBAR 14.1
EXAMPLE OF SHAME AS NEGATIVE AND POSITIVE

Shame can be seen in the following Old Testament passage. Jonathan is (falsely) shamed in Saul's eyes (and therefore loses face before Saul) for siding with David (negative shame). At the same time, however, Jonathan is grieved over Saul's shameful behavior and his understanding of Saul's real shame prevents him from also acting shamefully (shame as a positive motivator).

Saul's anger flared up at Jonathan and he said to him, "You son of a perverse and rebellious woman! Don't I know that you have sided with the son of Jesse to your own shame and to the shame of the mother who bore you? As long as the son of Jesse lives on this earth, neither you nor your kingdom will be established. Now send someone to bring him to me, for he must die!"

"Why should he be put to death? What has he done?" Jonathan asked his father. But Saul hurled his spear at him to kill him. Then Jonathan knew that his father intended to kill David.

Jonathan got up from the table in fierce anger; on that second day of the month he did not eat, because he was grieved at his father's shameful treatment of David. (1 Sam. 20:30–34)

REFLECTION AND DISCUSSION

1. Why did Saul throw his spear at Jonathan? What role do honor and shame play in that action?
2. What did Jonathan's mother have to do with the issue of shame?
3. Why, in Saul's eyes, did Jonathan's transgression of siding with David bring shame to Saul?

It is truly good news for people from honor cultures to realize that Jesus endured shame for us, as noted in Hebrews 12:1–3 (see DeSilva 1994):

> Therefore, since we are surrounded by such a great cloud of witnesses, let us throw off everything that hinders and the sin that so easily entangles. And let us run with perseverance the race marked out for us, fixing our eyes on Jesus, the pioneer and perfecter of faith. For the joy set before him endured the cross, scorning its shame, and sat down at the right hand of the throne of God. Consider him who endured such opposition from sinners, so that you will not grow weary and lose heart.

Further, Peter notes that we can count it an honor to bear shame in Christ's name (1 Pet. 4:13–16; see Elliott 1995):

> But rejoice inasmuch as you participate in the sufferings of Christ, so that you may be overjoyed when his glory is revealed. If you are insulted because of the name of Christ, you are blessed, for the Spirit of glory and of God rests on you. If you suffer, it should not be as a murderer or thief or any other kind of criminal, or even as a meddler. However, if you suffer as a Christian, do not be ashamed, but praise God that you bear that name.

Jesus is also very clear about the ultimacy of shame at the time of the judgment: "If anyone is ashamed of me and my words in this adulterous and sinful generation, the Son of Man will be ashamed of them when he comes in his Father's glory with the holy angels" (Mark 8:38).

HONOR EMBEDDED IN WORLDVIEW

If we want to understand how discipleship works in cross-cultural settings, we need to understand how people connect in cultures that deeply value honor and face and take shame very seriously. For that, we need to briefly explain how they value honor and face in the ways they connect with one another by exploring their local worldviews. As we noted in chapter 4, all worldviews have three primary components: the cognitive, the affective, and the evaluative (Hiebert 2008b). Figure 14.2 illustrates how these "surround" the concept of honor and enable people within the culture to live lives that value honor. The *cognitive* component of worldview includes what the people know about honor, especially the rules and regulations for maintaining, increasing, or losing it. The *affective* component involves their emotional attachment and stability in relation to honor and shame. It is how they feel about gaining face, and how they experience shame or other negative emotions. Finally, the *evaluative* component involves their moral decision-making rules about how to evaluate actions and attitudes that lead to increase or decrease of honor, such as what are appropriate and inappropriate ways to defend face when it is threatened.

Worldview: Cognitive

In justice-oriented societies, people focus on the idea that "all have sinned," while in honor-oriented societies people focus on the idea that "all fall short of the glory of God" (all are defiled and without face; see T. Chuang 1996; Strand 2000). Restoration in a justice-oriented worldview is based on how to pay the penalty and correct the wrong, whereas restoration in an honor-oriented worldview is based on how one can be restored to a pure state.

> *How can we "fix" the problem of face? If we accept that face is a fact, and engage it not as an issue to eliminate but to reorient in cruciform ways, we are well on our way. By orienting face with reference to God, we can help bring about the type of face and facework that are both culturally appropriate and glorify God.*
>
> Flanders 2009, 19

As noted earlier, in justice-oriented societies guilt (of the self) controls behavior; thus conformity is centered on rules that apply equally to everyone. These rules can be abstracted from context as principles that apply across contexts. In these cultures members idealize treating everyone as an equal, and it is considered wrong to give in-group (or family) members preferential treatment. Thus many organizations in justice cultures will have policies regarding nepotism, which is considered wrong.

By way of contrast, in honor-oriented societies, shame (of the self or of the in-group) controls behavior, and conformity is centered on relationships and behaving in ways acceptable to the in-group. Thus, actions (and how they are evaluated) are always seen in their contexts. For example, in honor cultures a

> *Shame is a reaction to other people's criticism of self or in-group, an acute personal chagrin at our failure to live up to our obligations and the expectations others have of us. It is not limited to our actions, but affects our person.*
>
> *In true shame-oriented cultures, every person has a place and a duty in the society. One maintains self-respect not by choosing what is good rather than what is evil, but by choosing what is expected of one. Personal desires are sunk in the collective expectation.*
>
> Hiebert 1985, 212–13

person's own in-group is more important to him than the rest of society, so it will be important for him to favor his own in-group members and treat those not of his in-group as people of lower importance.

Worldview: Affective

The affective dynamic in a worldview is typically played out in myths and stories found in the culture. Heroes in literature and other media in honor-oriented settings live out rules of honor and shame through appropriate ritual action. In some settings, whether the hero lives or dies is immaterial (unlike in the West)—as long as the hero lives or dies honorably.

For example, the movie *Jesus Is My Boss* (2001) is a wonderful portrayal of a member of the Japanese *yakuza* (Mafia) who comes to Christ. Being from an honor-oriented culture, he is unable to imagine a simple forensic transaction of Jesus on the cross. As a result, he chooses to walk across Japan carrying a heavy cross, announcing that he is a sinner as a sign of his repentance for being part of such a shameful group as the *yakuza*. While it is true that Christ paid the complete penalty for his sin, it is also true that this man was unable to feel the connection to that truth without a concrete demonstration of his own shame before others. Simply offering a prayer to accept Christ was not enough for him to connect to what Christ had done on his behalf. He had to work through a ritual that demonstrated he was a changed person who was willing to endure shame to be restored to a relationship with God through Christ. The proverbs of honor and shame in sidebar 14.2 illustrate from a variety of cultures the sense of honor and how it is developed as well as the shame that comes with transgression.

Worldview: Evaluative

The evaluative dynamic is framed in terms of how actions and beliefs are evaluated as good or bad. Those from a justice-oriented culture will search

---

SIDEBAR 14.2
PROVERBS OF HONOR AND SHAME

Fools show their annoyance at once, but the prudent overlook an insult. (Prov. 12:16)

A courageous foe is better than a cowardly friend. (Chinese)

When the tree falls, any child can climb it. (Vietnamese)

Better to die than to live on with a bad reputation. (Vietnamese)

A thousand people bear one's fault. (Uighur)

The voice of a poor man does not carry very far. (Laotian)

---

for how they as the guilty individuals pay the penalty and correct the wrong. Their restoration of honor comes about through punishment and forgiveness. They have a deep appreciation for the concept of justification (Rom. 5:18) as the theological answer for guilt, as well as an intuitive connection to the penal substitutionary view of the atonement (that we deserved judgment and Christ took the penalty that belonged to us by dying on the cross). It is not surprising that in Western evangelical tradition this view of atonement is often deemed the most central.

However, those from an honor-oriented culture will search for the means by which they as shamed or unclean individuals can be cleansed or restored. Their restoration comes through some type of ritual for cleansing or restoration. They have a deep appreciation for the concepts of cleansing (Heb. 9:14) and restoration to a relationship (John 1:12–13) as the theological answers to their shame (Francis 1992). The atonement views that they intuitively resonate with are the moral view (Christ won a moral—i.e., honorable—victory over Satan) and Christus Victor (Christ was victorious over the powers of evil). This orientation does not deny penal substitution, but it does not resonate with it as much as with the moral or Christus Victor views.

CONCLUSION

Marvin Mayers has proposed that we ask what he calls the prior question of trust: "Is what I am doing, thinking or saying building or undermining trust?" (1974, 7). This is a crucial question, but we can best answer it when we understand how trust is built. In honor societies, it is built by maintaining

---

SIDEBAR 14.3
SELECTED WEB RESOURCES ON HONOR AND JUSTICE ORIENTATIONS

Beyond Intractability articles: Face (http://www.beyondintractability.org/essay/face/); Guilt and Shame (http://www.beyondintractability.org/essay/guilt_shame)

Face Saving (International Online Training Program on Intractable Conflict; Conflict Research Consortium; http://www.colorado.edu/conflict/peace/treatment/facesavr.htm)

"The Gospel for Shame Cultures: A Paradigm Shift," by Bruce Thomas (http://www.internetevangelismday.com/shame-cultures.php)

Shame Culture and Guilt Culture (http://www.doceo.co.uk/background/shame_guilt.htm)

Wikipedia articles: Face (http://en.wikipedia.org/wiki/Face_%28social_concept%29); Honor (http://en.wikipedia.org/wiki/Honor)

the face or honor of those with whom you interact and by keeping yourself pure in ways that make sense to them. Perhaps we need to add a corollary: "Is what I am doing, thinking, or saying building or undermining honor or face?" This is especially important for those who come from justice-oriented cultures ministering in honor-oriented cultures. Our case study for this chapter is a dilemma involving obligations to family, including honor and face.

CASE STUDY:
WHAT PRICE THE GOSPEL?

CARL K. KINOSHITA

Reprinted with permission from Hiebert and Hiebert (1987, 186–87).

At exactly the appointed hour, Second Lieutenant Seichi Miyazaki knocked on the office door of Carter Jackson, pastor of the Kalakaua Baptist Church. With military discharge only eight months away, Seichi needed the pastor's advice on a decision crucial to his future.

In the over thirty years he had been a pastor and missionary in China and Hawaii, Jackson had counseled many men about entering the Christian ministry. From what he had learned about Seichi since they first met three years ago, Jackson did not think the decision would be difficult to make. After all, the twenty-two-year-old Air Force officer had made good grades in college, was popular as a Sunday school teacher and counselor of junior-age boys, and was an active leader in the young people's department of the church. And although Seichi had been a Christian and church member for just over two and a half years, more than a few members had expressed their feeling that he should consider the ministry as a vocation.

Seichi and Jackson had talked about all of these things two months earlier. But today the more information Seichi shared about his family, the more Jackson understood the reason for the worried look on the young man's face. These were some of the data Seichi gave his pastor. . . . He was the first of seven children born to Kazuo and Matsue Miyazaki and was raised on Molaka, a small island of predominantly Japanese and Filipino people who worked for the most part as laborers for the Del Monte Pineapple Company on the island of Oahu. He was taken to the Buddhist temple most Sundays until his years at the high school he attended in Honolulu on the island of Oahu. At this point in his story, Seichi stressed the fact that his mother started working in the pineapple fields to help pay for his education at Lolani School, a private, college-prep, boarding institution. Upon finishing there, Seichi had enrolled at the University of Hawaii and lived with an aunt in Honolulu. In the meantime, his family moved to Kahjaluu, a rural community on Oahu, and leased five acres of land for truck farming. But when heavy rains ruined the crops on two consecutive years and put Mr. Miyazaki near bankruptcy, Seichi decided to drop out of college, find a full-time job, and help his family financially. But Mr. Miyazaki insisted that Seichi remain in school in pursuit of a business administration degree, an order impossible to disobey after being reminded of three facts: (1) for a quarter of a century Seichi's father (whose own parents had died while he was still in his teens) had dreamed of running a family-owned store; (2) the second son, Fumio, who was a year younger than Seichi, was born mentally retarded; and (3) the last son and youngest child, Hitoshi, was also showing signs of mental retardation.

Relating the incident of two weeks ago was most painful for Seichi. His mother's father had died, and a Buddhist funeral service was held at the Kukui Mortuary. At the part of the service when family members and, later, everyone else in attendance were asked to light the incense sticks, Seichi had refused to participate. What he did out of a strongly felt loyalty to Christ resulted in severe criticism of his parents by relatives. And that, Seichi said, had hurt him deeply.

Until today, Pastor Jackson had known very few of these details. Now he realized that no longer was Seichi's dilemma just a matter of discovering God's call to a Christian vocation.

REFLECTION AND DISCUSSION

1. Do you agree with Seichi's decision to refuse participation? Explain your answer.
2. How might Pastor Jackson help the young man sort out the conflicting demands on his loyalty in a way that would be true to his Christian commitment?

Part 4

Developing Intercultural Expertise

xpertise is a strong word. Unfortunately, it is not often associated with missionaries in terms of intercultural communication. In part 1, we explored whether this reputation was justified. In this section, we explore what it takes to put into practice those things discussed in parts 2 and 3.

The foundations have been set, but putting them into practice and becoming a competent communicator involve more than just laying the foundation. For example, what steps actually need to be taken in order to adjust to a new culture? We explore this and related questions in chapter 15.

Why are some people more competent in language and culture learning than others? Just what does it take to develop competence in intercultural communication? Adjustment to the new culture was the first step; in chapter 16 we look at the next step of developing competence in the new cultural setting.

As followers of Christ, we cannot shrink from the responsibility we have to walk in obedience to his commands. Crucial to our ability to communicate Christ clearly in a new cultural setting is the ability to develop healthy relationships with people who are culturally different from us. This forms the basis of the discussion in chapter 17.

However, our relationships are not just for their own sake. The Christian engages in relationships as a result of her or his desire to reach people for Christ. What does that look like when those people are of a different culture? What issues do we need to take into account when trying to share the good news of Christ in ways that make sense in another culture? We explore these and related questions in chapter 18.

Beyond that, we want to see people grow to maturity in Christ. What does intercultural discipleship entail? How can we disciple people to be faithful to Christ in their own culture without simply remaking them into what we think a follower of Christ should be like? These issues are our focus in chapter 19.

Even more significant is ensuring that new believers in local cultures are connecting with one another in growing, vibrant fellowships or churches. What lessons from intercultural communication can church planters and developers learn to help them be more effective in building local Christ-centered bodies of believers who are engaging their own culture in light of the gospel? All these are crucial questions that are the focus of chapter 20.

To close out this part of the book, we have chosen three specific areas in which intercultural communication offers significant help to today's cross-cultural Christian: teaching, team formation, and conflict management.

Many who go to a new culture go as teachers or trainers. Even if that is not their focus, the process of becoming like Christ involves knowing how to teach and how people in different cultural settings prefer to learn. We examine what is involved in this process in chapter 21.

A recent trend, and one that seems sure to grow, is having people be part of teams in intercultural settings. More and more these teams are themselves multicultural. What does it take to build a strong team in which the gifts of its members are properly channeled into ministry for Christ? In chapter 22 we offer helpful ideas.

Inevitably conflict will be part of everyone's intercultural experience. Knowing how to engage in conflict in ways that are appropriate to Scripture and local culture is a challenging task. Therefore, in chapter 23 we discuss what is involved in dealing with conflict.

Finally, to close the book, in chapter 24 we briefly examine the future of intercultural communication. How can the discipline help Christians serve more effectively wherever God leads them? What further insights—and challenges—might we expect for and from the discipline in the years ahead? We hope you find the discussion as helpful as it is hopeful!

15

Cultural Adaptation

O ne of the significant elements that people who embark on short-term trips inevitably miss is the reality of cultural adaptation. While they may perceive themselves as going through a type of adaptation process, it is one thing to adapt when you know your sojourn will be for a month or less, but it is something else altogether when you realize that you have years ahead of you rather than weeks or months.

Most people who have undergone the process of cultural adaptation (also called acculturation or adjustment) recognize that it is not something that happens all at once. Rather, it is a process that requires emotional as well as intellectual adjustments. The mental earthquakes that are typically part of it are referred to as culture shock, and there is a wealth of literature on the entire process of adjustment as well as the attendant processes related to culture shock (e.g., Bochner and Furnham 1986; Steffen and McKinney Douglas 2008, 203–7). In this chapter we focus on the practical side

Adjustment to cross-cultural living is very stressful. For the missionary, this cross-cultural stress is also compounded by the stress of many life changes and the stress of very high expectations due to the missionary role. It is no surprise that many individuals exhibit abnormal behavior when subjected to missionary work.

Loss 1983, 113

of adjusting to a new culture (e.g., Sauter 2010), including the phases of cultural adaptation, the realities of culture shock, and strategies that help us to cope with the process.

PHASES OF CULTURAL ADAPTATION

While no two individuals experience cultural adaptation in the same way or for exactly the same duration, the full process is usually seen as a four-phase cycle (the following discussion draws from Kohls 1976, 64–68) that will take anywhere from several months to more than a year to complete. The four stages include (1) initial euphoria, (2) irritability and hostility, (3) gradual adjustment, and (4) adaptation. The actual time for any individual to reach the fourth stage will vary, depending on both the person and the amount of difference between home and host cultures. The process of adapting to a new cultural setting involves weathering the phases of culture shock, though even after culture shock is over, we must continue to live with the realities of ongoing stress—sometimes for years to come (Dye 1976, 61).

Initial Euphoria

In this initial phase, everything in the new culture is wonderful, curious, exotic, and exciting. There are a million things to learn, and each learning experience can be made into a game. Every day is full of discoveries about the culture, and each discovery opens a new door for further exploration. It is no wonder that this is called "the honeymoon phase"! While there is genuine wonder and excitement in this stage, in reality you are incompetent in the new culture, but (except for language) largely unaware of just how incompetent you are. It is the stage of unconscious incompetence.

Irritability and Hostility

Sooner or later the differences you see in your new culture lose their appeal, and you begin to resent that you never really feel "comfortable" or "relaxed." You long for items or circumstances that remind you of home. You experience events that make you uncomfortable or even angry. This is the beginning of culture shock.

CRITICAL INCIDENTS

All too often we do not have the time to simply observe everything that takes place around us. First, it happens too quickly. Second, and perhaps more important, even our observations are biased, for they are built on what we

214

were trained to observe as we were enculturated. However, there are times when observations of a negative kind are unavoidable. These occur when we are blindsided by something that we do not expect. Such events are called cultural (Storti 1990) or critical incidents:

> Critical incidents often revolve around a misunderstanding, a dispute, a linguistic error, or some other kind of cultural *faux pas*. They are the sorts of events that highlight different cultural assumptions and values. They are about attitudes and behaviors that might (read "probably will") be interpreted in different ways by different people, particularly when people from different cultural backgrounds interact. Thus, they help illustrate why you need to be aware of multiple cultural contexts in order to make sense of what happens between people when something goes wrong cross-culturally. Often what we consider "common sense" is seen in other cultures as neither common nor making much sense! And "just acting naturally" is seldom good enough or effective for very long as an adjustment strategy. (La Brack n.d.)

Craig Storti distinguishes these situations into two types of incidents (1990, 15–24). A type 1 incident is one in which the sojourner is baffled, unsettled, or offended by something a person in the host culture has done. A type 2 incident is one in which the sojourner baffles, unsettles, or offends those of the host culture. As a sojourner, you will be very aware of the type 1 incidents, while you might be completely unaware of the type 2 incidents unless a host-culture person explains to you what you have done.

In this phase of cultural adaptation, the type 1 incidents impact you on a regular basis. Even when they are relatively small, they are constant reminders that you are a stranger who does not know the (local) rules of living. Together, the type 1 incidents that you experience in the early time of your sojourn are part of the process of *culture shock*. It would be nice to think that these incidents would end

The finding in this study of the high level of dogmatism among missionaries, and the inverse relationship between dogmatism and effective cross-cultural communication-adaptation, suggests a need for considering this factor in the selection of missionary candidates. The gospel is not credited by being proclaimed by missionaries who hardly respect or value their host culture.

Goring 1991, 70

once the stage of culture shock has passed, but as long as you are still learning the culture—which will take years—they will be part of the reality of your life in the new culture.

Culture Shock

The term "culture shock" was initially coined by anthropologist Kalervo Oberg to describe a syndrome he regularly saw among Americans coming to live in Brazil, where he helped to orient American technicians and their families to Brazilian society. He called the sequence of behavior, from initial excitement through frustration and eventual recovery, "culture shock" (McComb and Foster 1974, 359; see also Oberg 1960). The term has been used since then to describe a critical component of this second phase of adjustment that people experience when they move from one culture to another. For some the experience is barely noticeable; for others it is so debilitating that they end up leaving the new culture and returning home. Most of us are somewhere between these two extremes.

Culture shock occurs simply because of the process it takes to learn to live in another culture. In a new cultural setting, everything is different, from greetings (whether or how to shake hands or bow) to buying groceries, knowing how to drive by local customs and laws, using public transportation, and getting a doctor's appointment. Sometimes it seems that every activity that you "know" from your home culture has a different set of rules for behavior in your new culture, and the normal cues you rely on to guide your behavior—facial expressions, gestures, language—are all different as well. At first this may be exciting, but eventually it becomes wearing. The frustrations with daily life add up, and eventually the total effect can be overwhelming.

SIDEBAR 15.1
WHAT IS CULTURE SHOCK?

Robert Kohls (1976, 63) notes two distinctive features of culture shock:

1. It does not result from a specific event or series of events. It comes instead from the experience of encountering ways of doing, organizing, perceiving or valuing things which are different from yours and which threaten your basic, unconscious belief that your enculturated customs, assumptions, values and behaviors are "right."

2. It does not strike suddenly or have a single principal cause. Instead it is cumulative. It builds up slowly, from a series of small events which are difficult to identify.

REFLECTION AND DISCUSSION

Based on Kohls's features, what questions might you ask someone who thinks that he is experiencing culture shock?

Symptoms of culture shock (see, e.g., Oberg 1960, 176; Smalley 1963, 51–53; and Kohls 1976, 65) include loneliness, anger, and anxiety. Symptoms can also show up in physical ways, such as sleeping problems, eating problems, and lack of energy. People may act differently as well; they may withdraw or become more aggressive or overly concerned with issues such as cleanliness and safety. Some feel homesick and have a corresponding loss of identity, while others disparage much of what they encounter in the new culture and perhaps cluster in an "expatriate ghetto" as a result (Taber 1983b, 193), and still others overidentify with the new culture by believing that everything there is superior to their home culture.

Typically people may undergo more than one phase of culture shock. This is a natural part of the cycle of adjusting to a new culture and should be expected. "It can be an important aspect of cultural learning, self-development and personal growth" (Adler 1975, 14). The most important consideration is not *whether* you will experience some form of culture shock but *how you will cope* with it. We offer several suggestions later in the chapter.

Gradual Adjustment

If you persist, you will eventually begin to change how you view the local culture. You start behaving as you see locals behaving: eating not just what they eat but the way they eat it, waiting (or not) for service the way they do, and driving as they do. You have started the process of being oriented to the new ways of living. These ways are no longer new and fascinating (or repugnant). Instead, they begin to feel normal. You have a much better understanding of what people really mean by what they say. You are starting to feel comfortable in responding to compliments and insults and are not offended by the questions you are asked or the stares you receive, and so on. Life has a quality of normalcy once again, though it is a new normalcy in which you begin to feel that you are coming to understand the culture in ways that make sense to you.

Adaptation

In this phase, the new way of life has become your normal way of life. There is no real sense of transition between the prior stage and this one; it is just that you suddenly realize that life as a whole in the new setting now seems completely normal to you—perhaps through the questions asked of you by newcomers from your home culture who are still baffled by what they are experiencing! You have not forgotten your previous cultural patterns; you simply operate in the new culture without having to think through things in the

SIDEBAR 15.2
FAILURES IN ADJUSTING

Kohls (1976, 54)

A survey taken of non-Americans who had worked with American experts on a variety of projects revealed the following common complaints about the American experts:

1. They display feelings of superiority; they know the answers to everything.
2. They want to take credit for what is accomplished in *joint* efforts.
3. They are frequently unable or unwilling to respect and adjust to local customs and cultures.
4. They fail to innovate in terms of the needs of the *local* culture.
5. They refuse to work through the normal administrative channels of the country.
6. They tend to lose their democratic ways of working and acting when in a foreign assignment.

REFLECTION AND DISCUSSION

1. How might the list change, if at all, if the survey had been asked about Christians working with American missionaries?
2. Identify the one or two behaviors that you might have the greatest tendency to exhibit. What are some constructive steps you can take to lessen your tendency to act this way?

same way anymore. The various life patterns in the new culture may feel better, worse, or the same as your old ones, but you have learned to live them out.

STRATEGIES FOR CULTURAL ADAPTATION

The work it takes to adjust to a new culture, especially accounting for culture shock, makes it clear that those who have coping strategies in mind prior

> *We speak of cultural adjustment, but in fact it is not to culture that we adjust but to behavior. Culture, a system of beliefs and values shared by a particular group of people, is an abstraction that can be appreciated intellectually, but it is behavior, the principal manifestation and most significant consequence of culture, that we actually experience. To put it another way: it is culture as encountered in behavior that we must learn to live with.*
>
> Storti 1990, 14, emphasis in original

to their sojourn will be better equipped to handle the stresses that arise. A helpful metaphor to follow in understanding the adaptation process is seeing Christians in cross-cultural service as cultural pilgrims (Dean 2012). As you examine each of the three following sections, it will help to keep the idea of a cultural pilgrim in mind.

Prescription for Culture Shock

Robert Kohls offers five positive steps you can take to work your way through culture shock (1976, 69–70). The first is to pursue knowing your host country and culture as well as you can. This is more than just a distraction; it lays a foundation for getting past culture shock as you find explanations for the things that baffle and/or frustrate you. Once things begin to make sense to you, your footing will solidify and your reactions can subside.

Based on what you learn, the second step is to *"look for logical reasons* behind everything in the host culture which seems strange, difficult, confusing, or threatening" (Kohls 1976, 69, emphasis in original). Kohls notes that even if your explanations are not correct, your search for them offers you the chance to recognize that people act as they do for reasons that make sense to them. Eventually you should be able to accept that the customs and behaviors you see are "right" in their own setting, even if you can never reach the stage of accepting them in such a way that you yourself practice what initially offended you (see Dye 1974, 66–67).

Third, avoid the temptation to disparage or otherwise talk negatively about your host culture. Expressing such thoughts can lead into a self-feeding cycle, especially when talking to other expatriates who do not understand the local culture well or who have already developed a negative attitude toward local customs. The ability to withhold inappropriate criticism is an important one to develop, and it may mean you have to avoid those who engage in it, simply to prevent yourself from following their lead.

We should add to Kohls's point that emotional security is essential if we are to avoid inappropriate criticism during our adjustment to a new culture. Wayne Dye offers a helpful perspective:

> Emotional security requires self-acceptance and self-forgiveness. But both of these must begin with self-awareness, because one's unconscious mind is constantly reacting to one's limitations and past failures. . . . Genuine self-acceptance recognizes and finds a way to live with these limitations. Self-forgiveness deliberately quits accusing or punishing oneself for these failures. For Christians this can be achieved by a deep awareness of God's forgiveness. Participating in sharing

> *Personally modeling the way of the cross of Christ rather than our home culture may be the greatest* cross-cultural challenge *missionaries face. We can claim to be* cross-cultural *missionaries if we attempt enculturation in a new place. But we can only claim to be* cross-cultural *missionaries if we consistently model the unique values of Jesus Christ. This* cross-cultural challenge *is infinitely harder than language learning and acculturation and even more vital to communicating Christ to those who do not know him.*
>
> Dent 2005, 315, emphasis in original

groups with these purposes and confession have both helped many people become emotionally secure.

One can also be strengthened by encouragement and other supportive measures from one's colleagues. Receiving understanding and love are especially valuable when one's inner self seems to be under attack, as it does during adjustment to a new culture. (Dye 1974, 75)

Fourth, Kohls recommends finding a host national with whom you can talk about what you have experienced and your feelings about those experiences. As you explain things from your perspective in a healthy way—without becoming judgmental—you provide the national the opportunity to explain in a way that puts things in perspective for you.

Kohls's fifth recommendation is to have faith in yourself and in the essential goodwill of your hosts. As Christians we can reframe this to recognize that God's hand is present in all circumstances we encounter, and the Spirit can lead us to recognize the goodness in what happens even when the outcomes are not what we may have preferred (see also suggestions in sidebar 15.3).

Coping Strategies

Educator and intercultural specialist Ted Ward (1984) notes that much of our adjustment in the intercultural setting is accomplished not through knowing more but through developing an appropriate set of coping strategies that enable us to absorb the shocks of living in a new culture. He stresses three primary strategies: empathy, observation, and exploration.

Empathy is critical for passing from the second to the third phase of cultural adjustment. Empathy does not come from simply trying to identify with what we see around us. It takes emotional connection, understanding

220

the local worldview, and the ability to frame the actions of others in ways that make sense to them rather than ways that make sense to you. As followers of Christ, how we relate to others is the foundation for competency in cross-cultural encounters, and your ability to relate to them in healthy ways necessitates that you understand the world as they do. Ultimately the answers to questions such as "Do I trust _____?" and "Can I accept help from _____?" will in large part depend on your ability to empathize with those of your new culture.

To *observe* you simply need to look around at what is happening. This will be harder than you may think, because your observation skills were developed in your own cultural setting, and much of what happens around you is constantly filtered. As Kohls notes, "We are selective in what we perceive. . . . In fact, most of what we are seeing, hearing, tasting or feeling at any moment is screened out by our conscious minds" (1976, 58). It should be evident that observing is an important coping strategy; learning how and what to observe in the new cultural setting will itself be a learning process. One tactic you will need to employ early in your sojourn is to delay your snap judgments because so many of them are built on your enculturated reading of what is happening around you, and that reading is far more likely to be wrong in your new cultural setting than at home.

Based upon personal experience, numerous contacts with missionaries representing many missions and many fields, and extensive reading of relevant literature, I estimate that only about one out of four missionaries function at a level near to that which was normal in their home culture.

Loss 1983, 3

After the initial shock of everything being new and feeling overwhelmed by different sensory data, do we respond by withdrawal or by maintaining an observer's attitude? Do we assume that things are the same everywhere and filter out significant clues in our contexts? How much attention do we give to details?

Finally, we must be willing to *explore* by trial and error the things we have observed. This can be harder for people who are not natural risk takers. We recommend that you find ways to try out your hunches, rather than withdraw as a passive participant. For those who are more comfortable taking risks, these attempts must be tempered with the willingness to see your explorations for what they are: tentative attempts to move in line with the things you have observed in order to fit into and more fully understand the new culture.

SIDEBAR 15.3
TIPS FOR SURVIVAL FOR NEW CROSS-CULTURAL WORKERS

Adapted from Loss (1983, 85–101)

Myron Loss suggests the following fifteen tips for survival for those who are living in a new cultural setting:

1. Set reasonable goals.
2. Don't take your job description too seriously.
3. Be committed to joy.
4. Maintain good emotional health.
5. Remember that you are human.
6. Don't be afraid to be a little bit eccentric.
7. Be flexible.
8. Don't take yourself too seriously.
9. Reduce your stress where possible.
10. Make your culture change gradual.
11. Forgive yourself; forgive others.
12. Establish some close friendships with people from the host culture.
13. Be thankful.
14. Be an encourager.
15. Take courage, someone (Jesus) understands.

REFLECTION AND DISCUSSION

1. Identify which tip you think might be the most important for you and why.
2. This list was written before the internet age. How might having instant access to loved ones, friends, and supporting churches through email, Skype, or instant messaging change the list?

The Field Observation Cycle

The Field Observation Cycle, used as part of advanced individual training by Campus Crusade for Christ, now known as CRU, expands on Ward's observation and exploration steps. Designed initially as a four-step process for systematically analyzing any particular component of culture, it also gives a person a coping mechanism to handle the stresses and strains involved in adapting.

The first step is to *observe*, following the advice given above. As an example to illustrate the Field Observation Cycle, imagine that you observe that people rarely look each other in the eyes even when speaking directly to each other.

The second step is to *assume*: make some assumptions about what you see. Why do people avoid eye contact when talking, when in your culture it is important to look each other in the eyes while talking? In this case, you may decide to assume that direct eye contact is impolite in your new culture, even though you do not know why this is so.

The third step is to *validate*. Your goal is to validate your observation about behavior you have noticed. This can be done in more than one way. For example, you may ask a cultural informant about it, or you might research your observation on the web, at a local bookstore or library, or by asking someone who has been in the country longer than you. Be sure to consult more than one source, and bear in mind that your observation of the action (not looking each other directly in the eyes while talking) may be substantiated even if no clear explanation can be found. After all, people in every culture of the world know *how* responsible adults should behave even if they do not always know *why* they should behave that way.

The fourth step is to *apply* what you have validated. Apply your newfound cultural knowledge in the cultural setting. In the example we have used, you can begin to cultivate the practice of looking away from the eyes of the person with whom you talk. You may find it strange or even uncomfortable at first, but as you persist you may experience a whole new level of conversation that had previously escaped you because of your behavior.

REENTRY OR REVERSE CULTURE SHOCK

Before we close this chapter, we need to offer a quick word about an often-overlooked reality. As hard as the shocks are in adjusting to a new cultural setting, it can be even harder once you have adapted and then return to your home culture to live (Gehman 2005; B. Hill 2005). It is important to note that it is considered normal to take six to twelve months to complete this adjustment (Austin 1983), which has a cycle parallel to the initial cultural adaptation (Storti 1997, 57–71).

The reality of reverse culture shock—or reentry shock—should not be surprising, since to the extent that you have succeeded in becoming bicultural, you will return home a different person. To complicate matters, depending

---

SIDEBAR 15.4
SELECTED WEB RESOURCES ON CROSS-CULTURAL ADAPTATION

Cultural Adjustment articles in Network for Strategic Missions Knowledgebase (http://www.strategicnetwork.org/index.php?loc=kb&view=b&fto=1275&sf=Y)

Missionary Care ebooks (http://www.missionarycare.com/ebook.htm)

On-line Cultural Training Resource for Study Abroad (University of the Pacific; http://www2.pacific.edu/sis/culture/)

Planet ESL: "Culture Shock" (http://www.planetesl.com/resources/shock.html)

What Missionaries Ought to Know about Culture Stress (http://www.missionarycare.com/brochures/br_culturestress.htm)

SIDEBAR 15.5
SELECTED WEB RESOURCES ON REVERSE CULTURE SHOCK

Peace Corps Online library: Culture, Culture Shock, Reverse Culture Shock (http://peacecorpsonline.org /messages/messages/2629/2027574 .html)

Reentry Shock articles in Network for Strategic Missions Knowledgebase

(http://www.strategicnetwork.org /index.php?loc=kb&view=b&fto =641&sf=Y)

What Missionaries Ought to Know about Re-Entry (http://www.mis sionarycare.com/brochures/br _reentry.htm)

---

on how long you have been gone, the people you know and your home culture will have changed as well. In addition to the normal fact of growth and development of your friends and family (just as you yourself have also grown and developed), in our globalized era it is increasingly true that *every* culture with any exposure to the larger world changes on a regular basis. Thus, when you learn that you are returning home (whatever the reason), it will be well worth your time to prepare for the shock of reentry. You may want to read some resources on reverse culture shock (sidebar 15.5), revisit lessons you learned to adjust in your new country, or see if your agency or business has materials for those who return to their home country.

CONCLUSION

If you plan to live in a culture other than your own for any time greater than one year, you can expect to go through the process of culture shock as you adjust to life in your new setting. In the next chapter, we explore what it means to develop competence as a communicator in your new setting. In the case study for this chapter, Scott describes elements of the process he went through learning how to drive on the other side of the road as a metaphor of cultural adjustment.

CASE STUDY:
DRIVING ON THE OTHER SIDE OF LIFE

Adapted from Moreau (1996)

One week after my arrival in Swaziland (a small country in southern Africa), I faced a daunting task. A group of us had ridden with a friend to Johannesburg to buy vehicles that we would use in Swaziland. Our job was to drive the vehicles from

Johannesburg to Swaziland, a journey of some three hundred miles all driving on (what was to me) the wrong side of the road. It was nerve-racking! I found myself grabbing the wheel as tightly as I could, making sure that I kept the lead vehicle in sight. Not only did I not know the way home, I didn't even know how to make a right-hand turn! I hadn't even adjusted to the new time zone, let alone driving a right-hand-drive vehicle with a stick shift on the column of the steering wheel on the wrong side of the road.

In my first driving experience on the left side of the road, I was a curious mixture of connection and independence. Traveling in the truck by myself, I was apparently independent. At the same time, following the leader and fearing what might happen if we were separated gave me an urgent need for connection! Over the course of several weeks of driving, I developed my own sense of being on the correct side of the road. Unconsciously, I anticipated that it was a good thing for me to be independent in my driving skills.

When learning how to drive on the left-hand side of the road, I found that the most difficult maneuver for me was making a right-hand turn across traffic. I found myself wanting to try to drive behind people crossing my lane instead of in front of me. It was months before I felt comfortable with this one simple act, let alone the hundreds of driving acts that were needed to drive safely in my new home country.

When I learned how to drive in the United States, I developed an instinctive reaction to being in a dangerous situation. When a car was coming toward me, I would pull off to the right to get off the road and out of its way. To use that same reaction in Swaziland would have resulted in a horrible accident, since pulling off to the right would have put me in the face of oncoming traffic. I had to develop a new "instinctive" reaction of pulling off to the left, the exact opposite of my old reaction. It took well over a year for this to develop, but it was a skill that served me well in my time in Africa.

Shortly before my first home leave, I dreamed I was back in the United States driving my parents' car down the streets of my hometown. In the dream I panicked, wondering if I was driving on the correct side of the road. Then I remembered the principle that the steering wheel should be toward the center of the road. As I checked it out, I discovered that I was driving properly. It was not until I woke up from the dream, and thought about it, that I realized that in my dream I had placed the steering wheel on the wrong side of the car! The fact that I was so adjusted to driving on the left side of the road that I couldn't even dream about driving on the right side is a metaphor for the bicultural identity of a person. We live, eat, sleep, and even dream in ways that reflect that we belong to more than one culture. We don't often think about "acting" biculturally; we simply do what is right in a given situation. We have gone beyond the process of having to learn the behavior to the stage of internalizing it so that it "feels" right to us. This cannot be reached without internal struggles, but it is worth the effort once the daily struggles are behind us and life feels normal in our new setting.

REFLECTION AND DISCUSSION

1. What are the strengths and weaknesses of this metaphor for cross-cultural adaptation?
2. What other metaphors might reflect the process of adapting to a new culture?

Intercultural Competence

There is no doubt that competence is critical for long-term healthy relationships in a new cultural setting. The ability to live well—in ways that honor your hosts *and* allow you to live out your Christian convictions in addition to appropriately performing your expected responsibilities—is of critical importance for Christians who choose to live in a cross-cultural context. In this chapter we explore what that involves by examining the concept of intercultural competence.

DEFINING INTERCULTURAL COMPETENCE

What do we mean by intercultural competency or effectiveness? Surprisingly, a consensus definition has yet to be developed. As Canchu Lin notes (2005, 9), it has been variously described as "the capacity to be culturally sympathetic and empathetic" (Bennett 1998), as "functional fitness, psychological health, acquisition of an intercultural identity, and emergence of intercultural person-hood" (Y. Y. Kim 2001a), or as consisting "of three interrelated components: intercultural sensitivity, intercultural awareness, and intercultural adroitness" (Chen and Starosta 1996; 2003).

Yet another way to think of it is to follow the lead of evangelicals such as David Livermore who focus on the concept of cultural intelligence, which involves four components: drive, knowledge, strategy, and action (2013; for academic resources, see http://culturalq.com/fouraspects.html).

Debate continues over whether intercultural competence should be seen as a general skill (the ability to adapt well to a variety of cultural environments) or as a specific skill set (the ability to accomplish a goal or to adapt well in a particular culture) (see Rathje 2007, 4–6). Our focus is on the latter.

We define intercultural competence as a composite of several things, including (1) the ability to adjust well by coping effectively with culture stress and dealing with adaptation; (2) the ability to facilitate adjustment and manage stress for family and significant others; (3) the ability to interact well, such as with appropriateness, friendliness, and clarity when training in skills or transferring information; and (4) the ability to carry out one's assigned task—that is, professional competency and actual job performance (Dodd 1991, 273; see also discussion in Rathje 2007, 3–4).

As Christians, our ultimate desire is to communicate Christ, and to do so in a cross-cultural setting, we must be effective in intercultural communication. In the long run, intercultural competence will also enable us to enjoy our new home more completely, leading to a decrease in burnout and greater longevity in the place of service.

APPROACHES TO INTERCULTURAL COMPETENCE

There are at least four approaches to understanding intercultural competence (summarized in table 16.2): the cognitive awareness model, the character traits model, the social skills model, and the interactionist model.

The Cognitive Awareness Model

Proponents of the *cognitive awareness model* suggest that intercultural communication is more or less a mental puzzle to be solved. This model assumes that any person able to "solve" the puzzle is capable of being a successful intercultural communicator. On the macrolevel, it is assumed that we need a general awareness of cultural dynamics as well as some type of model of the communication process. On the microlevel, it is assumed that we need awareness of the specific aspects of cultural dynamics as well as specific knowledge of the target culture. This model recognizes that more than mere academic knowledge is necessary—the knowledge must be personalized, integrated, and consciously utilized in order to facilitate better intercultural communication.

For those who use the cognitive awareness model, the best way to train people for competency is to identify the knowledge of the person, evaluate it in terms of suitability for a cross-cultural setting, and then develop a program in which the knowledge is enhanced to enable the person to understand the new context.

The Character Traits Model

Proponents of the *character traits model* assume that the key to intercultural communication is the character traits of the communicator. Several listings of necessary traits (and attitudes) have been proposed. Table 16.1 presents a summary of both positive traits to emulate and negative traits to avoid.

A critical element in understanding the characteristics in both columns is how the host culture communicates the attitudes or values presented. For example, in Japan you should not try to make excuses for why something did not work, as that is considered self-centered behavior. Rather, a simple apology is better.

For those who use the character traits model, the best way to train people for competency is to identify the person's character traits (which can include skills and attitudes; see table 16.1), evaluate them in terms of suitability for cross-cultural settings, and then develop a program through which the unsuitable traits may be changed.

The Social Skills Model

The basic thesis of the *social skills model* is that learning to live in a new culture should be considered the same as learning to live in one's own culture (e.g., socialization), and that preparing people to live in another culture should be thought of as a socialization process: "Cross-cultural problems arise because sojourners have trouble negotiating certain social situations. Therefore it is necessary to identify the specific social situations which trouble a particular sojourner and then train the person in those specific skills that are lacking" (Bochner and Furnham 1986, 15).

The critical idea is not so much that we *adjust* to a new culture as that we *learn the important techniques of social behavior* of the new culture. One weakness of this approach is that a person without relevant personal traits or good interpersonal attitudes can be trained in the correct social skills and still not adjust well in the new cultural setting (see Kealey 1989, 423).

For those who use the social skills model, the best way to train people for competency is to identify the person's various social skills, evaluate them in terms of suitability for the new setting, and then develop a program in which skills needing improvement are honed to a minimum standard level.

Traits for Effectiveness (Traits to Emulate)	Traits for Ineffectiveness (Traits to Avoid)
Higher emphasis on people, less on task; approachable: establishes contact with others easily; intercultural receptivity: interested in people, especially people from other cultures	Insistence on task behavior; self-oriented behavior (many self statements)
Ability to not criticize the host people; shows respect: treats others in ways that make them feel valued; capacity to communicate respect	Ethnocentrism; preconceptions and stereotypes
Tolerance of ambiguity	Intolerance of ambiguity; high anxiety
Flexibility; open to culture learning	Rigidity; insists on adherence to "comfortable" monocultural rules
Empathy (demonstrated through culturally appropriate means of listening and accurate perceiving of the other's point of view); cultural perspectivism: the capacity to imaginatively enter into another cultural viewpoint	Low empathy; poor listening skills; assumes similarity instead of difference
Openness in communication style; nondogmatic; social openness; the inclination to interact with people regardless of their differences	Less openness; more dogmatism in communication
High cognitive complexity (not quickly judging in black-and-white terminology; not accepting simplistic stereotypes); capacity to be nonjudgmental	Cognitive simplicity; tends to judge too quickly
Good personal relational skills in the home culture; ability to trust others; capacity for turn taking	Discomfort with personal relations; mistrust
Maintains a sense of personal control; positive orientation: expects that one can succeed living and working in another culture	Feels out of control; highly fatalistic
Innovativeness; enterprise: tends to approach tasks and activities in new and creative ways; venturesome: inclined toward that which is novel or different	Stodginess; lack of innovation
Proper self-esteem, including confidence in communication skills; forthrightness: acts and speaks out readily; social confidence: tends to be self-assured	Faulty self-esteem (in either direction)
Perseverance: tends to remain in a situation and feel positive about it even in the face of some difficulties	Gives up when difficulties arise
Capacity to personalize one's knowledge and perceptions	Doesn't integrate knowledge into the local scene

Developed from Dodd 1991, 279; M. Elmer 1986; Ruben 1982; L. Barna 1982; Dinges 1983; Kealey and Ruben 1983.

The Interactionist Model

The *interactionist model* envisions intercultural competence as an interaction of character traits, social skills, and situational factors (see Dinges 1983, 192–94; Kealey 1989; 1990; Lustig and Koester 2005; Arasaratnam 2006): "A competence is more appropriately inferred from a demonstrated behavior rather than the potential for behavior being inferred from a reported trait, knowledge area, or skill. Consequently, a good test of future performance should allow inferences about both competencies of knowledge and competencies of performance" (Dinges 1983, 193).

Two general areas and two skill sets compose this model. All four are important, and they all interact with one another in a holistic fashion. Significant weakness in any one of these areas lessens the possibility of the person developing competence.

The first general area is cognitive awareness, which involves not just a basic knowledge of cultures and cultural dynamics but also how well a person can personalize and apply what she knows. The second general area is that of personal character traits and attitudes, including such things as flexibility, a nonjudgmental attitude, the ability to tolerate ambiguity, and a high cognitive complexity (see table 16.1).

The first skill set encompasses the social and interpersonal skills for the immediate context. It includes a person's ability not only to socialize but also to feel comfortable in the social settings in the intercultural situation. The final skill set is that of the person's job or ministry-related skills. It

TABLE 16.2
SUMMARY OF MODELS OF INTERCULTURAL COMPETENCE

Approach	Description
Cognitive Awareness	Typically stressed in the academic arena, this approach seeks to prepare the intercultural communicator by giving her the theoretical background and cognitive skills necessary for intercultural communication. The focus tends to be on what constitutes a culture (in the broadest theoretical sense) and how we should think about the process of communicating in any new culture (M. Elmer 1986).
Character Traits	Commonly used in missionary preparation programs, this approach centers on developing a model of the character traits needed for a person to be an effective intercultural communicator. This is combined with a program designed to discover which of the actual traits the prospective missionary has and to see where changes need to be made. As with the cognitive model, the focus is very general, intended to apply across a variety of cultures.
Social Skills	The model's core idea is that the intercultural communicator in the new setting is similar to someone with poorly developed social skills. It focuses on identifying the necessary basic social skills in the particular target context and then developing a training program that will enable the communicator to gain these skills (Bochner and Furnham 1986).
Interactionist	This approach is based on the notion that competency in intercultural communication is related to a cluster of traits and skills, not just to knowledge, character traits, or social skills. It is not just the sum of each skill but the total interactive complex that accounts for the observed competency (Dinges 1983).

involves how well trained and capable the person is in the job or ministry, and whether she is secure or insecure with her responsibilities and the position she holds.

According to the interactionist model, the best way to train people for competency is to identify the complex of factors in each of the four interactive areas. Thus, a program is developed in which all factors (knowledge, character traits, social skills, and job/ministry skills) may be noted, evaluated, and improved to help ensure success in the intercultural setting.

A MODEL OF INTERCULTURAL COMPETENCE

We take our lead from the interactionist model, but use five interactive areas in our model of intercultural competence (adapted in part from Lustig and Koester 2010). Three of the components deal with the foundational issues of knowledge, motivations, and actions. The latter two involve our ability to choose good strategies and employ them appropriately in the context to achieve the effects or accomplish the goals we desire. The model is illustrated in figure 16.1.

FIGURE 16.1
THE INTERACTING COMPONENTS OF INTERCULTURAL COMPETENCE

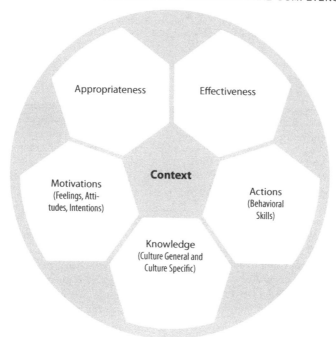

231

Foundational Base

Three foundational components constitute the base of our model of intercultural competence: knowledge, motivations, and actions. Although our internal apprehension of them is important, ultimately it is our hosts who will judge our competence based on their judgments of how well we are able to apply them to the specific setting in which we minister.

KNOWLEDGE

Though a basic knowledge of cultures and cultural dynamics is important, it is not just what we know but how well we can personalize and apply our knowledge in the intercultural setting that determines our competency in intercultural communication. As a foundation, and because learners construct meaning based on an existing knowledge schema (Zhu and Valentine 2001), the competent intercultural communicator needs to start by learning the general principles of communication, including the topics examined in parts 2 and 3 of this book.

SIDEBAR 16.1
ASSESSING OUR INTERPERSONAL COMMUNICATION SKILLS

The following questions can help you assess your own intercultural communication skills and identify areas of strength and areas that need improvement. As you read through them, consider which two you feel are your greatest strengths and which two you consider to be your greatest weaknesses. Bounce your ideas off a trusted friend and ask for her or his input.

1. Do I pay attention to contextual factors (time of day, tiredness of either party, illness of either party, etc.)?
2. When something feels strange to me, how do I handle it?
3. When I do not respond well to a person, am I simply "turned off" to his or her personality?
4. How do people of lesser social power show respect for those of greater power?
5. As a "stranger" here, what is my status? What is appropriate for people of my status?
6. Do I emphasize areas that will build credibility?
7. What is my understanding of being "on time"? How does that compare to the society in which I live?
8. How do people where I live express anger? How does that differ from the ways I express anger?
9. How much do I pay attention to things such as eye contact, physical distance, and touch between conversation partners?
10. In what ways do stereotypes affect my communication patterns?
11. How do I change my communication patterns when I am feeling stressed? How might that be helpful or harmful in my culture of service?

Also, once they are living in the new culture, intercultural communicators need culture-specific knowledge beyond the general principles (see, e.g., Snider and Starcher 2013). For example, is the society in which they live collectivistic? If so, how does that manifest itself in daily life? What specifics do they need to know to successfully navigate their daily lives as well as to handle the specialized tasks they are expected to perform? How can they utilize knowledge about the tendencies of people to interpret specific actions? Through all this, intercultural communicators must be aware of the danger of applying the general tendencies of a society (collectivistic) to every person or setting they encounter.

MOTIVATIONS

Understanding your own motives and how they impact the way you view the people among whom you live is another essential component of communication competency. Our motivations can be seen in three areas: our feelings, our character traits and attitudes, and our intentions.

The feeling area of our motivations refers to the emotional or affective states you experience when communicating interculturally. How do you experience and express your emotions, and what roles do they play in your communication patterns? Perhaps no emotion can cause more problems—especially in high-context cultures—than anger that is expressed publicly. You will do well to ask trusted cultural informants how people in the society handle anger, and what is acceptable in public settings.

Character traits and attitudes refer to the way we approach life and how we respond to various situations. Key traits, as noted in the previous discussion (see also table 16.1), include flexibility, a nonjudgmental attitude, the ability to tolerate ambiguity, and a high cognitive complexity. How do we know which traits we bring to the task? Psychological self-report studies have not been as useful as one would hope for predicting competency in a new setting (Kealey 1989, 410). Others' perceptions of us are a better predictor of competency than our self-evaluations (Kealey 1989, 422).

By *intentions* we refer to the ideals or motivations that guide the choices you make in developing strategies for communicating with strangers. What are the goals, plans, objectives, and desires through which you focus and direct your behavior? For example, stereotypes can short-circuit other positive skills by reducing the number of choices about and interpretations of others' actions you may make and thus lead to a less successful sojourn.

Of these three motivational areas, that of intentions is the murkiest. Often we even hide our intentions from ourselves; after all, who can know his or her own heart except God? We also face the problem of people attributing

SIDEBAR 16.2
TENTMAKING EFFECTIVENESS

Patrick Lai surveyed 450 tentmakers working in the least-reached countries of the world (2007). He found the following factors were more likely to be present in the lives of those who were more effective in ministry than in the lives of those who were not. As you read through this list, consider how each point correlates (or does not correlate) with the model used in this chapter.

1. *Spiritual life*: Those who fast are most likely to be effective; those who consistently set aside time for study of Scripture and prayer and read Christian literature or listen to sermon tapes are slightly more effective.
2. *Social and personal life*: Those who report most of their closest friends are nationals and who entertain nationals three times a week or more or who vacation with nationals are more effective.
3. *Home- or sending-church relationship*: Those who send out prayer letters, have 151 or more people praying for them, and who receive quarterly communication from their home church are slightly likely to be more effective.
4. *Identity and visa*: Those who are recognized by the locals as missionaries are more effective, while those who work on tourist or social-visit visas are slightly less effective.
5. *Field- or overseas-church relationship*: The most effective tentmakers are those who are regularly involved in a national congregation or a house church in the local language.
6. *Witnessing and ministry overseas*: Workers who live consistent, holistic Christian lives and who actively seek opportunities to verbally share their faith are more effective. Those

negative intentions to us when they do not understand or appreciate what we are doing. For example, many missionary couples think they are demonstrating healthy marriages or child-rearing practices, not knowing how they are being interpreted by those who are observing them. African students from several countries wrestled with Scott in various classes on the issue of helping their wives with household chores, especially in the kitchen. They saw American men doing this but felt it was potentially dangerous for them to follow the example, since their wives might be reprimanded or worse by their mothers or in-laws (whether Christian or not) for allowing their husbands to do what they considered women's work. With extended families living in the same house or compound, it would be extremely difficult to hide a man helping out. As a result, Africans wondered why the American men did this. At the same time, American men wondered why more Africans did not do so. Both attributed motivations to each other based on their own interpretations of what they observed.

who simply let their lives be a witness or do not initiate sharing are
less effective.

7. *Adopted people/country group:* When
there is no hindrance to sharing
faith, workers tend to be more
effective.

8. *Language:* Those who are fluent in
the local heart language rather than
a trade or national language are
more effective.

9. *Security:* Workers who lie to ensure
business success are less effective,
while workers who take appropriate
risks are more effective.

10. *Accountability:* Workers who have a
clear strategy for planting a church

and who meet with someone who
holds them accountable at least
once per month are more likely to
be effective.

11. *Team:* Those on a team of twelve to
fifteen members are most effective.

12. *Work/job overseas:* Workers who have
a job working alongside those they
are trying to reach are most effective, as are those who are good at
their jobs. Those whose jobs are a
front or cover are less effective.

13. *Money/salary:* Higher salary does not
impact effectiveness, though those
earning less than seven hundred
dollars per month were less effective.

ACTIONS—BEHAVIORAL/SOCIAL SKILLS

Cross-cultural learning can be like learning a new game where the game
and its rules are known intimately to the host (who expects other people to
already know them as well), but the guest must still learn them. Bochner and
Furnham have identified six types of social interactions (game settings) that
people find difficult when they are operating in a new culture (1986, 216):

1. Formal relations/focus of attention
2. Managing intimate relations
3. Public rituals
4. Initiating contact/introductions
5. Public decision making
6. Assertiveness

Learning how to successfully behave in each of these interaction areas is
critical to developing competency. Keep in mind that the skills necessary for
each of these types of interactions will vary from culture to culture as well
as among the people you serve. For example, there will be different rules for
interacting among street children than among the socially elite.

Social skills that are particularly important for the interaction areas include
those listed alphabetically in sidebar 16.3. As you read through the list, see if
you can think of people, books, or other resources that can help you to learn
these important skills. Finally, we add that a person with a sensation-seeking

235

SIDEBAR 16.3
SOCIAL SKILLS TO ACQUIRE

Adapted from Bochner (1982); Bochner and Furnham (1986); Lustig and Koester (2010)

Anxiety management: Coping with social anxiety during moments of stress or ambiguity.

Conversation: Appropriate speaker exchanges (timing, volume, clarity), topics, and self-disclosure.

Decision making, negotiation, and conflict management: Skills in handling the interchange of ideas during conflict that leads toward culturally appropriate resolution.

Emotional expression: Ability to express the full range of appropriate emotions in various situations; includes skills to appropriately express feelings of warmth, affection, and sexuality.

Humor: Understanding and being able to use humor appropriately.

Public performance: Skills at handling being the focus of public attention.

Synchrony: Coordinating verbal and nonverbal behavior, encouraging the communication partner, giving appropriate feedback.

Trust: Ability to generate and display trust, including skills in empathy, respect, and tolerance for personal differences.

---

orientation may, in combination with other factors, also be more successful in developing intercultural competence (Arasaratnam, Banerjee, and Dembek 2010).

Appropriateness and Effectiveness

Building on the foundation of knowledge, motivations, and actions, competent communicators will use appropriate and effective strategies for communication. If our communication methods are inappropriate, we may lose our audience before they even understand what we seek to communicate. What is appropriate, of course, is defined in light of the ways a biblical approach

---

SIDEBAR 16.4
A PARADOXICAL FINDING

In what seems to be a paradox, a large-scale study by Daniel Kealey of Canadian volunteers working in cross-cultural settings revealed "that at least some of the individuals who will be ultimately the most successful can also be expected to undergo the most severe acculturative stress" (1989, 408).

REFLECTION AND DISCUSSION

What reasons do you think could account for this finding?

SIDEBAR 16.5
SELECTED WEB RESOURCES ON INTERCULTURAL COMPETENCE

Alvino E. Fantini and Ageel Tirmizi. "Exploring and Assessing Intercultural Competence." (http://digital collections.sit.edu/cgi/viewcontent.cgi?article=1001&context=world learning_publications) Intercultural Competence Assessment Test (http://www.incaproject.org/)

The Interculture Project module: "Acquiring Intercultural Competence" (http://www.lancs.ac.uk/users/inter culture/mod.htm) Wikipedia article: Intercultural Competence (http://en.wikipedia.org /wiki/Intercultural_competence)

---

to living should be worked out in our new cultural setting rather than in our home setting. However, even if our methods are biblically and culturally appropriate, they may not be effective in helping us to reach our goals. Effectiveness should not be confused with efficiency, which is not part of this model. Efficiency in ministry is under the control of God, not people; our goal is to learn to follow the Holy Spirit's promptings so that God's will is accomplished, whatever the timing.

CONCLUSION

People do not cross cultural boundaries *hoping* to fail in their adjustment. They may very well fear that possibility, but they do not *hope* it happens unless there are external constraints that are abnormal (e.g., family expectations to be a missionary). Nevertheless, and unfortunately, people do sometimes fail to adjust. Knowing what to expect, being aware of our strengths and weaknesses, learning appropriate social skills, and then applying what we know in appropriate ways will help make the transition smoother and the ultimate adjustment healthier.

Sometimes, however, it is not ministry that is the source of stress. Instead, it is simply what is required for living in the new setting. Our case study explores that issue with a teacher who tried to approach the conflicted signals he was getting by telling a story to help people understand what he was experiencing. The method was appropriate, but the content of the story did not have the impact he intended.

CASE STUDY:
DOG IS NOT MAN'S BEST FRIEND

R. VANCE MASSENGILL

Andy had been in China for more than a year now. He had learned so much about the culture but was always eager to learn more. As an English teacher in a Chinese university, he had accomplished more than he had ever expected in his first year. He was very popular among the students and the school leaders. He had already established many close friendships among Chinese students and also had several students come to Christ. After his first year, he was voted the most popular teacher by the student body and spent all his free time with the Chinese. However, things were about to change.

After returning from his summer furlough, he noticed a change among many of his students from the previous year, especially the English majors with whom he was the closest. It seemed as if over the summer they had changed. Andy's teaching was a little stricter, and his assignments were more demanding, but that was his way of pushing them to be the best they could be. Many of the students stopped visiting, and Andy felt a strong tension in the classroom. He asked some of the students in the class what was wrong, but their answers never seemed to make much sense to him.

Three months into the school year, Andy could not take it any longer. He decided that he had to find out what was wrong and met with the few students who had continued to visit him regularly. They insisted that Andy had done nothing to deserve the cold treatment he was receiving by a majority of the class.

After reflecting with the students, Andy decided to approach the whole class about the way he felt, and the students agreed that it might help. From Andy's travels, he knew that sometimes a story was more effective in some cultures than a speech. He decided to use an analogy that he felt would best describe his feelings in a way that the students would understand.

Andy went to class the next day anxious to reestablish the relationship he once had. He was nervous but knew that he needed to open his heart. Andy shared a story about a man who owned a dog and loved the dog very much. He cared for the dog, fed the dog, and was always showing the dog how much he felt for it. Then one day the dog, for no reason, bit the man. The man's heart was broken. He had only shown love for the dog and was repaid for his efforts by being bitten.

As he concluded the story, many students were crying. They said they were sorry they had hurt Andy. He left class thinking things would now return to normal. However, later that day the Foreign Affairs Officer (FAO) called Andy to come to her office. She told Andy that the class was extremely angry and so was she. She said that students in the class had informed her that he had called Chinese people dogs and that the only reason he came to China was to make Chinese people become Christians.

Andy was shocked. He tried to explain the story to the FAO, but she would not listen. He felt his whole ministry had fallen apart. He was in jeopardy of being asked to leave China. It seemed like now the whole school hated him, and he wondered if there was any way he could convey the meaning he had intended for the story. Sighing in frustration, he felt like just leaving China and going home.

Andy just did not know what to do, but after he shared this event with a trusted friend, he was told that a century earlier the British had put a sign in a park that read: "No dogs and Chinese allowed" and that this type of ban remained a monument to the Chinese humiliation by Westerners. Suddenly he understood the strength of their reaction at his attempt to relate to his students using the story of a dog as man's best friend. He was shocked and deeply embarrassed to discover that his story had made everyone in the class lose face! How could he possibly patch things up with the people he had come to serve?

REFLECTION AND DISCUSSION

1. Do you think that Andy's friend has the best explanation? What other explanations might help Andy?
2. How would you advise Andy to deal with his problem?

17

Intercultural Relationships

One of the central goals for all Christians in cross-cultural settings is to develop healthy relationships with people of the new culture, which is at the core of partnership in the gospel (Michaels 2010). With those who are Christians, such relationships provide fellowship, the chance to grow in learning about our faith from a new set of perspectives, emotional and spiritual support in times of need, and opportunities to grow together spiritually. With those who do not know Christ, such relationships provide a chance to connect with people who have different perspectives on life, ways to grow as persons and sojourners in the new culture, and, of course, opportunities to respectfully and appropriately share the good news offered in Christ. They have gifts to offer us; we have gifts to offer them. Both are enriched by this mutual exchange, and each has the opportunity to contribute meaningfully in the life of the other.

While there are distinct advantages of living in our technologically connected age, when it comes to developing relationships in our new setting there are also significant disadvantages. For the first time in human history, those

Material in this chapter is drawn from chapter 14 of Moreau, Corwin, and McGee, *Introducing World Missions: A Biblical, Historical, and Practical Survey* (2004), with significant revision and expansion.

crossing into new cultural and geographic settings can electronically bring friends and family with them. Skype, email, blogging, and instant messaging are all wonderful tools to stay connected with those "back home," but they also can and will get in the way of developing friendships in your new environment.

The simple reality is that if your connections enable you to have your emotional relationship needs met electronically, there will be little motivation to go through the difficult task of forming friendships across cultural boundaries—especially the type of relationships in which your needs can be met by others. This ultimately is detrimental to local Christians, who will perceive that they have nothing to offer well-econnected cross-cultural workers. It robs local believers of the opportunity to minister to their guests and keeps the cross-cultural workers distanced from them. Surely this is not God's hope for those who serve him in new cultural settings.

> *It is puzzling when Americans apply the word "friend" to acquaintances from almost every sector of one's past or present life, without necessarily implying close ties or inseparable bonds.*
>
> visitor to the United States
> from Iran, in Kohls 1981, 8

PHASES OF CROSS-CULTURAL RELATIONSHIPS

Certainly, progression toward deep friendship is one of a cross-cultural worker's goals. Whatever the culture, there is an ebb and flow in developing relationships. While each relationship is unique and follows its own path, in general there are three phases in relationships across cultures: (1) initial uncertainty, (2) friendly relations, and (3) intimacy/friendship. The separation between the phases may be fuzzy, and relationships can proceed both backward and forward, but these phases typify progress in a relationship. As the relationship develops, people may wander back and forth through all three. Sidebar 17.1 carries the discussion further by helping you to think through five types of changes that take place in growing friendships.

PHASE 1: INITIAL UNCERTAINTY

Everyone has a certain level of anxiety in developing new relationships. For some people this is a significant factor, and for others it is not an issue.

Though friendships are the means by which we meet the emotional needs common to all people, we also share the experience of encountering anxiety when we enter new relationships. One early goal of any relationship is to

241

SIDEBAR 17.1
CHANGES IN DEVELOPING FRIENDSHIPS

Intercultural communication specialists Myron W. Lustig and Jolene Koester note five changes that take place in friendships crossing cultural boundaries (1996, 246):

1. Friends interact more frequently; they talk to each other more often, for longer periods of time, and in more varied settings than acquaintances do.
2. The increased frequency of interactions means that friends will have more knowledge about and shared experiences with one another than will acquaintances, and this unique common ground will probably develop into a private communication code to refer to ideas, objects, and experiences that are exclusive to the relationship.
3. The increased knowledge of the other person's motives and typical behaviors means that there is an increased ability to predict a friend's reactions to common situations. The powerful need to reduce uncertainty in the initial stages of relationships suggests that acquain-

tanceships are unlikely to progress to friendships without the ability to predict the others' intentions and expectations.

4. The sense of "we-ness" increases among friends. Friends often feel that their increased investment of time and emotional commitment to the relationship creates a sense of interdependence, so that individual goals and interests are affected by and linked to each person's satisfaction with the relationship.
5. Close friendships are characterized by a heightened sense of caring, commitment, trust, and emotional attachment to the other person, so that the people in a friendship view it as something special and unique.

REFLECTION AND DISCUSSION

1. What are the risks in each of the changes in a cross-cultural setting?
2. How might awareness of these areas of change impact the way you disciple someone in a cross-cultural setting?

---

reduce that anxiety through developing shared communication patterns with the other person. While this is moderately important when communicating with those of our own culture, it becomes crucial in cross-cultural settings.

Combining our need to develop relationships with our need to avoid uncertainty (see sidebar 17.2) yields a motivation that includes both the desire to approach and the desire to avoid. While we want to develop relationships with others in the intercultural setting, doing this results in greater uncertainty and anxiety for us, and we may tend to avoid them as a result. It is the avoidance tendency that makes our econnections even more attractive to us than they were before we entered the new culture.

242

In this initial phase of the relationship, we tend to base all our judgments on our respective cultural maps. Since we have no personal history of relating to the potential friend, we base initial impressions on what we perceive to be his culture, ethnic identity, and so on.

How do we reduce uncertainty, especially in the intercultural setting? Every society has established its own general procedures for reducing uncertainty and anxiety in the process of relational development. On the one hand, in more extreme collective cases it might even mean that you simply do not develop relationships with strangers, because you are born into all the relationships you anticipate you will ever need (Bell and Coleman 1999, 3). It can even be seen as a betrayal of the group to form too close of a relationship with an outsider. Thus collectivists moving to a more individualistic culture are often surprised by how friendly and willing to start a relationship people are. On the other hand, individualists moving to a strongly collective culture may be unaware that the socially marginalized will often be the ones most interested in developing a relationship with the stranger, since they do not have "normal" connections within their own society.

The procedures used to reduce uncertainty will include such things as the type of information you offer and need to receive, how you reveal such information, and appropriate boundaries for what is considered private or public. Americans working in China are offended when they are asked how much

---

SIDEBAR 17.2
NEEDS THAT MOTIVATE US TOWARD FRIENDSHIPS

J. H. Turner suggests seven basic needs shared by humans that motivate us to interact with others (from Gudykunst and Kim 1992, 190):

1. Our need for a sense of security as a human being.
2. Our need for a sense of trust (this need involves issues of predictability; "I trust you will behave as I think you will").
3. Our need for a sense of group inclusion.
4. Our need to avoid or diffuse anxiety.
5. Our need for a sense of a common shared world.
6. Our need for symbolic or material gratification.
7. Our need to sustain our self-conception.

REFLECTION AND DISCUSSION

1. Do you agree that these are universal needs found in every culture?
2. In what ways do you think these needs match needs for all people seen in the Bible? What might you add to the list? What might you remove?

money they make—information considered private by most Americans but public in China. Japanese business people, for example, have enough information printed on their business cards so they can know the relative status of each other when they exchange cards. This enables each to avoid making status-related mistakes early in the relationship that could damage it irreparably.

The particular strategies available for reducing uncertainty are built on the society's values and understanding of relationships, including such things as gender roles; social power, status, and role; and even the very definition of friendship itself. These strategies are learned as children grow up and are simply thought to be "natural" to them. People might not even be consciously aware that they use them.

> *Making friends across cultures requires time and work and frustration. Understanding does not turn on like a light. But at the end is unparalleled satisfaction. You are bringing into being, in a partial way, the climax of history.*
>
> Stafford 1984, 38

A Ugandan at a small midwestern Christian college asked an intercultural communication class one day why people he passed as he was walking around campus—even strangers— smiled at him when they saw him. To him the smile meant that they wanted to engage in conversation, but whenever he approached them they were surprised and seemed to be put off. In asking the question, it dawned on many American students in the class that they did this without even thinking about what they were doing; it was simply a way of being polite. The Ugandan read the smile as an invitation; to the Americans it was nothing more than a polite acknowledgment. No wonder he was confused!

One American couple serving in Kenya was confused when they invited Kenyans over to dinner but were not invited to their homes in turn. Then they learned that people who are friends in Kenya just drop by rather than wait for an invitation (Stafford 1984). As noted in chapter 10, this was also explained to Scott in an African class setting when a student told him that he would love it if Scott would just drop by some day *without* scheduling an appointment or offering a reason for coming. By scheduling an appointment or giving a reason for being there, Scott was communicating that this was a business visit rather than friendship. If he came without a reason, then he was showing that he was a friend.

During this early exploration, two barriers can stop the growth of the relationship. The first comes from the human tendency to stereotype. Before intimacy can have a chance to grow in a cross-cultural relationship, each person must be able to stop seeing the other as "one of them" and instead see that person as an individual. To overcome this barrier, we need to reduce our

---

SIDEBAR 17.3
AFRICAN PROVERBS OF FRIENDSHIP

A man who does not quarrel about neglected friendship does not love his friend.

Words are easy, but real friendship is difficult.

Friendships are like mushrooms: they cannot be forced (when getting them out of the ground).

Friendship is like fat; you eat it while it is still hot.

Friendship is like the body; you do not scratch where it does not itch.

REFLECTION AND DISCUSSION

1. Discuss what you think is the meaning behind each proverb.
2. All these proverbs come from the Luganda of Uganda. What do they value in friendship?
3. How do their values differ from your own? How are they the same?

---

reliance on stereotypes and our uncertainty about the other person. This is a skill that is developed within the culture, and each culture will have its own rules about how this uncertainty is best reduced (Lustig and Koester 1996, 260–63; see also Walker 2013).

It may be apparent to the reader that our discussion is built on the presupposition that relationships, and especially friendships, are *voluntary* associations. That is, at any time either party in a relationship can choose to pull out or deepen the ties. This ideal fits well with an individualistic orientation to life but, as mentioned earlier, not as well in collective cultures, where people are born into extensive in-group relationships that they must maintain for life. However, as outsiders who have crossed cultural boundaries, missionaries are never born into the collectives of the people they seek to reach; thus missionary relationships with members of the local culture are by definition voluntary relationships.

This fact plays an important role in the potential for a relationship to develop. For example, Americans may look for common interests, hobbies, skills, and the like before they "volunteer" friendship. Chinese, however, want to know the extent of *yuan* in a relationship before they will progress (Chang and Holt 1991). According to Chang and Holt, *yuan* accompanies all relationships, determining the extent to which they can develop. *Yuan* is not the cause of a relationship but the context in which relationship causes take place. Metaphorically speaking, if the direct cause of relationship development is a seed, *yuan* may be understood as the sunshine, the soil, and the rain (Chang and Holt 1991, 34). To the American missionary, this may sound fatalistic, but to the Chinese it traditionally plays an important role in determining the extent of a relationship with a stranger.

The second barrier to a deeper relationship can be framed in a simple question: "Are you *enough like me* to commit to a deeper relationship?" The question may not be asked out loud, but it is implicit in your desire to get to know the other person. At least initially, you may be attracted *because* of the differences. Even so, too many differences will eventually make it difficult to develop genuine intimacy. If mutual satisfaction, acceptance, and trust for each other develop during this stage, then the relationship can move on to the next level.

PHASE 2: FRIENDLY RELATIONS

The second stage of relationships requires both parties to consider the risks of changing enough to accommodate each other. Both must make some compromises if the friendship is to be mutually valued. Because you are a stranger in a new culture, nationals who form relationships with you are taking certain risks. They may see advantages in those risks, which can include status and access to the relative wealth you represent or simply an opportunity to connect to someone who represents new opportunities. However, they may think that the advantages do not outweigh the disadvantages and decide that pursuit of a deeper relationship is too risky.

During this phase, you will be able to coexist at a certain level of comfort with the other person. Missionaries of the past often felt that they should not show any weaknesses to the nationals. They were afraid that the message of the gospel would be diluted or weakened if they were weak themselves. The resulting "glittering image" they presented was of people who needed no help. Nationals, however, could see through this disguise and recognized that there was an unfathomable distance between themselves and the missionaries. Intimacy was difficult to develop in this relational climate. Contemporary cross-cultural sojourners from the West are less likely to deny their own weaknesses. However, learning how to be emotionally open with people who you feel do not understand you is still a risk that is difficult for many people to take.

A basic truth that all missionaries must learn if they want to effectively disciple in another culture is this: when missionaries do not allow others to help them, they deny those others dignity. In refusing to admit that they hurt and need help and support, missionaries effectively deny those of the host culture the chance to see themselves as people who have something to offer the missionaries. Relationships developed in this way will be one-dimensional because the missionary only gives and the indigenous people only receive. That situation is not healthy for discipleship or local church development.

During this phase you will still rely to a great extent on your own values and understanding (your "cultural map"). However, if you desire to move on in your friendship, you must move beyond this. Since you now have a history of relating in which you have discovered through individual observations who the other person is, you will rely less on your cultural map and more on the personal history of the relationship.

> *Without a clear-cut decision to pursue friendship, missionaries could find themselves filling their time with an assortment of other relationships and activities.*
>
> H. Hill 1993, 266

Handling conflict is an important part of this stage. Inevitably relationships face conflict sooner or later, and the coping strategies people use to resolve conflict are engrained deeply in them as they grow up. Cultures value differing ways of handling, or even admitting to, conflict. Learning the ways people do this in your new culture is an important step not only in your culture-learning process but in helping you to develop deeper relationships with those you have come to serve.

In order to move into a genuine friendship, you must continue the mutual satisfaction, acceptance, and trust built in the first phase of the relationship. You must also now experience emotional sharing and openness and put into practice appropriate conflict-resolution strategies (discussed in chap. 23).

One of the barriers to reaching the third phase of friendship is that of getting past dissimilarities. The less you are like someone, the more anxiety and uncertainty you will experience in moving toward a more intimate relationship. Dodd has captured a means of explaining this through proposing the homophily principle (1991, 229–39; see also Gudykunst and Kim 1992, 197–99), which is the idea that we tend to share more of ourselves with people who are similar to us and less with those who are less like us.

A second significant barrier in this stage of the relationship is the need for truly mutual accommodation. When we cross cultures to engage in relationships, significant differences will remain, and we need to find ways to accommodate them. In trying to understand perceptions of time and scheduling in Kenya, Scott asked a Kenyan friend this question: "If I invited you to come to dinner at my house at 6 p.m., and you wanted to show me that we are friends, when might you come?" The friend replied, "A little late." Scott followed this up, "What do you mean by 'a little late'?" The friend answered, "About one hour." You can imagine how Scott would need to accommodate himself to this friendship if the friend showed up one hour past the scheduled time! At the same time, you can imagine how the friend would have to accommodate himself to Scott's sense of scheduling.

Theoretically we have rightly placed the responsibility of accommodation on the cross-cultural worker. After all, she is the new one in the culture and as a guest should learn how to "do as the Romans do." It gets very sticky in friendships, however, and especially in discipleship, when the cross-cultural worker feels responsible for the spiritual development of the national. The discipler will feel constrained to "shape" the national to fit her image of what a disciple should be (e.g., shows up on time, schedules things, does not waste time—all deeply held cultural values) rather than asking what a disciple should look like in light of the national's values.

> *Trying to establish an interpersonal relationship in the United States is like trying to negotiate over or break down a wall; it is almost like a series of concentric circles. You have to break down different levels before you become friends.*
>
> visitor to the United States
> from Ethiopia, in Kohls 1981, 8

A particular problem is that the cross-cultural worker may have been trained to read "being on time" as a biblical value and may have the verses to back it up. The national, however, will have a different set of values and will have her own verses to back those up. This is where the ability to mutually accommodate is critical in the relationship. Both parties can learn from each other. What can get in the way are issues of power and local expectations of how a good host should accommodate to the guest as well as the guest's understanding of what being an ambassador of Christ means—all focused around the concept of sin (see, e.g., Dye 1976; Priest 1994; T. Chuang 1996; and Strand 2000).

The final barrier in moving to a closer friendship is the need for one of the partners to make a conscious movement toward this type of intimacy. Simply put, if neither initiates this movement, it will not happen.

One challenge in this area is the difficulty of even recognizing when such a move is being made. Another is understanding how to initiate in a way that the other party will see as appropriate. For example, what signals closeness to a collective person may be an invasion of privacy for the individualist. Someone from a patron-client culture may be signaling a desire to engage the missionary as a patron, while the missionary does not understand the rules of the game and rejects even the possibility of a positive relationship as a patron. A monochronic individualist may schedule more frequent times to meet a person in a collectivist culture in the hopes of moving the friendship along, not knowing that scheduling itself communicates a lack of desire for greater intimacy. The signals of a person from an obligation-oriented society can be interpreted as stiff and formal by someone from a culture that values spontaneity and improvisation. The case study at the end of the chapter provides a personal look at the confusion that can result in cross-cultural friendships.

PHASE 3: INTIMACY/FRIENDSHIP

Ideals of intimacy will vary from culture to culture, especially when the two friends are on opposite sides of the individualism-collectivism spectrum. The collective person identifies intimacy in terms of the amount of time spent together, the relative lack of privacy, mutual dependence, and issues of face (discussed in chap. 14). The individualist may prefer to maintain a level of privacy and independence that seems distancing to the collectivist. Note the feelings of an Asian American toward American friendships:

> I grew up for a good portion of my life in the United States. In the course of living here, I've made many American friends. My relationships with them are very close, in that I even confide in them, but somehow I feel something is missing. There seems to exist a barrier against how close we can really be. I guess this is especially noticeable to me because of the fact that my early childhood was spent in a culture that put a great deal of value on friendship. (cited in Lustig and Koester 1996, 245)

Further, for the individualist, face is more the responsibility of the individual, while for collectivists it is more the responsibility of the group. The polarity in defining responsibilities may make it difficult for the friends to know how (or whether) to help each other out when face is threatened. For individualist missionaries moving to a collective culture, understanding the issue of face in that culture will be important in developing intimate relationships.

SIDEBAR 17.4
SEVEN REALITIES OF CROSS-CULTURAL FRIENDSHIPS

(H. Hill 1993, 266–68)

1. Cross-cultural friendship must be intentional. In monocultural situations, we often gravitate effortlessly toward those who become our friends. But establishing cross-cultural friendships requires more intent. . . .

2. Cross-cultural friendship requires proximity. Reflecting on his cross-cultural experiences, Daryl Whiteman speaks of one experience as successful and another as less successful. In the first, he lived in a village and developed good relationships. In the

second, he taught in a school, lived on the school compound, and came away with very few relationships with nationals. His values or model hadn't changed, but his proximity to the people had. Those who can live in the middle of the community have a great advantage. Those who cannot must regularly get close to the people.

3. Cross-cultural friendship must appreciate differences and similarities. Anthropology greatly helps us understand people of different cultures, but it can also hinder us. . . .

   If differences are our primary focus, we will not be able to have real relationships. We must balance the understanding of our differences with a realization of our common humanness. . . .

4. Cross-cultural friendship will cross economic classes. This barrier seems at times more difficult than crossing cultures. We can understand another's etiquette, values, and social structure, but the contrast of our income and theirs spews out a host of problems. We feel guilty about having so much, both materially and in terms of opportunity. We are accustomed to a certain lifestyle and function very poorly when all of our props are removed. . . .

5. Cross-cultural friendship involves vulnerability. . . . When cross-cultural workers experience the death of a child, they often report suddenly being taken into a new level of intimacy with the people. In the depths of their grief, all modeling and role playing set aside, bonding with the people occurs to an extent never thought possible.

6. Cross-cultural friendship must be selective. On any continent, you can only relate meaningfully to a handful of people. The same holds true in most cross-cultural situations. Without selecting a few people as close friends, your attention will be too diffused to be significant. But with a few friends, you will gain a window on the culture.

7. Cross-cultural friendship must be flexible. The goal is friendship, but the strategies must remain flexible. Each situation is different, and each missionary is different. Your lifestyle might look significantly different than someone else's, but if you both have good relationships with the people, you've both succeeded.

REFLECTION AND DISCUSSION

1. Identify which of the above areas you would consider an area of strength for you. Do you think it would still be a strength in a cross-cultural setting? Why or why not?

2. Choose one of the items above that you find most difficult and explain what it might take for you personally to grow in this area.

Finally, any intimate friendship will sooner or later have to face the need for forgiveness. The fact that everyone not only makes mistakes but also at times acts in sinful ways toward even those who mean the most to them underscores the need for missionaries to know both how to forgive and how to repent (see Allender and Longman 1992; J. White 1992). Relationships without these spiritual disciplines will rarely pass from friendships to the

SIDEBAR 17.5
SELECTED WEB RESOURCES ON CROSS-CULTURAL RELATIONSHIPS

"A Cross-Cultural Perspective on Friendship Research." Monika Keller. Max Planck Institute for Human Development, Berlin. (http://www.mpib-berlin.mpg.de /en/institut/dok/full/keller/acrosscu /ISSBD.pdf)

Intercultural Relationship Resources (focus is on intercultural marriage; http://gorigirl.com/inter cultural-relationship-resources) InterVarsity: "Making Friends Cross-Culturally" (http://www.intervarsity .org/ism/article/470)

deeper intimacy that Christ wants all Christians to experience as part of his body. Those who are working in a new culture must also take the time to see how forgiveness and repentance are expressed in that culture, so that they know how to read cues that are important to the survival—not to mention the growth—of relationships.

CONCLUSION

Discipleship is built on relationships. Relational values and skills are culturally learned, and the wise cross-cultural worker will invest significant time in learning how friendships are developed in that culture so that he can disciple well. In the end, developing deep relationships in the host culture is not an option for missionaries who want to faithfully call others to worship Christ (Bruce 2011). The question is not *whether* missionaries develop significant relationships; it is *how well* they do it. The case study that follows offers an example where one set of cultural values directly clashes with another and illustrates the trauma of finding ways to deal with the conflicting values in the process of developing a relationship.

CASE STUDY:

FRIENDSHIP LIMITS?

ANGELA RHODES

When Estelle first came to China to be an English teacher in August 2002, she had no idea what the term "collectivism" really meant. She couldn't even tell that it existed. Besides the bargaining, things in China seemed to work relatively the same way as things did in North America. She didn't quite understand what all the talk of the importance of relationships was until she met her first Chinese friend, Ji Yubing.

It was then that the collectivistic idea of living became a surprising reality to her.

After only a couple months of knowing Yubing, it seemed as though Yubing was very comfortable with Estelle. She often came to Estelle's apartment unannounced and always entered without knocking or as she was knocking. Estelle sometimes found herself locking the door just so that Yubing might get the hint that her actions were a little rude. It never seemed to work though.

Yubing also had a habit of demanding things. For example, "I want to use your washing machine" or "Give me those chopsticks." After a while, Estelle started feeling that Yubing was acting like a spoiled child always demanding something from her parents. She couldn't stand constantly being told what to do. Estelle understood that there were cultural differences between herself and Yubing, but it seemed as though every time Yubing came over, Estelle couldn't help but let her frustrations keep building on top of one another.

One day, Yubing walked into the apartment, as she usually did, but this time looking very tired. Before Estelle could even greet her, Yubing immediately told her that she wanted to sleep on her bed until her next class. Estelle told her, "Sure," but on the inside she couldn't believe what had just happened. Her emotions were all over the place. At that point, Estelle couldn't even imagine opening the door to her teammates' apartments without knocking, let alone telling them she wanted to sleep in their bed for a little while. Plus, Estelle had a lot of work she had to get done and was actually thinking about taking a nap herself before she got started, but now that was not an option. Her apartment was too small, and she had only one bed.

Estelle noticed Yubing going into the kitchen. She grabbed a glass and helped herself to some water before she went to lie down. Estelle rolled her eyes, thinking how she never had to remind Yubing to make herself at home. She tried to brush it all off and actually did end up getting a little bit of work done while Yubing was sleeping; however, when Yubing woke up, she almost pushed Estelle to the limit. She walked right into the bathroom on her, again without knocking, and then just started using her hairbrush, without asking.

After Yubing left, Estelle just collapsed on her bed, almost in tears. She was so confused, because she had been overseas several times before and had always developed great bonds with the people she came to know. Based on these experiences, Estelle always thought that she could adapt to new situations well, that she was flexible, and that nothing in the cultural realm could ever bring her negative feelings, because that is what she loved, culture.

Yubing was one of Estelle's closest friends, but Estelle had come to a point where she couldn't stand being around Yubing. Estelle felt guilty for her thoughts and her lack of ability to adjust to Yubing, but she just didn't know what to do. How could she ever tell Yubing what she was feeling? She knew that this would crush Yubing. Even worse, she didn't know how to do this in the appropriate way or even if there was an appropriate way. Nevertheless, she knew that something definitely had to be done; otherwise her closest national friend might become the person she most wanted to avoid.

REFLECTION AND DISCUSSION

1. How might Estelle express her needs for privacy and boundaries to Yubing?
2. In what sense are our needs in these areas determined by culture?
3. Based on your discussion, what might you say to Estelle?

18

Intercultural Evangelism

E ven in one's own culture evangelism can be difficult. People may be indifferent, they may be antagonistic, and in cultures where the church has had a long presence people often have preconceived ideas about the gospel message that make it hard to present the truth in a way that connects with who they are. When you add to this the reality of communicating in a new culture, the difficulties are compounded almost exponentially. Yet, as Scott learned in his years while working with Campus Crusade for Christ, successful evangelism is simply sharing Christ in the power of the Holy Spirit and leaving the results to God. Further, as Cecil Stalnaker notes (2012), God is the "silver bullet" in evangelism, not any particular strategy or method.

Thus, in spite of the complexity of intercultural evangelism, God has successfully used Christians crossing cultural boundaries to share the good news of Christ for millennia, and vibrant, healthy churches exist in many of the ethnolinguistic groups of the world. Certainly there is more work to be done, and in this chapter we explore several issues involved when we cross cultures and seek to communicate Christ.

ISSUES IN INTERCULTURAL EVANGELISM

C. Thomas Wright defines contextualized evangelism as "presenting the uncompromised gospel of Jesus Christ in the sociocultural, ethnic, and linguistic

---

SIDEBAR 18.1

MYTHS ABOUT COMMUNICATING THE GOSPEL

Charles Kraft has identified several myths about the communication of the gospel (for the full list, see Kraft 1991a, 35–54; note also the critique and notations in Hesselgrave and Rommen 1989, 193–96). As you read through the list, can you identify any that you have believed? If you think it is not a myth, how would you respond?

1. Hearing the Gospel with one's ears is equivalent to "being reached" with the gospel.
2. The Holy Spirit will make up for all mistakes if we are sincere, spiritual, and prayerful enough.

3. As Christians we should severely restrict our contacts with "evil" people and refrain from going to "evil" places lest we "lose our testimony" and ruin our witness.
4. Preaching is God's only ordained means of communicating the gospel.
5. The sermon is the most effective vehicle for bringing about life change.
6. The only key to effective communication is the precise formulation of the message.

---

context of the hearers so they may respond and be discipled into a church" (1998, 453). Too often evangelicals have tended to export linear methods that have been effective in their home culture to a new location expecting the same positive results they saw at home (see, e.g., Gener 2005).

Contextualized evangelism and discipleship models must take into account such issues as local understandings of sin (Priest 1994; T. Chuang 1996; Strand 2000), repentance (Pesebre 2005), decision making (Hesselgrave 1978; Gener 2005), conversion (Rambo 1995; McKnight 2002), Bible translation (Nehrbass 2012), and religious ritual (Zahniser 1997), lest we push people to convert to our culture rather than to come to faith in Christ. Research into methods that are fruitful is not only desired but also necessary (Burke 2010; Daniels 2010; Daniels and Allen 2011; Gray et al. 2010; Woodberry 2011). While methods in and of themselves do not produce spiritual fruit, God uses patterns of ministry to draw people to himself, and it is worth our time to study those patterns that bear fruit in order to learn from one another in cross-cultural evangelism.

Sin in Cultural Context

One of the core concepts of the gospel message is the bad news that "all have sinned and fall short of the glory of God" (Rom. 3:23). While in English we tend to think of one word for the concept of "sin," in the biblical languages there are numerous terms encompassing many ideas. For example,

> *"I became a Christian while living in Eastern Europe," a student once confessed to me.*
>
> *"How did that happen?" I asked him.*
>
> *"I stopped praying. I ate pork and drank wine," he said.*
>
> *"You did not become a Christian," I told him. "You stopped being a Muslim."*
>
> *"There's no difference," he retorted. "When a man falls from Islam he becomes a Christian."*
>
> In the ensuing discussion we sorted out the most serious challenge to Christians who are seeking to penetrate Islam with the gospel of Jesus Christ: how to demonstrate the spiritual validity of Christianity. To do so, we must develop relationships with Muslims that are based on integrity and respect. Muslims do not accept the faith of people for whom they have no respect, or from whom they receive no respect.
>
> B. Bradshaw 1988, 358

Greek terminology includes such ideas as missing the mark, transgression, unrighteousness, lawlessness, impiety, depravity, and evil desire. Sin, then, is a multifaceted concept involving who we are on the inside (impious, depraved, unrighteous) and what we do on the outside (miss the mark, transgress, disobey).

Unfortunately, our tendency is to take our own understanding of sin—not just who we are on the inside but our ideas of which acts are sinful and which are not—into our new cultural setting. Although there is overlap between our understanding and the understanding of people in the new culture about what individual sins are, there is also discontinuity (Priest 1993, 1994).

For monochronic people, missing an appointment or arriving too late may be interpreted as sin. For indirect people, public displays of anger and appearing out of control may be understood as sin. For collective people, not supporting the honor of the group will likely be seen as sin. For large gender-role separation people, switching male and female roles may be considered sin. This list does not even begin to address issues such as public displays of affection or dress (what to cover up and what may be revealed, appropriate use of cosmetics and jewelry), let alone the much more difficult issues of bribery and corruption (see B. Adeney 1995).

255

SIDEBAR 18.2
IS THERE A "CORE" MESSAGE OF SALVATION?

Is there a core message of salvation? If so, is it possible to extract it from the Bible? The Western forensic approach distills ideas and organizes them into categories and outlines; other worldview logics do not use the same pattern (e.g., they use stories; see Hiebert 2008b). With this in mind, the following points are suggested content for the evangelistic message of good news:

1. Humanity's relationship with God is broken.
2. That broken relationship cannot be restored by human efforts.
3. Christ died on behalf of humanity as the means to restore that relationship.
4. Our relationship with God is not restored until people respond to God's offer through Christ.

5. Those who have a restored relationship with God will demonstrate it in the way they live their lives.

REFLECTION AND DISCUSSION

---

1. As you consider this list, how might you change it?
2. If you were to weave this list of points into a story rather than an evangelistic tract, how would you do it?
3. How might the understanding of each statement be impacted by cultural values?
4. If you agree that this list captures the essentials, how do your cultural values shape the way you might choose to "package" them?

Robert Priest advocates that we look for areas in which we understand sin in the same ways that the local culture does and use those areas in our attempts to communicate the biblical view of sin more adequately (1994). This will be far more effective for our evangelistic efforts than speaking out about things that we consider sin but the local culture does not.

As an example, consider Mark Strand's explanation of why Chinese people have such a difficult time understanding sin as used in Chinese translations of the Bible:

> Chinese people, especially unbelievers, misunderstand the meaning of the biblical doctrine of sin for three reasons. First, Chinese people are more oriented to the group than to the individual. Attention tends to be diverted away from the individual, and with it, away from responsibility for personal behavior. Chinese people tend to blame society for their personal shortcomings or sins. Second, the foundation on which Chinese culture has been built teaches the inherent goodness of humanity. Finally, *zui*, the primary Chinese word used to translate sin, means to violate the country's laws. Law-abiding people would not consider themselves sinners by these terms. (2000, 432)

Strand notes that the term used for sin by the initial translators was not the best choice, and much of this problem could have been avoided by a better translation.

Tsu-kung Chuang (1996), arguing along the same lines as Strand, proposes an alternate version of the Four Spiritual Laws that would be more understandable to a non-Christian Chinese audience, because it incorporates local views of not hitting the mark (one of the Greek ideas of sin). Rather than stating that we are all sinful, as in the original version, he states that no one can become the ideal perfect person, a point well known in Chinese culture. Further, he changes the statement about Christ being our provision for sin to Christ being the one who can restore our relationship with God. Finally, he removes the individualistic emphasis on receiving restoration with God.

Chuang's version takes the same gospel message found in the Four Spiritual Laws and frames it in terms of honor and shame rather than justice and forensics, which will have greater appeal to his intended audience. We would do well to consider this type of adaptation for any condensation of the gospel message that comes from within a monocultural setting. Doing so, however, assumes that such a condensation is the best approach (see sidebar 18.3), something that has been recently challenged by narrative approaches (Steffen 1996, 1999, 2000, 2005), especially that of Chronological Bible Storying (http://www.chronologicalbiblestorying.com).

TABLE 18.1
FOUR SPIRITUAL LAWS REVISED FOR A CHINESE AUDIENCE

Four Spiritual Laws	Four Spiritual Laws—Chinese Version
1. God loves you and offers a wonderful plan for your life.	1. No one can become the ideal, perfect person he wants to be because man is sinful and separated from God.
2. All of us are sinful and separated from God. Therefore we cannot know and experience God's love and plan for our life.	2. We are all created in the image of God. Since God created us, he also has a plan for every one of us.
3. Jesus Christ is God's only provision for our sin. Through him we can know and experience God's love and plan for our life.	3. God loves us; therefore, he sent his only son, Jesus Christ, to restore the relationship between himself and us. When our relationship with God is restored in our life, the process of becoming the godly person he wants us to become will start, and we can enjoy the abundant life he plans for us.
4. We must individually accept Jesus Christ as Savior and Lord; then we can know and experience God's love and plan for our life.	4. To restore our relationship with God, we must receive Jesus Christ as Savior and Lord.

Adapted from T. Chuang 1996.

Repentance in Cultural Context

Just as there can be cultural confusion over sin, so can there be cultural confusion over repentance. Many Westerners see repentance as an individualized, private admission in prayer before God of our sin and a commitment to turn away from it. This is an appropriate understanding of the biblical term, which at root means to turn away from something.

However, the individualized and the privatized approaches are not the only ways to express repentance that are found in the Bible. Public repentance before an in-group is demonstrated through the ritual of baptism (e.g., Acts 2:37–41; 10:47–48), which is not separated from salvation in the New Testament (Dunn 1977, 96–97). The possibility of entire families (Acts 16:14–15) or groups of people coming to Christ simultaneously (Acts 2:37–41; 10:47–48) is also found in the New Testament and in collective cultures today.

It will be well worth our time to look at the many ways repentance was expressed biblically—in groups, individually, spontaneously, through ritual, by acts of penitence, by changed lives—and to ensure that the means we use to enable people to express repentance is something they can understand from within their own cultural perspective.

Decision Making in Cultural Context

It is a simple fact that in order for someone to come to faith in Christ he or she must make a series of decisions over the course of time (fig. 18.1; Kraft 2005a, 260–56; see also Engel and Norton 1975). Some of these decisions are easy to identify: Should I believe these new ideas? Can I turn my back on old ways of living? Dare I forsake my gods?

Other elements of the decision-making process are more buried. Culture plays a role in decision making, from determining whether a decision must be made to providing the criteria for making a decision. Figure 18.2 indicates some of the questions that must be answered in light of cultural values if we are to understand local decision-making processes.

In what ways does culture—or at least communication patterns discussed in part 3 of this book—affect the answers to the questions in figure 18.2? In table 18.2 we offer suggestions to indicate some possibilities. Because our focus is on decisions related to coming to Christ, we focus on that issue in particular.

We offer opposing orientations for selected communication patterns as simple contrasts for each question. They are intended only to illustrate divergent answers to the questions that come from the selected communication patterns. We want to illustrate the types of intercultural decision-making

FIGURE 18.1
DECISIONS TOWARD CHRIST (ADAPTED FROM KRAFT 2005A, 264)

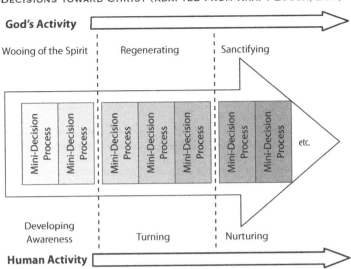

FIGURE 18.2
DECISION-MAKING QUESTIONS TO ANSWER IN LIGHT OF CULTURAL VALUES

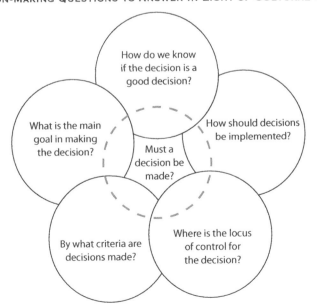

TABLE 18.2
COMMUNICATION PATTERNS IN RELATION TO DECISION MAKING

Question	Communication Patterns and Impact on Decision Making
Must a decision for Christ be made?	*Honor/Justice*: If the decision will bring shame, it should not be made until circumstances change *versus* a decision must be made if a person wants to avoid hell and live in heaven eternally.
Where is the locus of control for the decision?	*Power Distance*: The responsibility to make decisions lies with the patron or leader *versus* each individual is responsible for making his or her own decision. *Collectivism/Individualism*: Decisions are made in light of the needs and interests of a person's in-group *versus* individuals make decisions in light of their own needs. *Gender-Role Separation*: Religious decisions are limited by gender *versus* individuals of each gender are free to make a decision for Christ.
What are the criteria for the decision for Christ?	*Power Distance*: What are the consequences for those above and below a person if he makes a decision for Christ *versus* what are the consequences for a person if she makes a decision for Christ? *Collectivism/Individualism*: Are the decision makers motivated by self-related or group-related obligations? *Gender-Role Separation*: How do personal relationships, competition, or performance factors motivate a decision? Is "getting ahead" (e.g., personal salvation) more important than interpersonal harmony (waiting for the rest to decide)? *Honor/Justice*: In what ways might a decision for Christ bring shame (or honor) to a person's in-group or patron?
What is the main goal in making the decision for Christ?	*Power Distance*: Satisfying the needs of the patron or group *versus* satisfying the individual's needs. *Collectivism/Individualism*: Helping the person's in-group *versus* personally connecting with Christ. *Honor/Justice*: Bringing honor to the person's in-group or patron *versus* dealing with the person's own sin.
What determines if the decision for Christ is a good decision?	*Collectivism/Individualism*: It benefits the in-group *versus* it benefits the individual personally. *Gender-Role Separation*: It will enable people to maintain gender-role separation *versus* it will not force people to separate gender roles. *Honor/Justice*: It does not bring shame *versus* it is the right thing to do.
How should a decision for Christ be implemented?	*High/Low Context*: It should come through a change in life without needing to be verbally articulated *versus* the verbal component should play a prominent role (perhaps through a formulated prayer). *Power Distance*: A patron or mentor should lead the way and people should follow *versus* each individual should decide for himself or herself. *Collectivism/Individualism*: People in the in-group should wait until the entire group has expressed in some way a willingness to come to Christ *versus* each individual should make a personal decision. *Honor/Justice*: The means of coming to Christ should not bring shame or dishonor to the in-group *versus* since it is the right thing to do, it should be done no matter how it impacts others.

issues you need to be aware of and stimulate your thinking about them in relation to evangelism.

Conversion in Cultural Context

Biblically speaking, conversion is the process of turning one's life over to Christ. There is no single set way this happens. People come to Christ for a variety of reasons in a variety of ways. It should be understood, then, that conversion also has cultural connotations. Lewis Rambo (1995) has studied conversion in multiple settings as well as from the perspective of different religions and developed a seven-stage picture of the process. The stages are not linear; people may move back and forth among them or work through multiple stages simultaneously (see fig. 18.3). At the risk of so reducing his exploration that we distort it, the following is a synopsis of those stages. As you read through each, consider the implications for evangelism in intercultural encounters.

1. *Context*: Refers not only to the actual immediate context of the conversion but also to the range of types of conversion and the motifs of the conversion process. It is in these contexts that all conversions are seen.
2. *Crisis*: Rarely do people simply convert without something in their lives driving them in the direction of conversion. Typically it is some form of psychological or social crisis ranging from personal mystical experiences to lifestyle changes to impending calamity.
3. *Quest*: People respond to the crisis by either actively seeking a solution or passively waiting for whatever will happen. They explore the resources available to them and are driven by internal motivations toward a resolution that makes sense.
4. *Encounter*: In the process of their quest, people will encounter an advocate. This advocate in some way—whether consciously or not—demonstrates to the potential convert the advantages of conversion, and they engage in a relationship.
5. *Interaction*: The interaction of the potential convert and the advocate results in the potential convert interacting not only with the advocate in rituals and rhetoric but also with the possibility of conversion and all that it entails.
6. *Commitment*: In moving toward conversion, the convert goes through a decision-making process and then commits herself to the act of conversion involving some form of ritual such as separation from the old life and surrendering to the new one. The convert now has a story of conversion that she can share with others. She reframes how she thinks about herself prior to the conversion event.

261

7. *Consequences*: There are multiple types of consequences of conversion, including psychological, familial, social, and cultural. Some of them the convert could anticipate; some are unexpected. These need to be worked through if the conversion is to "stick."

FIGURE 18.3
SEVEN STAGES OF CONVERSION (ADAPTED FROM RAMBO 1995)

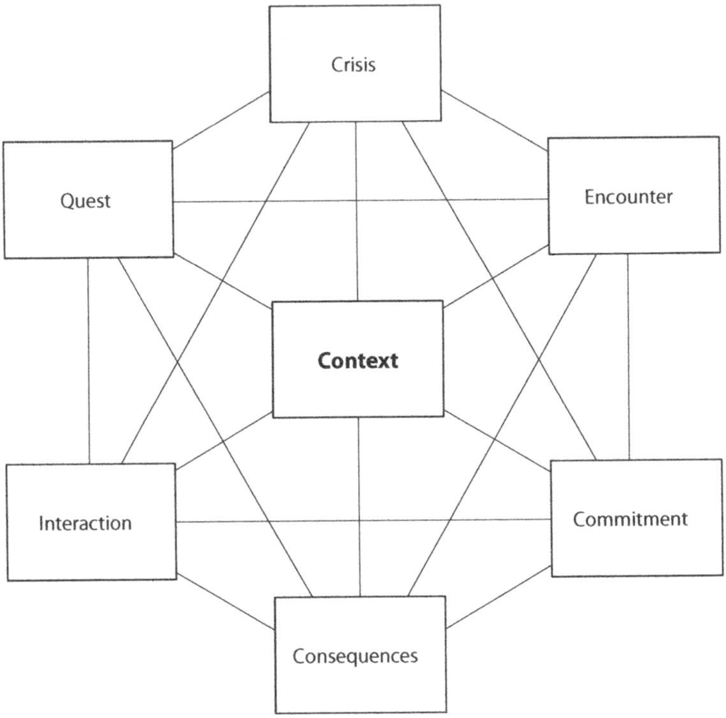

INTERCULTURAL EVANGELISTIC METHODS

Evangelicals are willing to try a wide variety of evangelism methods in the hope of being more effective (Waldrep 2007, 17–18; e.g., see sidebar 18.3). From using the Jesus film in the vernacular; performing Christian weddings in Japan (Midgley 2003); finding meaningful starting points (Andy Smith 2009); telling Muslims how to "live under the law" (Greer 2002) to finding a Muslim "man of peace" (Greeson 2004); storytelling among Muslims (Morton 2004), Hindus (Hoefer 2005), and postmoderns (R. Richardson 2006); and starting with historical reflection (Smither 2009), evangelicals have long experimented with new ways to more clearly communicate Christ.

Evangelicals are not simply interested in theories that are well articulated or orderly; they also look for and evaluate (Richard 2001) practices or models that will "work"—typically in terms of the process of conversion (Meral 2006), more people coming to Christ (Otis 1980), more churches being formed (Dixon 2002; Garrison 2004b) or mobilized for outreach (Parshall 2001), understanding why churches grow or struggle (Song 1997), or better teaching of core truths (Wakely 2004).

Effectiveness is a key issue for many evangelicals, especially in light of the reality that people perish apart from Christ. Thus they are concerned with better understanding the hardest areas for outreach, such as the Muslim (Parshall 1994; Musk 1988, 2008), Hindu (Richard 1998), or Buddhist (DeNeui 2005) worlds. They also look for practices that have been successfully used in a cross-cultural setting, such as Don Richardson's redemptive analogies (1974, 2000; see also Gilliland 2005, 508), other cultural bridges to understanding the gospel (R. Brown 2006a, 2006b, 2006c), or church-planting strategies (Talman 2004).

Narrative Evangelism

Taking a lead from postmodern deconstruction of the idea of an "objective" approach to communication, many evangelicals are working to show how the use of narrative is a viable form of contextualizing evangelism and discipleship (Redford 2005, 236–37), though this method is not really as new as it may seem (Steffen and Terry 2007). Applications include the following:

1. Using biblical parables to communicate truth to younger generations in the United States (M. Shaw 1993) and to oral learners in Majority World settings (R. Brown 2004a; Goforth 2011).
2. Recognizing that it is through the story of the Bible that we see God's truth enfleshed (H. Cole 2005; Achoba 2005).
3. Helping missionaries to learn how to use proverbs (Moon 2009, 2012) and stories in evangelism (R. Richardson 2006, 82–97) and discipleship work (Franklin 2005) among Muslims (Morton 2004), Hindus (Hoefer 2005), oral learners (http://www.chronologicalbiblestorying.com), and postmoderns (W. T. Kim 2005).
4. Learning from the stories developed in local settings that portray Christ in a way that people understand from within their own worldview (Miller 2009, 473; D. Richardson 1974, 1977; Ritchie 1996).

Much more could be said that space does not allow. Sidebar 18.3 offers a set of helpful questions for developing effective means of using story to

---

SIDEBAR 18.3
DEVELOPING EFFECTIVE STORYING

Franklin (2005, 11)

For the re-telling of Bible stories to be effective, storytellers must know how to select the stories, and how to tell them well so they can be retold easily and accurately. It is especially important to know the differences between Bible stories and other types of stories. Questions such as the following must be answered:

- What information in the story do the listeners already have at their disposal?

- How are the stories told in the source text?
- Who tells them?
- What is the general purpose of the stories?
- For whom are they told?
- In what ways can the stories be enhanced to make them more appropriate for this context?

---

communicate Christian truths. For a listing of over fifty websites providing resources for using stories in evangelism and discipleship, browse http://www.mislinks.org/communicating/storying.

Bible stories will hopefully be the first step in developing an interest in the vernacular, so they should be developed using various tools, such as dramatization, pictures, and recordings. Perhaps in some cases they will lead naturally to requests for videos of Luke or the story of Jesus. However, this will depend on the interest of the people and the availability of trained vernacular speakers.

Power Evangelism

Perhaps no term is seen more often in models contextualizing spiritual power than "power encounter." Coined by Alan Tippett in 1971 to refer to the "confrontation that tested the power of their [i.e., peoples in the South Pacific] ancestral gods against that of the Christian God, resulting in an obvious victory for the latter," the current usage of the term has been expanded to include healing and deliverance from demons (Kraft 2000, 774–75).

Possibly the most controversial approaches to evangelism among Westerners have been those related to power evangelism (Wimber 1990; Yip 1995), including practices such as spiritual mapping (e.g., Otis 1993) and strategic-level spiritual warfare (SLSW) (Wagner 1996, 1998). Advocates of SLSW exhort Christians to identify and confront territorial spirits, seen as ruling spirits that supervise other spirits in a particular territory (the more powerful the territorial spirit, the larger the area and the greater the bondage of its inhabitants).

The foundation for engaging SLSW is established through the process of spiritual mapping, in which we research the history and spiritual forces that exercise power over a locale. After uniting local churches and repenting before God as a body, local church leaders confront territorial spirits through prayer until they sense that their power is broken (Caballeros 1993; Otis 1993). Criticized for going beyond what Scripture teaches, a poor theological foundation, and exaggerated claims (see, e.g., Lowe 1998; Moreau 2002; Reid 2002), SLSW is still practiced, though with less fanfare than in the 1990s.

Infiltration Evangelism

Building on Paul's model of acting like a Jew to win the Jews (1 Cor. 9:20), in 1974 Kraft advocated "that we encourage some Christians to become Christian Muslims in order to win Muslims to Muslim Christianity" (1974b, 144). Most agree that those who come to Christ from Muslim, Hindu, or Buddhist backgrounds should be given time to determine how their new relationship with Christ fits with their existing social identity. This particular method, however, has missionaries who have not come from any of these backgrounds going "underground" and taking on the appearance of Muslims, Hindus, or Buddhists in order to reach them for Christ. Some have even gone to the extreme of changing their legal religious identity in countries that require a religious identity.

While such things as missionaries keeping the Muslim fast of Ramadan seem to be less an issue (Speers 1991; Parshall 1998b), there is significant controversy over missionaries participating in mosque rituals and calling themselves "Muslims" (as "ones who submit") with the intention of winning Muslims for Christ (Schlorff 2006; Tennent 2006; Woodberry 2007). This type of "infiltration" method is fraught with ethical dangers (Guthrie 2004, 133) and not advocated even by some of the strongest advocates of highly contextualized ministry among Muslims (Travis 2000, 55).

Evangelistic Appeals

Those engaged in intercultural evangelism must recognize that appeals that work in their home culture may very well not be as effective in their new culture. What types of appeals may the intercultural communicator make in seeking to lead people to Christ? The answer, of course, will depend on the cultural context. Several types of appeals should be kept in mind as options (the following draws from Hesselgrave 1991b, 602–11):

SIDEBAR 18.4

SELECTED WEB RESOURCES ON INTERCULTURAL EVANGELISM

"God's Amazing Diversity in Drawing Muslims to Christ," by Joshua Massey (http://www.ijfm.org/PDFs_IJFM/17_1_PDFs/Drawing_Muslims.pdf)

InterVarsity: A Code of Ethics for Christian Witness (http://www.intervarsity.org/slj/fa00/fa00_code_of_ethics.html); Basic Bibliography and Resource List for 1990–2000 (http://www.intervarsity.org/ism/article/26); International Witnessing Communities (http://www.intervarsity.org/ism/cat/53)

Network for Strategic Missions articles: Cross-Cultural Evangelism (http://www.strategicnetwork.org/index.php?loc=kb&view=b&fto=1624&sf=Y); Story Telling (http://www.strategicnetwork.org/index.php?loc=kb&view=b&fto=888&sf=Y)

"What Must One Believe about Jesus for Salvation?" by Rick Brown (http://www.ijfm.org/PDFs_IJFM/17_4_PDFs/02_Brown_Beliefs_hw.pdf)

The X Spectrum (http://www.internetevangelismday.com/x-spectrum.php)

---

1. The appeal to *selfhood* (useful among people who are individualistic).
2. The appeal to *authority* (useful among people who value large power distance or honor).
3. The appeal to *security* (useful among people who value large power distance and collectivism).
4. The appeal to *reason and logic* (useful among people who are low context and justice oriented; not as useful among people who are higher-context "folk" religious practitioners).
5. The appeal to *shame* (useful among people who are honor oriented and collective).
6. The appeal of *guilt* (useful among people who are justice oriented and individualistic).

CONCLUSION

There is much more that could be said about intercultural evangelism. We hope we have provided some foundational considerations that will enable you to better understand how evangelism can work in your own setting. In the midst of all this analysis, however, we must not lose track of how ultimately God is the one who draws people through the Holy Spirit. We may be catalysts, tools, or even simply observers whom God chooses to use in the process. At the outset of this chapter, we mentioned that successful evangelism is simply sharing Christ in the power of the Holy Spirit and leaving the results to God. Given the material we have covered in this chapter, we should revise that definition: successful evangelism is simply sharing Christ in the power of the Holy Spirit *and in light of cultural sensitivities* and leaving the results to God. In the case study for this chapter, we look at one of the issues seen in many settings: How can we tell if a conversion, or a promise to convert, is legitimate?

CASE STUDY:
CONVERSION OR SOCIAL CONVENTION?

PAUL G. HIEBERT

Reprinted by permission from Hiebert and Hiebert (1987, 161–63).

"Leela is already twenty-one, and by our customs she should have been married five or six years ago. It is not good for a woman to remain unmarried in the village. Already the people look down on Leela and suggest that she is cursed by the gods and brings bad luck. Soon the people will accuse her of prostitution. So it is urgent that we arrange a marriage for her right away. But we are now Christians, and there are no Christian young men of our caste for her to marry. We have searched widely. The only good prospect is Krishna, a young Hindu who is willing to become a Christian if we give Leela to him as his wife. Is it sin if we marry Leela to him? Is his conversion genuine if he becomes a Christian in order to marry Leela?"

Virginia Stevens looked at the anxious mother who was pouring out her heart to her. Then she looked at the young woman sitting expectantly on the mat before her. What should she say?

For years the Lutheran missionaries had worked in Andhra Pradesh on the east coast of South India. They had many converts, but most had come from the *harijan*, or untouchable castes. A few scattered individuals had become Christians from the lower clean castes, but none from the high castes.

Then a leading South Indian evangelist, a converted Brahmin from the highest caste, held meetings in the area, and five families of Reddys became Christians. The Reddys are farmers and rank high in the caste order. Because of their land holdings, they are wealthy and control much of the regional politics.

The new Christians met in a house church led by Venkat Reddy, one of the converts. He was well educated and could read the Scriptures, but he knew little about Christian doctrine and practice. So he contacted Sam and Virginia Stevens, Lutheran missionaries serving in Guntur, a hundred miles away. They visited the new church and encouraged it in its new faith. They also spent time with Venkat Reddy to help him grow in his understanding of Christianity. The church had grown spiritually and had won three other Reddy families to Christ, but one urgent problem persisted. How should the parents arrange marriages for their children?

Indian village culture requires that parents marry their children to members of their own caste. To marry outside of caste carries a great social stigma. Those involved and their families are put out of caste and shunned. Even the untouchables will have little to do with them. But there were few Reddy Christians, and many of the new converts could find no Christian Reddys to marry their children. There were many Christian young people in the old established churches, but they were all *harijans*, and it was unheard of for Reddys to marry untouchables. To do so would bring disgrace on the Christian Reddy families and cut them off totally from their non-Christian relatives. The door for further evangelism among the Reddys would then be largely closed.

Three years had passed since the Reddy congregation was formed, and the problem was becoming more acute as the young men and women grew older. One young man ran away from home and married a Christian woman he met in college. She was from an untouchable background, so they moved to the city of Madras where they could hide from the censure of their rural communities. But this had caused great pain to the young man's parents, who remained in the village.

Then a distant relative of Leela approached her parents about the possibility of Leela marrying their son. Ram and Shanta, Leela's parents, at first said no, that a Christian should not marry a non-Christian. But two months later, when the relative returned and said that Krishna, the young man in question, was willing to become a Christian and be baptized if the marriage took place, they began to reconsider.

Ram was not sure. "He will become a Christian in name only," he said.

"But he will listen to us and to Leela," said Shanta. "She is a strong Christian, and can help him grow in faith. Look at her! She's well past the age of marriage. If we pass up this opportunity, she may never get married. You don't want to condemn her to that, do you?"

Ram looked at Leela, his only daughter, and said, "I know. But we have always said that our Christian God would care for us in important matters such as this. Certainly he can provide us a Christian husband."

The next time the evangelist came to the village, Ram Reddy asked him if there were any Christian Reddy men in other parts of Andhra for his daughter. He also made several trips himself to distant towns in search of a husband. But none of his efforts turned up a suitable groom.

It was then that Krishna Reddy's father approached Ram and Shanta, urging them to arrange the marriage and reminding them that his son was willing to become a Christian and be baptized before the wedding. Ram and Shanta began to wonder whether this was God's way of opening the door for their daughter's marriage. Or was this a temptation they had to resist? Was such a conversion genuine? Did God want them to marry Leela to a Christian from an "untouchable" background instead? Could they bear the shame and ostracism that this would bring upon them in the village?

Now, as Virginia heard Shanta's story, she realized that the problem affected not only these parents, but also the future of the church among the Reddys. If Christians could not find spouses for their children, many Reddys would be afraid to convert. On the other hand, what did the Scriptures mean when it said that Christians should not be unequally yoked with unbelievers? Would Krishna's conversion be genuine if he took baptism so that he could marry Leela? What would happen if such marriages became an accepted practice in the Reddy church? And how would she feel if her own daughter were denied marriage because her mother herself had become a Christian? Virginia breathed a prayer before she responded . . .

REFLECTION AND DISCUSSION

1. Why does caste continue to be so important to the Indian church? How might it compare to ethnic identity in Western settings?

2. How do you think Virginia should respond?

Intercultural Discipleship

A s with intercultural evangelism, intercultural discipleship is the process of connecting people who are from a different culture than we are to Christ. Again, cultural values have a clear role to play in the discipleship process. To explore this, we first look at discipleship, then cultural issues of connecting people more deeply to Christ, followed by the use of rituals to help people make connections. Building on these three topics, we close the chapter with some suggestions on how we can use rituals as a part of the discipleship process.

WHAT IS DISCIPLESHIP?

In order to understand how to disciple, we must answer in the most basic form the question "What is discipleship?" The linguistic root of the New Testament term (*manthano*) is "to learn." The basic sense, then, is to direct one's mind to something. The noun form (*mathetes*) is in the most general sense a pupil. It implies both a relationship with a particular teacher and an intellectual link with those who are distant in time (e.g., Socrates was a *mathetes* of Homer).

In New Testament terms, disciples are described as people who have a deep, abiding commitment to a person (Christ), not a philosophy. They hold to Jesus's teaching (John 8:31–32), love one another (John 13:35), help one another (Matt. 10:42), bear fruit for Christ (John 15:8), are partners with him in service (Luke 5:1–11), make other disciples (Matt. 28:18–20), are the family of Jesus (Matt. 12:46–50), and put Jesus ahead of all other earthly commitments (Matt. 8:21–22; Luke 14:26–27), which involves a call to suffering for the sake of the gospel (Matt. 10:17–25).

Certainly this issue merits more space than we can give here. However, we have provided enough to define discipleship as follows in light of the New Testament and our definition of evangelism in the previous chapter: *Discipleship is the process of providing a culturally appropriate environment through the power of the Holy Spirit in which people can be connected to Christ so that they can grow to be more like him, thereby empowering them to progress toward completion in Christ while leaving the results to God.*

There are two sides of this connection and empowerment: people who know Christ need to (1) connect ever more deeply with him and (2) connect ever more deeply with other members of Christ's body for the purposes of building one another up. The question then becomes, "How do we help people connect?" Certainly a crucial way is to enable them to grow as Christ followers. Table 19.1 offers perspectives from the New Testament on how we grow, though in

TABLE 19.1

GROWTH IN THE NEW TESTAMENT

	Individually	Growth in:
Growth in Our Relationship with God		• faith (2 Cor. 10:15; 2 Thess. 1:3; 2 Pet. 1:5–8) • knowledge of God (Col. 1:10) • grace and knowledge of Christ (2 Pet. 3:18) • all aspects into Christ (Eph. 4:15) • respect to salvation (1 Pet. 2:2)
	Corporately	Growth: • as the body of Christ (Col. 2:19) • into a holy temple in the Lord (Eph. 2:21) • in giving thanks to God (2 Cor. 4:15)
Growth in Godliness	Individually	Growth in: • faith, moral excellence, knowledge, self-control, perseverance, godliness, brotherly kindness, and Christian love (2 Pet. 1:5–8) • walking as we ought to walk (1 Thess. 4:1) • behaving properly toward outsiders (1 Thess. 4:9–12) • love (Eph. 4:16; Phil. 1:9; 1 Thess. 3:12; 2 Thess. 1:3) • generosity (2 Cor. 8:7; 9:10–11)
	Corporately	Growth in: • edifying the church (1 Cor. 14:12) • the work of the Lord (1 Cor. 15:58) • love of outsiders (1 Thess. 3:12)

> Disciples *are people "who have heard and understood what*
> *Jesus taught during His lifetime—they are* earwitnesses"—
> *people "who hear and understand the commands and teaching*
> *of Jesus so it can be said that they do the will of God."*
>
> O'Brien 1976, 75, emphasis in original

any cross-cultural setting we need to consider carefully how cultural values frame both growth and discipleship, the latter of which may not even have an equivalent in the local language (see Mtange 2010).

DISCIPLESHIP: HELPING PEOPLE CONNECT

Culture plays a fundamental role in how people connect with one another. Collectivists have different ideas of friendship and connecting than do individualists. People who value large power distance will connect in different ways from those who value low power distance. On the one hand, what might seem to be a method of connecting with a low-context person may be perceived as insulting to a high-context person. On the other hand, what might seem to be connecting to a high-context person may be indecipherable to a low-context person. Each of these differences will have an impact on the discipleship process in intercultural settings. To explore them all would take a book by itself.

For that reason, and because it is an issue in so many locations around the world, in this chapter we largely confine our discussion to points that will help those from justice-oriented societies see how they can help people from honor-oriented societies grow in their discipleship. By this means we hope to chart a path that can be followed for developing models for other settings as well.

In chapter 14 we explored the worldview of honor-oriented societies. We noted that they are typically more collectivistic, higher in context, and larger in power distance than justice-oriented societies. We extend that description here in relation to discipleship by briefly discussing how they emphasize the *value of connecting*. Second, we explore their *rules for connecting* by seeing how they are embedded in the local cultural values. Finally, we will discuss how you can utilize *means of connecting* by understanding—and contextualizing—appropriate bonding practices seen in rituals that we can use to lead them to more meaningful encounters with Christ and with one another.

Value of Connecting

People in honor-oriented societies value connecting primarily with their patron or their in-group. Ultimate allegiance is owed the patron, and to be without a patron is to be unprotected. To be without an in-group is to be shamed so deeply as to become a nonperson, since it is through in-group relations that honor-oriented people define themselves. Connecting in long-term intimate relationships is essential for honor-oriented people, and they favor those with whom they have such connections over others (and expect such favoritism in return).

Honor-oriented people who come to see Christ as their patron and the body of Christ as their in-group will desire to connect as deeply as they can with both. Thus one foundational goal in discipleship in honor-oriented cultures will be to nurture this view of Christ and the church.

For people in these cultures, learning that Christ endured shame can be a hurdle. To acknowledge that God allowed such a person as Christ to suffer shame may contradict their idea of Christ as a patron deserving glory and honor. The idea that Christ achieved great honor by means of bearing shame does not fit their worldview. However, making this connection cognitively, affectively, and volitionally will be critical for them so that they can connect to Christ's enduring the shame for the sake of obedience to God.

A difficulty that justice-oriented people working in honor-oriented settings face is the need to serve as appropriate patrons who point people to Christ (1 Cor. 11:1). People from justice-oriented societies typically grow up individualistically and do not learn the rules of the patron-client system, and they feel uncomfortable practicing it (they may call it unbiblical or unchristian). They will need to explore in greater depth patron-client relationships in Scripture to identify healthy ways to connect honor-oriented people to Christ and the church.

Rules for Connecting

The rules a society uses for connecting are embedded in the local cultural values. Most honor-oriented cultures are collectivist and high context. They tend to value large power distance and utilize patron-client systems of relationships. As a result, in many honor-oriented societies, social debt acts as a type of glue holding the society together, and the rules of connecting are extensions of developing social debt. This practice was illustrated in the steps of social exchange for a patron and a client described in chapter 12.

People from independent, individualistic cultures typically do not understand this practice. Indeed, they value *avoiding* social debt rather than accumulating it. Thus, if you invite an independent individualist to dinner he or she will have an obligation to return the favor in some way to zero out the social account. This zeroing out is just the opposite of honor-oriented peoples' rules for connecting.

Imagine an independent person borrowing something from or granting a favor to an honor-oriented person. There is now a social debt between them. The independent person will feel constrained to balance the account and pay off the debt. By doing this, however, the independent person may be communicating either a lack of interest in a connecting relationship or interest in pursuing a patron-client relationship with the honor-oriented person. Unfortunately, the unprepared independent person will not even be aware of the meaning given to his actions and will not understand further acts by the honor-oriented person.

Means of Connecting

We have seen how people who are honor-oriented value connecting, and we have touched on their rules for connecting (the following discussion draws from Moreau 2005, 2006). How do we engage such people in discipleship? Many honor-oriented societies deeply value *rituals* as a means of embedding the values and engaging the rules of connecting.

Thus it is essential that we explore the role of rituals and how they enable people to bond (or connect) more deeply with Christ and his body. Rituals are used for multiple purposes in societies. People in honor-oriented cultures expect to use rituals for such things as affirming their social and historic identity, transitioning from one type of status to another, and reminding them of who they are and how they are expected to properly relate to others.

However, many North American evangelicals have been leery of ritual, at least in part as a reaction formulated in the Reformation and solidified in the contemporary distancing from mainline denominations. Our Pietistic forefathers criticized the use of empty ritual and focused on developing a personal relationship with Christ through prayer and Bible study rather than through formal ritual. Similarly, many evangelicals who come to faith after

> *Rituals serve a variety of purposes in religions. They establish or affirm the social and historic identity of the participants, reminding them of who they are and how they relate to others in the culture. They help people move from one social status to another. They serve as cultural drama libraries in which the history, values, and beliefs of the people are symbolized and reenacted.*
>
> Moreau 2005, 339

leaving mainline churches have mixed feelings at best about the rituals practiced in their former denominations, especially when they have experienced a vibrant relationship with Christ apart from formal ritual and in contrast to their former church life.

As a result, evangelicals can be reluctant to consciously focus on ritual as a means of discipleship. By doing so, however, they overlook the simple fact that many of their discipling activities (small group Bible studies, corporate worship, one-on-one discipleship, devotional times) are inherently ritualistic. They have lost sight of how they were created as ritualistic beings—the worship of the multitudes in heaven bearing witness that we will all engage in meaningful rituals as an integral part of our experience of eternal, abundant life (Rev. 7:9–12).

Cross-cultural communicators from these types of churches can overlook ritual altogether. At best they may work to contextualize liturgical New Testament rituals such as communion and baptism. However, they are likely to ignore or suppress important indigenous rituals that may be adaptable to church life, such as rituals for conflict resolution, life transitions, and socialization—in other words, rituals important for discipleship. Wise cross-cultural workers, however, will become students of the rituals found in the society they serve. They will constantly explore ways in which these rituals can be used for the important kingdom-building activities of evangelism, discipleship, and social transformation (see, e.g., Moon 2012, 2013; Smythe 2011).

Ritual scholars have identified three distinct types of ritual (R. Shaw 2000): (1) rituals of transformation (changing from one state to another, such as in baptism or becoming a member of a church); (2) rituals of intensification (renewal or growth, such as in corporate or private worship and fellowship); and (3) rituals of crisis (dealing with setbacks, problems, or emergencies, such as anointing with oil and prayer for healing).

Such rituals lead us to encounters with Christ, with his followers, and with the God who made us. Charles Kraft has identified three types of such encounters that are critical in discipleship (1991c): (1) allegiance encounters, in which we commit ourselves to Christ and his kingdom; (2) truth encounters, in which we commit ourselves to the truth of the Word of God and its consequences for our lives; and (3) power encounters, in which we engage those spiritual powers that would hinder our growth in Christ.

In the rest of this chapter, we survey ways to combine different types of rituals to enable appropriate encounters as a means of discipleship in honor-oriented societies. In addition to the following discussion, John Travis (2008) offers very helpful applications using the types of encounters identified by Kraft in discipling Muslims.

USING RITUALS IN INTERCULTURAL DISCIPLESHIP

Rituals of Transition

Rituals of transition enable people to shift from one stage of life to another. They include such things as graduation ceremonies, weddings, and initiation rites. Prior to the ritual, the participants were limited in terms of recognition for tasks or responsibilities; after the ritual, they have full community status to engage in these tasks or responsibilities. Many cultures of the world still have initiation rituals to bring a person from childhood to adulthood, and some churches are working to take advantage of these for the purposes of connecting their youth to Christ (e.g., http://tinyurl.com/kwujm8y). These rituals take place in three stages (fig. 19.1): separation, transformation, and reincorporation (Zahniser 1997, 192).

Separation, the first phase, is the severing of the person from normal life. This is often accomplished through a symbolic act such as moving to special living quarters, wearing clothes indicating the separation, or being ritually sent away from the community.

FIGURE 19.1
THREE STAGES OF TRANSITION RITUALS (MOREAU 2005, 340)

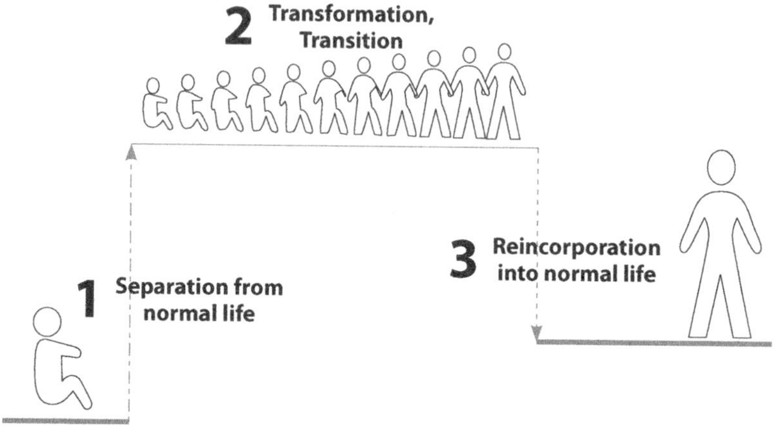

Transformation, the second phase, involves the process that is required for the individual to be changed. While separated and cut off from normal support systems, those in the transformational process may be required to perform special deeds, undertake various trials, pass tests, overcome challenges, or make special commitments. Those undergoing transformation are in what is called a *liminal* state (Hertig 2000). As a result of the shared experience, they often develop a close-knit community whose bonds may be even stronger than kinship. They are also bonding to new roles they will have once they complete the transformational stage, which may happen in a few minutes (a wedding) or over the course of several years (a degree program, an apprenticeship) (Zahniser 1997, 94–98).

Once the trials or training are completed, the final phase of *reincorporation* happens. This often includes a ceremony indicating the successful completion of the transition, such as a graduation ceremony. This ceremony socially affirms that the transition is complete and the person is now qualified to enjoy all the rights and privileges of one who has completed the ritual, from being allowed to drive, to qualifying for certain types of occupations, to being able to enter into further transition rituals such as graduate school or elder training.

Rituals of Intensification

Rituals of intensification are used to strengthen or shore up beliefs, identity, or other important cultural values. Saluting the flag and saying some type of pledge is intended to invigorate patriotism, wedding anniversaries revitalize a marriage, and weekly church services refresh our faith. People growing in their faith need regular renewal opportunities, and rituals of intensification play an important role in the life of every believer. From weekly worship to small group Bible studies to devotional times to prayer gatherings, all are important in connecting believers to Christ and to one another. At the same time, no ritual takes place in a "cultural vacuum." When properly contextualized, rituals draw on and reinforce cultural values related to connectedness and religious devotion, bringing people closer to Christ and his body.

Rituals of Crisis

Rituals of crisis help us to cope with calamities or other emergencies as they arise. The actual crisis may be minor, such as feeling a cold coming on. Our ritual response in these cases may be as simple as taking medicine and going to bed early.

The crisis may also be major, such as when someone is suddenly diagnosed with life-threatening cancer. In these cases, the importance of the ritual to handle the crisis is more deeply felt. In more-secular societies, this ritual may include marshaling major medical resources. Among Christians in those societies, it can also include calling Christians together to pray or setting up special healing services. In many cultures around the world, however, people go to shamans, diviners, or healers for help. All these practices are still ritual in the sense that they follow patterned responses to deal with the crisis.

These rituals give us a way to fight back when things are going wrong or spinning out of control. They give people hope that a higher power (e.g., God, spirits, luck, and fate) will intervene on their behalf and provide relief. For Christians, crisis rituals can play an important part in the discipleship process, for learning how to go to God and trust him in such times is a significant way we connect with Christ.

Using Rituals to Initiate Connecting Encounters

We have presented three types of encounters and three types of rituals. Together they provide a total of nine types of ritual encounters that can be used in discipleship settings. To help you to see how this can be worked out to develop a culturally sensitive discipleship strategy, in the following discussion we offer suggestions for discipleship and rituals based on three of the communication patterns that are part of the honor game as discussed earlier: high context, collectivism, and patron-client relationships. This discussion and table 19.2 are not intended to be exhaustive. Rather, consider the examples offered as no more than suggestions to stimulate your own thinking and experimentation within biblical boundaries.

Discipleship in *high-context settings* differs from that in low-context settings. This is especially true when the discipler and those being discipled are of the same in-group and share in the ocean of information in such a way that a high-context approach will work. We offer the following characterizations of discipleship in high-context settings as suggestions to consider and to stimulate your own thinking.

First, we might expect that excessive verbal self-expression is discouraged. People attend to nonverbal communication skills. Those being discipled are expected to pay careful attention to the nonverbal behavior of the discipler for cues on how to respond. It is more likely that ideas will be taught indirectly rather than directly. For example, leaders may "beat around the bush" or use stories or parables to communicate their point. In small group settings, silence in the group is not seen as indicative of noncommunication and is welcomed as part of the group's time together. Finally, discipline is more likely to be indirect, for an outburst of verbal anger by the discipler might indicate lack of control or derangement. How discipline is actually handled, however, is moderated by power distance (in which the more powerful are free to berate the less powerful) and the severity of the issue being addressed.

Discipleship in *collectivist settings* differs from discipleship in individualistic settings. This is especially true when the discipler and those being discipled are members of the same in-group. We offer the following characterizations of discipleship in collectivist settings as suggestions to consider and to stimulate your own thinking.

First, connection in collective groups is rooted in concrete relationships that are long term and intimate. Connecting involves living through concrete situations rather than learning abstract ideas. Further, in-group members feel a direct sense of responsibility for the face of their in-group members. Thus teamwork means thinking of others' needs before your own. Conversely, others are responsible for thinking of your needs. Collectivists may also have a strong desire for maintaining hierarchy rather than developing equality. For example, the leader is always the leader (just as the older person is always older).

Discipleship in *patron-client settings* differs from discipleship in independent/individualistic settings. This is especially true when the discipler and those being discipled are of the same patron-client group. We offer the following characterizations of discipleship in patron-client settings as suggestions to consider and to stimulate your own thinking.

First, in patron-client settings people stress personal "wisdom" rather than impersonal "truth." This wisdom is transferred in the relationship of leader and disciple, and the effectiveness of learning is related to the excellence of the spiritual leader. Further, a spiritual leader is responsible for disciplining his or her disciples and merits their respect and support. Therefore, the leader is only rarely—if at all—contradicted or publicly criticized. Disciples in this setting may be in some type of hierarchy (e.g., Jesus had the twelve, but three were special to him). Finally, the disciples want their spiritual leader to initiate communication and outline the paths they are to follow.

Based on the suggestions for high-context, collectivist, and patron-client settings, then, what types of rituals might be used in discipling people in honor-oriented settings? Table 19.2 offers a suggestion for each of the encounters under each type of ritual.

SIDEBAR 19.1
SELECTED WEB RESOURCES ON CROSS-CULTURAL MINISTRY

Ethnic Harvest Resources for Multicultural Ministry (http://www.ethnicharvest.org/links/linkindex.htm) Network for Strategic Missions articles: Cross-Cultural Ministry (http://www.strategicnetwork.org /index.php?loc=kb&view=b&fto =1665&sf=Y); Discipleship (http:// www.strategicnetwork.org/index .php?loc=kb&view=b&fto=762&sf =Y)

TABLE 19.2
SUGGESTIONS FOR DISCIPLESHIP RITUALS IN HONOR-ORIENTED SETTINGS

Type of Ritual	Encounter	In the ritual, have people connect by:
Transformation (changing one status to another)	Allegiance	committing themselves to Christ as their patron and his in-group as their collective. They may do this through making a group verbal pledge or performing some task that demonstrates everyone's allegiance.
	Truth	taking an oath declaring specific truths from God's Word (e.g., a creed) when transitioning into a new position of leadership in the fellowship (e.g., deacon, elder, other church officer).
	Power	having them participate under the authority of a respected and experienced leader in anointing and praying for the oppressed as a way of preparing them to engage in a ministry of deliverance.
Intensification (strengthening beliefs or identity)	Allegiance	worshiping under the direction of a spiritual leader who follows Christ and reordering priorities demonstrating allegiance to Christ and his church.
	Truth	developing a specific group statement of faith on a topic of spiritual growth under the guidance of a church leader.
	Power	sharing in a group setting visions, dreams, prophecies, power encounters, or other experiences of the supernatural that people have had that have strengthened their faith and, with a respected leader, seeking God's wisdom to understand his purposes through them.
Crisis (coping with a calamity or other emergency)	Allegiance	corporately confessing allegiance to Christ when a crisis is disturbing the community. When necessary, shunning a person who has been disciplined for allegiance to someone other than Christ.
	Truth	developing a Bible-centered and culturally sensitive statement of faith on a crisis faced by the group, under the direction of a leader.
	Power	gathering to have those in authority anoint and pray for people undergoing a crisis (health, family, job) and allowing the Spirit to pray on the group's behalf with groans beyond words (Rom. 8:26–27).

CONCLUSION

Christians living in new cultural settings are not exempt from the command to make disciples of all nations (Matt. 28:18–20). Chances are, however, if you were discipled in your home culture by someone of the same culture, you will make assumptions about discipleship that will not be true in the intercultural setting. As we have seen, discipleship requires a good understanding of the biblical ideal together with a good understanding of how it can be worked out in a given culture. Our case study illustrates the issues involved in intercultural discipleship, including biblical teaching, cultural values, and religious values.

CASE STUDY:
THE VULNERABLE AGE

PAM BARGER

Nancy didn't know what to do. She and Painge had constantly read the Bible, prayed, and even fasted about the difficult situation. Painge was confused and struggled over a strong, emotional division in her heart. How could she love God without further hurting her family? How could she honor her mother and father without dishonoring God?

Nancy taught English as a second language at an American university. It was there that she first met Painge, a Thai American whose family was still in Thailand. Painge was an ambitious undergraduate motivated to pursue a career as a psychologist. She and her family were Buddhists, as all Thai are expected to be. Although she consistently prayed to Buddha, worked hard for her good grades, and had a close family who loved her very much, Painge still felt an emptiness in her heart. Over the months of her English studies under Nancy, she began to question the true meaning of life.

Early in her junior year at the university, through her friendship with Nancy, a deep longing was filled as Painge entered into a brand-new relationship with Jesus. Having given her life over to Christ, she began to experience healing of the hurts that had wounded her over the years. Having found a purpose for life in her commitment to Christ, Painge was to be taken by surprise at the harsh and negative impact her decision had on her family.

During a term break in her junior year, Painge went home to Thailand. As she gradually began to share her testimony of Christ with family, they became dismayed. Her mother particularly took Painge's conversion very hard; she angrily and tearfully told her daughter that if she accepted Christ, then she could not be a part of the family anymore. Painge's mother conveyed to her that for a person to be Thai, she must be Buddhist. With pain Painge remembered that over the course of her teen years, her mother had often mentioned that she felt as if Painge was not her daughter but a mere stranger to her. This new decision for Christ seemed to be the final straw, and Painge's family refused to associate with her.

Painge returned to the United States to continue her studies heavy in heart. Through the grace of God and prayers from her friends, however, she persisted in her walk with the Lord. She constantly prayed that God would prepare her heart whenever she would see her family again.

A year after graduation, Painge had an unexpected opportunity to return to Thailand and be with her family for a year. Though her parents, especially her mother, still had a difficult time with her faith, things seemed to improve. Painge was allowed to attend church and continue involvement in her Christian faith.

During the year she was in Thailand, Painge consistently attempted to show the light of Christ to her family. She was able to get a job in which she saved up money to attend a well-known Christian graduate school. She had a strong desire to know more about her personal relationship with God and his will for her in the future. Her parents, though somewhat resistant, slowly began to appreciate her hard academic work and accomplishments.

281

The year passed quickly, and once again Painge left her family and returned to the United States, this time to attend the graduate program for which she had been saving. During her second semester, however, she experienced in rapid sequence two events that left her confused and hurt, wondering what course of action she should take.

During the first term Painge had turned twenty-four and reached the period of "the vulnerable age," which is the age of twenty-five. Originally a superstition but now adapted as part of Thai Buddhism, turning twenty-five marks the transition from childhood to the beginning of adulthood. Just prior to turning twenty-five and during this critical stage, the young adult is considered extremely vulnerable in almost all aspects of life. Illness, loss of job, and family problems are all associated with the vulnerable age. Thus the vulnerable age not only affects the individual but also his or her family. Painge's mother, knowing this stage was coming, had started hinting that her daughter could make amends with the family by undergoing the Buddhist ritual that would give protection through the vulnerable age. In that ritual, Buddhist monks chant and sprinkle holy water on the supplicant, who is expected to give *bun*, or money, to them so that they will pray for the supplicant and family for protection and a prosperous life.

About the time Painge began to feel serious pressure from her mother, a Thai friend, Aucha, received devastating news. Aucha, who was not a follower of Christ, reached the age of twenty-five without having performed the ritual. Shortly afterward, her family learned that Aucha's father was in an advanced stage of cancer and had only a few months to live. Aucha's grandmother commented to Painge's mother that she believed that the illness was caused by Aucha not performing the ritual. Aucha's family, terrified at the prospect of losing her father, immediately decided to have a Buddhist ritual for Aucha and her father in the hopes that it would restore his health. Painge's mother was deeply alarmed at the situation and immediately began to apply even greater pressure on Painge, insisting that Painge perform the ritual and thereby protect Painge and her family.

To complicate things, a week after the news of Aucha's father's cancer, Painge and her brother were in a car accident. In the accident, Painge hit her head on the windshield. She went to the emergency room and was soon released with only a minor concussion. Her parents were terribly shocked about the incident, especially since she had hit her head. In Thai culture, the head is considered the most precious part of the body, a symbol of intellect, wisdom, success, and life. Painge's parents believed that the car accident was a warning sign from Buddha that she and her family needed to protect themselves from any possible accidents in the future. They increased the pressure on Painge to honor and protect herself and them by performing the ritual.

Painge was confused and hurt. She agonized over what to do. The window of vulnerability stretched out over the next few months, and she loved her family more than any other people on earth. Feeling torn between the desire to be a faithful, loving child of her human family and a faithful, loving child of her heavenly family, Painge was filled with conflicting thoughts. On the one hand, she knew God would protect her. On the other hand, she could not help thinking of the coincidental events that had happened in such rapid succession and how her parents, and even her whole culture, interpreted them. Though she trusted God, she also loved her family and wanted to respect as well as please them. She did not know what to do.

It was then that she turned to Nancy, who had been instrumental in helping her come to Christ. Together they prayed, asking God for wisdom. They searched the Scriptures as well as resources on Thai culture and the Buddhist ritual. Though initially confused and not sure how to proceed, eventually they both sensed God's quiet, still voice leading them to decide that Painge should . . .

REFLECTION AND DISCUSSION

1. In what ways does Painge's crisis reflect common issues for people coming to Christ from non-Christian families and societies?

2. What would you suggest Painge do?

20

Intercultural Church Planting

Going beyond intercultural evangelism and discipleship, intercultural church planting is the process of connecting people with Christ and gathering them together as an organized living body (or bodies) of believers. From decision making to leadership and organizing, cultural values have a clear role to play in the church-planting and developing process. It should be obvious that church planting needs to use indigenous forms of worship (Krabill 2012; Schragg and Krabill 2012; Taylor 2012) and organization—from Native American (Woodley 2000) to Muslim (Trueman 1989; Goble and Munayer 1989; Baker 2009; Hoefer 2009) to Hindu (Hoefer 2001). However, it must also take into account the social structures of the population among which the church is being planted (Hiebert and Meneses 1995; Hiebert 1999b; Nida 1999; Waldrep 2007, 12–15; Woodberry 2011).

To explore this process, in this chapter we introduce various types of church planting models but give particular attention to the lead of David Hesselgrave (see fig. 20.1) in using Paul's process of church planting as portrayed in Acts. Although this is not the only viable model for church planting in cross-cultural settings (see sidebar 20.1), because it is drawn from Scripture it merits special consideration.

A Church-Planting Model

Throughout the history of the church, numerous viable church-planting methods have been used to establish healthy, long-lived churches (see, e.g., Garrison 2004a; Nichols, Moreau, and Corwin 2011; Payne 2009; Ott and Wilson 2011; Zdero 2011). Peter Wagner (1990) presents twelve models divided into two categories based on terminology applied to mission by Ralph Winter (1971, 1974): (1) seven *modality* models, or those that are one church giving birth to another, and (2) five *sodality* models, or those that are an agency or other parachurch group giving birth to a church. For example, in the New Testament, Paul used a sodality model based on his apostolic gift.

> *A contextual missiology will result in a church—large or small, growing or stable in membership—that faithfully understands its relationship to its own context, its nature as the church, its own forms of worship, and its own expressions of Christian discipleship.*
>
> Taber 1983a, 128

SIDEBAR 20.1
TWELVE MODELS OF CHURCH PLANTING

Adapted from Wagner (1990, 59–75)

MODALITY MODELS

Hiving Off: A nucleus for a new church is formed from members of another established church.

Colonization: Like hiving off, except the nucleus actually moves to a new geographic area to form the new church.

Adoption: An older denomination or church establishes a relationship with a recently established church.

Accidental Parenthood: As a result of a church split (for whatever reason), two churches are formed.

The Satellite Model: A new church is (or new churches are) formed with a semiautonomous relationship with the mother church.

Multicongregational Churches: Many different (usually ethnic) congregations share the same facilities.

The Multiple-Campus Model: One congregation, having one staff, one budget, and one membership roll, has more than a single facility.

SODALITY MODELS

The Mission Team: A team of missionaries is sent out to form a new church.

The Catalytic Church Planter: This person starts a new church and then leaves for another area (Paul is the model for this planter).

The Founding Pastor: The sending agency designates the one being sent as the founding pastor who stays with the church once it has been planted.

The Independent Church Planter: These planters operate apart from any agency (they serve as their own agency). They may follow any of the models listed but operate on their own.

The Apostolic Church Planter: Among groups that recognize the gift of apostleship, an apostle is sent out to plant a new church.

Examples of each of these twelve models can be found in church history, but that does not mean that all manifestations of them are desirable (e.g., the "accidental parenthood" that happens when a church splits).

The model we utilize as the outline for this chapter comes from the Apostolic Church Planter method, with the specific outline derived from Paul's ten-step church-planting cycle found in Acts as explained by Hesselgrave and shown in figure 20.1 and table 20.1. This approach has been taught to and used by numerous church-planting missionaries since the first edition of *Planting Churches Cross-Culturally* was published in 1980 (the second edition was published in 2000 and is still in print).

FIGURE 20.1
PAULINE CHURCH-PLANTING CYCLE (ADAPTED FROM HESSELGRAVE 1980B)

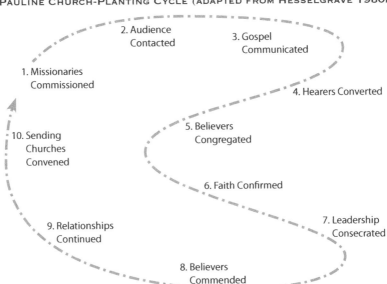

While this church-planting method has a beginning and an end, it is cyclical and so will continue until the Lord returns. It is a process that the planter can proceed through step by step even though in many cases multiple steps will be happening simultaneously. It is intended to apply to a church in any stage of its existence as well as to pioneer situations (Hesselgrave 1980b, 49–51).

The ten steps of the cycle are identified in table 20.1. Because steps 2 through 4 involve the evangelism process (discussed in chap. 18), we do not discuss them in this chapter. Further, because our focus on the commissioning component noted in step 1 involves the commissioning of new church planters who are from the cross-cultural setting at the end of the process, we present it as the last step rather than the first.

TABLE 20.1
PAULINE CHURCH-PLANTING STEPS

Step	What Is Involved
1. The Missionaries Commissioned	Local congregations, as part of larger fellowships such as denominations and as led by the Holy Spirit, set aside people for the missionary task of church planting. The church planters are provided opportunity for suitable training and are offered prayer and other appropriate support.
2. The Audience Contacted	The church planters cross cultural boundaries for the purpose of contacting the people among whom they intend to plant churches. They learn the language and culture of the people, working to become effective communicators of Christ.
3. The Gospel Communicated	The church planters sow the gospel by engaging in biblically centered and culturally appropriate evangelism in the society where they live. This may range from one-on-one to mass evangelism, but it is contextualized and as bold as God's leading requires.
4. The Hearers Converted	As people come to Christ out of true understanding and through culturally appropriate patterns of decision making, the church planters seek to disciple them into people who are genuine, persevering, and able to produce their own spiritual fruitfulness.
5. The Believers Congregated	Those who have come to Christ are gathered together on a regular basis. This may be in small discipleship groups initially, though the eventual goal is the development of viable fellowships. These may take the form of cell groups, house churches, or larger congregations, depending on the setting and circumstances.
6. The Faith Confirmed	Within the fellowships, believers are discipled toward maturity in Christ. They learn to exercise their gifts in service to the fellowship, to worship with all they are, to give sacrificially, and to share their faith as led by the Spirit.
7. The Leadership Consecrated	As leadership arises, it is recognized by the church planters and fellowships in ways that allow it to function in contextualized fashion. When appropriate, local leaders are formally consecrated by the fellowships they lead, and they are empowered to organize and lead the fellowships in appropriate ways.
8. The Believers Commended	The church planters ensure (if they have not already done so) that they are phasing out of leadership. This may involve a formal ritual of commending the local congregation and leaving the location. At the same time, they remain in touch with the congregational leaders, providing assistance and advice at the local leaders' discretion.
9. The Relationships Continued	The congregations develop and establish appropriate relationships with the church planters, the agency of the church planters, and with other local fellowships.
10. The Sending Churches Convened	The congregations mature to the point where they are in the process of sending their own cross-cultural church planters, and they organize themselves (perhaps developing a new mission agency) for the purpose of training, sending, and supporting their own missionaries.

Adapted from Hesselgrave 2000a.

The Believers Congregated

People who have come to Christ need connection with other Christians. In the milieu of the early church, groups met in homes, at synagogues, and in public places (at least when they were not being persecuted). While the Sabbath (Saturday) was set aside as a special day for worship, there was no prohibition against meeting at other times or in places other than the synagogue. In the history of the church, Sunday—the day Jesus rose from the dead—was eventually recognized as the Lord's Day and became the Christian Sabbath. However, no scriptural passage demands that Christians observe the Sabbath on Sunday.

It will be helpful to briefly consider what these churches should look like, how they should "feel" in the local setting, and what impact they should have. The best-known model for dealing with these important issues, though not without controversy, was developed by Charles Kraft and is called "dynamic equivalence churchness":

> A "dynamic equivalence church," then, is the kind of church that produces the same kind of impact on its own society as the early church produced upon the original hearers. In that equivalence the younger church will have need of leadership, organization, education, worship, buildings, behavioral standards, means of expressing Christian love and concern to unconverted people. A dynamically equivalent church will employ familiar, meaningful, indigenous forms, adapting and infilling them with Christian content. (Kraft 1973a, 49)

The term "dynamic equivalence" was initially developed by Eugene Nida in linguistic theory for use in translation (North 1974, xii). Borrowing from the linguistic and communicational frames, the goal of Kraft's approach is "to see expressed in the lives of the receptors the meanings taught in Scripture" (Kraft 2005c, 168).

In maintaining that contextualization should be dynamic, Kraft is essentially proposing a "calculus" approach to revelation and contextualization. For our purposes, the more significant—and less controversial—implications of the *dynamic* nature of contextualization are (adapted from Kraft 2005a):

- Contextualization is a process, not a product.
- Learning is best done by self-discovery rather than impartation of information.
- The goal is the transformation of lives of individuals and groups; God accepts people where they are and leads them in a process of transformation.

·In molding his approach around equivalence of *impact* rather than of *form*, Kraft draws from the disciplines of linguistics, translation, communication, and anthropology. He posits that God's intent is for us to attempt to reproduce the *impact* of God's revelation rather than the cognitive content. In essence, Kraft attends to the *stimulus* generated in the receptors rather than in God's own work of *illuminating* the Scriptures for the receptors' benefit. The primary implications of the *equivalence* component of dynamic equivalence are (adapted from Kraft 2005a):

- Equivalence is in impact, not in information transfer.
- Equivalence is ever changing (as cultures are ever changing).
- Since all cultures are "adequate and equal in potential usefulness as vehicles of God's interaction with humanity," (43) we focus on methods that will enable people to be impacted with the significance of Christ and align their allegiance with God through a minimum of worldview shift.

In sum, by following these and other principles as developed by Kraft, when we congregate believers we work to produce a dynamic-equivalent church that

(1) conveys to its members truly Christian meanings, (2) functions within its own society in the name of Christ, meeting the felt needs of that society and producing within it the same Christian impact as the first century Church in its day, and (3) is couched in cultural forms that are as nearly indigenous as possible.

What is desired is a church that will possess indigenous forms for Christ, adapting them to Christian ends by fulfilling indigenous functions and conveying Christian meanings through them to the surrounding society. (Kraft 1973a, 40; see also 1979b, 295–97)

Kraft is certainly correct that churches should adapt practices and forms in their culture and connect them to Christ. However, doing so must have boundaries. For example, he has been sharply criticized for enjoining the church to draw from animistic practices, fill them with Christian meaning, and use them in Christ's authority for God's glory in spiritual warfare (see Priest, Campbell, and Mullen 1995; Kraft 1995).

This approach has also been critiqued for ignoring the historical particularity of the text: can we really expect the contemporary Western urban reader to have the same response to Leviticus as the rural, nomadic Hebrews without some kind of radical change in the original meaning of the text (Carson 1985, 202–5)? It has also been criticized for making the Bible subject to our understanding of ancient culture (McQuilkin 1980, 117; see also Inch 1984, 745–46), making us dependent on the anthropologist to understand the meaning of Scripture and know how to generate the right response as well as potentially leading to the "death of the apostolic Christianity which he proposes to champion" when Kraft's former students go beyond his own intentions (Hesselgrave 1984, 723).

Dynamic equivalence in translation has been extremely helpful when applied with appropriate safeguards. In the same way, it must be moderated when applied to church planting and development. For example, rather than seeing response as the emotional reaction, it is better to see dynamic "equivalence in linguistic categories, i.e. in terms of the removal of as many as possible of the false linguistic barriers (along with the associations each linguistic category carries) which actually impede the communication of truth" (Carson 1985, 205). Ultimately, Donald Carson concludes that an insurmountable problem is "the unwitting assumption that 'response' is the ultimate category in translation. Strictly speaking, that is not true; theologically speaking, it is unwise; evangelistically speaking, it is uncontrolled, not to say dangerous" (205).

Our goal in congregating believers, then, is not to focus solely on producing a dynamic-equivalent response in our day to the New Testament church in its time, but to develop faithful fellowships that understand the Bible and are able to enflesh it in their own cultural milieu. That will include elements of dynamic equivalence, to be sure. But the ultimate goal will be focused not so much on local response as on faithfulness to God's intended meanings for the church as revealed in the Bible.

The Faith Confirmed

While this step is also part of the discipleship process, the element that is of significance for establishing a local church is our focus. Beyond the initial follow-up, the purpose of this step is to enable the new Christians to begin the process of learning to trust Christ and to be connected more with one another than with the church planter. Using the discipleship methods and rituals discussed in chapter 19, the church planter enables them to exercise their spiritual gifts, to worship God in contextual fashion, to give to God's work, and to become infectious witnesses for Christ as the Holy Spirit leads.

Of critical importance, of course, is that the methods used to confirm the new believers' faith be biblically grounded and understandable within the culture. The point is not to make the new church indistinguishable from the culture, for no church is to be so culturally bound. Rather, the goal is that the forms of faith exhibited by the new believers be understandable to them and to nonbelievers within their culture. We want new believers made over not in

---

SIDEBAR 20.2
ENABLING THE DEVELOPMENT OF A LOCAL WORSHIP STYLE

The following story tells how David Learner enabled the church he planted in an unreached part of the world to develop a corporate worship service that fit the local setting (for other reflections related to songs, see Atkins 2012 and Smythe 2011).

The most obvious areas where I needed to strip away my own culture and cultural expectations were in my styles of worship, both private and public. As I taught my new friends worship, I taught the elements of worship, not style or form. This was not easy. What was natural for me was foreign for them. I learned to ask questions as I taught. When I introduced prayer, I asked them how they would pray. The Bible teaches we are to pray. They began to pray in a way that was familiar to them and directed toward the God we all knew and loved. When I introduced singing, I asked them what songs they would sing. They had none. I gave them none. They were inspired by the Holy Spirit to write their own. It sounded like their music, and it gave glory and honor to God. When I introduced teaching, I asked them how they would teach God's word. The style was different from mine, but normal for their culture. When I introduced preaching, I asked them how they would exhort others to follow the teachings of Christ. The resulting form of preaching was different from what I was used to, but it met their needs and was acceptable to their culture. When I introduced church leadership, I asked them how they would lead a group in their community. The results were different from the congregational approach I would have taken, but it fit them and their way of doing things. (Learner 1997, 22–23)

REFLECTION AND DISCUSSION

1. It almost sounds too easy; what do you think the difficulties were?
2. Consider extending the questions Learner asked beyond the worship service to other areas of church life, such as decision making, leadership, or pastoral counseling. Choose an area, and develop questions you could ask that would have the same impact as Learner's questions on worship.

---

our image but in what Christ's image would be if he took on their language and culture.

In 1973 Kraft wrote about "the possibility of 'Muslim Christians' or 'Christian Muslims' to signify those who, while committing themselves to God through Christ simply remain *culturally* Muslim (as an American remains culturally American)" (1973d, 119, emphasis in original). Though the term "Christian Moslem" can be dated back to 1936 (Pickens 1936), during the past several decades, this notion has developed into the idea of *insider movements* composed of people situated in Islamic, Hindu, Buddhistic, or other

> *The fact of the matter is that the Jesu bhakta [insider Christian in Hindu settings] typically feels no particular need to participate in public worship. The Hindu tradition of bhakti worship takes place primarily in the home and in private. The church's rites seem like external shells. Why not get to the heart of it all directly and personally?*
>
> *The words "church" and "Christian" are notorious among high caste Hindus and Muslims. Also in the West, we can find this same revulsion with what these words have come to stand for, especially in Europe and among post-modern Americans. Clergy still are welcomed and respected if they live up to their spiritual calling.*
>
> Hoefer 2002, 41

non-Christian contexts who come to Christ but remain inside their social/cultural frames (for an overview, see Moreau 2012, 159–65).

To cultural outsiders, these people look like Muslims, Hindus, or Buddhists in dress, language, and even religious rituals. However, their allegiance is to Christ within the context of their cultural constraints (Higgins 2006, 2007; R. Brown 2007), even though many of them do not want to be called "Christians" because of the negative connotations of the term in their societies (Richard 2001, 312). Instead, they are referred to by a variety of terms: "Messianic Jews" and "followers of Yeshua" (Goble 1975); "Muslim Culture Believers" and "new creation Muslims" (Brislen 1996), "Messianic Muslims" (Travis 2000), "Messianic Cultural Muslims" (R. Brown 2006d), and the more common "Muslim Background Believers"; "Hindu Christ-Followers" or "Hindu Yeshu Bhaktas" (Brian K. Peterson 2007, 87); and "New Buddhists" (Decker 2005, 8; Kraft 2005a, xxvi).

While the practice of working to purposefully develop insider movements has become a contextual model followed by more and more field practitioners over the past twenty years, the new practices and terms have not come without cautions or challenges (e.g., Corwin 2006, 2007; Hyatt 2009; Parshall 1998a; Schlorff 2006; Tennent 2006).

The Leadership Consecrated

One of the most difficult tasks for the intercultural church planter is to identify and develop local leadership. The difficulties arise from the temptation to choose people who express their faith in ways closest to the planter's own.

If he is monochronic, he will prefer local leadership that is monochronic even when the culture is polychronic. If she is an independent individualist, she will value as potential leaders people whose style fits hers and avoid patronage even when that fits the culture's ideals (Tino 2008, 327). Certainly this tendency can be overcome, but the church planter must be aware of this bias in seeking those who will take on the mantle of leadership in the fledgling fellowship.

Duane Elmer has wonderfully captured the concept of servanthood as essential to leadership in intercultural settings. He defines serving as "becoming like Christ to others" and walks through a process that he learned as he as listened to leaders from other cultures for almost two decades. The process is outlined in figure 20.2. Rick Kronk's description (2010) of an American missionary team planting a church composed of North African immigrants in a French Brethren church in Grenoble and Andy Johnson's account (2013) of listening to West African Church leaders depict ways in which this attitude of serving has worked successfully in a multicultural setting.

Those who lead by serving may not be flashy or dynamic. However, the local congregation trusts and respects them as people of integrity whom they will follow. It is critical that the church planters give time for this leadership

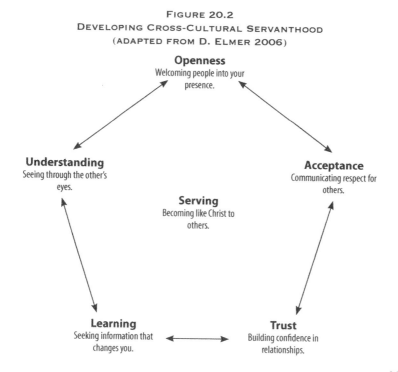

FIGURE 20.2
DEVELOPING CROSS-CULTURAL SERVANTHOOD
(ADAPTED FROM D. ELMER 2006)

Openness
Welcoming people into your presence.

Understanding
Seeing through the other's eyes.

Acceptance
Communicating respect for others.

Serving
Becoming like Christ to others.

Learning
Seeking information that changes you.

Trust
Building confidence in relationships.

> *There is a great difference between what is worshipful to a Westerner and what is worshipful to a Muslim. In fact, the Zwemer Institute tells American Christians who are witnessing to Muslims never to take them to church! It will greatly undermine the witness. The predictable counterpart of this is that a good church service in an Islamic culture will leave the Western missionary uncomfortable.*
>
> Trueman 1989

to develop and avoid identifying who they think will be leaders too early. At the same time, however, delaying this step will result in too much dependence on the church planter, and it should be taken as early in the process as possible. In our case study at the end of the chapter, we present an overview of issues for cross-cultural planning for church growth that show where leadership development fits into the picture.

The Believers Commended

It is critical in the church-planting process that the church planters begin with a phase-out in mind (Steffen 1997). Those who do not will often overstay their time and in the process impede the development of indigenous leadership.

Phasing out is not simply abandonment, however. It is the deliberate strategy of exiting while enabling the local church to meet its needs by means of locally available resources through the power of the Holy Spirit. Tom Steffen notes the following principles and methods as significant in passing the baton successfully to local leadership (1997, 217–18):

1. Build deep relationships;
2. Make sure the national believers own the vision;
3. Organize to disperse power;
4. Call for ministry involvement immediately;
5. Expect mistakes;
6. Believe in the nationals;
7. Announce departure plans discreetly;
8. Plan programmed absences; and
9. Expect ministry to increase after the church planter's departure.

To this we add that in a patron-client setting, it will be critical for the church planter to have the next pastor installed and seen as the new patron before leaving the church. When that does not happen, the resulting power struggle after the withdrawal of the church planter can devastate the church (Tino 2008, 326).

The Relationships Continued

With indigenous leadership in place, the church planters should not expect to simply sever their relationship with the new fellowship. Rather, they establish appropriate boundaries for the relationship and keep the new body in contact with the larger body of Christ. If the church is part of a larger denomination, then it needs to be connected with the denomination. Churches that are not part of a larger denomination face an even greater need for connection, since they do not have the advantages of a denomination to help them in their growth.

The Sending Churches Convened

As a vision for missions develops in the indigenous churches, they will want to organize themselves to send out their own missionaries. Recently a host of mission agencies and mission agency fellowships have sprung up around the world. Five of the many Majority World national and international missions associations are:

1. The Nigeria Evangelical Missions Association (NEMA), founded in 1982, is a coalition and fellowship forum for more than 90 mission agencies and churches. These agencies have some 4,000 missionaries worldwide serving in 40 countries. In 2005, NEMA announced a plan to mobilize 50,000 Nigerians over the next fifteen years for its Operation Samaria, which seeks to take the gospel through the North African Islamic nations back to Jerusalem (http://www.nematoday.org).

2. The India Missions Association was founded in 1977 to connect and enhance missions and churches to establish Jesus-worshiping fellowships among every people group within India and beyond. It has some 210 Indian mission organizations, agencies, and church groups as members, and it oversees some 40,000 Christian workers within India and beyond (http://www.imaindia.org).

3. The Back to Jerusalem Movement followed a vision to send 100,000 Chinese church planters across the old Silk Route to Jerusalem, planting churches along the way (http://www.backtojerusalem.com).

4. COMIBAM (Cooperación Missionaria Iberoamerica, Ibero-American Missionary Cooperation Congresses) held its first congress in 1987. The vision of COMIBAM is to help the Ibero-American church become a missionary community, able to take the gospel of Jesus Christ to all nations (http://www.comibam.org).

5. The Korean World Missions Association (KWMA) was established in 1990. It works to bring together Korean churches and denominational mission boards and agencies to share in all its mission-related activities.

By 2007 it had sent 16,616 missionaries from 130 agencies and boards. By 2030 the organization hopes to have more than 50 percent of Korean churches take part in mission, with 100,000 fully supported missionaries and 1,000,000 self-supported missionaries (http://www.kwma.org).

The Missionaries Commissioned

With local organization for mission, the churches are now ready to commission their own missionaries and start the cycle again. Commissioning comes as a culmination of events leading up to the public recognition that God has set some aside for the task of crossing cultures. The ritual used should enable the one being commissioned and the local body to feel his or her transition from one status to another. In addition to the actual commissioning ceremony, this step includes the church's method of recognizing that God has indeed set some aside for this ministry, training them and also preparing the congregation to be involved in the total effort through prayer, giving, and other means of support.

CHURCH-PLANTING MOVEMENTS

Though space limitations preclude more than a cursory introduction and list of resources, a brief word about church-planting movements is in order. Initially church-planting movements were *discovered* rather than intentionally developed (Garrison 1999). Church-planting movements are typically composed of house or cell churches that grow along natural social webs. The growth of the movement must be so rapid that there is not enough time to build church structures. Within the movement, all the Pauline steps are in progress simultaneously, though within a culture rather than from one culture to another. The rapidity of the growth and the lack of church structures ensure that the movements are decentralized, require the rapid development of local leadership, and, in sensitive locations, make it easier to stay under the radar when a public presence would result in persecution. The larger frame also means that those on the periphery may be more amenable to being reached in a church-planting movement than those at the heart of a society, and strategies may be developed to reflect this reality (McGuire 2010).

> *A Church Planting Movement is a rapid multiplication of indigenous churches planting churches that sweeps through a people group or population segment. There's a lot more we could add to this definition, but this one captures its essence.*
>
> Garrison 2004a, 27

Since the discovery of such movements in multiple locations around the world, practitioners have strategized ways to consciously enable and develop

SIDEBAR 20.3

SELECTED WEB RESOURCES ON INTERCULTURAL CHURCH PLANTING

Church Planting Resources (http://www.missionresources.com/church planting.html)
Cross-Cultural Church-Planting Resources (http://www.rmuller.com/cccpr.html)
Ethnic Church Planting (http://www.ethnicharvest.org/links/plant-links.htm)
International Journal of Frontier Missions archives (http://www.ijfm.org/archives.htm; search on the page for several articles on church planting)

MisLinks Church Planting page (http://www.mislinks.org/index.php?cID=840)
Network for Strategic Missions articles: Church Planting (http://www.strategicnetwork.org/index.php?loc=kb&view=b&fto=540&sf=Y)
"Urban Cross-Cultural Church Planting Models," by Jerry Appleby (http://ethnicharvest.org/links/articles/appleby_models.htm)
YWAM Church-Planting Coaches (http://www.cpcoaches.com)

such movements (Arlund 2013; Garrison 2004b, 2004c; Rebecca Lewis 2004; Naja 2007; Ponraj and Sah 2003; Zdero 2004, 2005) as well as how not to hinder them (Garrison 2004d)—but this effort is not without those who caution against an excessive focus on multiplication (e.g., Seipp 2010).

CONCLUSION

Ultimately a goal for all Christians is the development of local fellowships of believers wherever they are. Not all Christians are church planters or pastors, but they all should be deeply concerned with the health and development of the local church. In the intercultural setting, where the rules for just about everything related to church life may be different from what the missionary was used to at home, enabling a church to develop within its cultural context takes special care and attention. Rather than pose a dilemma in a case study in this chapter, we present selected issues on planning and culture as they relate to growing a church. We hope the questions will enable you to be better prepared to play a role in that process wherever you live.

SIDEBAR 20.4
ISSUES IN CROSS-CULTURAL PLANNING FOR CHURCH GROWTH

Scott Moreau

Step One: Together with a team of national leaders, consider what things are essential for a church to grow (in all senses of the word). What biblical essentials can be discerned? The following skeletal outline can be used as a starting point:

    a. Dependence on God as the one who brings growth (1 Cor. 3:6–7)
    b. Being firmly rooted in Christ (Eph. 3:16–19)
    c. Leadership that is equipping the saints for service, which they do by the exercise of their spiritual gifts (Eph. 4:7–16)
    d. Being filled with the Spirit (Eph. 5:18) in order to
        i. Produce the fruit of the Spirit (Gal. 5:22)
        ii. Obey the "one another" commands (e.g., 1 John 4:7–8)
        iii. Walk in obedience to

    (1) the Great Commandment ("Love your neighbor as yourself"; Matt. 22:39)
    (2) the Great Commission (Matt. 28:18–20)
    (3) the Greatest Commandment (love God with all your heart, soul, mind, and strength; Matt. 22:37)

Step Two: Come to grips with the cultural expectations of planning. On the basis of those expectations (and within the framework of biblical revelation), develop a planning approach that is appropriate for the context.

Step Three: Using the planning approach from the previous step, develop and implement plans to enable the growth of indigenous management of the fellowship in its own cultural context.

QUESTIONS FOR REFLECTION AND DISCUSSION CONCERNING CROSS-CULTURAL CHURCH ORGANIZATION

1. Is there a single biblical model of organization?
2. Given no outside influence, what is the most likely organizational model that will develop in this particular local setting?
3. What are the most likely expectations of a church organizational structure? If some of those elements are not biblical, how can we help guard against their development in our church?
4. Within the allowable framework of biblical guidelines, what organizational structure will be best for this culture?

QUESTIONS FOR REFLECTION AND DISCUSSION CONCERNING CROSS-CULTURAL CHURCH LEADERSHIP

1. Is there a single biblical style of leadership? Is it possible to blend servant leadership with all styles of leadership?

2. Given no outside influence, what is the most likely leadership style that will develop in this local culture?

3. What are the most likely expectations of a church leadership? If some of those elements are not biblical, how can we help guard against their development in our church?

4. Within the allowable framework of biblical guidelines, what leadership style will be best for this culture?

QUESTIONS FOR REFLECTION AND DISCUSSION CONCERNING CROSS-CULTURAL CHURCH MANAGEMENT

1. Is there a single biblical style of management?

2. Given no outside influence, what is the most likely management model that will develop in this local culture?

3. What are the most likely expectations of managing in a church setting? If some of those elements are not biblical, how can we help guard against their development in our church?

4. Within the allowable framework of biblical guidelines, what managing model(s) will be best for this culture?

Cross-Cultural Teaching and Learning

Many cross-cultural workers find themselves in situations where they are looked to as teachers or trainers in a variety of settings. From leading small group Bible studies to preaching to teaching in training institutions, colleges, or seminaries, the reality is that some form of teaching is often an integral part of missionary service. In this chapter we provide an overview of important issues related to teaching in a new culture. Our focus is on more formal teaching settings rather than on less formal ones (e.g., apprenticeships or coaching), and more on teaching and learning among adults than among children, since these are more typical of mission-related ministry and work than their counterparts.

CULTURAL VALUES IN THE LEARNING SETTING

One obvious question is the extent to which the contrasting sets of cultural values we discussed in part 3 impact teaching and learning. Space permits only a cursory listing of possible implications for the types of patterns we explore from the perspectives of teachers and learners, with the caveat that we must be careful not to apply general statements too quickly (see, e.g., Pelissier 1991;

Ryan and Louie 2007). It is important to keep in mind that all settings include a blending of various cultural values, and some of the values will carry more weight than others. For example, in large power-distance, high-context settings, it would not be surprising if teachers, who have larger power, correct learners by direct communication—including shaming—rather than by indirect communication, since to keep order in a learning environment large power-distance communication patterns are given higher priority than high-context communicating patterns. Further, in some societies there is a "school" culture that differs from "home" culture and "social" culture, depending on the history of educational processes in those societies, and these cultural values will affect such things as the motives of the learners, which also play an important role in the learning process (see Salili 1996, 72–74).

> *Indigenous African education was never a process of unconscious imitation. It was deliberate, in many cases conducted by teachers in a particular manner aimed at achieving definite goals. Children were taught different things at different ages. The teachers included parents, brothers, sisters, relatives, neighbors, and members of the age group. The period of active participation can begin at the age of eight and continue throughout life.*
>
> Bangura 2005, 21

Contexting

Teachers and learners in high-context settings are less likely to directly address issues. For example, these teachers might not give as much information for assignments or expectations as those who value low-context communication, since such information may be considered part of the general pool of knowledge shared by people in the setting. Further, they are more comfortable telling stories or using maxims, and learners are expected to make connections from the concrete stories to the abstract ideas. In low power-distance, high-context settings, teachers are less likely to directly correct wrong answers to questions (see the Luganda proverb on p. 302), and the questions themselves tend to be more indirect. Learners do not expect precise information from teachers and appreciate those teachers who expect them to "fill in the blanks" about assignments, answers to questions, and solutions to dilemmas.

Those who value low-context communication patterns, however, expect issues to be directly addressed and consider the words used in teaching and learning more important than the context in which the words are used. They

301

tend to value answers couched in abstract principles more than concrete examples and expect all assignments and responsibilities to be clearly spelled out.

Time

People who value polychronic communication patterns are less concerned with deadlines and more willing to pursue "off-track" discussion instead of sticking to a schedule of completing a certain amount of material by a given date. They prefer learning environments that are more fluid and flexible, allowing space for relational issues as they come up rather than keeping strictly to content. In small power-distance settings, learners feel more free to interrupt one another as well as the teacher.

> *The misshaped pot of a learner is rejected by the buyer. But he takes it all the same, to encourage the learner.*
>
> *Explanation: The buyer can appreciate the efforts, if not of the results, of the learner.*
>
> Luganda [Uganda] proverb

Teachers and learners who value monochronic communication patterns, however, prefer setting a schedule and adhering to it. Missing deadlines and interruptions are seen as disruptive, as are deviating from the topic scheduled for discussion. They prefer stability in the class schedule, well-defined starting and ending times for learning, and arranging private meetings in advance.

Individualism and Collectivism

People who value collective communication patterns (the following discussion draws from Hofstede 1986, 312; see also Salili 1996, 57–58; and Trumbull and Rothstein-Fisch 2008) tend to focus more on concrete examples than universal principles, and learners focus more on learning how to do than how to learn. Learners tend to avoid speaking out or otherwise distinguishing themselves from their fellow learners, and those who do such things are put in their place by the teacher or their peers. Formation of groups tends to be along in-group lines, with competition *between* in-groups more likely than competition *within* in-groups (which focus on harmony). Conflict is generally less frequent than in individualistic societies and more disruptive when it does occur. Teachers who are of the same in-group as some of the learners are expected to give preferential treatment to those learners. Sharing resources (such as answers on exams) within in-groups is valued, regardless of the stated rules. Shaming of the group because of an individual's action is more likely to be used as a motivator than guilt of an individual. One important goal of completing a learning cycle is to increase the status of the in-group, and certificates or diplomas may be more valued than actual skill development or competency.

Teachers and learners who value individualistic communication patterns appreciate universal principles more than concrete examples, and learners focus more on learning how to learn than how to do. Learners are more likely to volunteer responses to questions asked of the class as a whole, and learners who stand out are more likely to be valued by the teacher. Small groups are easily formed and disband once a task is complete with little or no expectation of ongoing bonds. Conflict among learners is considered normal and has little impact on the other learners. Nonpreferential treatment of all learners is expected. The focus of learning tends to be more directed toward self-improvement than toward group goals, and competency is valued more than certificates or diplomas.

> *A canoe is known by the one who launches it.*
>
> *Explanation: Parents know their children, teachers know their pupils.*
>
> Luganda [Uganda] proverb

Social Power

Those who value larger power distance (the following discussion draws from Hofstede 1986, 313) tend to stress the personal "wisdom" of the teacher, which is transferred to the learners in the relationship, especially when filial piety is valued (Salili 1996, 59–60). The teacher merits the respect of the learners inside as well as outside the learning setting, especially when the teacher is older. The educational approach is teacher centered, and learners expect the teacher to initiate communication and to outline paths to follow in the learning process. Learners rarely contradict or criticize the teacher in public, and when teacher-learner conflicts arise, the community is expected to side with the teacher simply because he or she is the teacher.

> *The first time my professor told me: "I don't know the answer—I will have to look it up," I was shocked. I asked myself, "Why is he teaching me?" In my country a professor would give a wrong answer rather than admit ignorance.*
>
> visitor to the United States from Iran, in Kohls 1981, 8

Teachers and learners who value smaller power distance tend to stress impersonal truth, which any competent teacher is expected to be able to communicate. The educational approach is learner centered, and learners are expected to initiate communication with the teacher and participate actively in finding their own paths to follow. A teacher should respect the independence of the learners, and the effectiveness of learning is related to the amount of two-way communication in class. Learners may prefer younger teachers, and they have more freedom to contradict or criticize the teacher in class. When teacher-learner conflicts arise, the community is free to side with the learner based on the community's understanding of the impersonal facts of the conflict.

Gender Roles

Women and men who value a greater separation of gender roles (the following discussion draws from Hofstede 1986, 315) typically follow a more "masculine" approach to learning. Teachers openly praise good learners and use the best learners as the norm in a system that encourages competition and rewards learners' academic performance. In parallel fashion, learners admire brilliance in teachers. A learner tends to choose academic subjects in view of career opportunities and along traditional gender lines, and failure in school can be a severe blow to his or her self-image. Women and men who value a smaller separation of gender roles typically follow a more "feminine" approach to learning. Teachers avoid openly praising learners and use the average learner, rather than the best learner, as the norm. Learners, however, admire friendliness in teachers. The learning system rewards learners' social adaptation rather than pure academic performance, and in general learners practice mutual solidarity and try to behave modestly. Learners tend to choose subjects that are intrinsically interesting to them, and fewer subjects are considered "masculine" or "feminine" in these societies. Finally, a learner's failure in school is considered a relatively minor issue.

Honor and Justice

Teachers and learners who value honor-related communication patterns pay close attention to face issues. The face of the teacher is valued by all learners, while (depending on the orientation to social power) the teacher values shaming techniques as part of the learning process. Learners who have great face—whether achieved or ascribed—are treated differently than those who have relatively little face. While some face may be granted to a learner on the basis of performance, the recipient needs to ensure that it is handled appropriately. Learners who promote their own face inappropriately are shamed by teachers and fellow learners, and learners who lose face for their in-group strive to find ways to help the in-group recover. Groups that lose face work to find ways either to restore their face or to avenge their loss on the person or group deemed responsible.

People who value justice-related communication patterns pay close attention to fairness and right and wrong. All learners are expected to be treated equally, and the guilt of one learner is not passed on to a larger group (especially in individualistic settings). Learners are expected to separate performance in learning settings from personhood. Teachers are expected to play a neutral role in evaluating and disciplining learners as well as in favors offered to learners and relationships with them. Likewise, learners are expected to play a neutral role in evaluating teachers.

CULTURE AND LEARNING STYLES

It is generally agreed that people's preferred ways of learning are based on personality and genetic traits. At the same time, culture impacts how people prefer to learn and what they value as learners.

For example, based on observations of papers written by international students, Robert Kaplan has proposed the following diagrammatic representation (fig. 21.1) of the thought flow of selected linguistic groups (1966, 15). While agreeing with Marshall Singer that we must be careful not to think that everyone from the listed cultures follows the same logic flow, or that all prose in these languages is always constructed according to the diagram (1987, 189), there are still obvious implications for teaching and learning in intercultural settings. It is easy to imagine that teachers among Semitic (Middle Eastern) cultures might value presenting information or ideas through repetition in ever-increasing chunks, while someone from an Asian setting might prefer to talk around the central topic. However, while this oversimplification is helpful in a general sense, it does not take into account such things as the expectations of the students when the teacher is recognized as foreign to their culture.

> *A child does not begin learning to trade with big capital.*
>
> *Explanation: A learner or apprentice must start with small beginnings.*
>
> Akan [Ghana] proverb

Assumptions about Learning Styles

In exploring learning styles we need to recognize that there are actual stylistic preferences in the learning process. People really do differ in how they prefer to learn. Some learn best through physical exercises that link motions to memory, others prefer seeing visual images that support or explain underlying

Figure 21.1
Flow of Thought Patterns Illustrated (Adapted from Kaplan 1966, 15)

English Semitic Asian Romance

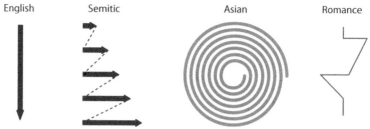

ideas, and still others prefer hearing an idea explained without added imaginative content. Learning theorists assume that these styles are a product of nature (genetic inheritance), nurture (things reinforced through childhood), and enculturation (the process of learning how to be an adult in the particular cultural setting).

To date, most learning-styles inventories that assess thinking patterns have not been tested as well interculturally as they have been in the developer's own culture. A resulting danger is that developers tend to universalize their measurements and scales.

Below we briefly describe two major orientations toward learning styles. The first focuses on *information*, seeing learning as a two-step process: how we (1) *take in* or *perceive* information and (2) *process* or *transform* information once we have taken it in. Several means of assessing learning styles following the information focus have been developed, such as David Kolb's Learning Styles Inventory (Kolb 1984; Baker, Jensen, and Kolb 2002), Anthony Gregorc's Learning Styles Assessments (Gregorc 1985), and the Myers-Briggs Temperament Analysis applied to learning (Lawrence 1993). The second major

The way people think is part of the general theory of culture. All people are born with an innate knowledge of logical structure, which they use to produce different logical patterns in different linguistic and cultural settings. The logic found in college textbooks — Western logic — is one example of how people think. Other logical forms evolved outside western European culture; any anthropology of human reasoning must treat these forms as equal to European forms.

Hamill 1990, 3

orientation focuses on *intelligence*, following Howard Gardner's seven types of intelligence as the key to unlocking learning preferences (1999).

Information-Focused Approaches

For the first step, those who promote learning-styles thinking generally assume that people take in information in two ways: either by concrete experience or by abstract thinking. One way to illustrate the extremes is to think of the difference between the person who buys a cell phone and simply starts randomly opening apps to see what happens versus the person who reads the owner's manual in its entirety before doing anything with the phone. Both are legitimate processes of learning, and all people tend to learn through one approach or the other, though typically not at the extremes described here.

For the second step, promoters of learning styles again assume two ways of processing information once it has been taken in: either by random experimenting or by sequenced analysis. In the cell phone illustration, how do people who initially simply opened apps take what they learn and process it? Do they discover how to work an app and then repeat it until memorized or simply move on to another app, trusting that they can figure the first one out again if necessary? Similarly, how do the people who prefer to read the manual first process what they have learned? Do they prefer to walk through every step with the phone in the order found in the manual, or choose an app that interests them and turn to the page in the manual and open it up to learn that particular app first?

> *The stone cannot tell the ground to push away so that it will sit down.*
>
> *Explanation: There are some dependent human relationships—such as teacher-student—that are absolute, and such relationships must be accepted with humility.*
>
> Ewe [Ghana] proverb

Learning-styles thinking indicates that everyone prefers one way to take in information and one way to process it. Though people can use a way they do not prefer, they will not learn as well as they will using their preferred methods. On the one hand, it is assumed that theoretical scientists generally prefer to take information in through abstract thought and process it sequentially. Engineers, on the other hand, are assumed to take in information through concrete experience and process it sequentially, while "tinkerers" might prefer to take information in through concrete experience and process it by random experimentation.

307

SIDEBAR 21.1
BENEFITS OF LEARNING-STYLES THINKING

There are several benefits in utilizing learning-styles thinking in teaching settings. These include:

1. Learning-styles assessment can help teachers understand themselves and why they feel more comfortable with particular teaching methods.
2. Learning-styles thinking helps teachers and learners focus on the varieties of processes by which people learn.

3. Learning-styles thinking enables teachers to be more flexible and able to focus on learners as people rather than as consumers of content.
4. With judicious planning, teachers can both play to the strengths and help overcome the weaknesses of all their learners.
5. At times simply introducing the idea of learning styles may be helpful to learners and teachers.

The general rule of thumb for learning-styles thinking is that teachers tend to teach by their preferred style, and that this is most helpful for those learners who prefer the same style and least helpful for those learners who prefer the opposite style. Good teachers, then, need to proactively develop a range of teaching activities that play to the strengths of all types of learners rather than to those students most like them.

Intelligence-Focused Approaches

Those who focus on intelligence—"the ability to solve problems or create products that are valued within one or more cultural settings" (Gardner 1999, 33)—as the lens through which to understand learning follow Gardner's scheme of types of intelligence. He originally posited seven types and later added an eighth (1999, 48–52; the following definitions come from http://www.thomasarmstrong.com/multiple_intelligences.htm; for an excellent overview and discussion, see http://en.wikipedia.org/wiki/Intelligences):

1. Linguistic intelligence ("word smart")
2. Logical-mathematical intelligence ("number/reasoning smart")
3. Spatial intelligence ("picture smart")
4. Bodily-kinesthetic intelligence ("body smart")
5. Musical intelligence ("music smart")
6. Interpersonal intelligence ("people smart")
7. Intrapersonal intelligence ("self smart")
8. Naturalist intelligence ("nature smart")

The focus in these approaches is not so much on *how* we take in or process information as on our native capacity in the *types of information* (whether physical or cognitive) that we are able to process and use creatively. While intelligence-focused approaches are very popular in US educational circles, criticisms have been leveled both at the underlying concepts (e.g., Stahl 1999; Waterhouse 2006) and at the way they have been employed without careful thinking (Gardner 1999, 79–80).

Limitations of Using Learning Styles

While utilizing learning-styles theories certainly can enhance learning experiences for both teachers and learners, there are limitations to the promotion of learning styles as seen in the literature. First, learning-styles theories are still only theories, and their application should be appropriately limited. For example, it is far too common to find learning styles linked to personality types without corresponding confirmation through solid empirical research. Second, it is helpful to keep in mind that learning-style assessment tools are nothing more than tools—almost all of which rely on self-reporting rather than external (ethnographic and statistical) assessment methods. Further, most of these tools have not been validated cross-culturally and are therefore susceptible to cultural bias.

Third, some learning "styles" that have been identified are in reality *skills*, which may be acquired, rather than *styles*, which are inherent. As a result, those who rely too much on learning-styles approaches may use a low rating in a particular learning strategy as an excuse to limit growth or experimentation. For example, the person who *prefers* to randomly open apps as a way to learn how to work a new cell phone could also learn how to read the manual, even if he or she did not prefer to read the manual. Most learning-style assessment takes place in an isolated environment rather than in everyday settings. By way

---

Every training or educational situation has a cultural context of teaching and learning. Usually the organization that plans and funds the school or workshop establishes the context. The definition of curriculum, the scheduling of time, and the organization of learning are structured around a set of cultural expectations that belong to the sponsoring organization. While teaching from a single cultural perspective can work, teachers will be more effective if they recognize the importance of cultural context.

Lingenfelter and Lingenfelter 2003, 17

---

of contrast, more recent anthropologists focus not on learning-style "capacities" but on the actual use of cognitive skills in real life. They do not try to determine capacity but rather observe how people think through problems they actually face (see Pelissier 1991, 79–81). They thus avoid locking people into categories of "learning-style jail" from which they can never escape.

Finally, learning-styles approaches in practice rarely take into account prior knowledge of the ideas being learned. This factor can radically shift how we assess differences in learning styles, since having a prior body of skills can change how a person takes in and processes new skills in the same area of learning. A person who has memorized hundreds of verses from the Bible, for example, will have a set of skills that he brings to the memorization task, and this will impact his preferences for the task of memorizing additional verses.

COMPETENCY IN CROSS-CULTURAL TEACHING

Becoming competent as a cross-cultural teacher is a step-by-step process. Just as learning a new language takes time, so learning to teach well in a new cultural setting will take time. Give yourself space to make mistakes, to try new methods, and to learn as you watch the learners. Do not expect to become a master teacher in the space of a few years; even those teaching in their own cultures take longer than that to develop into good teachers! What follows are some suggestions that will get you started in the process.

In a twelfth-grade social studies class, the teacher gave choices of assignment for the next class. I didn't like the idea of pupils choosing the assignment. I wonder what these pupils will do later in life when there are no choices in the duty assigned to them. They must learn while they are in school how to do well the jobs assigned to them from above.

visitor to the United States
from Korea, in Kohls 1981, 10–11

Observe, Observe, Observe!

Those who are new to the setting in which they serve can best learn how to teach by developing their own observational skills. They can observe not only national teachers but also learners who are being taught by them, paying attention to evidences of cultural values at work (e.g., the level of cooperation, the respect given to the teacher, gender roles in the classroom). With more than fifty years of teaching experience among us, Evvy, Susan, and Scott all affirm that this type of observation needs to be a lifetime habit rather than limited to an early career practice. We could also add that this involves not only observing but also asking good and culturally appropriate questions (Parro 2012). The best teachers are *always* learning new ways to enable their learners to learn.

Recognize the Realities of Social Power

Judith and Sherwood Lingenfelter note that "it is in the contest of wills that students and teachers struggle for power in their relationships with one another" (2003, 18). It is particularly important for teachers to admit to themselves the power they wield over learners and to discover how to act appropriately in their new cultural settings. Teachers from small power-distance settings who teach in large power-distance settings may attempt to develop friendships or egalitarian relationships with learners that the learners consider inappropriate. Teachers from large power-distance settings may be seen by learners from smaller power-distance settings as dictators who lord it over them. While it may feel strange initially, learning how to act appropriately toward learners based on what the learners value will be critical for teachers, especially early in their sojourn in the new culture. No matter what the cultural frame of reference, however, we cannot escape the need for appropriate teacher-learner relationships if we want to have a lasting impact (Nichols 2012).

Develop New Teaching Methods

Good teachers recognize that certain types of teaching methods simply will not work for them, whether because of their personality, their skill level, or other elements of their "wiring" as people. However, they also are willing to experiment on a regular basis with different teaching methods, not to confuse their learners but to grow in their capacity to teach in a variety of ways to meet the needs of their learners (see sidebar 21.2).

At the same time, they also realize that they should not try out too many methods too quickly, which can frustrate everyone involved. If they will be teaching for the foreseeable future, they might add at least one or two new methods annually with the intention of developing a wide variety of methods that will be at their disposal for years to come. They should also attend to local expectations in trying out new methods, paying attention to the possibility of violating cultural sensibilities before attempting a new method.

Expectations and Teaching

Teachers and learners both enter learning settings with expectations based on culture, perceived goals, community needs, and so forth. Good teachers

SIDEBAR 21.2
TEACHING METHODS AND TECHNIQUES BRAINSTORMING

The following is a list of teaching strategies, methods, and techniques developed by brainstorming in several classes. Look it over to see the range of ideas.

Analogies	Displays	Interpreting	Playing	Silence/reflection
Answers	Dissection	poetry	instruments	Silent reading
Apprenticeship	Drama	Interviews	Portfolio	Simple to com-
Arts and crafts	Drills	Introspection	Pottery	plex thinking
Asking questions	Error correction	Jazz chants	Practice	Simulations
Audio visual	Examples	Journaling	Practice teaching	Singing
Authentic	Exams	Lab experiments	Prayer	Skits
assessments	Exercise	Lecture	Presentations	Speeches
Brainstorming	Exhibits	Listening	Problem solving	Sports
Card games	Exploration	exercises	Punishment/	Standardized
Case studies	Field trips	Live	discipline	tests
Charts	Fill in an infor-	performances	Puppet shows	Storytelling
Chewing	mation gap	Making lists	Puzzles	Street learning
Collaboration	Fill in the blank	Memorization	Questions	Summarizing
Collage	Filmstrips	Mime	Quizzes	Surveys
Compare/	Finger painting	Modeling	Recess	Synthesis/
contrast	Flannel graph	Multimedia	Reflection	analysis
Competition	Flash cards	Multiple choice	Reinforcements	Tapes
Computer games	Games	Networking	Repetition	Tests
Construction	Getting rest	Note taking	Reporting	Time lines
Cooking	Graphic	Observation	Research	Total physical
Costumes	organizers	Opinion polls	Reviewing	response
Creative projects	Group	Oral reading	Rewards	Transcribing
Creative writing	discussions	Outlining	Riddles	Trial and error
Dance	Group projects	Overheads	Ritual	Tutoring
Debate	Hammering	Panel discussions	Role play	Venn diagrams
Demonstration	Hands on	Parables	Scavenger hunt	Videos
Destruction	manipulation	Paraphrasing	Sculpting	Web browsing
Devotions	Highlighting	Peer evaluation	Self-assessment	Webpage
Diagramming	Homework	Peer teaching	Self-discovery	development
Dialogue	Humor	Pen pals	Sewing	Worksheets
Dictation	Hypnosis	Picture cards	Shared	
Discourse	Immersion	Pictures	experience	
analysis	experiences	Planting	Show and tell	
Discussion	Inferring		Sign language	

REFLECTION AND DISCUSSION

1. As you look over the list, consider the cultural factors that may make each one more successful or less successful when implemented in different cultures.

2. In cases where cultural constraints might make a method less successful, what types of adjustments could be made to the method to increase the chance of success in its use?

SIDEBAR 21.3
SELECTED WEB RESOURCES ON CROSS-CULTURAL TEACHING

Educational Resources Information Center (ERIC; http://www.eric.ed.gov/)
MisLinks Cross-Cultural Teaching and Learning page (http://www.mislinks.org/ministering/cross-cultural-teaching-and-learning)

Network for Strategic Missions articles on Cross-Cultural Teaching (http://www.strategicnetwork.org/index.php?loc=kb&view=b&fto=2809&sf=Y; most require a premium subscription to the site)

will take these into account and refuse to develop negative stereotypes when their own expectations are not met.

CONCLUSION

If teaching in your own cultural setting brings enough challenges to last a lifetime, teaching in a new cultural setting is about as big a challenge as you can face. Strategic thinking will help you stay focused, enable you to learn how to best emulate culturally sensitive learners and teachers, and expand your own repertoire of teaching skills. All are important steps in learning how to help those who are culturally different from you become learners (and teachers) in their own right. In the case study for this chapter, a teacher faces the reality of cultural clashes in the classroom around the idea of cheating—or sharing—among students.

CASE STUDY:
HELPING ON EXAMS

NORM GRANDERSON

Greg Nelson had been teaching in China for one and a half years. Other Americans had warned him that the Chinese cheated rampantly on exams, but he had not had serious problems with this among his students. In his three semesters at Heping University, he had caught only two or three students cheating. He had given them zeros on their exams and, as is the Chinese custom for anyone who fails a final exam, had given them makeup exams to allow them another chance to pass.

Now, for the first time, Greg was teaching large classes with too many students for him to really know everyone. Since the largest classrooms at the university held fewer than 150 students, Greg's students sat crowded shoulder to shoulder as they took his midterm exam. The conditions were ideal for copying one another's answers and terrible for catching anyone who was copying.

Greg warned the students that he considered cheating a serious offense; he told them he had given zeros to students he had found cheating earlier, and that he would do the same thing for any students who cheated on this exam. Since the midterm would count for 50 percent of the class grade, this meant that anyone caught cheating would fail the class and would have to take a makeup exam the following fall.

With this warning and the relatively few people who had cheated on his previous exams, Greg expected that cheating would not be a big problem on this exam. However, when he marked the exams and began to compare answers, he found that almost one-third of the students had identical or nearly identical answers to those of at least one other student in the class. Still more students had some parts of the exams that were the same as others. Greg had no way of knowing which students had copied, which had allowed others to copy—intentionally or inadvertently—because of the crowded conditions, and which had independently chosen the same answers; yet it was clear that a very significant amount of cheating had occurred.

Having said that he would give zeros to anyone who copied, but knowing that it would not be acceptable to fail 30 percent of the class, Greg didn't know how to handle the situation. He started looking into the Chinese approach to dealing with cheating more carefully, only to find what seemed to him to be contradictory ideas. The university considered cheating to be very serious—so serious that anyone caught cheating would not be allowed to graduate. Teachers, however, didn't want to be the cause of keeping their students from graduating, so they usually ignored cheating. Even though they made threats like Greg had before the exam, they would almost certainly look the other way when faced with such massive cheating.

In talking with teachers and students, Greg also began to learn more about why cheating was so widespread. All students had to pass this class before they could graduate, but many had a command of English that was far too poor for them to pass it on their own. While many Chinese teachers would choose to pass everyone regardless of their ability, the students knew Greg was unlikely to do that. Thus the students with weaker English felt that they had no option but to copy from their classmates.

The better students also felt trapped. Since true friends should help one another in any way that they can, it would be a betrayal of friendships for them not to help their classmates pass the exam. Many of them felt it wasn't fair for those who didn't know English as well to get the same grades they did, but they still thought it was their responsibility to give answers to their friends.

With this new information in mind, Greg walked into the next class and said . . .

REFLECTION AND DISCUSSION

1. Why was helping someone on an exam so important to Greg's students? Can you think of an equivalent obligation in your own culture (if so, explain)?

2. What would you advise Greg to say to the class?

22

Intercultural Ministry
through Teams

In the late twentieth century, teams had become so important in missions
that they dominated many mission agencies by the 1990s (Pocock, Van
Rheenen, and McConnell 2005, 252). Today agencies are far more reluctant
to send out the lone ranger than they were thirty years ago, especially into
pioneer settings. As the missionary force has become more global, the teams
being assembled have typically become more multicultural.

This presents a challenge for mission simply because having a multicultural
team working in a culture that is not home to any of them raises a host of new
issues (e.g., Dunaetz 2010; R. J. Lewis 2009; Plueddemann 2009, 2011). What
is the team language and culture? How does leadership operate? How do the
leaders make decisions? How should conflict be resolved? How is discipline
to be handled? We might generalize by asking what types of core convictions
are important in building healthy teams and partnerships (Lederleitner 2010).
With that in mind, in this chapter we introduce several issues that we hope
will help make your experience on a team—whether multicultural or not—in
an intercultural setting more successful.

ADVANTAGES AND DISADVANTAGES OF TEAMS

Taking a team approach can be difficult for those who are used to being independent. It will help to recognize the many advantages of working in teams, provided the team is able to function in a healthy way. What are the advantages from the perspective of an individualistic society (the following are adapted from Leaver 1997)?

First, teams can approach more-complicated issues directly using the differing gifts of members. Rather than relying on one individual to be a "master of all trades," a team brings in a variety of perspectives as well as gifts, and often the team can make a better decision than an individual acting alone.

Related to this factor, teams focus more "brainpower" and energy on key tasks and strategic choices. Because team members are committed to common goals and share a common purpose, the vantage points of multiple people looking at the same goals can result in a synergy that is more effective than each individual pursuing her own agenda.

Further, teamwork can result in a more humane process of making decisions because of the variety of perspectives that must be considered in the decision-making process. Insights that an isolated leader would not have are generated by team members if they feel listened to and appreciated. This is even more important for international teams, when the insights of teammates come from different cultural perspectives and not just different personalities.

Fourth, teams are able to serve as positive culture shapers within the organization, especially if it is not accustomed to having healthy teams working

One thing is clear: a multicultural team is far more complex than a monocultural team. And it's not fair to the team members to operate the team under certain one-sided cultural assumptions. A few of the assumptions which have caused problems are: (1) the majority culture or the culture of the team leader rule the team culturally, (2) English is the team language, (3) only men do the leading, (4) only the wives carry the responsibility for the family and household, (5) the salaries are fixed in the home country without respect to the host country, (6) leadership is from the top down. Such assumptions as these are initially cultural blind spots but, if insisted upon, can cause deep rifts in the lives of individuals and the team as a whole.

Roembke 2000, 109–10

in unity. It should be noted that this is more the case when the organization has greater exposure to the team (e.g., in an urban setting) than when the team is isolated.

Fifth, teams enable interdependent thinking that is more likely to keep the larger goals of the organization in mind rather than shifting to goals that are independent of the organization. Teams can get stuck in ruts, but they have greater resources to draw on to get them out and can bring more creative energy to tasks at hand.

Finally, teams in a team-oriented organization can recruit their own members (from within the organization or from without) rather than wait for the agency to assign them someone to fill roles. This decentralizes the mobilization element of the work and enables teams to choose people who they feel are suited to the needs and responsibilities they face.

As you look over this list, consider how it might need to be changed for collective cultures. It might not even be necessary to convince collectivists that there are advantages to working in teams; they might need a parallel list that shows the advantages of working as individuals.

Just as there are general advantages of teamwork in individualistic settings, there are further advantages when working in multicultural teams in mission. First, a multicultural team can model the diversity of the body of Christ (Cho and Greenlee 1995, 179). This is important whether the team is focusing on church planting or on development in heterogeneous or homogeneous settings. In the former, people see team members deal with issues and remain unified despite their differences. In the latter, the team acts as a reminder that people must think beyond those who are like them, and it can help to develop a world vision for local homogeneous fellowships.

Second, it is obvious that multicultural teams can demonstrate more clearly God's transforming power in intercultural relations (Cho and Greenlee 1995, 179). Teams that struggle with this should bear in mind that they cannot really hide their differences, especially in high-context cultures. They will be watched as they wrestle with differences, and the way they handle those differences will potentially point the way for the local believers to deal with their own.

Third, multicultural teams, composed of people of multiple viewpoints, have a built-in, heightened sensitivity to their own cultural orientations (Cho and Greenlee 1995, 179). If all members are valued in decision-making processes, and all have the freedom and the awareness to point out their own as well as other members' cultural values, they are less likely to find monocultural solutions to problems or to simply make disciples in their own cultural image.

Finally, multinational teams are far less likely to be confused with political agents and so are less likely to be considered subversive by residents of the host country (see Stetzer 2003, 500).

Of course, teams are not always the best solution to ministry or other needs in intercultural settings. At times they simply may not be feasible. Even when they are, however, certain issues must be considered. For example, forcing people into teams might hinder individual creativity. Alternatively, a team can slavishly follow a model that does not meet the particular team's needs or gifts. Even worse is the potential that a strong team can develop into an independent "foreign ghetto" that hinders ministry. This development is more likely with a monocultural team than a multicultural one.

Another possible problem is that continually adding people to teams can result in teams that become unwieldy and too bureaucratic (too much like an organization itself). One study found that for each person added to the team after the fifteenth member, the effectiveness of the team's ministry decreased (Lai 2007, 174).

> *Getting to know one's teammates is, at first, most exciting. It's a smorgasbord of inviting nuances promising to enrich one's own life. But reality soon sets in when the most normal ways of interacting become gnawing irritations or puzzling encounters.*
>
> Roembke 2000, 105

Finally, we need to be aware of the trap of thinking that teams are the answer to every problem, even when they may not be the best strategy. This can become a form of idolatry that must be guarded against (see Zehner 2005).

For those involved in ministry on multicultural teams, there are different sets of potential problems. For example, leadership problems can include communication styles, counseling styles, and gender-role issues. A low-context, confrontational leader may offend high-context, nonconfrontational teammates; conversely, a high-context, indirect leader may confuse and frustrate low-context, direct teammates (Cho and Greenlee 1995, 180).

Second, lifestyle issues (one's values and feelings) can be the most emotionally difficult ones to handle on multicultural teams. These include team language, the freedoms and constraints of those who are single in contrast to those who are married, values and feelings of husbands and wives on the team, child-rearing practices, what various members consider to be "white" lies, and cross-cultural romances. For example, many international teams use English as their language for all team meetings and events, as that is often the only language they have in common (at least until they learn the local language).

SIDEBAR 22.1
WHAT WOULD YOU SAY?

Cho and Greenlee (1995, 182)

David Wilson, the American field director for Central Asia, is visiting one of his multi-national teams. He knows that some of the Koreans on the team do not yet speak English very well although they make a heroic effort to learn. During his individual interviews with each of the team members, he asks if there are any personal problems of which he should be aware. He is particularly impressed with how cheerful and pleasant Soo Jung, a newcomer, is and comments on this to the Brazilian team leader. Later, the team leader writes to David. As it turns out, Soo had smiled but actually had hardly understood a word that he had said. In reality she was facing a personal crisis related to the illness of her non-Christian father back home in Korea. "But how was I to know?" protests David to himself. "I asked her and she did not tell me anything!" What could David do differently in the future? Any advice for Soo or the team leader?

This can hamper those whose English is weaker and who have difficulty expressing their hearts in English (Cho and Greenlee 1995, 180).

Third, problems can arise from preferred ministry patterns. These can range from personal spirituality to worship styles to means of evangelism and church planting. Each member of the team will have to flex with the others, as it is highly unlikely that any one pattern or style will be shared by all members of the team (Cho and Greenlee 1995, 180).

Fourth, in ministry settings, teams might unnecessarily prolong their existence out of misguided thinking about unity or Christian fellowship. If the team is especially tight, when the local task is completed the temptation will be to find new tasks simply to keep the team together, which can stifle local church or ministry development.

"TEAMONOMICS"

Economics is essentially the exchange of goods and services. Team economics—"teamonomics"—plays a vital role in the team's development and success. Every team member brings "goods and services" to the team, and all team members can benefit from engaging in exchange with one another. Additionally, the team as a unit has "goods and services" to offer the community in which the teammates live and work. Understanding both the internal and external "teamonomics" is vital to team effectiveness, for the team needs to overcome those things that hinder good cross-cultural team development (P. Shaw 2010).

One of the internal socioeconomic realities for teams is the understanding and use of the social power of each member. This will play out in leadership styles, team language fluency, and how well teammates relate to one another and to the team leader. On the one hand, teammates who value large power distance will defer to the leader and be dismayed at small power-distance teammates who seem to have little or no respect for leadership (see Mackin 1992, 138). These differing views can become so disruptive that the team can fall apart if team members are not aware of the role that cultural values play in communication patterns. On the other hand, teammates who value small power distance will be frustrated with large power-distance teammates who never challenge ideas from the leader and do not seem to pull their own weight in team discussions.

This factor is also important in how the team operates in the intercultural setting. In countries where missionaries are not welcome, a team can be expelled because of one independent or overzealous individual who does not stay within the parameters of team policy for engagement with the local culture. At the same time, however, team members who are seen as productive and important by locals can lift up the reputation of the rest of the team and give them more freedom to pursue ministry. It is critical for those putting teams together for service in areas where security is an issue to impress on the smaller power-distance individualists the need to respect team leadership in a way that the leaders—especially if they are national—understand.

An important area of the give-and-take dynamics of a team is that of sacrifice. Everyone on the team will have to give up something, but everyone also gains by

---

SIDEBAR 22.2
WHAT WOULD YOU SAY?

Cho and Greenlee (1995, 182)

On the flight back to his Middle Eastern home, returning from a mission executive meeting, Martin, an American, told himself that the main thing he wanted was time with his family. The day he returned he promised his wife and two young teens that next Saturday was to be their special day. On Saturday morning, as the family was getting things together for a special outing, Paulo, a Brazilian colleague, arrived at the door with Kamal, a new believer. Inside Martin groaned. If they had gotten up a half hour sooner, they would have been gone by now. Now the only option was to invite Paulo and Kamal in, prepare some tea, and talk at least for a while hoping that nobody else showed up for a visit. Martin and his family have come to minister to people like Kamal. But they also need time as a family. How do you think that Martin and his wife should handle the immediate and future situations involving family time?

being part of the team, as Liann Roembke notes: "It is wise to remind oneself during the process that there is a sense of sacrifice for the privilege of being a missionary in that culture and a sense of giving up something for the good of the group as a whole. Dwelling on the sacrifice alone as a loss will distort the perspective and rob the missionaries (and their coworkers) of joy" (2000, 116).

We should not overlook that an important advantage of a team in terms of social power is that it will have greater potential for developing social capital within the new setting. In many cases, the team members bring with them educational levels and expertise that gives them high social status in the new setting. They also come with some level of training in ministry and personal spiritual maturity that is a form of spiritual capital (they may even be considered religious experts, depending on the setting). Finally, as qualified foreigners, they may have enough status to interact with public officials who are inaccessible to the indigenous Christians. In economic terms, their status can be utilized as *linking* capital to help gain favor for the national church or to enable national leaders to make connections they otherwise would never be able to make. While this can be an advantage, a different reality is that nationals will be reticent to openly criticize the team in any way because of the team's status. This especially applies to short-term missions teams, which may never know what the local Christians really think of them because the local Christians don't wish to be the cause of the team members losing honor or status due to local criticism—even when it is fully justified.

SUCCESSFUL TEAMS

Successful teams typically do not just happen. It takes commitment, hard work, and a willingness to pull together over the long haul, especially in intercultural settings, for a team to be effective. There are several characteristics of successful teams (the following discussion draws from Huszczo 1990, 38). First, they have a clear sense of direction as evidenced by their goals and the awareness of those goals by all team members. However, they see themselves as a "temporary scaffold" and not the building itself, which is the national church (Patterson and Currah 2003). Additionally, they have the training as well as the talent needed to fulfill their goals, and that training and talent are being harnessed appropriately. Third, all members recognize their roles on the team and feel valued for the roles played. Fourth, effective and efficient ministry and service procedures are well established and followed by all. Fifth, members get along with one another; they trust one another, communicate well, and resolve conflicts as they arise. Sixth, rewards (e.g., an agency commendation) and disciplinary systems (e.g., accountability) are in place in the larger organization to reinforce and sustain teamwork. Finally, the team has a positive and constructive relationship with that team's organization leadership as well as with local officials and is not constantly wrestling over continued viability with either of them. We can add to this list that the teammates have learned how to handle their differing cultural values in ways that honor each member and maintain the cohesion of the team despite varying values (Hegeman 2010).

In a study of some 450 tentmakers, 93 percent of whom served on teams, Patrick Lai discovered several team-related factors that were directly associated with an individual's effectiveness in ministry (2007, 174). First, those who were team leaders or had successfully recruited people for the team (or even for other teams) were more effective. So were those serving on a multinational team or a team which included nationals. For each member added on a team from three to twelve people, likelihood of success increased. From twelve to

---

SIDEBAR 22.3
TEAM LEADERSHIP ROLES

Leaver (1997)

The following have been identified as the types of roles team leaders play in US businesses. Read through them and discuss them as a group. See if you can identify people you know who tend to take on these roles in team settings as well as which role(s) you prefer in those who lead you.

Animator: Who brings to life passion and images by using member's language and introducing new language via media such as poetry.
Teacher: Who patiently transfers knowledge from experts to members of the team.
Eccentric: Who takes bold strides away from the center and lets loose.
Broker: Who overtly (and covertly) connects those who must learn to work together.
Storyteller: Who weaves myth and mystery into tales and amplification of the truth.

Change Agent: Who pushes and cajoles to bring forth a new order.
Theater Director: Who focuses on backstage, onstage, and on the back of the theater before, during, and after each team session; knows "what's going on" and what is around her or him.

REFLECTION AND DISCUSSION

1. Which of these leader roles works well for teams engaged in cross-cultural ministry?
2. What cultural values are seen in each of the types of leader roles?
3. Imagine you are leading a team of people from collective, large power-distance cultures. Which of these leader roles might be most successful? Which might be least successful?

SIDEBAR 22.4
WHAT WOULD YOU SAY?

Cho and Greenlee (1995, 182)

An [American] mission agency's executive committee faces a perplexing situation. One of their team leaders living in a male-dominated Muslim land has had to step down. A replacement must be named soon. There is one clear choice to succeed him in terms of gifts, skills, and experience: Elisabet, a single Brazilian woman. But that is just it—she is a woman, and a single woman at that. The issue for many is her gender and marital status and not her abilities. If nominated, doubtless she would humbly decline but the committee believes she would accept if they encouraged her to take on the responsibility. But, even if she did accept, the committee wonders if her multi-cultural team would accept her as leader. How would she relate to the handful of leaders, all men, from the fledgling national church? How do you think the executive committee should proceed? Assuming they appoint Elisabet, how can they help her to succeed?

---

fifteen members it was relatively steady, and (as noted previously) once the team grew larger than fifteen the effectiveness began to decrease. Finally, those who were members of a team that met weekly or biweekly (rather than less frequently) were more likely to be effective in ministry.

FACTORS IN BUILDING STRONG MULTICULTURAL TEAMS

People who are part of a team almost always want the team to succeed. What ingredients are important to build such a team? Using the acronym CACTUS, Kelly O'Donnell notes eight such core characteristics of resilient teams (1999), which he calls the CACTUS Kit (table 22.1).

TABLE 22.1
CACTUS KIT CHARACTERISTICS

C	Coping ability and commitment
A	Appreciation
C	Communication
T	Time together
U	Understanding
S	Structure and spiritual wellness

A resilient team has the coping ability to accept the challenges that ministry in a different culture brings. The decision to choose to believe the best of one another and the willingness to work through impasses and struggle together through problems are critical skills for team cohesion.

Second, the team members are committed to goals that they share, tasks that they need to accomplish, and to one another (Dyer 1985). They are willing to persevere in spite of setbacks, though this is not a blind perseverance that seeks to overcome all opposition.

Third, a resilient team expresses appropriate appreciation for each person. These expressions can be planned (e.g., a team appreciation night) or spontaneous. If properly cultivated this practice can be an infectious attitude that is characteristic of the team, and those who are able to persevere through hardships can do so more consistently if they know that they are appreciated by the rest of their teammates.

Fourth, resilient teams are able to communicate well. This is especially important when dealing with conflict, which will inevitably arise within the team. Team leadership will lead by example and ensure that members in conflict find appropriate ways to communicate with one another about it (taking into account such communication patterns as contexting and power distance).

Fifth, resilient teams spend time together. This is especially important in the early stages of team building and during transitions that come later. While this time together is important, the team leaders also need to ensure that the team does not become a type of enclave in which members spend more time with one another than they do with those among whom they serve. As noted earlier, Lai's research indicates that people who spend quantity and quality time with nationals are more likely to be effective than those who do not (2007, 170).

Sixth, members of resilient teams understand one another to the extent that they are able to overlook weaknesses and know why teammates behave the way they do. They can distinguish sin from cultural values and work toward continual growth in their relationships.

Seventh, resilient teams have appropriate structure, including clear roles for the leaders and agreed-upon methods for decision making, accountability (Dyer 1985), and conflict resolution.

Eighth, resilient teams are spiritually healthy. They are led by godly people (Dyer 1985), there is recognition and utilization of the spiritual gifts of each person (Love 1996, 313–14), and they unite in prayer regularly (Dyer 1985). As Roembke notes, "A multicultural team is a hothouse in which spiritual growth is accelerated. It is accelerated in the sense that one is confronted more often with the negative effects of one's own culture on another" (2000, 110).

Dealing with negative things requires humility and a willingness to forgive as well as to repent. While, for example, forgiveness is experienced differently in individualistic versus collectivistic societies (Fujino 2009), it is a Christian imperative that is possible only with God's working in and through us.

SIDEBAR 22.5
WHAT WOULD YOU SAY?

Cho and Greenlee (1995, 182–83)

It has been a real struggle to accomplish much work during the last three weekly meetings of a multinational team in China. One of the single Brazilian men has fallen in love with a Korean team member, and this has led to some division. The Korean team leader and his wife believe it is better not to encourage this relationship. The other three members of the team, an American couple and their 20-year-old son, see no serious problem with it, provided they go slowly and remain accountable. The leader tries to instruct the Brazilian man privately but they end up arguing. The oldest American tries to act as a mediator between both parties as this issue is brought up during the team meetings. The Korean woman is confused, the team leader feels his authority is being overlooked, the Americans want to move on and focus on ministry issues, and the Brazilian is afraid that he will lose a potential wife. Take the part of one of the seven team members, and describe what you might do to help resolve this situation.

CONCLUSION

The ability to play a role in building a strong team is an essential skill for those engaging in cross-cultural ministry. Even if you do not start out as part of a team, the odds are high that eventually you will become a team member,

---

SIDEBAR 22.6
SELECTED WEB RESOURCES ON TEAMS AND TEAM BUILDING

"Cross Cultural Conflict Resolution in Teams," by John Ford (http://www.mediate.com/articles/ford5.cfm)
The Leader's Institute: free team-building resources (http://www.leadersinstitute.com/teambuilding/team_building_tips/index.html)

NETWORK FOR STRATEGIC MISSIONS ARTICLES

International Teams (http://www.strategicnetwork.org/index.php?loc=kb&view=b&fto=678&s f=Y)
"The Power of Team Leadership," by

Roberta Hestenes (http://youthspecialties.com/articles/the-power-of-team-leadership)
TeamBuilding, Inc. free articles (http://www.teambuildinginc.com/ei_news.htm)
Team Building Activities, Initiative Games, and Problem-Solving Exercises (http://wilderdom.com/games/InitiativeGames.html)
Teams in Missions (http://www.strategicnetwork.org/index.php?loc=kb&view=b&fto=1086&sf=Y)
Wikipedia: Teamwork (http://en.wikipedia.org/wiki/Teamwork)

---

whether in the church you attend or with other members of your sending organization. The benefits of working as a team in accomplishing work for God's kingdom far outweigh the possible risks associated with teams. This is especially important to recognize because so much of the world's population—and especially the unreached—are collectivist in orientation and do not understand the independent individual. The case study for this chapter illustrates the types of decisions that teams face and gives you a chance to explore dealing with the tensions they can bring.

CASE STUDY:
HURRY TO THE HURAM?

SHAWNA WALSH DUVALL AND SCOTT MOREAU

Tormod, slightly out of wind from the uphill walk, knocked on the door, and Allen invited Birger and him in for their weekly team meeting. Tormod and his roommate, Birger, had been living in the countryside of Mongolia for three years. Allen and John had been serving with them for the past year after two years of language and culture study in Ulaanbaatar, the capital of Mongolia. After a time of prayer focused on team unity, all four of them looked at each other. Finally, Tormod, the team leader, asked, "We can't put it off any longer, since we'd have to start on arrangements today if we are to make it on time. Should we go or not?"

During the past year the four men of the team had seen the young local church grow in adult attendance as an answer to their fervent prayers. A particular young couple with a one-year-old son had been such nominal members in the fellowship throughout the year that the team had strong reservations about their faith.

During the past two months, however, the couple had pursued a relationship with Birger and Tormod. They also were much more active in the church body, showing positive signs of Christian growth. To show how much they valued their forming relationship with the two workers, the young couple invited the whole team to their *huram*.

A *huram* is the traditional Mongolian wedding ceremony strongly resembling a wedding feast. The couple's best friends and relatives attend, give gifts, speak blessings, and share in a great feast. The wedding, although reflecting certain strong Buddhist elements, is void of any nuptial agreements, vows, or any kind of legal matters. Commonly in the Mongolian culture a couple will cohabit after the woman becomes pregnant, and they are then considered married in the eyes of the community.

The invitation posed a problem for the team that highlighted differences in ministry and theology. John and Allen, conservative American evangelicals, refused to attend the *huram* because they wanted to make a stand against general acceptance of cohabitation as well as the richly symbolic Buddhist wedding rituals. They strongly felt that the Christian couple should renounce all former ties with their Buddhist background and demonstrate their new faith by marrying in the church. They also felt that the fledgling fellowship was watching their decision, and this could set the course for years to come.

Tormod and Birger, European evangelicals who had grown up in a more lenient theological atmosphere, also recognized the importance of their decision in the eyes of the church. But they disagreed with John and Allen's refusal, arguing that avoiding the wedding would make the couple lose face and jeopardize their relationship with them. It might even drive them from the church. When John had suggested that Tormod and Birger go, Tormod responded that if only half of the team went, it would send a mixed message in this collective culture.

The *huram* was in two days, and they had not yet made transportation arrangements, which would take at least a day to finalize, so they had to make their decision today. Both sides appealed to Scripture, and both acknowledged that team unity was important. How they made the decision today could affect the way they handled dilemmas in the future. If they went, what were the implications of their participation in the Buddhist rituals? If they did not go, what were the implications for the young couple and the church?

After talking through everything they could think of, Tormod realized that they would not be able to agree quickly enough to make the arrangements in time for the celebration, which would be a decision against going. He realized that in this instance it would fall to him as the team leader to make the final decision, as a vote would obviously result in a tie. With a quick prayer for wisdom, he said . . .

REFLECTION AND DISCUSSION

1. What would you suggest Tormod decide?
2. Identify several strategies that might help the team members to come to common ground on approaching issues like this in ministry.

23

Conflict and Culture

Many Christian graduate schools and seminaries have on-campus housing. Placing roommates from different cultures together in one apartment provides an interesting laboratory for cross-cultural conflict management. A US student complains of her Korean roommate, "She says I am too loud. Yet she thinks my closing a cabinet door in the kitchen is a loud noise!" A South Asian woman insists on having the doors and windows open every time she cooks, which makes her roommates uncomfortable and cold in the middle of winter. She persists in maintaining her practice because "when cooking hot, spicy food, one must have ventilation to be healthy!" An Asian student reports to the housing office that his German roommate plays music too loudly and when asked to turn it down the roommate just laughs and tells him to get some headphones.

In one team situation, a Chinese ministry fellowship elected a new president, who had spent a decade as a missionary in another country and had adopted some of the cultural practices and values of that country. The leadership team soon spoke to a non-Chinese third party in a higher position within the organization about the new president, asserting that his communication and interaction styles were no longer Chinese and that he was ineffective as a president. After a number of sessions using the third party as a mediator, the president was allowed to retain his post, although he was quite hurt by the

---

---

experience, and relationships within the fellowship continued to be strained. He continued to meet with the third-party mediator about his sense of shame, leading the mediator to believe that he had not been successful in resolving the problem.

These examples illustrate types of conflict that can occur between individuals and within teams. The individual conflict may be easier for you to assess using the cultural values that you have learned about in this book. Team conflicts are far more difficult to maneuver because there are not only individual conflict styles and cultural values to navigate but also an exponential increase of factors based on the cultural backgrounds, personalities, and conflict styles of each team member interacting with individual team members or combinations of team members. Our goal in this chapter is to give you some models based on cross-cultural conflict research to help you better understand conflict dynamics and ideas and tools to resolve conflict in creative and productive ways.

WHAT IS CONFLICT?

Conflict involves "a perceived or real incompatibility of goals, values, expectations, processes, or outcomes between two or more interdependent individuals or groups" (Martin and Nakayama 2005, 195), leading to emotional frustration and interpersonal or intergroup tensions. A simple definition of conflict is offered by Clara Cheng: conflict is "the emotional tension of the people involved over their differences in common issues of concern" (2012, 3).

According to David Augsburger, conflict is elicited by "a crisis that forces us to recognize explicitly that we live with multiple realities and must negotiate a common reality; that we bring to each situation differing—frequently contrasting—stories and must create together a single shared story with a role for each and for both" (1992, 11). Particularly in intercultural teams, creating

329

a common story, vocabulary, and means for resolving conflict is crucial. Conflict can be a useful catalyst for self-reflection, negotiation, and redefinition of the group's interaction and communication style, leading to greater group cohesion (Van Meurs and Spencer-Oatey 2009).

CONFLICT IS UNIVERSAL, INDIVIDUAL, AND CULTURAL

The image of iron sharpening iron in interpersonal relationships supports the notion that conflict is a human universal; it is unavoidable and is not necessarily bad. It can provide the necessary stress to stimulate creative response and growth. Conflict can occur in many forms and is inevitable when there are scarce resources that must be shared, differences in access to power, division of roles that may be unclear or in dispute, and differences of opinion about a course of action. And, of course, cultures differ in each of these dimensions. Thus "conflict in all cultures is characterized by multilevel communication, alternate movement between subtle cues and visible behaviors, intricate combinations of covert responses and overt reactions, ambivalent feelings, and polarized perspectives, defensive strategies of concealment and offensive attempts to provoke a crisis, and so on" (Augsburger 1992, 24).

> *As iron sharpens iron, so one person sharpens another.*
>
> Proverbs 27:17

Many of us dislike conflict and have difficulty responding well to it within our own families, close relationships, and others within our own culture. People typically develop an individual default style of managing conflict based on family dynamics and personal history (Martin and Nakayama 2013). That default acts as the "normal" setting, and when a conflict experience is outside that normal range, new strategies for managing conflict must be learned. If unhealthy patterns of conflict resolution have been learned because of dysfunctional family dynamics, those patterns can become troublesome defaults, particularly under stress. Our individual conflict style interacts with our cultural conflict style and level of self-awareness, creating a complex reaction to conflict that is rooted in our overall emotional health.

The intensity of the conflict makes a difference in our ability to respond in positive ways. In everyday interactions, the minor conflicts that erupt are usually dealt with in effective ways. We are able to calmly determine the impact of differing cultural values on the situation. When situations are highly ambiguous or conflict intensifies, we can become emotionally flooded and less able to use our full range of conflict-resolution strategies. For example, research conducted on interactions between American and Russian astronauts on joint missions indicates

> that in situations where uncertainty increased, conflicts erupted, emergencies arose, and interpersonal relations were stressed—cultural differences did arise and powerfully affected the ability of the space and ground crews to accomplish mission goals. In short, under conditions of stress and conflict, people reverted to their cultural programming rather than relying on the training protocols developed over years of effort. (Hammer 2009, 221)

Living and working in unfamiliar contexts in cross-cultural ministry likely increase our stress in ways that may impede our ability to approach conflict as a potentially positive catalyst for learning.

In cross-cultural settings, conflict is much more likely to occur because of misattribution, defined as "ascribing meaning or motive to behavior based on one's own culture" (Lane 2002, 118). Differences in values and conflict-resolution styles, lack of fluency in a common language and misinterpretation of nonverbal cues, ambiguous situations, and degree of individual social competence can all contribute to misunderstandings leading to conflict (Lane 2002; Martin and Nakayama 2013). Imagine the challenge of negotiating conflict when you may be unaware that there is a conflict at all or have no idea that what you have said or done has been interpreted as offensive!

> *The context of conflict management is the emotional wholeness of a cross-cultural worker . . . [including] self-awareness of the impact of one's national character on their personality.*
> Cheng 2012, 2

Ironically, a Christian worldview may intensify the perception of incompatibility with others because people of faith often hold so tightly to their cultural way of being Christian as a matter of principle. "One of the major temptations of Christians in conflict situations is to elevate their position to a matter of principle. This artificial production of a value conflict implies that to change is to compromise" (Bates 1980, 97). And compromising principles that are interpreted as biblical and faith based can be very uncomfortable for Christians. Taking this idea further, US Christians are likely to see Matthew 18 as the primary Scripture informing conflict management, forgetting that the context for that passage is sinning against another (Cheng 2012). Using this Scripture implies that the conflict is due to a spiritual problem and that the person you are approaching is the sinful one. Assuming that conflict arises from the sin of another person rather than from differences in cultural values and resolution style may sabotage the conflict-resolution process from the beginning.

TABLE 23.1

CROSS-CULTURAL CONFLICT CASE STUDIES IN SCRIPTURE

Read through each of the Scripture passages and identify the cause of conflict and principles of conflict resolution. Look for ways to expand your understanding and appreciation of a variety of biblical models of conflict resolution.

Old Testament	New Testament
Abraham and Pharaoh (Gen. 12:10–20)	Jesus and the Pharisees (Matt. 21:36–46; John 8:1–11)
Sarah and Hagar (Gen. 16; 21)	
Abraham and Abimelek (Gen. 20; 21:22–31)	Jesus and Pilate (Matt. 27:11–14)
Isaac and Abimelek (Gen. 26)	Feeding the Greek-speaking widows (Acts 6:1–6)
Jacob's sons and the Shechemites (Gen. 34)	
Israel and Egypt (Exod. 1–15)	Peter and Simon (Acts 8:9–24)
Moses and the exiles (Exod. 32)	Peter and Herod (Acts 12)
Israel and Gibeonites (Josh. 9)	Paul and Elymas (Acts 13:6–12)
Elijah and the prophets of Baal (1 Kings 18)	Jerusalem Council (Acts 15:1–35)

THE IMPORTANCE OF CULTURAL VALUES

Before presenting the research on cross-cultural conflict, it is important to acknowledge the limitations of the typical methodologies. "One of the very major weaknesses of virtually all the research into the role of communication in conflict processes that is carried out in management, cross-cultural psychology and communication studies is that it is nearly always based on self-report data, using Likert-style responses to questionnaire items" (Van Meurs and Spencer-Oatey 2009, 109). Also, much of the research is done in secular and business settings. Self-reports are likely to elicit responses that show oneself in a positive light, and Likert-style scales are most familiar to the Western mind. Keeping these limitations in mind is important before applying research to intercultural ministry settings.

In this section, a few of the familiar cultural values are applied to conflict situations. Although the sections are separated by cultural value, there is significant overlap between values, reflecting the actual complexity of real-life cross-cultural conflict.

Individualism versus Collectivism

Individualistic and collectivistic orientations are significant contributors to cross-cultural conflict. In individualistic cultures, people tend to separate instrumental goals from task goals. Task goals focus on how to solve a problem or achieve a specific goal; in other words, the task-oriented person wants to get the job done. Instrumental goals are concerned with interpersonal or relationship problems, such as antagonism between persons. "The distinction therefore focuses on conflict about ideas versus conflict about people" (Lustig and Koester 2010, 269). An individualist is typically able to discuss an idea rather heatedly and then transition to friendly conversation afterward. After all, for the individualist, the conflict isn't personal; it's about an idea. A collectivist, however, does not separate the instrumental from the task issues and sees conflict as personal. It does not take much imagination to see how these differing goals could escalate a rather minor conflict into a major one.

> *A taboo outside the circle of awareness of one party may completely frustrate an amicable solution to what appears to the Westerner to be a very straightforward situation. More often the cultural baggage is latent, outside of the awareness of both the carrier and the other party, but nevertheless highly dynamic in the situation.*
>
> Bates 1980, 95

This focus on task goals in combination with a lack of awareness of the influence of culture on conflict may be particularly problematic for Westerners, who are more apt to minimize the impact of culture and emphasize aspects of the "problem" when attempting to resolve conflict. Westerners tend to overfocus on the issues and lack appreciation for cultural and value influences.

Because cultural ways of addressing conflict are so ingrained, they are unlikely to be questioned, further inflaming conflict situations. Table 23.2 contrasts the cultural perspectives of individualists and collectivists, emphasizing the individualist's concern for task completion and the collectivist's concern for process and preservation of relationships.

TABLE 23.2
INDIVIDUALIST AND COLLECTIVIST CONFLICT LENSES

Individualist Conflict Lens	Collectivist Conflict Lens
Outcome-focused	Process-focused
Content goal-oriented	Relational goal-oriented
Doing-centered	Being-centered
Use personal equity norms	Use communal norms
Self-face concern	Other-face concern
Low-context conflict styles	High-context conflict styles
Competitive/dominating behaviors	Avoiding/obliging behaviors
Conflict effectiveness	Conflict appropriateness

Ting-Toomey and Chung 2012, 184.

333

In general, people in individualistic societies tend to see resolution of conflict as a step to be completed so that the greater task can be achieved. In order to accomplish that goal, the individualist is likely to appeal to the best idea or principle and become more assertive in promoting that ideal. This style is in direct opposition to the strategies of collectivists, who are more likely to use indirect methods of resolving conflict in order to preserve relationships.

Large Power Distance versus Small Power Distance

This dynamic is further aggravated when power distance is added to the equation. The greatest danger lies in situations where there is large power distance between those engaged in conflict (see fig. 23.1). For the individualist (and recall that the United States scores the highest of any nation on this trait), personal status and achievement are utilized to resolve the situation. For the collectivist, a large power distance is likely to elicit a benevolent conflict approach in which deference is given to the person(s) with higher status. For example, it is quite possible that a person from the United States in this situation may have greater status because of country of origin and educational/professional background, yet may be unaware of this advantage because of the high cultural value placed on equality, democracy, and straight talk. The individualist in this scenario may believe that a resolution has been achieved, when the collectivist is actually being submissive. In this case, a solution based on dominance, when collaboration is most desired by the individualist and the collectivist, is apt to be disappointing for all parties.

In contrast, small power distance allows for more collaboration and emotional distance from the situation, which likely leads to a more desirable outcome for all parties. Yet it is important to emphasize that cultures in which high power distance is valued must be engaged on their own terms, and the power differences must be respected. If power has been ascribed to you, even though you

> *Cross-cultural studies on interpersonal conflict clearly indicate that the competing style of conflict resolution (i.e., high assertiveness, low cooperativeness) is more favored by members of individualistic cultures . . . than it is by members of collectivist cultures . . . and that the opposite pattern occurs for the avoiding (i.e., low assertiveness, low cooperativeness) and accommodating (i.e., low assertiveness, high cooperativeness) styles.*
>
> Kim-Jo, Benet-Martinez, and Ozer 2010, 265

do not wish it to be so, that power must be accepted and used carefully. And if more power has been given to another, respectful engagement is crucial for conflict to be resolved.

FIGURE 23.1
CULTURAL CONFLICT GRID: FOUR CONFLICT APPROACHES
(TING-TOOMEY AND CHUNG 2012, 184)

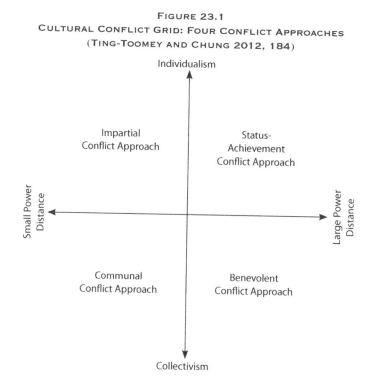

High Context versus Low Context

Let us return for a moment to the opening scenario involving Christian seminary on-campus housing and residents from many cultures. A US resident assistant comes to her supervisor complaining about her international residents: "Every time there is any roommate conflict, the international student comes to me and expects me to fix the problem. Why can't she just talk to her roommate directly without putting me in the middle?"

The resident assistant does not understand that the international residents are approaching conflict in the preferred style for their culture. Using a third-party intermediary would allow the roommate relationship to be preserved and prevent loss of face. Yet for the United States resident assistant, the role of mediator is unfamiliar, uncomfortable, and unexpected for minor issues. Resolution of conflict among high-context and low-context people can be especially challenging because the key questions regarding conflict are answered in very different ways (see table 23.3).

People from low-context settings tend to believe that conflict is best dealt with directly and as soon as it arises. Culturally bound sayings such as "Let's nip this in the bud" or "Put your cards on the table" communicate the desire to address issues early and openly. For the low-context person, conflict most likely arises because expectations are not communicated adequately or behavioral norms are not sufficiently understood. Once those things are clearly and logically communicated, the persons engaged in conflict can brainstorm ideas for resolution, agree on a solution, and everything will be fine. Because problems can be separated from people, directly addressing the issue is not considered personally threatening. Indirect strategies for communicating displeasure can be seen as confusing at best or passive-aggressive at worst.

People from high-context cultures prefer to use indirect strategies to let another person know that a cultural norm has been violated or that there is tension in the relationship. Because the person and the problem cannot be separated, high-context societies desire to preserve the relationship and allow the person a way to address the problem without shaming him. Direct confrontation would create an emotionally charged and personally demeaning dynamic, creating unnecessary shame and putting the relationship at risk.

TABLE 23.3

A SUMMARY OF BASIC CHARACTERISTICS OF LOW-CONTEXT CONFLICT
AND HIGH-CONTEXT CONFLICT

Key Questions	Low-Context Conflict	High-Context Conflict
Why?	Analytic, linear logic, goal-oriented, dichotomy between conflict and persons involved in conflict	Synthetic, spiral logic, expressive-oriented, integration of conflict and persons involved in conflict
When?	Individualistic-oriented, low collective norm expectations, violations of individual expectations create conflict potential	Group-oriented, high collective norm expectations, violations of collective expectations create conflict potential
What?	Revealing, direct, confrontational attitude, action/solution-oriented	Concealing, non-confrontational attitude, face/relationship-oriented
How?	Explicit communication codes, linear/factual rhetoric, open/direct strategies	Implicit communication codes, intuitive-affective rhetoric, ambiguous/indirect strategies

Reprinted from Ting-Toomey 1985, 82.

The intensity and use of emotional expression in conflict-resolution style plays a significant role in how communication is perceived. For some, high emotionality emphasizes the importance of one's view; for others, emotionally

> The concept of directly managing conflict simply does not exist in a high context culture. High context people who are involved in conflicts usually have to resolve the emotional tensions within their hearts while letting the problem continue. Or, they may go to a third party to seek help. This method of conflict management intrinsically has . . . underlying dangers. As long as the problem is not resolved, the emotional tension may lead to unresolved spiritual sins, like bitterness, resentment and so on.
>
> Cheng 2012, 4

charged communication is seen as threatening and out of control (see, e.g., Kochman 1981). However, low emotional expression may communicate rational calmness to one person and detachment or disinterest to another. Mitchell Hammer (2004) offers a model of intercultural conflict style that explores the relationship between directness of approach and level of emotional expression (see fig. 23.2).

Hammer offers detailed descriptions of the various conflict styles (2004, 30). The discussion style (direct, emotionally restrained) of engaging conflict utilizes precise language, emotional control, and objective facts to address concerns and uses caution in introducing personal feelings into the situation. The engagement style (direct and emotionally expressive) is also verbally direct but with more emotional intensity, focusing on sincerity, and using emotion to communicate a high degree of concern. Accommodation style (indirect, emotionally restrained) uses more-ambiguous language to keep the situation from getting out of control. With this style, a calm demeanor combined with indirect messages may preserve harmony, a highly valued state of being. Finally, the dynamic style (indirect, emotionally expressive) uses exaggeration and repetition in engaging conflict. With this style, a third-party mediator is

---

SIDEBAR 23.2
SELF-REFLECTION

Take a moment for self-reflection. Do you tend to be more direct or indirect in your conflict style? Do you prefer interpersonal communication during conflict to be less or more emotional? Do any of these styles make you feel especially uncomfortable? How do these two aspects of conflict style intersect in your personal conflict style? What are positive qualities of other approaches to conflict resolution? Can you imagine scenarios where each style might be the better approach?

more likely to be used, and the more intense emotional expressivity is believed to communicate the credibility of the speaker.

FIGURE 23.2
A MODEL OF INTERCULTURAL CONFLICT STYLE (HAMMER 2004, 30)

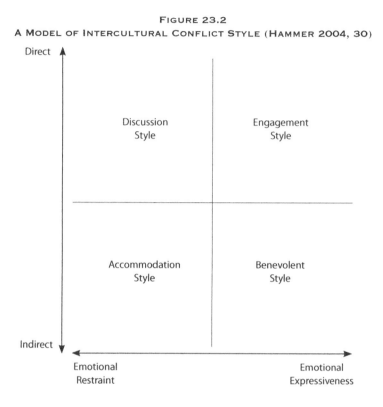

The Importance of Saving Face

The concept of face is commonly attributed to Chinese culture, yet many cultures have a concept that reflects the importance of maintaining personal or group honor. Judith Martin and Thomas Nakayama assert that "conflict strategies usually relate to how people manage their self-image in relationships" (2005, 199), regardless of the person's cultural identity. When conflict arises, often there is fear of losing resources, power, relationship, or trust. If conflict is not resolved in the desired way, self-image is threatened because others may see one as weak or ineffective. In other words, loss of face is a basic human fear.

Face refers to a "claimed sense of desired social self-image in a relational or international setting. Face loss occurs when we are being treated in such a way that our identity claims are either being directly or indirectly challenged or ignored. Face-loss can occur either on the individual level or the identity group level, or both" (Ting-Toomey 2007, 256). To maintain face we employ strategies that protect our group or self-image, a goal that may compete with resolution of the conflict. These self- or group-protective strategies are called *facework* and are used to manage one's own face or the face of another. Attempting to control the face of another can be positive and supportive or undermining and threatening (Neuliep 2009, 330).

In general, individualists prefer defending self-face and use confrontation strategies, showing less concern about saving the face of others. Collectivists tend to prefer strategies that save face for the other person and are more likely to avoid direct confrontation, seek mediation, or give in so that the other person does not lose face. Recent research has focused on integrating both individualist and collectivist perspectives into face-saving communication theory. For example, Stella Ting-Toomey has expanded her earlier face-negotiation theory to include the Asian collectivist perspective in order to broaden the applicability of the concept of facework to fit a range of cultures. Her theory is based on the following assumptions (2007, 257):

1. People in all cultures try to maintain and negotiate face in all communication situations.
2. The concept of face is especially problematic in emotionally threatening or identity-vulnerable situations.
3. The cultural value spectrums of individualism-collectivism and small/ large power distance shape facework concerns and styles.
4. Individualism and collectivism value patterns shape members' preference for self-oriented facework versus other-oriented facework.
5. Small and large power distance value patterns shape members' preference for horizontal-based facework versus vertical-based facework.
6. The value dimension in conjunction with individual, relational, and situational factors influence the use of particular facework behaviors in particular cultural scenes.
7. Intercultural facework competence refers to the optimal integration of knowledge, mindfulness, and communication skills in managing vulnerable identity-based conflict situations.

Self-face concern is about preserving one's own image and relies more on dominating behaviors. Other-face concern is mindful of preserving the face of others and relies more on avoiding and integrating styles (see fig. 23.3 for an illustration of conflict strategies related to self-face and other-face concerns). Westerners tend to see avoidance behaviors in a negative light and interpret them as running away from the problem. Cultures that value saving the face of the other tend to see domination and confrontation as unnecessarily aggressive and humiliating. Interestingly, third-culture approaches tend to be integrative, assessing the situation and using various strategies to solve problems, which suggests that a multicultural approach involving multiple conflict-resolution tools and sensitive application may be an effective response to conflict situations.

FIGURE 23.3
SELF-FACE CONCERNS, OTHER-FACE CONCERNS, AND COMMUNICATION STYLES
OF MANAGING CONFLICT (NEULIEP 2009, 332)

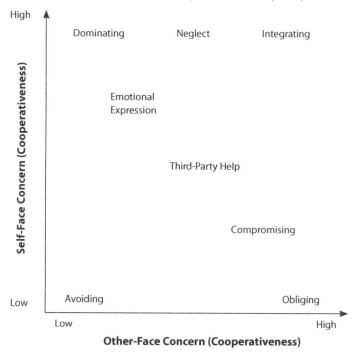

For those who are less familiar with the concept of saving face, Ting-Toomey (1999, 227–28) suggests the following ways to improve facework management. First, start with a foundation of increased awareness; be mindful of ways for mutual face-saving in a collectivist culture through sensitivity to one's words, nonverbal communication, or other means that may cause others to lose face. Second, proactively engage low-conflict situations before things get out of control. If any tension is sensed, consult a cultural informant to gain help in understanding where misunderstanding or misattribution may have occurred, and if an issue is identified, seeking mediation may be desirable. Third, give face whenever possible. Allowing another person a gracious way out of the conflict saves face and preserves the relationship. Fourth, patiently observe the contextual clues. For example, is past history impacting the situation? Individualists need to refrain from asking too many "why" questions, recollecting that collectivists focus more on nonverbal "how" questions and process. Fifth, practice good listening skills by attending to verbal communication, nonverbal signals, and the emotionality of the other person. Sixth, be prepared to soften direct communication styles. The use of qualifiers, disclaimers, indirect refusal, and tentative statements will help persons from indirect cultures feel less threatened. Finally, remember that avoiding a problem may save face and is not necessarily a poor strategy. If the other person is unwilling to engage directly, find the courage to let it go.

CONFLICT RESOLUTION

Most of us desire peaceful relationships with others and will work toward those ends. The problem usually is not the desire to seek peace and pursue resolution, but rather confusion over how to do so in ways that are understood by others and reach true reconciliation. And what we have learned as "good strategies" in our home culture may not be appreciated or understood by those in other cultures. Thus we need to constantly expand our conflict-resolution skills so that we can effectively engage others, pursuing mutual understanding and valuing relationships.

Westerners have key assumptions affecting how mediation is handled that often conflict with the assumptions of other cultures. For example, Westerners believe that people and problems can be separated, whereas many people from Majority World cultures do not believe this is possible or desirable. Being goal directed, Westerners tend to value directness, decisiveness, and immediacy in making decisions. Westerners tend to be open about expectations and provide bottom-line requests, whereas Majority World people may inflate demands, assuming that the other side will be doing the same. For a Westerner, a yes means yes and a no means no; one's word is considered binding and final, whereas people in many Majority World societies may use more-nuanced meanings and indirect replies. Once agreement is reached, a Westerner expects implementation to take place as a logical consequence of a mutual understanding, not realizing that someone from a Majority World setting may interpret the agreement differently and thus see implementation differently (Augsburger 1992, 206–9).

> *Whoever of you loves life and desires to see many good days, keep your tongue from evil and your lips from telling lies. Turn from evil and do good; seek peace and pursue it.*
>
> Psalm 34:12–14

341

These key assumptions, based on sincere motivation and limited cultural understanding, can limit the range of approaches to conflict, assuming that one's own cultural response is morally or, perhaps, spiritually superior. As we have been learning throughout this chapter, at times it may be best to respect the other culture by choosing to operate by its rules. Alternately, finding a new or "third way" through creation of a common story, a common vocabulary, and an agreed-upon approach to conflict (Van Meurs and Spencer-Oatey 2009) may be the best means of pursuing peace. In any event, at all times we need to be flexible, adaptable, and creative.

Before Engaging in Conflict Resolution

Engaging in conflict resolution requires some familiarity with the culture of the persons involved in the disagreement. If you are a guest in the host culture, you should proactively learn about the culture because it will have a bearing on how conflict resolution should be approached. Recall that conflict will eventually happen, and preparation will expand your skills and likely increase your effectiveness.

Duane Elmer (1993) suggests reflecting on the following principles, which can be implemented prior to engagement in conflict resolution and are especially effective when undertaken in conversation with a cultural informant. First, the degree to which shame, face, and honor are core cultural values will determine your use of indirect methods. It is possible that persons in the host setting have had exposure to other cultures and may be more accepting of more direct conflict-resolution strategies; however, do not assume that directness will be tolerated or understood. Familiarity with the stories, parables, fables, legends, and heroes of a particular society and their use in conflict situations will expand your repertoire of culturally appropriate resolution strategies. Understanding and practicing the various indirect methods and their usage in the culture will also help you be sensitive and act appropriately in resolution strategies.

Second, look to God and Scripture for support. Seeking God in prayer for wisdom and insight is critical before pursuing conflict resolution (Lane 2002). Asking for God's help in using unfamiliar, culturally appropriate resolution strategies is also appropriate (D. Elmer 1993). As we look to Scripture for wisdom, it is important to be mindful that our cultural lenses impact our interpretation of biblical passages; in other words, our understanding of Scriptures related to conflict and peace are likely skewed by our cultural biases. As Elmer asserts, "Scripture is the final judge of all cultural forms" (1993, 181). Yet we must be prayerful and open to the leading of the Holy Spirit in sensitively interpreting Scripture in conflict situations.

Patty Lane (2002) suggests reflecting on issues that may have contributed to the conflict. Are there communications that could have been misunderstood by either party? Are there behaviors that may have been misinterpreted? Do the parties have different expectations regarding others' behavior? Where might misattribution have occurred? Is it possible to clarify motives? Are cultural factors influencing the conflict? Is it possible to distinguish between differences in culture and differences in personality? Where might there be common ground between the parties' positions? How might your understanding of the cause change if long-term goals are kept in mind? Lane also urges those in conflict to remember that a preserved relationship is a solution (2002, 131–33).

Possible Strategies for Resolving Conflict

Let us assume that you have a cultural informant and that you are reasonably familiar with the cultures of those involved in conflict. You have taken the time to learn, to pray, to seek biblical insight, and have done your best to figure out what went wrong. You are now ready to pursue peace through exploration of conflict-resolution strategies with an important reminder: when a person is in the midst of conflict, it is natural to have an emotional response. Some people manage their feelings fairly well, and others are easily flooded by emotion. Under these stressful circumstances, we are more apt to use default strategies for dealing with conflict and lose the flexibility and intentionality that we have cultivated. It is also important to acknowledge that not all persons engaged in a conflict will strive to use positive resolution strategies, and we need to recognize harmful responses and redirect maladaptive strategies toward healthier dynamics and avoid the wounds caused by these negative strategies. Table 23.4 charts several approaches in which conflict is managed, sometimes without resolution being achieved.

AEIOU Conflict Negotiation Model

The AEIOU Conflict Negotiation model outlined in table 23.5 uses a familiar English mnemonic device for naming vowels in the English alphabet to list five styles for negotiating conflict; the model appears to value direct interaction more highly than indirect strategies. It is fairly clear that *attacking* is not a preferable negotiating style (it would seem to permit very little negotiation). Yet if we honestly self-reflect, we will recognize that attacking is a familiar strategy for many and is used regularly by some, particularly in cultures that value confrontation. Although *evading* may seem undesirable, it does fit within

TABLE 23.4
NONCONFRONTATIONAL CONFLICT MANAGEMENT

Strategy	Behavior
Anticipatory management	Preventative; defusing conflict before it occurs.
Negative communication	Silence, avoidance, and/or evasion to communicate disagreement.
Situational friendliness	People in conflict avoid one another unless interaction is necessary (i.e., show friendliness in the presence of important persons/guests or in an emergency).
Triadic mediation	Conflict between two persons is mediated indirectly by a third person who acts as a go-between and uses his or her power to negotiate a solution.
Displacement	Anger or disapproval toward one party is expressed toward a third party who is more vulnerable and less able to retaliate (e.g., gossip, blaming another for one's request to solve a problem).
Self-aggression	Expressing a grievance by overassuming responsibility (e.g., apologizing when not at fault, accepting blame to save the face of another, self-accusation).
Acceptance	The conflict is seen as fate or destiny, which diffuses negative emotion because the conflict is no longer personal.

Content drawn from Augsburger 1992 and Lebra 1984.

the range of useful indirect strategies. *Informing* has similarities with the direct, emotionally restrained discussion style offered by Hammer (2004). *Opening* still requires a certain level of directness as questions are asked about the needs and feelings of others. *Uniting* looks for commonalities among those involved in the conflict and seeks to find the common story and vocabulary that could be a "third way" forward. The model does not specifically engage culture and is likely more applicable to conflict among Westerners.

TABLE 23.5
CONFLICT NEGOTIATION STYLES:
THE AEIOU COLLABORATIVE NEGOTIATION TRAINING MODEL

Negotiation Style	Behaviors
A = attacking	Threats, hostile tones/gestures, judgmental questions, criticizing, blaming, defending, patronizing, stereotyping, discounting others' ideas/input
E = evading	Abrupt topic change, ignoring incoming information, withdrawal from the scene of conflict, emotional/mental disengagement
I = informing	Stating a need, explaining why the need is important, justifying one's position with facts/opinions, disclosure of feelings
O = opening	Nonjudgmental questions regarding others' needs/feelings and position, active listening, testing understanding via use of paraphrase
U = uniting	Sharing to build rapport, establishing common ground, reframing issue to meet needs of opposing sides

Adapted from Raider, Coleman, and Gerson 2006.

Flexible Cross-Cultural Conflict-Resolution Styles

Other models for conflict resolution consider culture a primary factor in developing responses to conflict. For example, Duane Elmer (1993) suggests strategies that are sensitive to intercultural dynamics. To begin with, mediation could be considered because it is normal and appropriate for many cultures. If a person has successfully learned about the host culture, use of storytelling and proverbs may be a sensitive means of approaching conflict. Indirect responses, such as inaction, silence, or vague response can serve as ways to diffuse a tense situation or to say no without the other losing face.

One interesting strategy is taking the one-down position, which, by making yourself vulnerable, allows you to take the heat in a difficult situation. This strategy is often useful in writing cross-cultural emails. Rather than directly confronting the recipient of the email, the writer may choose to graciously give the recipient a way out by acknowledging that any misunderstanding may be due to the writer's gaffe. For example, when collaborative work has not been received by an agreed-upon deadline, the writer might choose to say, "I am confused and I hope that you can help me. I had thought we were to have our draft done by Tuesday, but I am probably mistaken about the date. Could you please let me know the correct date?" By putting yourself in the one-down position, saving face becomes much easier for the recipient.

For Stella Ting-Toomey and Leeva Chung, flexibility in intercultural conflict skills is key (2012, 199–203). Building on the facework management abilities as the first skill set, they list additional skills as creative means for seeking resolution.

The second category of skills focuses on mindful listening, which is considered face validating and power sharing. Ting-Toomey and Chung believe the skill is best explained by the Chinese word for listening; *ting* is defined as "attending mindfully with our ears, eyes, and a focused heart" (2012, 199). This skill set also includes paraphrasing skills in which the listener summarizes the content of another's message and conveys the emotional meaning of the other's message gleaned through observation of nonverbal cues.

The third skill set is called cultural empathy, which is defined as the ability to accurately perceive the self-experiences of others from diverse cultural viewpoints and relate that understanding effectively. Adding cultural sensitivity to empathy skills makes the practice of that skill that much more complex. A culturally empathic listener must have "cultural ears" (Ting-Toomey and Chung 2012, 201) that can identify with culturally different others who are part of the conflict.

The fourth skill set is called mindful reframing, an ability that is highly creative and allows for mutual face-saving. Mindful reframing is "using language to change the way each person defines or thinks about experiences and views the conflict situation" (Ting-Toomey and Chung 2012, 201). Some specific strategies for mindful reframing involve restating the situation in terms that identify and magnify common interests, changing complaint statements into respectful requests, moving from assigning blame to problem solving, helping others see solutions that are beneficial to both parties (a win-win situation), and helping others to see the "big picture" encompassing long-term desires.

Finally, Ting-Toomey and Chung identify adaptive code-switching as a desirable skill for flexible intercultural conflict engagement. Adaptive code-switching is defined as "the act of purposefully modifying one's behavior in an interaction in a foreign setting in order to accommodate different cultural norms for appropriate behavior" (Molinsky 2007, 264). In other words, some people are able to intentionally learn multiple sets of cultural norms and move fluidly between these differing sets of norms, depending on the context and situation. Minorities living in majority societies and children raised outside their parents' birth country, such as missionary kids and third-culture kids, have typically developed these skills in order to daily navigate the differing cultures of home, public life, and school, as a matter of survival.

Both models place a great deal of responsibility on the person to take a learning posture, to be willing to be flexible, and to acquire proficiency in intercultural conflict skills. The more skills the person attains, the more flexible and adaptive she will become in engaging cultural conflict in positive and creative ways.

Preserving Relationships

An important long-term goal for any effective cross-cultural ministry is preservation of relationships. Broken relationships are a poor witness to those we are ministering to, and without relationships, genuine ministry is difficult. Based on decades of cross-cultural ministry, Elmer (1993, 108–9) suggests the following guidelines for approaching conflict, focusing on the importance of pursuing relationship and mutual understanding.

1. Ask whether this is worthy of attention or should be let go.
2. Make your approach one of concern for the person and for preservation of the relationship.
3. Seek understanding through inquiry before forming judgments and making accusations (blaming).
4. Separate facts from rumor, partial information, feelings, and interpretation.

5. Consider how much stress the relationship can bear; this will help you to determine how much time and sensitivity will be required to address the conflict.

6. Put yourself in the other person's place and try to appreciate his or her perspective on the matter.

7. Address behaviors rather than motivations.

8. When you detect tense emotions or defensiveness, back up and give assurances of friendship and your desire to understand.

9. Frequently acknowledge and summarize what the other person has said to assure accuracy of understanding for both parties.

10. Believe a win-win resolution is possible if both parties can remain calm, understand each other's interests, and negotiate with integrity and fairness.

Common themes begin to emerge from the suggested ways of resolving conflict. Mutually satisfying conflict resolution requires empathy, humility, a strong concern for the others involved, compromise, patience, a willingness to not have to "be right," flexibility, adaptability, and, perhaps most important, recognition that resolution strategies are culturally bound and that your favored way of addressing conflict may not be appropriate to the context. Remember that despite best efforts and practiced skills, not all conflict is resolved. Yet it is incumbent on the peacemaker to be proactive in acquiring conflict-resolution skills and to seek to grow in maturity through using them. As Paul exhorts believers in Romans 12:18, "If it is possible, as far as it depends on you, live at peace with everyone."

> *Forgiveness is the key that can unshackle us from a past that will not rest in the grave of things over and done with. As long as our minds are captive to the memory of having been wronged, they are not free to wish for reconciliation with the one who wronged us.*
>
> Smedes 2008, 352

Whether or not conflict is resolved, forgiveness should be offered. Forgiveness opens a door for healing of the one forgiven, the one who forgives, and the relationship. Forgiveness is also a sign to those who are aware of the conflict of the power of forgiveness, offered by people through the power of God. As Paul notes, wrongs against one person grieve all in proximity to that wrong (2 Cor. 2:5–10), and a lack of forgiveness allows discord to fester. Further, forgiveness is asked of us in order to receive God's forgiveness (Matt. 6:14–15). Forgiveness from the heart is often difficult and comes through a process, involving forgiving anew when bitterness threatens to resurface. Truly letting go of past hurts

347

> ### SIDEBAR 23.3
> ### SELECTED WEB RESOURCES ON CROSS-CULTURAL CONFLICT RESOLUTION
>
> A Campaign for Forgiveness Research (http://www.forgiving.org) Mediators and Everything Mediation (http://www.mediate.com) Peacemaker Ministries (http://www.peacemaker.net)
>
> The Sociological Concept of Face (http://en.wikipedia.org/wiki /Face_(sociological_concept))

and interpersonal struggles is part of becoming more Christlike in our interactions with others.

THE FUTURE OF CROSS-CULTURAL CONFLICT RESOLUTION

Much research remains to be done on cross-cultural conflict. Most models are based on fairly simple interpersonal dynamics, such as conflict between two individuals from different cultures or the interaction of only two values. As more people are added and more cultural values are represented in conflict, research becomes more complicated. Yet this multicultural and multidirectional dynamic is becoming the normative reality. "As the world we live in is becoming more globalized, the one-way flow of population and adaptation assumed in current theories are to be joined by reciprocal flow and two-way adaptation. The tendency of having one dominant group in intercultural encounters will be no longer held true" (Ma 2005, 210). Embracing cross-cultural conflict as normal offers a positive opportunity to learn more about oneself and others and to practice conflict-resolution skills for a globalizing world.

> *But the wisdom that comes from heaven is first of all pure; then peace-loving, considerate, submissive, full of mercy and good fruit, impartial and sincere. Peacemakers who sow in peace reap a harvest of righteousness.*
>
> James 3:17–18

In the concluding case study for this chapter, the dynamics of negotiating conflict stemming from a hiring decision are front and center. As you read it, consider how the cultural values involved and the conflict resolution strategies discussed in the chapter might help you understand the situation and develop an appropriate approach to solving the dilemma faced at your school.

CASE STUDY:
THE HIRING DECISION

Adapted from Peace Corps (2011, 125).

You are being asked to take sides in a faculty dispute at your Bible school, where you are in your second year of teaching. A few weeks ago a vacancy occurred in the department where you teach. The two candidates for the position, both with master's degrees, were an older man (Mr. Tanakan) who has worked in another capacity at the school for fifteen years and a younger man with more up-to-date credentials, a superior educational background, and two years of experience on the faculty. From a qualification standpoint, the younger man was a much stronger candidate and also a more dynamic teacher. He was selected for the position by the chair of the department, a British missionary, who has been at the school for five years.

Mr. Tanakan and many of his (and your) colleagues were stunned by the decision, regarding it a rejection of his years of experience and loyalty to the school. Mr. Tanakan is extremely embarrassed at being passed over and has not appeared on campus since the announcement was made. Now his colleagues are circulating a petition to the chairman to reconsider his decision and put Mr. Tanakan into the job he deserves. They have asked you to sign the petition, already signed by all of them as well as dozens of students, and to join them in presenting the petition to the department chair.

REFLECTION AND DISCUSSION

1. Explain the issues involved from the perspectives of each side.
2. Will you sign the petition? If not, how will you explain your refusal?

The Future
of Intercultural Communication

here can be no doubt that as the speed of communication and people's access to one another across the globe increase, the need for
understanding communication across cultural boundaries will also
increase. Misunderstandings previously buffered by time and space now take
place instantaneously all over the globe. One might think that this would
make communication easier, but in reality it can make it harder. Mistakes are
no longer between two individuals but between the organizations they each
represent in ways that can be played out internationally in a matter of minutes.
From CNN to YouTube to blogging to tweeting and RSS feeds, what was previously hidden is now publicly accessible—at times even as it happens. This
presents major challenges to Christians in our increasingly connected world.

In our closing chapter we highlight issues that are relevant to the discipline
and to Christians who are or will be serving interculturally. These include the
ferment in the field of intercultural studies itself, selected ethical issues that
loom in significance in the years to come, and the effects of globalization on
intercultural communication. The challenges are enormous and will require
every tool that we can bring to the table to face them with faithfulness to the
gospel and integrity in our walks.

FERMENT IN THE FIELD

The discipline of intercultural communication seems to be at a threshold, with challenges ranging from the conceptual (Levine, Park, and Kim 2007) to the pragmatic. Depending on how they are handled, the discipline of intercultural communication may take a central role as a type of "clearing house" within the social sciences (Kim and Hubbard 2007). Several challenges that are part of the ferment may be noted.

First, during the past decade fewer scholars have held a positivist orientation that there are general rules and regulations that can be tested empirically. Instead, more have shifted to an interpretive approach in which each case stands on its own, and the interpreter cannot readily be separated from the event (Starosta and Chen 2003). In other words, fewer are looking at broad, global thinking, and more tend to take each communication event as a singularity with the interpreter as part of the event.

> *Formerly, [intercultural communication] was necessary for empire, or trade. Today, it is a matter of survival for our species.*
>
> Kim and Hubbard
> 2007, 223

Second, the discipline has been challenged by questions about whether the extent of the intercultural communication is itself truly intercultural (e.g., Kim and Hubbard 2007). For example, we are now challenged to move beyond the current Eurocentric approach ("in which we structurally and systematically privilege certain theorizing and research methods of Western origin over others" [Miike 2003, 244]) to draw upon an Asiocentric approach ("the theoretical notion that insists on placing Asian values and ideals at the center of inquiry" [Miike 2003, 251; see also Frykenberg 2003b, 1]).

This development has an impact on such instances as studies of cultural imperialism in the colonial era that deny any role played by the indigenous populations in the colonial process. Such an approach is built on the premise that it was only the colonizing Europeans whose actions were important, and the indigenes can be safely ignored in the historical picture, which is ultimately a form of Eurocentrism:

> With reference to cross-cultural exchanges in particular, a view that sees cultural change as the result of external impositions leads ultimately to a conception of modern world history in which the West has wielded a determining influence on global culture, in which modernity reduces to Westernization. Thus, the discourse of cultural imperialism, originating in opposition to Western cultural hegemony, can ironically lead to a conclusion which is profoundly Eurocentric in its denial of agency or autonomy to non-Western populations. (Dunch 2002, 307)

It is an exciting and maybe disturbing thing—the idea that biblical faith can be clothed in any language and culture. Witness the awesome reality in the so-called mission lands today. Whether Africa, India or China, it may well be that the largest number of genuine believers in Jesus Christ do not show up in what we usually call Christian churches!

Can you believe it? They may still consider themselves Muslims or Hindus (in a cultural sense).

Winter 2005, 5

An Asiocentric view of the same phenomena does not see all "cultural imperialism" as necessarily evil. At one end of the spectrum, it is evil. At the other end, however, it is at least neutral and is termed "cultural exchange" by contemporary Chinese scholars: "Chinese scholarship has tended to juxtapose (bad) cultural imperialism to (benign or at least neutral) cultural exchange, with the trend toward viewing missionaries increasingly in the latter category" (Dunch 2002, 316).

For Christians these challenges will be increasingly important. Already Christians from the Majority World outnumber Christians from the Western world (for multiple fascinating stories, see M. Adeney 2009). In 2008 roughly two-thirds of the total workers for US agencies were non-Americans (Moreau 2010, 40–42). Missionaries from Majority World settings have taken a significant portion of the load of crossing cultures for Christ, and we must ask how the Western tradition of missions will relate to the Majority World tradition of missions (Ward 1982, 3).

This shift has also led to the need to develop local multicultural churches as a sign of the larger multicultural nature of the body of Christ. Unfortunately, "people group" thinking, if not buffered with the full teaching of Scripture, can lead to the development of ethnocentric churches that avoid heterogeneity because leaders fear it may stop numerical growth or because they are not willing to overcome their prejudices. But a church that is exclusively homogeneous certainly does not portray the fullness of the body of Christ to a watching world. Henry Wilson proposes that

to build a healthy intercultural communion, the dynamic balance between independence and interdependence of communities should be respectfully maintained. Therefore, the mission commitment today involves multidirectional engagements of the promotion of intercultural relations/communion locally, as well as facilitating intercontextual relations and fellowships globally, with the prime aim of promoting fullness of life for all (John 10:10b). (2004, 28)

Even among Westerners there are intergenerational issues, as Richard Tiplady notes: "Anecdotal evidence of the personal experience of 'Xers' shows that we do not find it easy to fit into the culture and structures of much of the contemporary Western church, especially in its organizational forms, such as mission agencies" (2002, xi). The types of challenges that are fermenting in the field of intercultural communication are also being seen among missionaries and mission organizations. Christians can and should learn from the discipline without being dominated by it (or its conclusions).

ETHICAL ISSUES

More than ever, the reality of ethical challenges will be part of intercultural communication. First, we have seen an ongoing erosion of positive connotations associated with the concept of mission, and we increasingly see statements such as "numerous Westerners are sincerely convinced that an imposition of their own cultural values and systems constitutes their religious/moral duty and serve [sic] the best interest of the non-western 'brothers'" (Gawlikowski 2003, 17). This and similar challenges to mission in the framework of intercultural communication are likely to increase in the coming decades.

Second, all communication involves issues of power in some shape or form, and intercultural communication can help or hinder how that power is understood and exercised (Kim and Hubbard 2007). On the negative side, the social power of short-term missions teams (they are wealthy; they are guests who have sacrificed to come a long way; they have set objectives to accomplish) is something that is rarely understood by the participants themselves. Having no clear understanding of the power they wield, they are susceptible to abusing the power they have in relation to their hosts.

Third, we must beware of the temptation to turn intercultural communication principles into mechanistic techniques that we use to guarantee success in bringing more people to Christ. The particularly American penchant for discovering "keys" that will lead to "success" is a chief concern. It will be increasingly important for Christian communicators to know how to develop a better understanding of the cultures in which they serve and to utilize that knowledge to call the nations to worship without turning their approaches into manipulative sales pitches that are successful because they take inappropriate advantage of human psychology or sociology rather than relying on the work of the Holy Spirit.

GLOBALIZATION/FLATTENING ISSUES

Widely read *New York Times* columnist Thomas Friedman posits that the world is flattening as globalization expands (2005). By "flattening" Friedman refers to the leveling of the table in competition for manufacturing and industrial processes, especially in high-tech areas. Indicators of this flattening include such disparate things as the massive increase in quantity and quality of China's industrial capabilities, the strengthening of India's educational systems, the outsourcing of everything technological to both countries, the ever-deeper linking of financial markets, and the ability of companies to develop manufacturing facilities literally anywhere in the world that offers them the greatest economic advantages.

Questions remain, however. While there is indeed a flattening process in some economic and technological areas, is there a corresponding flattening in terms of the development of some type of global, international, homogenous culture? More important for our purposes, how might this impact churches that are at home in the high-tech, digitally connected world and the communication processes that are part of the lives of those churches?

> *A paradox, occasionally noted but not very deeply reflected upon, lies in the present state of what we so casually refer to as "the world scene": this world is growing both more global and more divided, more thoroughly interconnected and more intricately partitioned, at the same time. Cosmopolitanism and parochialism are no longer opposed. They are linked and reinforcing. As the one increases, so does the other.*
>
> Geertz 1999

The answers to these questions are mixed. While we may certainly note what has been termed the "International Society" (international travelers in every country that still hold American cultural values and who group together; Vincent 2007), at the same time there are newer types of cultures such as Japanese "knowledge communities" that blend older ideals (collectivism) with newer communication methods (e.g., low contexting; Yamazaki 2004).

The anticipated influence of ongoing flattening has significance in terms of such areas as cross-cultural argumentation and conflict resolution, areas for which intercultural communication skills will be not optional but essential (Wanis-St. John 2003), especially in fields such as human rights and cultural values (Liu 2007; Baraldi 2006). It even has implications for the very foundations of personhood, identity (Y. Y. Kim 2007; Kim and Hubbard 2007), and nationality (Wiley 2004). Dunch notes:

354

The emerging consensus in recent work on the cultural dimension of globalization since the nineteenth century recognizes that, while standardization and homogenization—through the construction of supposed "universal" standards and normative categories from Greenwich Mean Time to human rights—have been one aspect of globalization, cultural differentiation and heterogeneity have not only persisted in the face of globalization, they have actually been *produced* by it. (2002, 319, emphasis in original; see also Wilson 2004)

Some envision the internet as a homogenizing force, but studies indicate that the equation is not as simple as it might seem. It might not be surprising to discover that culture has an impact on emailing practices (Hasan, Bichelmeyer, and Cagiltay 2005; Widlic, Briggs, and Rivas-McMillan 2007). At the same time, the impact of homogenization can be seen in such things as the difficulty of using a conversational "warm-up" in an email the way we do in face-to-face interaction or of conveying high-context communication via email (where emoticons cannot really *replace* the subtlety of actual facial or bodily reactions). Such realities will shape how we communicate without necessarily controlling it. While it may be true that the medium is the message, this does not mean that the medium is not amenable to change in its use when a different message is desired. We can also note that even when English is used, websites intended for higher-context audiences tend to be designed to communicate to their audiences in ways that are not as low context as some might suppose (Würtz 2005).

A significant challenge of flattening involves the reality that our more deeply interconnected and ever more urban world enables connections of more radical fringes that would have been isolated from one another in centuries past. While it is true that almost all the religions of the world have some form of web presence (Ess, Kawabata, and Kurosaki, 2007), it is also true that groups ranging from American militia groups to German neo-Nazis to Islamic fundamentalists have found the internet an effective place to locate and mobilize others of like mind, recruiting them to join their cause, and indoctrinating them in the beliefs and methods of the group. This challenge is more frightening than any other, simply because there seem to be no limits to the information obtainable online, from the manufacture of sophisticated weapons to the testimonies of suicide bombers.

CONCLUSION

One dramatic difference between our world and the world fifty years ago is that the pace of change has accelerated significantly. Unfortunately, it appears that this acceleration will continue into the foreseeable future. Being available

---

SIDEBAR 24.1
MISSIONARIES AS AGENTS OF SIMULTANEOUS FLATTENING
AND DIVERSIFYING

Ryan Dunch notes that the missionary movement needs to be seen at both the macro—or larger—level and the micro-level when we are trying to understand the role it has played in history:

> On the macro level, can we trace a general missionary role in disseminating some of the categories claiming normative validity in the modern order on the basis of their "universality"—the nation, rationality, science and technology, the autonomous individual, religion itself—from European to non-Western societies? On the micro level, might there be ways in which missionaries generated cultural differentiation within and between societies, whether through appropriations of parts of their message or through reactions against them? The first question points us towards the global picture and the role of Christian missionaries relative to other vectors of change in non-Western societies; the second points us towards questions of translation and to indigenous agency in the reception, local expression, transformation, and/or rejection of missionary teachings in local settings. While much work remains to be done, recent scholarship on modern missions suggests affirmative answers to both questions. (2002, 319)

REFLECTION AND DISCUSSION

1. In what ways does this fit and not fit your idea of the roles of missionaries?
2. Do you think missionaries were aware of their role in either process? If so, should they have changed their approach?

24/7 is initially exciting, but the stress of having to be able to make important decisions 24/7 and not having downtime even on days off or while on vacation is already a draining reality faced by many missionary leaders.

Knowing and understanding the issues we have discussed will be increasingly important for agency and church leaders in the years to come (see Borthwick 2012), especially as they both become more diversified in composition and more skillful in reaching the unreached with the good news. In our case study, Jim Reapsome, the founding editor of *Evangelical Missions Quarterly*, reflects on how missionaries have news to deliver in a world that is already full of news, and in a world that increasingly is dissatisfied with traditional religious answers.

CASE STUDY:
DELIVERING BAD NEWS

Reprinted with permission from Reapsome (2000, 8).

I was sitting at home, enjoying a nice lunch with my wife, when the phone rang. Without any preliminaries, the doctor told me I had lymphoma and that I should schedule an appointment with an oncologist right away. That was two and a half years ago and, praise God, I'm alive and well.

Delivering bad news is one of a doctor's toughest tasks. Most doctors get little training in how to do it. They talk to older physicians and try to learn as they go along. Now some medical schools are stepping up their efforts to improve doctors' communication skills.

Delivering bad news is one of the missionary's hardest tasks. For that matter, it's hard for all Christians who take the gospel seriously and love their neighbors. We don't have to tell people they have cancer, but we do have to tell them that they are doomed without faith in the Lord Jesus Christ.

Our bad news is especially painful when we recognize the sincere efforts many of our friends make to please God. They try to be good, decent people. They are as devoted to their religious belief systems as we are to ours. Are they really spiritually bankrupt, with as much hope for life as a freshly cut flower?

This question cuts to the heart of our missionary enterprise. When we insist that Jesus meant it when he said, "Whoever believes in me is not condemned, but whoever does not believe stands condemned already," we face the world's opprobrium. We're like the guy who shows up at a fancy dress ball in his sneakers and blue jeans. It's downright embarrassing.

One day at a gathering of scholars a veteran missionary to the Muslim world was put on the griddle. These people knew that he had built lasting friendships with his Muslim neighbors. One of the men had become his very dear friend. "Do you really believe your good friend is lost and going to hell?" one of the scholars asked. The missionary stood up to the heat. He stared at his notes momentarily, and then with a catch in his throat, he replied, "As deeply as I wish I could say no, on the basis of the word of God I have to say yes." Profound silence reigned.

At another time in another setting, an evangelical theologian explained to a Hindu scholar, "Scripture is clear about Jesus saying, 'I am the way, the truth and the life,' but it does not authorize me to decide who is saved and who is lost. It's God who knows the hearts of the people." To which the Hindu asked, "So a Hindu could be saved without professing faith in Christ?" The Christian answered, "I am not God to tell who is to be saved or not."

He tried to deliver the bad news in a more palatable way. He did not want to be judgmental. It's true, only God knows who is saved and who isn't, but why try to sugarcoat the bad news? Why not say something like, "I'm sorry to say this, but whether you are a Hindu or not doesn't make any difference. Anyone—Protestant, Catholic, or Jew—who refuses to confess Jesus Christ as Lord and Savior will not be saved."

When asked about the eternal destiny of unbelievers, we cannot just wimp out and say, "I don't know. I'll leave that to God." The fact is that we do know the answer, and it makes us uncomfortable, too. People must see our tears and hear the clutch in our throats when we remind them that Jesus said, "No one comes to the Father except through me."

As with doctors so with us, and our missionaries and our pastors. We have to learn how to deliver the bad news truthfully, but without meanness and rancor. We can do this when our own hearts have been melted by God's love and Christ's forgiveness.

REFLECTION AND DISCUSSION

1. Do you agree with Reapsome's analysis? Use biblical reasoning to support your answer.

2. How can intercultural communication skills help us to deliver bad news when we do not have a choice?

Reference List

Achoba, E. 2005. "A Locus for Doing Theologies: Theological Stories at the Front Lines of Grassroots Mission Engagement." In *Doing Theology in the Philippines*, edited by John Suk, 24–36. Quezon City, Philippines: Asian Theological Seminary.

Achtemeier, Paul J. 1969. *An Introduction to the New Hermeneutic*. Philadelphia: Westminster Press.

Adeney, Bernard T. 1995. *Strange Virtues: Ethics in a Multicultural World*. Downers Grove, IL: InterVarsity.

Adeney, Miriam. 2009. *Kingdom without Borders: The Untold Story of Global Christianity*. Downers Grove, IL: InterVarsity.

Adler, Peter S. 1975. "The Transitional Experience: An Alternative View of Culture Shock." *Journal of Humanistic Psychology* 15:13–23.

Allen, Ralph K. 1955. "Mass Media and Intercultural Communication." *Journal of Communication* 5:65–76.

Allender, Dan, and Tremper Longman. 1992. *Bold Love*. Colorado Springs: NavPress.

Allison, Norman. 1984. "Make Sure You're Getting Through." *Evangelical Missions Quarterly* 20 (2): 165–71.

Andersen, Peter. 1991. "Explaining Differences in Nonverbal Communication." In *Intercultural Communication: A Reader*, edited by Larry A. Samovar and Richard E. Porter, 6th ed., 286–96. Belmont, CA: Wadsworth.

Anderson, William B. 1977. *The Church in East Africa, 1840–1974*. Nairobi: Uzima Press.

Applbaum, Ronald L., Karl W. E. Anatol, Ellis R. Hays, Owen O. Jensen, Richard E. Porter, and Jerry E. Mondel. 1973. *Fundamental Concepts in Human Communication*. San Francisco: Harper & Row.

Arasaratnam, Lily A. 2006. "Further Testing of a New Model of Intercultural Communication Competence." *Communication Research Reports* 23 (2): 93–99.

Arasaratnam, Lily A., Smita C. Banerjee, and Krzysztof Dembek. 2010. "Sensation Seeking and the Integrated Model of Intercultural Communication Competence." *Journal of Intercultural Communication Research* 39 (2): 69–79.

Argyle, Michael. 1982. "Inter-cultural Communication." In *Cultures in Contact: Studies in Cross-Cultural Communication*, edited by Stephen Bochner, International Series in Experimental Social Psychology 1, 61–79. Oxford: Pergamon Press.

Arlund, Pam. 2013. "Church Planting Movements among Oral Learners." *Orality Journal* 2 (1): 27–41.

Atkins, Wendy. 2012. "Transforming Worldview through Song." *Evangelical Missions Quarterly* 48 (1): 36–43.

Augsburger, David. 1992. *Conflict Mediation across Cultures: Pathways and Patterns.* Louisville: Westminster John Knox.

Austin, Clyde. 1983. "Reentry Stress: The Pain of Coming Home." *Evangelical Missions Quarterly* 19 (4): 278–87.

Axtell, Roger E. 1991. *Gestures: The Do's and Taboos of Body Language around the World.* New York: John Wiley & Sons.

Baker, Ann C., Patricia J. Jensen, and David A. Kolb. 2002. *Conversational Learning: An Experiential Approach to Knowledge Creation.* Westport, CT: Quorum Books.

Baker, Ken. 2009. "Church Planting and Kingdom Building: Are They the Same?" *Evangelical Missions Quarterly* 45 (2): 160–68.

Bangura, Adbul Karim. 2005. "Ubuntugogy: An African Educational Paradigm That Transcends Pedagogy, Andragogy, Ergonagy and Heutagogy." *Journal of Third World Studies* 22 (2): 13–53.

Baraldi, Claudio. 2006. "New Forms of Intercultural Communication in a Globalized World." *International Communication Gazette* 68 (1): 53–69.

Barna, George. 1991. *What Americans Believe: An Annual Survey of Values and Religious Views in the United States.* Ventura, CA: Regal.

Barna, LaRay M. 1982. "Stumbling Blocks in Intercultural Communication." In *Intercultural Communication: A Reader*, edited by Richard E. Porter and Larry A. Samovar, 3rd ed., 322–30. Belmont, CA: Wadsworth.

Barrett, Charles K. 1987. *A Commentary on the First Epistle to the Corinthians.* Harper's New Testament Commentaries. Peabody, MA: Hendrickson.

Bates, Gerald E. 1980. "Missions and Cross-Cultural Conflict." *Missiology: An International Review* 8 (1): 93–98.

Batten, Alicia. 1997. "Dishonour, Gender and the Parable of the Prodigal Son." *Toronto Journal of Theology* 13 (2): 187–200.

Beamer, Linda. 2000. "Finding a Way to Teach Cultural Dimensions." *Business Communication Quarterly* 63 (3): 111–18.

Bediako, Kwame. 1995. *Christianity in Africa: The Renewal of the Non-Western Religion.* Maryknoll, NY: Orbis.

———. 1998. "Understanding African Theology in the 20th Century." In *Issues in African Christian Theology*, edited by Samuel Ngewa, Mark Shaw, and Tite Tiénou, 56–72. Nairobi: East African Educational Publishers.

Bell, Sandra, and Simon Coleman. 1999. "The Anthropology of Friendship: Enduring Themes and Future Possibilities." In *The Anthropology of Friendship*, edited by Sandra Bell and Simon Coleman, 1–19. New York: Berg.

Benedict, Ruth. 1946. *The Chrysanthemum and the Sword: Patterns of Japanese Culture.* Cambridge, MA: Riverside Press.

Bennett, Milton J. 1998. "Overcoming the Golden Rule: Sympathy and Empathy." In *Basic Concepts of Intercultural Communication: Selected Readings*, edited by Milton J. Bennett, 191–214. Yarmouth, ME: Intercultural Press.

Bensley, Ross Everard. 1982. "Towards a Paradigm Shift in World View Theory: The Contribution of a Modified Piagetian Model." PhD dissertation. Pasadena: Fuller Theological Seminary.

Bentley, Jerry H. 1996. "Cross-Cultural Interaction and Periodization in World History." *American Historical Review* 101 (3): 749–70.

Berger, Peter. 1967. *The Sacred Canopy: Elements of a Sociological Theory of Religion.* Garden City, NY: Doubleday.

Berlo, David Kenneth. 1960. *The Process of Communication: An Introduction to Theory and Practice.* New York: Holt, Rinehart & Winston.

Berry, J. W. 1995. "Psychology of Acculturation." In *The Culture and Psychology Reader*, 457–88. New York: New York University Press, 1995.

———. 2001. "A Psychology of Immigration." *Journal of Social Issues* 57 (3): 615–31.

Blake, Joanna, Grace Vitale, Patricia Osborne, and Esther Olshansky. 2005. "A Cross-Cultural Comparison of Communicative Gestures in Human Infants during the Transition to Language." *Gesture* 5 (1): 201–17.

Blincoe, Robert. 2001. "Faces of Islam: Honor and Shame." *Mission Frontiers* 23 (4): 18–20.

Bochner, Stephen. 1982. "Social Difficulty in a Foreign Culture: An Empirical Analysis of Culture Shock." In *Cultures in Contact: Studies in Cross-Cultural Interaction*, edited by Stephan Bochner, 161–98. Oxford: Pergamon.

Bochner, Stephen, and Adrian Furnham. 1986. *Culture Shock: Psychological Reactions to Unfamiliar Environments.* New York: Routledge.

Borthwick, Paul. 2012. *Western Christians in Global Mission: What's the Role of the North American Church?* Downers Grove, IL: InterVarsity.

Bowen, Nancy R. 1991. "Damage and Healing: Shame and Honor in the Old Testament." *Koinonia* 3 (1): 29–36.

Bradshaw, Bruce. 1988. "Integrity and Respect Are Keys to Muslims Witness." *Evangelical Missions Quarterly* 24 (4): 358–62.

Braman, Sandra, Hemant Shah, and Jo Ellen Fair. 2001. "'We Are All Natives Now': An Overview of International and Development Communication Research." *Communication Yearbook* 24:159–87.

Bresner, Lisa. 1997. "The Fathers of Sinology." *Diogenes* 45 (2): 107–24.

Brewster, E. Thomas, and Elizabeth S. Brewster. 1978. "What It Takes to Learn a Language and Get Involved with People." *Evangelical Missions Quarterly* 14 (1): 101–6.

———. 1982. "Language Learning Is Communication—Is Ministry!" *International Bulletin of Missionary Research* 6 (4): 160–64.

Brislen, Mike. 1996. "A Model for a Muslim-Culture Church." *Missiology* 24 (3): 355–67.

Brown, Rick. 2004a. "Communicating God's Message in an Oral Culture." *International Journal of Frontier Missions* 21 (3): 122–28.

———. 2004b. "How to Make Oral Communication More Effective." *International Journal of Frontier Missions* 21 (4): 173–78.

———. 2006a. "Muslim Worldviews and the Bible: Bridges and Barriers (Part I: God and Mankind)." *International Journal of Frontier Missions* 23 (1): 5–12.

———. 2006b. "Muslim Worldviews and the Bible: Bridges and Barriers (Part II: Jesus, the Holy Spirit and the Age to Come)." *International Journal of Frontier Missions* 23 (2): 48–56.

———. 2006c. "Muslim Worldviews and the Bible: Bridges and Barriers (Part III: Women, Purity, Worship and Ethics)." *International Journal of Frontier Missions* 23 (3): 93–100.

———. 2006d. "Contextualization without Syncretism." *International Journal of Frontier Missions* 23 (3): 127–33.

———. 2007. "Biblical Muslims." *International Journal of Frontier Missions* 24 (2): 65–74.

Bruce, Joe W. 2011. "The Critical Role of Relationships in Missions." *Evangelical Missions Quarterly* 47 (3): 312–17.

Brucker, Joseph. 1912. "Matteo Ricci." Transcribed by John Looby. In *The Catholic Encyclopedia*, vol. 13. New York: Robert Appleton. http://www.newadvent.org/cathen/13034a.htm.

Buechner, Frederick. 1973. *Wishful Thinking: A Theological ABC*. New York: Harper & Row.

Burgoon, Judee K. 1995. "Cross-Cultural and Intercultural Applications of Expectancy Violations Theory." In *Intercultural Communication Theory*, edited by Richard L. Wiseman, 194–214. International and Intercultural Communication Annual 19. Thousand Oaks, CA: Sage.

Burke, L. R. 2010. "Describing Fruitful Practices: Communication Methods." *International Journal of Frontier Missions* 27 (3): 147–56.

Burnett, David. 1988. *Unearthly Powers: A Christian Perspective on Primal and Folk Religion*. Eastbourne, UK: MARC.

———. 2000. *World of the Spirits*. London: Monarch.

Caballeros, Harold. 1993. "Defeating the Enemy with the Help of Spiritual Mapping." *Breaking Strongholds in Your City: How to Use Spiritual Mapping to Make Your Prayers More Strategic, Effective and Targeted*, edited by C. Peter Wagner, 123–46. Ventura, CA: Regal.

Cardon, Peter W. 2006. "Reacting to Face Loss in Chinese Business Culture: An Interview Report." *Business Communication Quarterly* 69 (4): 439–43.

Carson, Donald A. 1985. "The Limits of Dynamical Equivalence in Bible Translation." *Evangelical Review of Theology* 9 (3): 200–213.

Chan, Chung-Yan Joyce. 2003. "Commands from Heaven." *Missiology: An International Review* 31 (3): 270–88.

Chang, Hui-Ching, and G. Richard Holt. 1991. "The Concept of *Yuan* and Chinese Interpersonal Relationships." In *Cross-Cultural Interpersonal Communication*, edited by Stella Ting-Toomey and Felipe Korzenny, 28–57. Newbury Park, CA: Sage.

Chapman, Roger. 1998. "Using an Interpreter: Less than Ideal, but Not All Bad." *Evangelical Missions Quarterly* 34 (1): 54–57.

Chen, Guo Ming, and William J. Starosta. 1996. "Intercultural Communication Competence: A Synthesis." *Communication Yearbook* 19:353–84.

———. 2003. "Intercultural Awareness." In *Intercultural Communication: A Reader*, edited by Larry A. Samovar and R. E. Porter, 344–53. Belmont, CA: Wadsworth/Thomas Learning.

———. 2005. *Foundations of Intercultural Communication*. 2nd edition. Washington, DC: University Press of America.

Cheng, Clara. 2012. "Spirituality in Cross-Cultural Conflict Management." *William Carey International Development Journal* 1 (3): 2–12.

Chinchen, Del. 1995. "The Patron-Client System: A Model of Indigenous Discipleship." *Evangelical Missions Quarterly* 31 (4): 446–51.

Cho, Yong Joong, and David Greenlee. 1995. "Avoiding Pitfalls on Multi-Cultural Mission Teams." *International Journal of Frontier Missions* 12 (4): 179–84.

Choi, Bongyoung, and Gyuseog Han. 2009. "Psychology of Selfhood in China: Where Is the Collective?" *Culture & Psychology* 15 (1): 73–82.

Chu, Godwin C. 1964. "Problems of Cross-Cultural Communication Research." *Journalism Quarterly* 41 (Fall): 557–62.

Chua, Elizabeth G., and William B. Gudykunst. 1987. "Conflict Resolution Styles in Low and High Context Cultures." *Communication Research Reports* 4 (June): 32–37.

Chuang, R. 2003. "A Postmodern Critique of Cross-Cultural and Intercultural Communication Research: Contexting Essentialism, Positivist Dualism, and Eurocentricity." In *Ferment in the Intercultural Field: Axiology/Value/Praxis*, edited by William J. Starosta and Guo-Ming Chen, International and Intercultural Communication Annual 26, 24–55. Thousand Oaks, CA: Sage.

Chuang, Tsu-kung. 1996. "Communicating the Concept of Sin in the Chinese Context." *Taiwan Mission Quarterly* 6 (2): 49–55.

Coertze, R. D. 2000. "Intercultural Communication and Anthropology." *South African Journal of Ethnology* 23 (2/3): 116–32.

Coffey, Steve. 2011. "The Cycle of Christ-Honoring Transformation in Communities." *Evangelical Missions Quarterly* 47 (2): 186–90.

Coggins, Wade T. 1972. "Study Attacks Mission Work among Latin American Indians." *Evangelical Missions Quarterly* 8 (4): 202–8.

Cohick, Lynn H. 2009. *Women in the World of the Earliest Christians: Illuminating Ancient Ways of Life*. Grand Rapids: Baker Academic.

Cole, Harold L. 2005. "Stories Aren't Just for Kids Anymore: A Case for Narrative Teaching in Missions." *Journal of Asian Mission* 7 (January): 23–38.

Comaroff, Jean, and John L. Comaroff, eds. 1991. *Of Revelation and Revolution: Christianity, Colonialism, and Consciousness in South Africa.* Chicago: University of Chicago Press.

Condon, John C. 1964. "Value Analysis of Cross-Cultural Communication: A Methodology and Application for Selected United States-Mexican Communications, 1962–1963." PhD diss., Northwestern University.

Condon, John C., and Mitsuko Saito, eds. 1974. *Intercultural Encounters with Japan: Communication-Contact and Conflict; Perspectives from the International Conference on Communication across Cultures Held at International Christian University in Tokyo.* Tokyo: Simul Press.

———, eds. 1976. *"Communication across Cultures for What?" A Symposium on Humane Responsibility in Intercultural Communication.* Tokyo: Simul Press.

Condon, John C., and Fathi S. Yousef. 1975. *An Introduction to Intercultural Communication.* Indianapolis: Bobbs-Merrill.

Conn, Harvie M. 1979. "Conversion and Culture—A Theological Perspective with Reference to Korea." In *Gospel & Culture: The Papers of a Consultation on the Gospel and Culture, Convened by the Lausanne Committee's Theology and Education Group,* edited by John Stott and Robert T. Coote, 195–239. Pasadena, CA: William Carey Library.

Cornett, Terry, and Robert Edwards. 1984. "When Is a Homogeneous Church Legitimate?" *Evangelical Missions Quarterly* 29 (1): 22–29.

Corradini, Piero. 1990. "Matteo Ricci's Approach to Chinese Civilization." *Dialogue and Alliance* 4 (2): 51–59.

Corrigan, Gregory M. 1986. "Paul's Shame for the Gospel." *Biblical Theology Bulletin* 16 (1): 23–27.

Cortez, Mark. 2005. "Creation and Context: A Theological Framework for Contextual Theology." *Westminster Theological Journal* 67:347–62.

Corwin, Gary. 2006. "A Second Look: Insider Movements and Outsider Missiology." *Evangelical Missions Quarterly* 42 (1): 10–11.

———. 2007. "A Humble Appeal to C5/Insider Movement Muslim Ministry Advocated to Consider Ten Questions." *International Journal of Frontier Missions* 24 (1): 5–20.

———. 2011. "Bounded and Centered Sets." *Evangelical Missions Quarterly* 47 (4): 390–91.

Crook, Zeba. 2009. "Honor, Shame, and Social Status Revisited." *Journal of Biblical Literature* 128 (3): 591–611.

Cunningham, Loren, and David Joel Hamilton. 2000. *Why Not Women? A Fresh Look at Scripture on Women in Missions, Ministry, and Leadership.* Seattle: YWAM.

Dahl, Stephan. 2004. "Intercultural Research: The Current State of Knowledge." Middlesex University Discussion Paper 26. http://papers.ssrn.com/sol3/papers.cfm?abstract_id=658202.

Daniels, Gene. 2008. "Event-Speech as a Form of Missionary Education." *Evangelical Missions Quarterly* 44 (1): 80–87.

————. 2010. "Describing Fruitful Practices: Relating to Society." *International Journal of Frontier Missions* 27 (1): 21–26.

Daniels, Gene, and Don Allen. 2011. "Fruitful Practices: Studying How God Is Working in the Muslim World." *Evangelical Missions Quarterly* 47 (4): 412–18.

Davis, Stephen M. 2008. "The Challenge of Missions in the Twenty-First Century." *Lausanne World Pulse*. http://www.lausanneworldpulse.com/perspectives.php/924.

Dean, Marcus W. 2012. "The Missionary as Cultural Pilgrim." *Evangelical Missions Quarterly* 48 (1): 10–14.

Dearborn, Tim A. 1991. "Spiritual Disciplines Born of the Travail of Language Learning." *Evangelical Missions Quarterly* 27 (1): 26–29.

Decker, Frank. 2005. "When 'Christian' Does Not Translate." *Mission Frontiers* (September–October): 8.

De Jong, Lowell. 2011. "Insider Believers and the Empathy of God." *Evangelical Missions Quarterly* 47 (1): 10–12.

DeNeui, Paul H. 2005. "A Typology of Approaches to Thai Folk Buddhists." In *Appropriate Christianity*, edited by Charles Kraft, 415–36. Pasadena, CA: William Carey Library.

Dent, Don. 2005. "Cross-Cultural Challenge." *Evangelical Missions Quarterly* 41 (3): 314–19.

DeSilva, David A. 1994. "Despising Shame: A Cultural-Anthropological Investigation of the Epistle to the Hebrews." *Journal of Biblical Literature* 113 (3): 439–61.

————. 1996. "'Worthy of His Kingdom': Honor Discourse and Social Engineering in 1 Thessalonians." *Journal for the Study of the New Testament* (64): 49–79.

————. 1998a. "Honor Discourse and the Rhetorical Strategy of the Apocalypse of John." *Journal for the Study of the New Testament* 71:79–110.

————. 1998b. "'Let the One Who Claims Honor Establish That Claim in the Lord': Honor Discourse in the Corinthian Correspondence." *Biblical Theology Bulletin* 28:61–74.

————. 2000. *Honor, Patronage, Kinship and Purity*. Downers Grove, IL: InterVarsity.

Dickerson, Lonna. 2004a. "Planning for Success in Language Learning" *ICCT Learner-notes for Second Language and Culture Learners*. Wheaton: Institute for Cross Cultural Training.

————. 2004b. "Steps to More Effective Missionary Language and Culture Learning." *Evangelical Missions Quarterly* 40 (1): 78–81.

————. 2008. "Getting a Jump Start on Language Learning before Leaving Home." http://www2.wheaton.edu/bgc/ICCT/pdf/LN%20jump%20start.pdf.

Dierks, F. A. J. 1983. "Communication and World-View." *Missionalia* 11 (1): 43–56.

Dinges, Norman. 1983. "Intercultural Competence." In *Handbook of Intercultural Training*, edited by Dan Landis and Richard W. Brislin, vol. 1: *Issues in Theory and Design*, 176–202. New York: Pergamon Press.

Dixon, Roger. 2002. "The Major Model of Muslim Ministry." *Missiology* 30 (4): 443–54.

Dodd, Carley H. 1991. *Dynamics of Intercultural Communication*. 3rd ed. Dubuque, IA: Wm. C. Brown.

————. 1998. *Dynamics of Intercultural Communication*. 5th ed. New York: McGraw-Hill.

Dsilva, Margaret U., and Lisa O. Whyte. 1998. "Cultural Differences in Conflict Styles: Vietnamese Refugees and Established Residents." *Howard Journal of Communications* 9 (1): 57–68.

Dunaetz, David. 2008. "Transforming Chaos into Beauty: Intentionally Developing Unity in Church Plants." *Evangelical Missions Quarterly* 44 (3): 358–65.

————. 2010. "Good Teams, Bad Teams: Under What Conditions Do Missionary Teams Function Effectively?" *Evangelical Missions Quarterly* 46 (4): 442–48.

Dunch, Ryan. 2002. "Beyond Cultural Imperialism: Cultural Theory, Christian Missions, and Global Modernity." *History and Theory* 41 (3): 301–25.

Dunn, James D. G. 1977. *Baptism in the Holy Spirit: A Re-examination of the New Testament Teaching on the Gift of the Spirit in Relation to Pentecostalism Today*. Louisville: Westminster John Knox.

Dye, Wayne T. 1974. "Stress-Producing Factors in Cultural Adjustment." *Missiology* 2 (1): 61–77.

————. 1976. "Toward a Cross-Cultural Definition of Sin." *Missiology* 4 (1): 27–41.

Dyer, Kevin. 1985. "Crucial Factors in Building Good Teams." *Evangelical Missions Quarterly* 21 (3): 254–58.

Dzubinski, Leanne. M. 2008. "Contrasting World Views and Their Implications for Missions in Spain." *Evangelical Missions Quarterly* 44 (1): 48–55.

————. 2011. "Integrating Women into Leadership in Mission Agencies." *Evangelical Missions Quarterly* 47 (3): 356–59.

Earley, P. Christopher, and Soon Ang. 2003. *Cultural Intelligence: Individual Interactions across Cultures*. Palo Alto, CA: Stanford University Press.

Eilers, Franz-Josef. 1999. "The Meaning of Intercultural Communication." *Journal of Dharma* 24 (3): 235–43.

Eitel, Keith. 1987. "The Transcultural Gospel—Crossing Cultural Barriers." *Evangelical Missions Quarterly* 23 (2): 130–37.

Elfenbein, Hillary Anger. 2006. "Learning in Emotion Judgments: Training and the Cross-Cultural Understanding of Facial Expressions." *Journal of Nonverbal Behavior* 30 (1): 21–36.

Elgstrom, Ole. 1994. "National Culture and International Negotiations." *Cooperation and Conflict* 29 (3): 289–301.

Ellingsworth, Huber W. 1978. "Conceptualizing Intercultural Communication." *Communication Yearbook* 1:99–106.

Elliott, John Hall. 1995. "Disgraced Yet Graced: The Gospel According to 1 Peter in the Key of Honor and Shame." *Biblical Theology Bulletin* 25:166–78.

Elmer, Duane. 1993. *Cross-Cultural Conflict: Building Relationships for Effective Ministry*. Downers Grove, IL: InterVarsity.

————. 2002. *Cross-Cultural Connections: Stepping Out and Fitting in around the World*. Downers Grove, IL: InterVarsity.

———. 2006. *Cross-Cultural Servanthood: Serving the World in Christlike Humility.* Downers Grove, IL: InterVarsity.

Elmer, Muriel Irene. 1986. "Intercultural Effectiveness: Development of an Intercultural Competency Scale." PhD diss., Michigan State University.

Engel, James F., and William A. Dyrness. 2000. *Changing the Mind of Missions: Where Have We Gone Wrong?* Downers Grove, IL: InterVarsity.

Engel, James F., and H. Wilbert Norton. 1975. *What's Gone Wrong with the Harvest? A Communication Strategy for the Church and World Evangelization.* Grand Rapids: Zondervan.

Escobar, Samuel. 2002. *Changing Tides: Latin America and World Mission Today.* American Society of Missiology Series 31. Maryknoll, NY: Orbis.

Ess, Charles, Akira Kawabata, and Hiroyuki Kurosaki. 2007. "Cross-Cultural Perspectives on Religion and Computer-Mediated Communication." *Journal of Computer-Mediated Communication* 12 (3): 939–55.

Fabian, Johannes. 1983. *Time and the Other: How Anthropology Makes Its Object.* New York: Columbia University Press.

Falk, Peter. 1979. *The Growth of the Church in Africa.* Grand Rapids: Zondervan.

Fee, Gordon D. 1987. *The First Epistle to the Corinthians.* Grand Rapids: Eerdmans.

Filbeck, David. 1985. *Social Context and Proclamation: A Socio-Cognitive Study in Proclaiming the Gospel Cross-Culturally.* Pasadena, CA: William Carey Library.

Fiori, Katherine L., Edna E. Brown, Kai S. Cortina, and Toni C. Antonucci. 2006. "Locus of Control as a Mediator of the Relationship between Religiosity and Life Satisfaction: Age, Race, and Gender Differences." *Mental Health, Religion and Culture* 9 (3): 239–63.

Flanders, Christopher. 2009. "Fixing the Problem of Face." *Evangelical Missions Quarterly* 54 (1): 12–19.

Florean, Dana. 2007. "East Meets West: Cultural Confrontation and Exchange after the First Crusade." *Language & Intercultural Communication* 7 (2): 144–51.

Fountain, Daniel E. 1975. "The Church and Cross-Cultural Communication in Public Health." *Missiology* 3 (1): 103–11.

Francis, Glen R. 1992. "The Gospel for a Sin/Shame-Based Society." *Taiwan Mission Quarterly* 2 (2): 5–16.

Frankl, Viktor E. 1984. *Man's Search for Meaning: An Introduction to Logotherapy.* New York: Simon & Schuster.

Franklin, Karl. 2005. "Re-thinking Stories." *International Journal of Frontier Missions* 22 (1): 6–12.

Friedman, Thomas L. 2005. *The World Is Flat: A Brief History of the Twenty-First Century.* New York: Farrar, Straus & Giroux.

Frykenberg, Robert Eric. 2003a. "Christians in India: An Historical Overview of Their Complex Origins." In *Christians and Missionaries in India: Cross-Cultural Communication since 1500 with Special Reference to Caste, Conversion, and Colonialism,* edited by Robert Eric Frykenberg and Alaine Low, 33–61. Grand Rapids: Eerdmans.

———. 2003b. "Introduction: Dealing with Contested Definitions and Controversial Perspectives." In *Christians and Missionaries in India: Cross-Cultural Communication since 1500 with Special Reference to Caste, Conversion, and Colonialism*, edited by Robert Eric Frykenberg and Alaine Low, 1–32. Grand Rapids: Eerdmans.

Fujino, Gary. 2009. "Toward a Cross-Cultural Identity of Forgiveness." *Evangelical Missions Quarterly* 45 (1): 22–28.

Gardner, Howard. 1999. *Intelligence Reframed: Multiple Intelligences for the 21st Century*. New York: Basic Books.

Garrison, David. 1999. *Church Planting Movements*. Richmond: International Mission Board of the Southern Baptist Convention.

———. 2004a. *Church Planting Movements: How God Is Redeeming a Lost World*. Bangalore, India: WIGTake.

———. 2004b. "Church Planting Movements vs. Insider Movements: Missiological Realities vs. Mythological Speculations." *International Journal of Frontier Missions* 21 (4): 151–54.

———. 2004c. "Church Planting Movements: The Next Wave?" *International Journal of Frontier Missions* 21 (3): 118–21.

———. 2004d. "How to Kill a Church-Planting Movement." *Mission Frontiers* 26 (6): 14–17.

Gawlikowski, Krzysztof. 2003. "The 'Civilization of Struggle' in the West and Appreciation of Harmony in East Asia: Philosophical and Social Implications of the Two Approaches." *Dialogue and Universalism* 13 (7/8): 17–48.

Geertz, Clifford. 1973. *Interpretation of Culture*. New York: Basic Books.

———. 1999. "What Is a Culture if It Is Not a Consensus?" *Grantmakers in the Arts Newsletter* 10 (2). http://www.giarts.org/article/what-culture-if-it-not-consensus.

Gehman, Richard J. 2005. "Transitioning Cross-Culturally—to the Good Old USA." *Evangelical Missions Quarterly* 41 (2): 174–78.

Geisler, Norman L., and William D. Watkins. 1989. *Worlds Apart: A Handbook on World Views*. 2nd ed. Grand Rapids: Baker.

Gener, Timoteo D. 2005. "Every Filipino Christian a Theologian: A Way of Advancing Local Theology for the 21st Century." In *Doing Theology in the Philippines*, edited by John Suk, 3–23. Quezon City, Philippines: Asian Theological Seminary.

Gilliland, Dean. 2005. "The Incarnation as Matrix for Appropriate Theologies." In *Appropriate Christianity*, edited by Charles Kraft, 493–519. Pasadena, CA: William Carey Library.

Gladwell, Malcolm. 2005. *Blink: The Power of Thinking without Thinking*. New York: Little, Brown.

Gmelch, George. 1985. "Baseball Magic." In *Magic, Witchcraft, and Religion: An Anthropological Study of the Supernatural*, compiled by Arthur C. Lehmann and James E. Myers, 231–35. Palo Alto, CA: Mayfield.

Goble, Phillip E. 1975. "Reaching Jews through Messianic Synagogues." *Evangelical Missions Quarterly* 11 (2): 80–87.

Goble, Phillip E., and Salim Munayer. 1989. *New Creation Book for Muslims*. Pasadena, CA: Mandate Press.

Goforth, Zeke. 2011. "Rice Farming & Church Planting." *Evangelical Missions Quarterly* 47 (4): 404–9.

Gordon, Robert C. 1973. "The Silent Language Every Missionary Must Learn." *Evangelical Missions Quarterly* 9 (4): 230–36.

Goring, Paul A. 1991. *The Effective Missionary Communicator: A Field Study of the Missionary Personality.* Wheaton: Billy Graham Center.

Gosnell, Peter W. 2006. "Honor and Shame Rhetoric as a Unifying Motif in Ephesians." *Bulletin for Biblical Research* 16 (1): 105–28.

Graham, Jean Ann, and Michael Argyle. 1975. "A Cross-Cultural Study of the Communication of Extra-Verbal Meaning by Gestures." *International Journal of Psychology* 10 (1): 57–67.

Gration, John. 1981. "The Homogeneous Unit Principle: Another Perspective." *Evangelical Missions Quarterly* 17 (2): 197–204.

Gray, Andrea, Leith Gray, Bob Fish, and Michael Baker. 2010. "Networks of Redemption: A Preliminary Statistical Analysis of Fruitfulness in Transformational and Attractional Approaches." *International Journal of Frontier Missions* 27 (2): 89–95.

Greenlee, David, and James Stück. 2004. "Individualist Educators in a Collectivist Society." *Missiology* 32 (4): 491–505.

Greer, Bradford. 2002. "Free to Live under the Law: A Model for Islamic Witness." *Evangelical Missions Quarterly* 38 (4): 444–53.

Greeson, Kevin. 2004. *Camel Training Manual.* Bangalore, India: WIGTake.

Gregorc, Anthony F. 1985. *Inside Styles: Beyond the Basics; Questions and Answers on Style.* Maynard, MA: Gabriel Systems.

Gudykunst, William B. 1995. "Anxiety/Uncertainty Management (AUM) Theory: Current Status." In *Intercultural Communication Theory*, edited by Richard L. Wiseman, International & Intercultural Communication Annual 19, 8–58. Thousand Oaks, CA: Sage.

Gudykunst, William B., and Young Yun Kim. 1984. "Preface." In *Methods for Intercultural Communication Research*, edited by William B. Gudykunst and Young Yun Kim, 7–10. Beverly Hills, CA: Sage.

———. 1992. *Communicating with Strangers: An Approach to Intercultural Communication.* 2nd ed. New York: McGraw-Hill.

Gudykunst, William B., and Bella Mody. 2002. *Handbook of International and Intercultural Communication.* 2nd ed. Beverly Hills, CA: SAGE.

Gudykunst, William B., and Tsukasa Nashida. 1986. "Attributional Confidence in Low- and High-Context Cultures." *Human Communication Research* 12 (June): 525–49.

Gudykunst, William B., and Stella Ting-Toomey. 1988. "Culture and Affective Communication." *American Behavioral Scientist* 31:384–400.

Guthrie, Stan. 2004. *Missions in the Third Millennium: 21 Key Trends for the 21st Century.* Waynesboro, GA: Authentic.

Hall, Edward T. 1959a. "The Anthropology of Manners." *Scientific American* 1 (3): 9–10.

———. 1959b. *The Silent Language.* Garden City, NY: Anchor Press.

———. 1976. *Beyond Culture*. Garden City, NY: Anchor Press.

———. 1983. *The Dance of Life: The Other Dimension of Time*. New York: Doubleday.

———. 1990. *Understanding Cultural Differences: Germans, French, and Americans*. Yarmouth, ME: Intercultural.

———. 1991a. *The Dance of Life*. New York: Doubleday.

———. 1991b. "Monochronic and Polychronic Time." In *Intercultural Communication: A Reader*, edited by Larry A. Samovar and Richard E. Porter, 6th ed., 334–39. Belmont, CA: Wadsworth.

———. 1993. *An Anthropology of Everyday Life: An Autobiography*. New York: Anchor.

Hall, Edward T., and Mildred Reed Hall. 1990. *Understanding Cultural Differences: Germans, French, and Americans*. Yarmouth, ME: Intercultural Press.

Hall, Edward T., and William Foote Whyte. 1960. "Intercultural Communication: A Guide to Men of Action." *Human Organization* 19 (1): 5–12.

———. 1963. "Intercultural Communication: A Guide to Men of Action." *Practical Anthropology* 10 (5): 216–29, 232.

Hamill, James F. 1990. *Ethno-Logic: The Anthropology of Human Reasoning*. Urbana: University of Illinois Press.

Hammer, Mitchell. 2004. "The Intercultural Conflict Style Inventory: A Conceptual Framework and Measure of Intercultural Conflict Approaches." IACM Seventeenth Annual Conference Paper. http://papers.ssrn.com/sol3/papers.cfm?abstract_id=601981.

———. 2009. "Solving Problems and Resolving Conflict Using the Intercultural Conflict Style Model and Inventory." In *Contemporary Leadership and Intercultural Competence*, edited by Michael A. Moodian, 219–32. Thousand Oaks, CA: Sage.

Hardage, Jeanette. 2002. "The Legacy of Mary Slessor." *International Bulletin of Missionary Research* 26 (4): 178–81.

Harms, L. S. 1973. *Intercultural Communication*. New York, NY: Harper & Row.

Harris, Philip R., and Robert T. Moran. 1982. "Understanding Cultural Differences." In *Intercultural Communication: A Reader*, edited by Richard E. Porter and Larry A. Samovar, 3rd ed., 62–72. Belmont, CA: Wadsworth.

Hart, William B. 2005. "Franz Boas and the Roots of Intercultural Communication Research." In *Taking Stock in Intercultural Communication: Where to Now?*, edited by William J. Starosta and Guo-Ming Chen, International and Intercultural Communication Annual 28, 176–93. Washington, DC: National Communication Association.

Hasan, Cakir, Barbara A. Bichelmeyer, and Kursat Cagiltay. 2005. "Effects of Cultural Differences on E-Mail Communication in Multicultural Environments." *Electronic Journal of Communication* 15 (1–2). http://www.cios.org.ezproxy.wheaton.edu/EJCPUBLIC/015/1/01512.html.

Haugen, Gary A. and Victor Boutros. 2014. *The Locust Effect: Why the End of Poverty Requires the End of Violence*. New York: Oxford University Press.

Heddendorf, Russell. 1982. "Status and Role." In *Christian Perspectives on Sociology*, edited by Stephen A. Grunlan and Milton Reimer, 90–108. Grand Rapids: Zondervan.

Hegeman, Benjamin L. 2010. "The Flight of the Swans: Discerning Hidden Values in Global Cultures." *Evangelical Missions Quarterly* 46 (2): 166–71.

Hellerman, Joseph H. 2000. "Challenging the Authority of Jesus: Mark 11:27–33 and Mediterranean Notions of Honor and Shame." *Journal of the Evangelical Theological Society* 43 (2): 213–28.

———. 2003. "The Humiliation of Christ in the Social World of Roman Philippi, Part P." *Bibliotheca sacra* 160 (639): 321–36.

Herskovits, Melville J. 1973. *Cultural Relativism*. New York: Random House.

Hertig, Young Lee. 2000. "Liminality." In *Evangelical Dictionary of World Missions*, edited by A. Scott Moreau, 579. Grand Rapids: Baker Books.

Herz, J. C. 2002. "The Bandwidth Capital of the World." *Wired* 10 (8):90–97.

Hesselgrave, David J. 1965. "The Modern Mission Apostolate." *Bulletin of the Evangelical Theological Society* 8 (4): 177–78.

———. 1972. "Dimensions of Cross-Cultural Communication." *Practical Anthropology* 19 (1): 1–12.

———. 1973. "Identification—Key to Effective Communication." *Evangelical Missions Quarterly* 9 (April): 216–22.

———. 1976. "Gold from Egypt: The Contribution of Rhetoric to Cross-Cultural Communication." *Missiology* 4 (1): 89–102.

———. 1978. *Communicating Christ Cross-Culturally: An Introduction to Missionary Communication*. Grand Rapids: Zondervan.

———. 1980a. "Gospel and Culture." *Missiology* 8 (2): 253–55.

———. 1980b. *Planting Churches Cross-Culturally: A Guide for Home and Foreign Missions*. Grand Rapids: Baker.

———. 1982. "The Third Horizon and Missionary Communication." *Trinity World Forum* 7 (3): 5–6.

———. 1983. "Missionary Elenctics and Guilt and Shame." *Missiology* 11 (4): 461–83.

———. 1984. "Contextualization and Revelational Epistemology." In *Hermeneutics, Inerrancy, and the Bible*, edited by Earl D. Radmacher and Robert D. Preus, 693–738. Grand Rapids: Zondervan.

———. 1985. "The Three Horizons: Culture, Integration and Communication." *Journal of the Evangelical Theological Society* 28 (4): 443–54.

———. 1986. "Culture-Sensitive Counseling and the Christian Mission." *International Bulletin of Missionary Research* 10 (3): 109–13.

———. 1987. "Fitting Third-World Believers with Christian Worldview Glasses." *Journal of the Evangelical Theological Society* 30 (2): 215–22.

———. 1990. "Christian Communication and Religious Pluralism." *Missiology* 18 (2): 131–38.

———. 1991a. "Christian Communication and Religious Pluralism: Capitalizing on Differences." *Evangelical Review of Theology* 15 (3): 223–32.

———. 1991b. *Communicating Christ Cross-Culturally: An Introduction to Missionary Communication*. 2nd ed. Grand Rapids: Zondervan.

———. 1997. "Worldview, Scripture and Missionary Communication." *International Journal of Frontier Missions* 14:79–82.

———. 1999. "Third Millennium Missiology and the Use of Egyptian Gold." *Journal of the Evangelical Theological Society* 42 (4): 577–89.

———. 2000a. *Planting Churches Cross-Culturally: North America and Beyond*. 2nd ed. Grand Rapids: Baker Books.

———. 2000b. "Third Millennium Missiology: 'Use of Egyptian Gold.'" *International Journal of Frontier Missions* 16 (4): 191–97.

Hesselgrave, David J., and Edward Rommen. 1989. *Contextualization: Meanings, Methods, and Models*. Grand Rapids: Baker.

Hiebert, Paul G. 1978. "Conversion, Culture and Cognitive Categories." *Gospel in Context* 1 (4): 24–29.

———. 1979a. "The Gospel and Culture." In *The Gospel and Islam: A 1978 Compendium*, edited by Don M. McCurry, 58–65. Monrovia, CA: MARC.

———. 1979b. "Sets and Structures: A Study of Church Patterns." In *New Horizons in World Mission: Evangelicals and the Christian Mission in the 1980s; Papers and Responses Prepared for the Consultation on Theology and Mission Trinity Evangelical Divinity School, School of World Mission and Evangelism March 19–22, 1979*, edited by David J. Hesselgrave, 217–27. Grand Rapids: Baker.

———. 1982. "The Flaw of the Excluded Middle." *Missiology* 10 (January): 35–48.

———. 1983. *Cultural Anthropology*. Grand Rapids: Baker.

———. 1985. *Anthropological Insight for Missionaries*. Grand Rapids: Baker.

———. 1989. "Form and Meaning in Contextualization of the Gospel." In *The Word among Us: Contextualizing Theology for Mission Today*, edited by Dean S. Gilliland, 101–20. Dallas: Word.

———. 1994. *Anthropological Reflections on Missiological Issues*. Grand Rapids: Baker.

———. 1999. "Cultural Differences and the Communication of the Gospel." In *Perspectives on the World Christian Movement*, edited by Ralph D. Winter and Steven C. Hawthorne, 373–83. Pasadena, CA: William Carey Library.

———. 2008a. "Clean and Dirty: Cross-Cultural Misunderstandings in India." *Evangelical Missions Quarterly* 44 (1): 90–92.

———. 2008b. *Transforming Worldviews: An Anthropological Understanding of How People Change*. Grand Rapids: Baker Academic.

Hiebert, Paul, and Frances Hiebert, eds. 1987. *Case Studies in Missions*. Grand Rapids: Baker.

Hiebert, Paul, and Eloise Hiebert Meneses. 1995. *Incarnational Ministry: Planting Churches in Band, Tribal, Peasant, and Urban Societies*. Grand Rapids: Baker.

Hiebert, Paul, Daniel Shaw, and Tite Tiénou. 2000. *Understanding Folk Religion: A Christian Response to Popular Beliefs and Practices*. Grand Rapids: Baker Books.

Higgins, Kevin. 2006. "Identity, Integrity and Insider Movements: A Brief Paper Inspired by Timothy C. Tennent's Critique of C-5 Thinking." *International Journal of Frontier Missions* 23 (3): 117–23.

———. 2007. "Acts 15 and Insider Movements among Muslims: Questions, Process and Conclusions." *International Journal of Frontier Missions* 24 (1): 29–40.

Highet, Gilbert. 1950. *The Art of Teaching*. New York: Knopf.

Hile, Pat. 1977. "Communicating the Gospel in Terms of Felt Needs." *Missiology: An International Review* 5 (4): 499–506.

Hill, Brad. 2005. "Perspectives: Reentering Worship during Home Assignment." *Evangelical Missions Quarterly* 41 (2): 144–46.

Hill, Harriet. 1993. "Lifting the Fog on Incarnational Ministry." *Evangelical Missions Quarterly* 29 (July): 262–69.

Hille, Rolf. 2000. "Ziegenbalg, Bartholomaeus." In *Evangelical Dictionary of World Missions*, edited by A. Scott Moreau, 1043–44. Grand Rapids: Baker Books.

Hoefer, Herbert. 2001. *Churchless Christianity*. Pasadena, CA: William Carey Library.

———. 2002. "Jesus, My Master: 'Jesu Bhakta' Hindu Christian Theology." *International Journal of Frontier Missions* 19 (3): 39–42.

———. 2005. "Gospel Proclamation of the Ascended Lord." *Missiology* 33 (4): 435–49.

———. 2009. "Muslim-Friendly Christian Worship." *Evangelical Missions Quarterly* 45 (1): 48–53.

Hofstede, Geert. 1980. *Culture's Consequences: International Differences in Work-Related Values*. Beverly Hills, CA: Sage.

———. 1983a. "The Cultural Relativity of Organizational Practices and Theories." *Journal of International Business Studies* (Fall): 75–89.

———. 1983b. "National Cultures Revisited." *Behavior Science Research* 18:285–305.

———. 1984. *Culture's Consequences: International Differences in Work-Related Values*, abridged ed. Newbury Park, CA: Sage.

———. 1986. "Cultural Differences in Teaching and Learning." *International Journal of Intercultural Relations* 10:301–20.

———. 1991. *Cultures and Organizations: Software of the Mind*. New York: McGraw Hill.

Hofstede, Geert, Gert Jan Hofstede, and Michael Minkov. 2010. *Cultures and Organizations: Software of the Mind*. New York: McGraw-Hill.

Hogan, Michael. 2007. *The Four Skills of Cultural Diversity Competence*. Belmont, CA: Brooks/Cole, Cengage Learning.

Hovey, Kevin G. 1986. *Before All Else Fails . . . Read the Instructions! A Manual for Cross Cultural Christians!* Brisbane, Australia: Harvest.

Howell, Brian M. 2006. "Globalization, Ethnicity, and Cultural Authenticity: Implications for Theological Education." *Christian Scholar's Review* 35 (3): 3–31.

Howell, Brian M., and Edwin Zehner. 2009. *Power and Identity in the Global Church: Six Contemporary Cases*. Pasadena, CA: William Carey Library.

Hsu, Francis L. K. 1977. "Individual Fulfillment, Social Stability, and Cultural Progress." In *We, the People: American Character and Social Change*, edited by Gordon J. DiRenzo, 95–114. Westport, CT: Greenwood.

Hunter, George G. 1992. "Communicating with Secular People. *Asbury Herald* (Fall): 3–5.

Huszczo, Gregory E. 1990. "Training for Team Building." *Training & Development Journal* 44 (2): 37–43.

Hyatt, Erik. 2009. "Christian Witness in Muslim Settings." *Evangelical Missions Quarterly* 45 (1): 84–92.

Inch, Morris A. 1984. "A Response to 'Contextualization and Revelational Epistemology.'" In *Hermeneutics, Inerrancy, and the Bible*, edited by Earl D. Radmacher and Robert D. Preus, 741–50. Grand Rapids: Zondervan.

Jackson, Ronald L., II, and Thurmon Garner. 1998. "Tracing the Evolution of 'Race,' 'Ethnicity,' and 'Culture' in Communication Studies." *Howard Journal of Communications* 9 (1): 41–55.

Jacobs, Donald R. 1979. "Conversion and Culture—an Anthropological Perspective with Reference to East Africa." In *Gospel & Culture: The Papers of a Consultation on the Gospel and Culture, Convened by the Lausanne Committee's Theology and Education Group*, edited by John Stott and Robert T. Coote, 175–94. Pasadena, CA: William Carey Library.

Jandt, Fred E., ed. 2004. *Intercultural Communication: A Global Reader*. Thousand Oaks, CA: Sage.

Jeyaraj, Daniel. 2005. "The First Lutheran Missionary Bartholomäus Ziegenbalg: His Concepts of Culture and Mission from a Postcolonial Perspective." *Svensk Missionstidskrift* 93 (3): 379–400.

Johnson, Andy. 2013. "Counsel from the Council: Five Jewels of Wisdom." *Evangelical Missions Quarterly* 49 (2): 204–10.

Johnson, Todd M., and Charles L. Tieszen. 2007. "Personal Contact: The Sine Qua Non of Twenty-First Century Christian Mission." *Evangelical Missions Quarterly* 43 (4): 494–501.

Jones, Larry B. 2009. "The Problem of Power in Ministry Relationships." *Evangelical Missions Quarterly* 45 (4): 404–10.

Jordan, Ivan, and Frank Tucker. 2002. "Using Indigenous Art to Communicate the Christian Message." *Evangelical Missions Quarterly* 38 (3): 302–9.

Kaplan, Robert B. 1966. "Cultural Thought Patterns in Inter-Cultural Education." *Language Learning* 16:1–21.

Kealey, Daniel J. 1989. "A Study of Cross-Cultural Effectiveness: Theoretical Issues, Practical Applications." *International Journal of Intercultural Relations* 13:387–428.

———. 1990. *Cross-Cultural Effectiveness: A Study of Canadian Technical Advisors Overseas*. Hull, Quebec: Canadian International Development Agency.

Kealey, Daniel J., and Brent D. Ruben. 1983. "Cross-Cultural Personal Selection Criteria, Issues, and Methods." In *Handbook of Intercultural Training*, edited by Dan Landis and Richard W. Brislin, vol. 1: *Issues in Theory and Design*, 155–75. New York: Pergamon Press.

Kelly, David C. 1978. "Cross-Cultural Communication and Ethics." *Missiology* 6 (3): 311–22.

Kim, Donghoon, Yigang Pan, and Heung Soo Park. 1998. "High- Versus Low-Context Culture: A Comparison of Chinese, Korean and American Cultures." *Psychology & Marketing* 15 (6): 507–21.

Kim, Min-Sun, Krystyna S. Aune, John E. Hunter, Hyun-Joo Kim, and Jung-Sik Kim. 2001. "The Effect of Culture and Self-Construals on Predispositions toward Verbal Communication." *Human Communication Research* 27 (3): 382–408.

Kim, Min-Sun, and Amy S. Ebesu Hubbard. 2007. "Intercultural Communication in the Global Village: How to Understand 'The Other.'" *Journal of Intercultural Communication Research* 36 (3): 223–35.

Kim, Wong Tok. 2005. "Discovering God's Prior Work in Bringing People to Himself." *Evangelical Missions Quarterly* 41 (1): 78–85.

Kim, Young Yun. 1984. "Searching for Creative Integration." In *Methods for Intercultural Communication Research*, edited by William B. Gudykunst and Young Yun Kim, 13–30. Beverly Hills, CA: Sage.

———. 1995. "Cross-Cultural Adaptation: An Integrative Theory." In *Intercultural Communication Theory*, edited by Richard L. Wiseman, International & Intercultural Communication Annual 19, 170–93. Thousand Oaks, CA: Sage.

———. 2001a. *Becoming Intercultural: An Integrative Theory of Communication and Cross-cultural Adaptation.* Thousand Oaks, CA: Sage.

———. 2001b. "Mapping the Domain of Intercultural Communication: An Overview." *Communication Yearbook* 24:139–56.

———. 2005. "Inquiry in Intercultural and Development Communication." *Journal of Communication* 55 (3): 554–77.

———. 2007. "Intercultural Personhood: Globalization and a Way of Being." Conference Papers—International Communication Association. http://search.ebscohost.com/login .aspx?direct=true&db=ufh&AN=26950368&site=ehost-live.

Kim-Jo, Tina, Veronica Benet-Martinez, and Daniel J. Ozer. 2010. "Culture and Interpersonal Conflict Resolution Styles: Role of Acculturation." *Journal of Cross-Cultural Psychology* 41 (264): 264–69.

Kingsolver, Barbara. 1998. *The Poisonwood Bible: A Novel.* New York: HarperCollins.

Kitao, Kenji. 1985. "A Brief History of the Study of Intercultural Communication in the United States." http://www.eric.ed.gov/ERICWebPortal/contentdelivery/servlet/ERIC Servlet?accno=ED278212.

Klaus, Byron. 2000. "Marginal, Marginalization." In *Evangelical Dictionary of World Missions*, edited by A. Scott Moreau, 597–98. Grand Rapids: Baker Books.

Klopf, Donald W. 2001. *Intercultural Encounters: The Fundamentals of Intercultural Communication.* 5th ed. Englewood, CO: Morton.

Kochman, Thomas. 1981. *Black and White Styles in Conflict.* Chicago: University of Chicago Press.

Kohls, L. Robert. 1976. *Survival Kit for Overseas Living.* Chicago: Intercultural Networks.

———. 1981. *Developing Intercultural Awareness: A Cross-Cultural Training Handbook.* Washington, DC: SIETAR.

Kolb, David A. 1984. *Experiential Learning: Experience as the Source of Learning and Development.* Englewood Cliffs, NJ: Prentice-Hall.

Krabill, James R., ed. 2012. *Worship and Mission for the Global Church: An Ethnodoxology Handbook.* Pasadena, CA: William Carey Library.

Kraft, Charles H. 1963. "Christian Conversion or Cultural Conversion." *Practical Anthropology* 10 (4): 179–87.

———. 1973a. "Church Planters and Ethnolinguistics." In *God, Man and Church Growth: A Festschrift in Honor of Donald Anderson McGavran*, edited by Alan R. Tippett, 226–49. Grand Rapids: Eerdmans.

———. 1973b. "God's Model for Cross-Cultural Communication—The Incarnation." *Evangelical Missions Quarterly* 9 (2): 205–15.

———. 1973c. "The Incarnation, Cross-Cultural Communication, and Communication Theory." *Evangelical Missions Quarterly* 9 (3): 277–84.

———. 1973d. "Toward a Christian Ethnotheology." In *God, Man and Church Growth: A Festschrift in Honor of Donald Anderson McGavran*, edited Alan R. Tippett, 109–26. Grand Rapids: Eerdmans.

———. 1974a. "Ideological Factors in Intercultural Communication." *Missiology* 2 (3): 295–312.

———. 1974b. "Psychological Stress Factors among Muslims." In *Report [of] Conference on Media in Islamic Culture*, edited by C. R. Shumaker, 137–44. Wheaton: Evangelical Literature Overseas.

———. 1978a. "Anthropological Apologetic for the Homogeneous Unit Principle in Missiology." *Occasional Bulletin of Missionary Research* 2 (4): 121–26.

———. 1978b. "Christianity and Culture in Africa." In *Facing the New Challenges: The Message of PACLA, December 9–19, 1976, Nairobi*, 285–91. Kisumu, Kenya: Evangel.

———. 1978c. "Interpreting in Cultural Context." *Journal of the Evangelical Theological Society* 21 (4): 357–67.

———. 1979a. *Christianity in Culture: A Study in Dynamic Biblical Theologizing in Cross-Cultural Perspective.* Maryknoll, NY: Orbis.

———. 1979b. "The Church in Culture: A Dynamic Equivalence Model." In *Gospel & Culture. The Papers of a Consultation on the Gospel and Culture, Convened by the Lausanne Committee's Theology and Education Group*, edited by John R. W. Stott and Robert T. Coote, 285–312. Pasadena: William Carey Library.

———. 1979c. "Communicating the Gospel God's Way." *Ashland Theological Bulletin* 12 (1): 3–60.

———. 1983. *Communication Theory for Christian Witness.* Nashville: Abingdon.

———. 1989. "Contextualizing Communication." In *The Word among Us: Contextualizing Theology for Mission Today*, edited by Dean S. Gilliland, 121–38. Dallas: Word.

———. 1991a. *Communication Theory for Christian Witness.* Rev. ed. Maryknoll, NY: Orbis.

————. 1991b. "Receptor-Oriented Ethics in Cross-Cultural Intervention." *Transformation* 8:20–25.

————. 1991c. "What Kind of Encounters Do We Need in Our Christian Witness?" *Evangelical Missions Quarterly* 27 (3): 258–65.

————. 1994. "Review of *Models of Contextual Theology: The Struggle for Cultural Relevance.*" *International Bulletin of Missionary Research* 18 (3): 131.

————. 1995. "'Christian Animism' or God-Given Authority?" In *Spiritual Power and Missions: Raising the Issues*, edited by Edward Rommen, 88–136. Pasadena, CA: William Carey Library.

————. 1996. "Roots of Acceptance: The Intercultural Communication of Religious Meanings." *Missiology* 24 (1): 131–32.

————. 1999. "Culture, Worldview and Contextualization." In *Perspectives on the World Christian Movement*, edited by Ralph D. Winter and Steven C. Hawthorne, 384–91. Pasadena, CA: William Carey Library.

————. 2000. "Power Encounter." In *Evangelical Dictionary of World Missions*, edited by A. Scott Moreau, 774–75. Grand Rapids: Baker Books.

————. 2005a. *Christianity in Culture: A Study in Dynamic Biblical Theologizing in Cross-Cultural Perspective*. 25th Anniversary ed. Maryknoll, NY: Orbis.

————. 2005b. "Contextualization in Three Crucial Dimensions." In *Appropriate Christianity*, edited by Charles Kraft, 99–115. Pasadena, CA: William Carey Library.

————. 2005c. "Meaning Equivalence Contextualization." In *Appropriate Christianity*, edited by Charles Kraft, 155–68. Pasadena, CA: William Carey Library.

Kramsch, Claire. 2002. "In Search of the Intercultural." *Journal of Sociolinguistics* 6 (2): 275–85.

Kristof, Nicholas D., and Sheryl WuDunn. 2009. *Half the Sky: Turning Oppression into Opportunity for Women Worldwide*. New York: Vintage Books, Random House.

Kroeber, Alfred Louis, and Clyde Kluckhohn. 1952. *Culture: A Critical Review of Concepts and Definitions*. Cambridge, MA: The Museum.

Kronk, Rick. 2010. "Successful Partnership: A Case Study." *Evangelical Missions Quarterly* 46, (2): 180–86.

Kuhn, Thomas S. 1970. *The Structure of Scientific Revolutions*. Chicago: University of Chicago Press.

Küster, Volker. 2005. "The Project of an Intercultural Theology." *Svensk Missionstidskrift* 93 (3): 417–32.

La Brack, Bruce. N.d. "What's Up with Culture? Module 1: What to Know Before You Go." http://www2.pacific.edu/sis/culture/index.htm.

Lai, Patrick. 2007. "Tentmaking Unveiled—'The Survey Says.'" *Evangelical Missions Quarterly* 43 (2): 168–75.

Landry, David T., and Ben May. 2000. "Honor Restored: New Light on the Parable of the Prudent Steward (Luke 16:1–8a)." *Journal of Biblical Literature* 119 (2): 287–309.

Lane, Patty. 2002. *A Beginner's Guide to Crossing Cultures: Making Friends in a Multi-Cultural World*. Downers Grove, IL: InterVarsity.

Larson, Donald N. 1966. "Cultural Static and Religious Communication." *Evangelical Missions Quarterly* 3 (1): 38–47.

Lawrence, Gordon. 1993. *People Types and Tiger Stripes*. 3rd ed. Gainesville, FL: Center for Applications of Psychological Type.

Learner, David L. 1997. "What Color Is Jesus? Or How Can We Present Jesus to a New Culture without Bringing Our Own?" *Mission Frontiers* (July–October): 22–24.

Leaver, Robert. 1997. "Teams in the Workplace: From 'Why' to Cautions." *Innovating* 7 (2): 12–18.

Lebra, Takie Sugiyama. 1984. "Nonconfrontational Strategies for Management of Interpersonal Conflicts." In *Conflict in Japan*, edited by Ellis Krauss, Thomas Rohlen, and Patricia Steinhoff, 41–60. Honolulu: University of Hawaii Press.

Lederer, William J., and Eugene Burdick. 1958. *The Ugly American*. New York: Fawcett.

Lederleitner, Mary M. 2010. "How Convictions Catalyze Fruitful Cross-Cultural Partnerships." *Evangelical Missions Quarterly* 46 (1): 54–59.

Lederleitner, Mary M., and Duane Elmer. 2010. *Cross-Cultural Partnerships: Navigating the Complexities of Money and Mission*. Downers Grove, IL: InterVarsity.

Leeds-Hurwitz, W. 1990. "Notes in the History of Intercultural Communication: The Foreign Service Institute and the Mandate for Intercultural Training." *Quarterly Journal of Speech* 76 (3): 262–81.

Lenchak, Timothy. 1994. "The Bible and Intercultural Communication." *Missiology* 22 (4): 457–68.

Lessard-Clouston, Michael. 2012. "Seven Biblical Themes for Language Learning." *Evangelical Missions Quarterly* 48 (2): 172–79.

Levine, Robert, and Ellen Wolff. 1985. "Social Time: The Heartbeat of Culture." *Psychology Today*, March, 28–35.

Levine, Timothy R., Hee Sun Park, and Rachel K. Kim. 2007. "Some Conceptual and Theoretical Challenges for Cross-Cultural Communication Research in the 21st Century." *Journal of Intercultural Communication Research* 36 (3): 205–21.

Lewis, J. David, and Andrew J. Weigert. 1981. "The Structures and Meanings of Social Time." *Social Forces* 60:432–62.

Lewis, Rebecca. 2004. "Strategizing for Church Planting Movements in the Muslim World: Informal Reviews of Rodney Stark's *The Rise of Christianity* and David Garrison's *Church Planting Movements*." *International Journal of Frontier Missions* 21 (2): 73–77.

Lewis, Richard J. 2009. "How Cultures Work: A Roadmap for Intercultural Understanding in the Workplace." *Evangelical Missions Quarterly* 45 (1): 38–45.

Liebau, Heike. 2003. "Country Priests, Catechists, and Schoolmasters as Cultural, Religious, and Social Middlemen in the Context of the Tranquebar Mission." In *Christians and Missionaries in India: Cross-Cultural Communication since 1500 with Special Reference to Caste, Conversion, and Colonialism*, edited by Robert Eric Frykenberg and Alaine Low, 70–92. Grand Rapids: Eerdmans.

Lieberman, Simma. N.d. "Gender Communication Differences and Strategies." http://www.simmalieberman.com/articles/genderstrategies.html.

Lienhard, Ruth. 2001. "A 'Good Conscience': Differences between Honor and Justice Orientation." *Missiology* 29 (2): 131–41.

Lin, Canchu. 2005. "Culture Shock, Social Support, and Intercultural Competence: An Investigation of a Chinese Student Organization on a U.S. Campus." *Conference Papers—International Communication Association*, 1–43. 2005 Annual Meeting. New York.

Lindquist, Jay D., and Carol Kaufman-Scarborough. 2007. "The Polychronic—Monochronic Tendency Model." *Time & Society* 16 (2/3): 253–85.

Lingenfelter, Judith E., and Sherwood G. Lingenfelter. 2003. *Teaching Cross-Culturally: An Incarnational Model for Learning and Teaching*. Grand Rapids: Baker Academic.

Lingenfelter, Sherwood G. 1992. *Transforming Culture: A Challenge for Christian Mission*. 2nd ed. Grand Rapids: Baker.

———. 1996. *Agents of Transformation: A Guide for Effective Cross-Cultural Ministry*. Grand Rapids: Baker.

Lingenfelter, Sherwood G., and Marvin K. Mayers. 1986. *Ministering Cross-Culturally: An Incarnational Model for Personal Relationships*. Grand Rapids: Baker.

Liu, Shuang. 2007. "Living with Others: Mapping the Routes to Acculturation in a Multicultural Society." *International Journal of Intercultural Relations* 31 (6): 761–78.

Livermore, David A. 2013. *Serving with Eyes Wide Open: Doing Short-Term Missions with Cultural Intelligence*. Updated ed. Grand Rapids: Baker Books.

Livingstone, William P. 1916. *Mary Slessor of Calabar: Pioneer Missionary*. New York: George H. Doran.

Loewen, Jacob A. 1972. "Language That Communicates." *Evangelical Missions Quarterly* 8 (3): 147–52.

Loss, Myron. 1983. *Culture Shock: Dealing with Stress in Cross-Cultural Living*. Winona Lake, IN: Light & Life Press.

Love, Rick. 1996. "Four Stages of Team Development." *Evangelical Missions Quarterly* 32 (3): 312–16.

Lowe, Chuck. 1998. *Territorial Spirits and World Evangelisation: A Biblical, Historical and Missiological Critique of Strategic-Level Spiritual Warfare*. Fearn, UK: Mentor/OMF.

Lustig, Myron W., and Jolene Koester. 1996. *Intercultural Competence: Interpersonal Communication across Cultures*. 2nd ed. New York: HarperCollins.

———. 2005. *Intercultural Competence: Interpersonal Communication across Cultures*. 5th ed. New York: HarperCollins.

———. 2010. *Intercultural Competence: Interpersonal Communication across Cultures*. Boston: Allyn & Bacon.

Luzbetak, Louis L. 1976. *The Church and Cultures*. Pasadena, CA: William Carey Library.

———. 1988. *The Church and Cultures: New Perspectives in Missiological Anthropology*. Maryknoll, NY: Orbis Books.

Ma, Ringo. 2005. "Communication between Hong Kong and Mainland Chinese: Rethinking Cross-Cultural Adaptation." In *Taking Stock in Intercultural Communication: Where to Now?*, edited by William J. Starosta and Guo-Ming Chen, International and

Intercultural Communication Annual 28, 197–213. Washington, DC: National Communication Association.

Mackin, Sandra L. 1992. "Multinational Teams: Smooth as Silk or Rough as Rawhide?" *Evangelical Missions Quarterly* 28 (2): 134–40.

Malina, Bruce, and Jerome Neyrey. 1991. "Honor and Shame in Luke-Acts: Pivotal Values of the Mediterranean World." In *The Social World of Luke-Acts: Models for Interpretation*, edited by Jerome Neyrey, 25–65. Peabody, MA: Hendrickson.

Martin, Judith N., and Thomas K. Nakayama. 2005. *Experiencing Intercultural Communication: An Introduction*. 2nd ed. Boston: McGraw-Hill.

———. 2013. *Experiencing Intercultural Communication: An Introduction*. 5th ed. Boston: McGraw-Hill.

Matsumoto, David, Harold G. Wallbott, and Klaus R. Scherer. 1992. "Emotions in Intercultural Communication." In *Readings on Communicating with Strangers: An Approach to Intercultural Communication*, edited by William B. Gudykunst and Young Yun Kim, 284–97. New York: McGraw-Hill.

Matthews, Victor H., and Don C. Benjamin. 1994. "Honor and Shame in the World of the Bible." *Semeia* 68:1–161.

May, David M. 1987. "Mark 3:20–35 from the Perspective of Shame/Honor." *Biblical Theology Bulletin* 17:83–87.

———. 1997. "Drawn from Nature or Common Life: Social and Cultural Reading Strategies for the Parables." *Review and Expositor* 94:199–214.

Mayers, Marvin K. 1974. *Christianity Confronts Culture: A Strategy for Cross-Cultural Evangelism*. Grand Rapids: Zondervan.

Mbiti, John S. 1975. *The Prayers of African Religion*. Maryknoll, NY: Orbis Books.

McClelland, David C. 1990. *Human Motivation*. Cambridge: Cambridge University Press.

McComb, Marlin R., and George M. Foster. 1974. "Kalervo Oberg, 1901–1973." *American Anthropologist* 76 (2): 357–60.

McConnell, C. Douglas. 1990. "Maps, Masses, and Mission: Effective Networks for Urban Ministry." 1989 Leonard Buck Lecture in *Missiology*. Lilydale, Victoria, Australia: Bible College of Victoria.

———. 1997. "Confronting Racism and Prejudice in Our Kind of People." *Missiology* 25 (4): 387–404.

McGavran, Donald A. 1955. *The Bridges of God: A Study in the Strategy of Missions*. New York: Friendship.

———. 1990. *Understanding Church Growth*. 3rd ed. Grand Rapids: Eerdmans.

McGuire, Dwight. 2010. "2½ Percent: Church Planting Movements from the Periphery to the Center." *Evangelical Missions Quarterly* 46 (1): 24–30.

McKinney, Carol V. 1990. "Which Language: Trade or Minority?" *Missiology* 18 (3): 279–90.

McKnight, Scot. 2002. *Turning to Jesus: The Sociology of Conversion in the Gospels*. Louisville: Westminster John Knox.

McQuilkin, J. Robertson. 1980. "Limits of Cultural Interpretation." *Journal of the Evangelical Theological Society* 23:113–24.

McVann, Mark. 1994. "Reading Mark Ritually: Honor-Shame and the Ritual of Baptism." *Semeia* 67:179–98.

"Men and Women in Partnership." 2011. In *The Cape Town Commitment*. Great Britain: The Lausanne Movement. End notes at http://www.lausanne.org/en/documents/ctcommitment.html#p2-6.

Meral, Ziya. 2006. "Conversion and Apostasy: A Sociological Perspective." *Evangelical Missions Quarterly* 42 (4): 508–13.

Merritt, Ashleigh. 2000. "Culture in the Cockpit: Do Hofstede's Dimensions Replicate?" *Journal of Cross-Cultural Psychology* 31 (3): 283–301.

Michaels, Timothy. 2010. "Friendship, Vodka, Money and the Gospel." *Evangelical Missions Quarterly* 45 (3): 344–49.

Michener, James. 1959. *Hawaii*. New York: Random House.

Midgley, Warren. 2003. "Christian Weddings in Japan." *Evangelical Missions Quarterly* 39 (1): 98–104.

Miike, Yoshitaka. 2003. "Beyond Eurocentrism in the Intercultural Field." In *Ferment in the Intercultural Field: Axiology/Value/Praxis*, edited by William J. Starosta and Guo-Ming Chen, International and Intercultural Communication Annual 26, 243–76. Thousand Oaks, CA: Sage.

Miller, David. 2009. "An Interview with Bruce Olson." *Evangelical Missions Quarterly* 44 (4): 472–78.

Miyashina, Toki. 1998. "Psalm 23 for Busy People." In *Bless the Day: Prayers & Poems to Nurture Your Soul*, compiled by June Cotner, 31. Tokyo: Kodansha.

Modell, Judith S. 1983. *Ruth Benedict: Patterns of a Life*. Philadelphia: University of Pennsylvania Press.

Molinsky, Andrew. 2007. "Cross-Cultural Code-Switching: The Psychological Challenges of Adapting Behavior in Foreign Cultural Interactions." *Academy of Management Review* 32 (2): 622–40.

Montgomery, Helen Barrett. 1910. *Western Women in Eastern Lands*. New York: Macmillan.

Moon, Jay. 2009. *African Proverbs Reveal Christianity in Culture: A Narrative Portrayal of Builsa Proverbs Contextualizing Christianity in Ghana*. American Society of Missiology Monograph Series 6. Eugene, OR: Pickwick.

———. 2012. "Holistic Discipleship: Integrating Community Development in the Discipleship Process." *Evangelical Missions Quarterly* 48 (1): 16–22.

———. 2013. "Using Rituals to Disciple Oral Learners: Part 1." *Orality Journal* 2 (1): 43–63.

Moreau, A. Scott. 1995. "The Human Universals of Culture: Implications for Contextualization." *International Journal of Frontier Missions* 12 (3): 121–25.

———. 1996. "Developing Bicultural Identity: Driving on the Other Side of the Road." *Bridges: A Cross-Cultural Quarterly* 1 (11): 9–12.

———. 2001. "Church Growth Movement." In *Evangelical Dictionary of Theology*, edited by Walter A. Elwell, rev. ed., 199–200. Grand Rapids: Baker Academic.

———. 2002. "Gaining Perspective on Territorial Spirits." In *Deliver Us from Evil: An Uneasy Frontier in Christian Mission*, edited by A. Scott Moreau, Tokunboh Adeyemo, David Burnett, Bryant Myers, and Hwa Yung, 263–78. Monrovia, CA: MARC.

———. 2005. "Contextualization: From an Adapted Message to an Adapted Life." In *The Changing Face of World Missions*, by Michael Pocock, Gailyn Van Rheenen, and Douglas McConnell, 321–48. Grand Rapids: Baker Academic.

———. 2006. "Contextualization That Is Comprehensive." *Missiology* 34 (3): 325–35.

———. 2009. "Paul G. Hiebert's Legacy of Worldview." *Trinity Journal* 30 (2): 223–33.

———. 2010. "Putting the Survey in Perspective." In *Mission Handbook: U.S. and Canadian Protestant Ministries Overseas 21st Edition*, edited by Linda Weber, 34–95. Wheaton: Evangelism & Missions Information Service.

———. 2012. *Contextualization in World Missions: Mapping and Assessing Evangelical Models*. Grand Rapids: Kregel.

Moreau, A. Scott, Gary Corwin, and Gary McGee. 2004. *Introducing World Missions: A Biblical, Historical, and Practical Survey*. Grand Rapids: Baker Academic.

Moreau, A. Scott, and Mike O'Rear. 2004. "Missions Resources on the Web: All You Ever Wanted on Short-Term Missions." *Evangelical Missions Quarterly* 40 (1): 100–105.

———. 2006a. "Missions Resources on the Web: And So the Story Goes; Web Resources on Storytelling, Myths and Proverbs." *Evangelical Missions Quarterly* 40 (2): 236–42.

———. 2006b. "Missions Resources on the Web: Intercultural Communication Resources." *Evangelical Missions Quarterly* 42 (4): 524–29.

Morgan, Timothy C. 2014. "Why We're Losing the War on Poverty." *Christianity Today* 58 (1): 56–58.

Morsbach, Helmut. 1988. "The Importance of Silence and Stillness in Japanese Nonverbal Communication: A Cross-Cultural Approach." In *Cross-Cultural Perspectives in Nonverbal Communication*, edited by Fernando Poyatos, 201–15. Göttingen: C. H. Hogrefe.

Mortensen, C. David. 1972. *Communication: The Study of Human Interaction*. New York: McGraw-Hill.

Morton, Jeff. 2004. "Narratives and Questions: Exploring the Scriptures with Muslims." *Evangelical Missions Quarterly* 40 (2): 172–76.

Moxnes, Halvor. 1988. "Honour and Righteousness in Romans." *Journal for the Study of the New Testament* 32:61–77.

———. 1993. "Honor and Shame." *Biblical Theology Bulletin* 23:167–76.

Mtange, Nebert. 2010. "Discipling Nations: A Kenyan's Perspective." *Evangelical Missions Quarterly* 46 (2): 206–12.

Mudimbe, V. Y. 1988. *The Invention of Africa: Gnosis, Philosophy, and the Order of Knowledge*. Bloomington: Indiana University Press.

Musk, Bill. 1988. *Touching the Soul of Islam*. Crowborough, UK: Broadway House.

———. 1996. "Honour and Shame." *Evangelical Review of Theology* 20 (2): 156–67.

———. 2008. *The Certainty Trap: Can Christians and Muslims Afford the Luxury of Fundamentalism?* Pasadena, CA: William Carey Library.

Mustol, John. 2004. "What Language to Learn First." *Evangelical Missions Quarterly* 40 (1): 74–83.

Naja, Ben. 2007. *Releasing the Workers of the Eleventh Hour: The Global South and the Task Remaining*. Pasadena, CA: William Carey Library.

Nehrbass, Kenneth. 2012. "How Translation Techniques Aid in Communicating the Bible Cross-Culturally." *Evangelical Missions Quarterly* 48 (2): 198–204.

Neill, James. 2006. "What Is Locus of Control?" http://wilderdom.com/psychology/loc /LocusOfControlWhatIs.html.

Neuliep, James W. 2006. *Intercultural Communication: A Contextual Approach*. 3rd ed. Thousand Oaks, CA: Sage.

———. 2009. *Intercultural Communication: A Contextual Approach*. 4th ed. Thousand Oaks, CA: Sage.

Neyrey, Jerome H. 1996. "The Trials (Forensic) and Tribulations (Honor Challenges) of Jesus: John 7 in Social Science Perspective." *Biblical Theology Bulletin* 26:107–24.

Ngai, Phyllis Bo-Yuen. 2000. "Nonverbal Communicative Behavior in Intercultural Negotiations: Insights and Applications Based on Findings from Ethiopia, Tanzania, Hong Kong, and the China Mainland." *World Communication* 29 (4): 5–35.

Ngaruiya, David. 2008. "The Trendy Giant Wounds: Some Lessons from the Church in Africa." *Evangelical Missions Quarterly* 44 (1): 58–66.

Nichols, Laurie Fortunak, A. Scott Moreau, and Gary Corwin. 2011. *Extending God's Kingdom: Church Planting Yesterday, Today and Tomorrow*. Wheaton: Evangelism & Missions Publishing Service.

Nichols, Mike. 2012. "Teaching outside the Classroom: The Power of Relationship." *Evangelical Missions Quarterly* 48 (1): 46–51.

Nida, Eugene A. 1954. *Customs and Cultures: Anthropology for Christian Mission*. New York: Harper.

———. 1955. "Cross-Cultural Communication of the Christian Message." *Practical Anthropology* 2 (2): 36–42.

———. 1972. *Message and Mission: The Communication of the Christian Faith*. Pasadena, CA: William Carey Library.

———. 1999. "Communication and Social Structure." In *Perspectives on the World Christian Movement*, edited by Ralph D. Winter and Steven C. Hawthorne, 429–37. Pasadena, CA: William Carey Library.

———. 2003. "A Contextualist Approach to Bible Interpretation." In *The Bible through Metaphor and Translation: A Cognitive Semantic Perspective*, edited by Kurt Fayaerts, Religions and Discourse 15, 289–98. Oxford: Peter Lang.

Nida, Eugene A., and William D. Reyburn. 1981. *Meaning across Cultures*. American Society of Missiology Series 4. Maryknoll, NY: Orbis.

Nida, Eugene A., and Charles Taber. 1974. *The Theory and Practice of Translation*. Leiden: E. J. Brill.

Nida, Eugene A., and William L. Wonderly. 1963. "Cultural Differences and the Communication of Christian Values." *Practical Anthropology* 10 (6): 241–58.

Nisbett, Richard E. 2009. "Living Together versus Going It Alone: How Asians and Western-ers Think Differently." In *Intercultural Communication: A Reader*, edited by Larry A. Sam-ovar, Richard E. Porter, and Edwin R. McDaniel, 11th ed., 134–44. Boston: Wadsworth.

Nixon, Yumi, and Peter Bull. 2005. "The Effects of Cultural Awareness on Nonverbal Per-ceptual Accuracy: British and Japanese Training Programmes." *Journal of Intercultural Communication* 9:63–80.

"The Nobel Peace Prize 2011." 2011. http://www.nobelprize.org/nobel_prizes/peace/laureates /2011.

North, Eric M. 1974. "Eugene A. Nida: An Appreciation." In *On Language, Culture and Religion: In Honor of Eugene A. Nida*, edited by Matthew Black and William A. Smal-ley, vii–xx. The Hague: Mouton.

Nuckolls, Charles W. 1991. "Culture and Causal Thinking: Diagnosis and Prediction in a South Indian Fishing Village." *Ethos* 19 (1): 3–51.

Oberg, K. 1960. "Cultural Shock: Adjustment to New Cultural Environment." *Practical Anthropology* 7:177–82.

O'Brien, Peter. 1976. "The Great Commission of Matthew 28:18–20: A Missionary Mandate or Not?" *Reformed Theological Review* 3 (September–December): 66–78.

O'Donnell, Kelly. 1999. "The 'Cactus Kit' for Building Resilient Teams." *Evangelical Mis-sions Quarterly* 35 (1): 72–78.

Oliver, Robert Tarbell. 1962. *Culture and Communication: The Problem of Penetrating National and Cultural Boundaries*. American Lecture Series 506. Springfield, IL: Thomas.

Olthius, James H. 1985. "On Worldviews." *Christian Scholar's Review* 14:153–64.

Olyan, Saul M. 1996. "Honor, Shame, and Covenant Relations in Ancient Israel and Its Environment." *Journal of Biblical Literature* 115 (2): 201–18.

Orbe, Mark P. 1997. *Constructing Co-cultural Theory: An Explication of Culture, Power and Communication*. Thousand Oaks, CA: Sage.

Otis, Gerald E. 1980. "Power Encounter: The Way to Muslim Breakthrough." *Evangelical Missions Quarterly* 16 (4): 217–20.

———. 1993. "An Overview of Spiritual Mapping." In *Breaking Strongholds in Your City: How to Use Spiritual Mapping to Make Your Prayers More Strategic, Effective and Targeted*, edited by C. Peter Wagner, 29–47. Ventura, CA: Regal.

Ott, Craig, and Gene Wilson. 2011. *Global Church Planting: Biblical Principles and Best Practices for Multiplication*. Grand Rapids: Baker Academic.

Padilla, Rene C. 1982. "The Unity of the Church and the Homogenous Unit Principle." *International Bulletin of Missionary Research* 6 (1): 23–30.

Parro, Craig. 2012. "Asking Tough Questions: What Really Happens When We Train Lead-ers?" *Evangelical Missions Quarterly* 48 (1): 26–33.

Parshall, Phil. 1979. "God's Communicator in the 80's." *Evangelical Missions Quarterly* 15 (4): 215–22.

———. 1994. *Inside the Community: Understanding Muslims through Their Traditions*. Grand Rapids: Baker.

———. 1998a. "Danger! New Directions in Contextualization." *Evangelical Missions Quarterly* 34 (4): 404–6, 409–10.

————. 1998b. "Other Options for Muslim Evangelism." *Evangelical Missions Quarterly* 34 (1): 38–42.

————. 2001. "Muslim Evangelism: Mobilizing the National Church." *Evangelical Missions Quarterly* 37 (1): 44–47.

"Patron-Client Systems: Overview." 2006. In *Political Theories for Students*, edited by Jaime E. Noce and Matthew Miskelly. http://www.enotes.com/political-encyclopedia/patron-client-systems.

Patterson, George, and Galen Currah. 2003. "MentorNet #12—Missionary Team Building." http://peopleofyes.com/mm/files/MentorNet_12_Missionary_Team_Building.htm.

Patterson, Miles, Yuichi Iizuka, Mark E. Tubbs, Jennifer Ansel, Masao Tsutsumi, and Jackie Anson. 2007. "Passing Encounters East and West: Comparing Japanese and American Pedestrian Interaction." *Journal of Nonverbal Behavior* 31 (3): 155–66.

Patterson, Miles, and Joann Montepare. 2007. "Nonverbal Behavior in a Global Context Dialogue Questions and Responses." *Journal of Nonverbal Behavior* 31 (3): 167–68.

Payne, J. D. 2009. *Discovering Church Planting: An Introduction to the Whats, Whys, and Hows of Global Church Planting*. Colorado Springs: Paternoster.

Peace Corps, ed. 2011. *Culture Matters: The Peace Corps Cross-Cultural Workbook*. http://wws.peacecorps.gov/wws/publications/culture/pdf/workbook.pdf.

Pearson, Helen Bruch. 1988. *The Bent Over Woman*. Wellspring 9. New York: Church Women United.

Pelissier, Catherine. 1991. "The Anthropology of Teaching and Learning." *Annual Review of Anthropology* 20:75–95.

Pesebre, John Ricafrente. 2005. "Balik-Loob: Towards a Filipino Evangelical Theology of Repentance." In *Doing Theology in the Philippines*, edited by John Suk, 117–30. Quezon City, Philippines: Asian Theological Seminary.

Peterson, Brian K. 2007. "The Possibility of a 'Hindu Christ-Follower': Hans Staffner's Proposal for the Dual Identity of Disciples of Christ within High Caste Hindu Communities." *International Journal of Frontier Missions* 24, no. 2 (Summer): 87–97.

Peterson, Brooks. 2004. *Cultural Intelligence: A Guide to Working with People from Other Cultures*. Yarmouth, ME: Intercultural Press.

Pickens, Claude L. 1936. "Moslem Country. A Christian Moslem" (photograph). http://via.lib.harvard.edu/via/deliver/deepLinkItem?recordId=olvwork172687&componentId=FHCL:81823.

Pilch, John J. 1995. "Death with Honor: The Mediterranean Style Death of Jesus in Mark." *Biblical Theology Bulletin* 25:65–70.

Plaisted, Robert L. 1987. "The Homogeneous Unit Debate: Its Value Orientations and Changes." *Evangelical Quarterly* 87 (3): 215–33.

Plueddemann, James E. 2009. *Leading across Cultures: Effective Ministry and Mission in the Global Church*. Downers Grove, IL: IVP Academic.

————. 2011. "Diversity and Leadership: The Challenge of Leadership in Multicultural Missions." *Evangelical Missions Quarterly* 47 (1): 100–103.

Pocock, Michael, Gailyn Van Rheenen, and Douglas McConnell. 2005. *The Changing Face of World Missions*. Grand Rapids: Baker Academic.

Ponraj, S. Devasahayam, and Chandon K. Sah. 2003. "Communication Bridges to Oral Cultures: A Method That Caused a Breakthrough in Starting Several Church Planting Movements in North India." *International Journal of Frontier Missions* 20 (1): 28–31.

Porter, Richard E., and Larry A. Samovar. 1982. "Approaching Intercultural Communication." In *Intercultural Communication: A Reader*, edited by Richard E. Porter and Larry A. Samovar, 3rd ed., 26–42. Belmont, CA: Wadsworth.

Poyatos, Fernando. 1983. *New Perspectives in Nonverbal Communication: Studies in Cultural Anthropology, Social Psychology, Linguistics, Literature, and Semiotics*. Oxford: Pergamon Press.

Priest, Robert J. 1993. "Cultural Anthropology, Sin, and the Missionary." In *God and Culture: Essays in Honor of Carl F. H. Henry*, edited by D. A. Carson and John D. Woodbridge, 85–105. Grand Rapids: Eerdmans.

———. 1994. "Missionary Elenctics: Conscience and Culture." *Missiology* 22 (3): 291–315.

Priest, Robert J., Thomas Campbell, and Bradford A. Mullen. 1995. "Missiological Syncretism: The New Animistic Paradigm." In *Spiritual Power and Missions: Raising the Issues*, edited by Edward Rommen, 9–87. Pasadena, CA: William Carey Library.

Proctor, J. H. 2000. "Serving God and the Empire: Mary Slessor in South-Eastern Nigeria, 1876–1915." *Journal of Religion in Africa* 30 (1): 45.

Prosser, Michael H. 1969. "Selected Sources on Modern International Communication." *Today's Speech* 17 (1): 48–57.

———. 1973. *Intercommunication among Nations and Peoples*. New York: Harper & Row.

Pryce-Jones, David. 2002. *The Closed Circle: An Interpretation of the Arabs*. New York: Harper & Row.

Pylkkänen, Anu. 1997. Women and Politics in Scandinavia. *SJFE: Women and Law in Europe*. http://www.helsinki.fi/science/xantippa/wle/wle14.html.

Raider, Ellen, Susan Coleman, and Janet Gerson. 2006. "Teaching Conflict Resolution Skills in a Workshop." In *The Handbook of Conflict Resolution: Theory and Practice*, edited by Morton Deutsch, Peter Coleman, and Eric Marcus, 2nd ed., 695–725. San Francisco: Jossey-Bass.

Rambo, Lewis R. 1995. *Understanding Religious Conversion*. New Haven: Yale University Press.

Rathje, Stefanie. 2007. "Intercultural Competence: The Status and Future of a Controversial Concept." *Language and Intercultural Communication* 7 (4): 254–66.

Reapsome, Jim. 1998. "Final Analysis: Our American Cake." *World Pulse* 33 (15): 8.

———. 2000. "Final Analysis: Delivering Bad News." *World Pulse* 35 (5): 8.

Redfield, Robert. 1957. *The Primitive World and Its Transformations*. Ithaca, NY: Cornell University Press.

Redford, Shawn B. 2005. "Appropriate Hermeneutics." In *Appropriate Christianity*, edited by Charles Kraft, 227–53. Pasadena, CA: William Carey Library.

Reed, Lyman E. 1985. *Preparing Missionaries for Intercultural Communication: A Bicultural Approach*. Pasadena, CA: William Carey Library.

Reese, Robert. 2006. "African Time." *Evangelical Missions Quarterly* 42 (4): 474–78.

Reid, Michael S. B. 2002. *Strategic Level Spiritual Warfare: A Modern Mythology?* Fairfax, VA: Xulon Press.

Rich, Andrea L. 1974. *Interracial Communication*. New York: Harper & Row.

Richard, H. L. 1998. *Following Jesus in the Hindu Context: The Intriguing Implications of N. V. Tilak's Life and Thought*. Pasadena, CA: William Carey Library.

———. 2001. "Evangelical Approaches to Hindus." *Missiology* 29 (3): 307–16.

Richardson, Don. 1974. *Peace Child*. Glendale, CA: Regal.

———. 1977. *Lords of the Earth*. Glendale, CA: Regal.

———. 2000. "Redemptive Analogies." In *Evangelical Dictionary of World Missions*, edited by A. Scott Moreau, 812–13. Grand Rapids: Baker Books.

Richardson, Rick. 2006. *Reimagining Evangelism: Inviting Friends on a Spiritual Journey*. Downers Grove, IL: InterVarsity.

Rickett, Daniel. 2012a. "Lean on Me: Part 1, the Problem of Dependency." *Evangelical Missions Quarterly* 48 (1): 62–68.

———. 2012b. "Walk with Me: Part 2, the Path to Interdependency." *Evangelical Missions Quarterly* 48 (2): 162–68.

Ritchie, Mark. 1996. *Spirit of the Rainforest: A Yanomamo Shaman's Story*. Chicago: Island Lake Press.

Roembke, Liann. 2000. *Building Credible Multicultural Teams*. Pasadena, CA: William Carey Library.

Rogers, Everett M. 1962. *Diffusion of Innovations*. New York: Free Press of Glencoe.

———. 2003. *Diffusion of Innovations*. 5th ed. New York: Free Press.

Rogers, Everett M., William B. Hart, and Yoshitaka Miike. 2002. "Edward T. Hall and the History of Intercultural Communication: The United States and Japan." *Keio Communication Review* 24:3–26.

Ross, Andrew C. 1998. "Slessor, Mary Mitchell." In *Biographical Dictionary of Christian Missions*, edited by Gerald H. Anderson, 623–24. Grand Rapids: Eerdmans.

Ruben, Brent D. 1982. "Human Communication and Cross-Cultural Effectiveness." In *Intercultural Communication: A Reader*, edited by Richard E. Porter and Larry A. Samovar, 3rd ed., 331–39. Belmont, CA: Wadsworth.

Ruby, Matthew B., Carl F. Falk, Steven J. Heine, Covadonga Villa, and Orly Silberstein. 2012. "Not All Collectivisms Are Equal: Opposing Preferences for Ideal Affect between East Asians and Mexicans." *Emotion* 12 (6): 1206–9.

Ryan, Janette, and Kam Louie. 2007. "False Dichotomy? 'Western' and 'Confucian' Concepts of Scholarship and Learning." *Educational Philosophy and Theory* 39 (4): 404–17.

Salili, Faridey. 1996. "Learning and Motivation: An Asian Perspective." *Psychology and Developing Societies* 8 (1): 55–81.

Samovar, Larry A., and Richard E. Porter. 1972. *Intercultural Communication: A Reader.* Belmont, CA: Wadsworth.

———. 2001. *Communication between Cultures.* 4th ed. Belmont, CA: Wadsworth.

Samovar, Larry A., Richard E. Porter, and Nemi C. Jain. 1981. *Understanding Intercultural Communication.* Belmont, CA: Wadsworth.

Samovar, Larry A., Richard Porter, and Edwin McDaniel. 2010. *Communication between Cultures.* Boston, MA: Wadsworth.

Saporito, Bill. 2012a. "Power Women." *Time*, August 20, 44, 46.

———. 2012b. "Survival of the Fittest." *Time*, July 30, 64.

Saral, Tulsi B. 1978. "Intercultural Communication Theory and Research: An Overview." *Communication Yearbook* 1:389–96.

Sauter, Kate. 2010. "Culture Shock! Successfully Navigating the Transition Phase of Ministry." *Evangelical Missions Quarterly* 46 (2): 142–48.

Schalück, Hermann. 2003. "The Challenge of Globalization and Intercultural Communication: A Missio Perspective." *Ecumenism* 149 (March): 25–31.

Schieleffelin, Bambi, and Don Kulick. 2003. "Language Socialization." In *A Companion to Linguistic Anthropology*, edited by A. Duranti, 349–68. Malden, MA: Blackwell.

Schlorff, Sam. 2006. *Missiological Models in Ministry to Muslims.* Upper Darby, PA: Middle East Resources.

Schragg, Brian, and James R. Krabill, eds. 2012. *Creating Local Arts Together: A Manual to Help Communities Reach Their Kingdom Goals.* Pasadena, CA: William Carey Library.

Schusky, Ernest L., and T. Patrick Culbert. 1987. *Introducing Culture.* 4th ed. Englewood Cliffs, NJ: Prentice-Hall.

Schwartz, Howard. 1969. "Communication and Non-Western Cultures: Parameters for Study." *Today's Speech* 17 (1): 39–42.

Seamands, John T. 1981. *Tell It Well: Communicating the Gospel across Cultures.* Kansas City, MO: Beacon Hill Press of Kansas City.

Seipp, Derek. 2010. "Written by the Hand of Paul: Church Planting Naturally." *Evangelical Missions Quarterly* 46 (3): 266–67.

Shank, David A. 1979. "The Problem of Christian Cross-Cultural Communication Illustrated." *Missiology* 7 (2): 211–32.

Shaw, Mark. 1993. *Doing Theology with Huck and Jim: Parables for Understanding Doctrine.* Downers Grove, IL: InterVarsity.

Shaw, Perry W. H. 2010. "Westerners and Middle Easterners Serving Together: Potential Sources of Misunderstanding." *Evangelical Missions Quarterly* 46 (1): 14–20.

———. 2013. "Patronage, Exemption, and Institutional Policy." *Evangelical Missions Quarterly* 49 (1): 8–13.

Shaw, R. Daniel. 2000. "Rituals and Ceremony." *Evangelical Dictionary of World Mission*, edited by A. Scott Moreau. Grand Rapids: Baker Books.

Shaw, R. Daniel, and Charles E. Van Engen. 2003. *Communicating God's Word in a Complex World: God's Truth or Hocus Pocus?* New York: Rowman & Littlefield.

Sheffield, Dan. 2007. "Assessing Intercultural Sensitivity in Mission Candidates and Personnel." *Evangelical Missions Quarterly* 43 (1): 22–28.

Shenk, Wilbert R. 1996. General Introduction to *American Women in Mission, 1910–1992.* Macon, GA: Mercer University Press.

Ships, Glover H. 1967. "A Survey of Communication for the Missionary with Special Emphasis on Its Cross-Cultural Applications." Master's thesis, Pepperdine College.

Shiraev, Eric, and David Levy. 2004. *Cross-Cultural Psychology: Critical Thinking and Contemporary Applications.* 2nd ed. Boston: Pearson.

Sider, Ron. 2007. "Injustice against Women." *Prism* 14 (1): 40.

"Sierra Leone Woman Barred from Becoming Chief." 2009. BBC News. http://news.bbc .co.uk/2/hi/africa/8413266.stm.

Siku. 2007. *The Manga Bible: From Genesis to Revelation.* New York: Doubleday.

Singer, Marshall R. 1987. *Intercultural Communication: A Perceptual Approach.* Englewood Cliffs, NJ: Prentice-Hall.

Sitaram, K. S. 1980. "Intercultural Communication: The What and Why of It." *Communication* 9 (2): 90–96.

Smalley, William A. 1963. "Culture Shock, Language Shock, and the Shock of Self-Discovery." *Practical Anthropology* 10 (2): 49–56.

Smedes, Lewis B. 2008. "From Forgiveness to Hope." In *Dimensions of Forgiveness: A Research Approach*, edited by Everett L. Worthington, 341–54. Danvers, MA: Templeton Foundation Press.

Smith, Alfred G. 1966. *Communication and Culture: Readings in the Codes of Human Interaction.* New York: Holt, Rinehart & Winston.

Smith, Andy. 2009. "Many Starting Points Can Lead to Jesus." *Evangelical Missions Quarterly* 45 (2): 198–203.

Smith, Arthur. 1971. "Interpersonal Communication within Transracial Contexts." In *Speech Communication Behavior*, edited by Larry L. Barker and Robert J. Kibler, 304–20. Englewood Cliffs, NJ: Prentice-Hall.

Smith, Donald K. 1971. "Changing People's Minds." *Practical Anthropology* 18 (4): 167–76.

———. 1992. *Creating Understanding: A Handbook for Christian Communication across Cultural Landscapes.* Grand Rapids: Zondervan.

Smither, Edward. 2009. "Remembering the Story: Historical Reflection Leading to Spiritual Dialogue." *Evangelical Missions Quarterly* 45 (3): 298–303.

Smythe, Julian. 2011. "Singing Ourselves into Being: The Music of West Papua." *Evangelical Missions Quarterly* 47 (4): 470–75.

Snider, Kimberly E., and Richard Starcher. 2013. "Six Things to Know before You Go." *Evangelical Missions Quarterly* 49 (2): 176–83.

Søgard, Viggo B. 1986. "Applying Christian Communication." PhD diss., Fuller Theological Seminary.

Song, Min-ho. 1997. "Constructing a Local Theology for a Second Generation Korean Ministry." *Urban Mission* (December): 23–34.

Speers, John. 1991. "Ramadan: Should Missionaries Keep the Muslim Fast?" *Evangelical Missions Quarterly* 27 (4): 356–59.

Spencer-Oatey, Helen. 2000. *Culturally Speaking: Managing Rapport through Talk across Cultures.* London: Continuum.

Stafford, Tim. 1984. *The Friendship Gap: Reaching Out across Cultures.* Downers Grove, IL: InterVarsity.

Stahl, Stephen. 1999. "Different Strokes for Different Folks? A Critique of Learning Styles." *American Educator* (Fall): 1–5. http://www.aft.org/pdfs/americaneducator/fall1999/DiffStrokes.pdf.

Stalnaker, Cecil. 2012. "Discovering 'Who' Is the Silver Bullet of World Evangelism: Eight Missiological Implications." *Evangelical Missions Quarterly* 48 (2): 216–22.

Stanley, Brian. 1990. *The Bible and the Flag: Protestant Missions and British Imperialism in the Nineteenth and Twentieth Centuries.* Leicester, UK: Apollos.

Starosta, William J., and Gou-Ming Chen. 2003. "'Ferment,' an Ethic of Caring, and the Corrective Power of Dialogue." In *Ferment in the Intercultural Field: Axiology/Value/Praxis*, edited by William J. Starosta and Guo-Ming Chen, International and Intercultural Communication Annual 26, 3–23. Thousand Oaks, CA: Sage.

———. 2005. "Where to Now for Intercultural Communication: A Dialogue." In *Taking Stock in Intercultural Communication: Where to Now?*, edited by William J. Starosta and Guo-Ming Chen, International and Intercultural Communication Annual 28, 3–13. Thousand Oaks, CA: Sage.

Steffen, Tom A. 1993. *Passing the Baton: Church Planting that Empowers.* LaHabra, CA: Center for Organizational and Ministry Development.

———. 1996. *Reconnecting God's Story to Ministry: Cross-Cultural Storytelling at Home and Abroad.* La Habra, CA: Center for Organizational and Ministry Development.

———. 1997. *Passing the Baton: Church Planting That Empowers.* Rev. ed. La Habra, CA: Center for Organizational and Ministry Development.

———. 1999. "Why Communicate the Gospel through Stories?" In *Perspectives on the World Christian Movement*, edited by Ralph D. Winter and Steven C. Hawthorne, 404–7. Pasadena, CA: William Carey Library.

———. 2000. "Reaching 'Resistant' People through Intentional Narrative." *Missiology* 28 (4): 471–86.

———. 2005. "My Journey from Propositional to Narrative Evangelism." *Evangelical Missions Quarterly* 41 (2): 200–209.

Steffen, Tom, and Lois McKinney Douglas. 2008. *Encountering Missionary Life and Work: Preparing for Intercultural Ministry.* Grand Rapids: Baker Academic.

Steffen, Tom A., and James O. Terry Jr. 2007. "The Sweeping Story of Scripture Taught through Time." *Missiology* 35 (3): 315–35.

Stetzer, Ed. 2003. "In the Workshop: Multi-cultural Teams in Church Planting." *Evangelical Missions Quarterly* 39 (4): 498–505.

Stewart, Edward C., and Milton J. Bennett. 1991. *American Cultural Patterns: A Cross-Cultural Perspective.* Rev. ed. Yarmouth, ME: Intercultural Press.

Storti, Craig. 1990. *The Art of Crossing Cultures*. Yarmouth, ME: Intercultural Press.

———. 1997. *The Art of Coming Home*. Yarmouth, ME: Intercultural Press.

Strand, Mark. 2000. "Explaining Sin in a Chinese Context." *Missiology* 28 (4): 427–41.

Strauss, Robert, and Tom Steffen. 2009. "Change the Worldview . . . Change the World." *Evangelical Missions Quarterly* 45 (4): 458–64.

Sweetman, Will. 2004. "The Prehistory of Orientalism: Colonialism and the Textual Basis for Bartholomäus Ziegenbalg's Account of Hinduism." *New Zealand Journal of Asian Studies* 6 (2): 12–38.

Taber, Charles R. 1983a. "Contextualization." In *Exploring Church Growth*, edited by Wilbert R. Shenk, 117–31. Grand Rapids: Eerdmans.

———. 1983b. "The Missionary Ghetto." *Practical Anthropology* 18 (5): 193–96.

Talman, Harley. 2004. "Comprehensive Contextualization." *International Journal of Frontier Missions* 21 (1): 6–12.

Tannen, Deborah. 1986. *That's Not What I Meant: How Conversational Style Makes or Breaks Your Relations with Others*. New York: Ballantine.

———. 1991. *You Just Don't Understand: Women and Men in Conversation*. New York: Ballantine.

———. 2003. *Communication Matters*. Course 1: "He Said/She Said: Women, Men and Language." Sound recording and text. http://www.modernscholar.com.

Taylor, Julie. 2012. "Beyond Song: Transforming the Reality of God's Kingdom through All the Arts." *Evangelical Missions Quarterly* 48 (1): 38–39.

Tennent, Timothy C. 2006. "Followers of Jesus (Isa) in Islamic Mosques: A Closer Examination of C-5 'High Spectrum' Contextualization." *International Journal of Frontier Missions* 2 (Fall): 101–15.

Thelle, Notto R. 2006. "Changed by the East: Notes on Missionary Communication and Transformation." *International Bulletin of Missionary Research* 30 (3): 115–18, 120–21.

Thoreau, Henry David. 1854. *Walden; or, Life in the Woods*. Boston: Ticknor & Fields.

Ting-Toomey, Stella. 1985. "Toward a Theory of Conflict and Culture." In *Communication, Culture, and Organizational Processes*, edited by William B. Gudykunst, Lea P. Stewart, and Stella Ting-Toomey, 71–86. Beverly Hills, CA: Sage.

———. 1989. "Intergroup Communication and Simulation in Low- and High-Cultures." In *Communication and Simulation: From Two Fields to One Theme*, edited by David Crookall and Danny Saunders, 169–76. Philadelphia: Multilingual Matters.

———. 1999. *Communicating across Cultures*. New York: Guilford Press.

———. 2007. "Intercultural Conflict Training: Theory-Practice Approaches and Research Challenges." *Journal of Intercultural Communication Research* 36 (3): 255–71.

Ting-Toomey, Stella, and Leeva C. Chung. 2012. *Understanding Intercultural Communication*. 2nd ed. New York: Oxford University Press.

Tino, James. 2008. "A Lesson from Jose: Understanding the Patron/Client Relationship." *Evangelical Missions Quarterly* 44 (3): 320–27.

Tiplady, Richard. 2002. "Introduction: Losing My Religion?" In *Postmission: World Mission by a Postmodern Generation*, edited by Richard Tiplady, xi–xxii. Waynesboro, GA: Paternoster.

Tippett, Alan R. 1972. "Taking a Hard Look at the 'Barbados Declaration.'" *Evangelical Missions Quarterly* 8 (4): 209–17.

Todd, Terry L. 1999. "Incarnational Learners: Overcoming Language and Culture Barriers Involves Repudiating One's Privileges." *Evangelical Missions Quarterly* 35 (4): 446–52.

———. 2001. "In the Workshop: If You Can't Stand the Heat." *Evangelical Missions Quarterly* 37 (2): 234–36.

Toulmin, Stephen. 1961. *An Examination of the Place of Reason in Ethics*. Cambridge: Cambridge University Press.

Travis, John. 2000. "Messianic Muslim Followers of Isa: A Closer Look at C5 Believers and Congregations." *International Journal of Frontier Missions* 19 (1): 53–59.

———. 2008. "Deep-Level Healing Prayer in Cross-Cultural Ministry." In Van Engen, Woodberry, and Whiteman 2008, 106–15.

Triandis, Harry C. 1992. "Collectivism v. Individualism: A Reconceptualisation of a Basic Concept in Cross-Cultural Psychology." In *Readings on Communicating with Strangers: An Approach to Intercultural Communication*, edited by William B. Gudykunst and Young Yun Kim, 71–82. New York: McGraw-Hill.

———. 1995. *Individualism and Collectivism*. Oxford: Westview Press.

Trueman, Tom. 1989. "Fresh Thinking on Muslim Missions." *Mission Frontiers* (November/December). http://www.missionfrontiers.org/issue/article/fresh-thinking-on-muslim-missions.

Trumbull, Elise, and Carrie Rothstein-Fisch. 2008. "Cultures in Harmony." *Educational Leadership* 66 (1): 63–66.

Tucker, Ruth, and Walter Liefeld. 1987. *Daughters of the Church: Women and Ministry from New Testament Times to the Present*. Grand Rapids: Zondervan.

Ueda, Keiko. 1974. "Sixteen Ways to Avoid Saying No in Japan." In *Intercultural Encounters with Japan: Communication-Contact and Conflict; Perspectives from the International Conference on Communication across Cultures Held at International Christian University in Tokyo Saito*, edited by John Condon and Mitsuko Saito, 185–92. Tokyo: Simul Press.

Unseth, Peter. 2013. "Using Local Proverbs in Ministry." *Evangelical Missions Quarterly* 49 (1): 16–23.

Van Engen, Charles E., J. Dudley Woodberry, and Darrell Whiteman, eds. 2008. *Paradigm Shifts in Christian Witness: Insights from Anthropology, Communication, and Spiritual Power*. Maryknoll, NY: Orbis.

Van Meurs, Nathalie, and Helen Spencer-Oatey. 2009. "Multidisciplinary Perspectives on Intercultural Conflict: The 'Bermuda Triangle' of Conflict, Culture, and Communication." In *Handbook of Intercultural Communication*, edited by Helga Kotthoff and Helen Spencer-Oatey, 99–120. Berlin: Mouton de Gruyter.

Van Rheenen, Gailyn. 1991. *Communicating Christ in Animistic Contexts*. Grand Rapids: Baker.

————. 1993. "Cultural Conceptions of Power in Biblical Perspective." *Missiology* 21 (1): 41–53.

Verryn, T. D. 1983. "What Is Communication? Searching for a Missiological Model." *Missionalia* 11:17–25.

Vincent, Cindy. 2007. "Becoming a Member of the International Society: A Closer Examination of the Globalized International Community." *Conference Papers—International Communication Association 2007 Annual Meeting*, 1–27.

Virts, Paul H. 1990. "Selecting Effective Communication Media for Evangelism." *Evangelical Missions Quarterly* 26 (3): 282–87.

Wagner, C. Peter. 1981. *Church Growth and the Whole Gospel: A Biblical Mandate*. San Francisco: Harper & Row.

————. 1990. *Church Planting for a Greater Harvest: A Comprehensive Guide*. Ventura, CA: Regal.

————. 1996. *Confronting the Powers: How the New Testament Church Experienced the Power of Strategic-Level Spiritual Warfare*. Ventura, CA: Regal.

————. 1998. *Confronting the Queen of Heaven*. Colorado Springs: Wagner Institute for Practical Ministry.

Wakely, Mike. 2004. "The Search for the Golden Key." *Evangelical Missions Quarterly* 30 (1): 12–22.

Waldrep, Richard Brent. 2007. "Contextualization and Church Planting." http://www.northamericanmissions.org/?q=node/365.

Walker, Keith. 2013. "All Cretans Are Liars: Reflections on Aspects of Cross-Cultural Analysis and Training." *Evangelical Missions Quarterly* 49 (2): 156–63.

Walls, Andrew. 1990. "The Translation Principle in Christian History." In *Bible Translation and the Spread of the Church: The Last 200 Years*, edited by Philip C. Stine, 24–39. Leiden: E. J. Brill.

Walsh, Brian J. 1992. "Worldviews, Modernity and the Task of Christian College Education." *Faculty Dialogue: Journal of the Institute for Christian Leadership* 18 (Fall): 13–35.

Wanis-St. John, Anthony. 2003. "Thinking Globally and Acting Locally." *Negotiation Journal* 19 (4): 389–96.

Ward, Ted. 1982. "Christian Missions—Survival in What Forms?" *International Bulletin of Missionary Research* 6 (1): 2–3.

————. 1984. *Living Overseas: A Book of Preparations*. New York: Free Press.

Waterhouse, Lynn. 2006. "Inadequate Evidence for Multiple Intelligences, Mozart Effect, and Emotional Intelligence Theories." *Educational Psychologist* 41 (4): 247–55.

Watzlawick, Paul, Janet Helmick Beavin, and Don D. Jackson. 1967. *Pragmatics of Human Communication: A Study of Interactional Patterns, Pathologies, and Paradoxes*. New York: W. W. Norton.

Wendland, Ernst R. 1995. "The 'Interference Factor' in Christian Cross-Cultural Communication." *Missiology: An International Review* 23 (3): 267–80.

White, John. 1992. *Changing on the Inside*. Ann Arbor, MI: Vine Press.

White, Mark. 1996. "Matteo Ricci's Lesson to a Modern Missionary." *America* 175 (4): 21.

Whiteman, Darrell L. 1981. "Some Relevant Anthropological Concepts for Effective Cross-Cultural Ministry." *Missiology* 9 (2): 223–39.

———. 1984. "Effective Communication of the Gospel amid Cultural Diversity." *Missiology* 12 (3): 275–86.

Widlic, Kevin, Rob Briggs, and Maria Rivas-McMillan. 2007. "Describe a Cultural Miscommunication That You Experienced and How You Would Handle It Differently Now." *Communication World* 24 (1): 14.

Wiley, Stephen B. Crofts. 2004. "Rethinking Nationality in the Context of Globalization." *Communication Theory* 14 (1): 78–96.

Willis, Mark. 1996. "Learning to Speak All Over Again." *Evangelical Missions Quarterly* 32 (4): 435–36.

Wilson, Henry S. 2004. "Mission and Cultures: Some Paradigms of Encounter." *Asia Journal of Theology* 18 (1): 14–32.

Wimber, John. 1990. "Power Evangelism: Definitions and Directions." In *Wrestling with Dark Angels: Toward a Deeper Understanding of the Supernatural Forces in Spiritual Warfare*, edited by C. Peter Wagner and F. Douglas Pennoyer, 13–42. Ventura, CA: Regal.

Wink, Walter. 1992. *Engaging the Powers: Discernment and Resistance in a World of Dominion*. Philadelphia: Fortress Press.

Winter, Ralph D. 1971. "Churches Need Missions because Modalities Need Sodalities." *Evangelical Missions Quarterly* 7 (4): 193–200.

———. 1974. "The Two Structures of God's Redemptive Mission." *Missiology* 2 (1): 121–39.

———. 2005. "Editorial Comment." *Mission Frontiers* (September–October): 4–5.

Wolterstorff, Nicholas. 1976. *Reason within the Bounds of Religion*. Grand Rapids: Eerdmans.

"Women in National Parliaments." 2013. Women in Parliaments: World and Regional Averages. http://www.ipu.org/wmn-e/world.htm.

Wong-McDonald, Ana, and Richard L. Gorsuch. 2004. "A Multivariate Theory of God Concept, Religious Motivation, Locus of Control, Coping, and Spiritual Well-Being." *Journal of Psychology and Theology* 32 (4): 318–34.

Wood, Beulah. 2011. "Injustice & Women in Families: Why Christian Ministries Must Fight for Change." *Evangelical Missions Quarterly* 47 (4): 450–56.

Woodberry, J. Dudley. 2007. "To the Muslim I Became a Muslim?" *International Journal of Frontier Missions* 24 (1): 23–28.

———, ed. 2011. *From Seed to Fruit: Global Trends, Fruitful Practices, and Emerging Issues among Muslims*. Rev. and enlarged 2nd ed. Pasadena, CA: William Carey Library.

Woodley, Randy. 2000. "Putting It to the Test: A Look at Congregations That Are Aiming to Worship with Native Forms." *Mission Frontiers* (September). http://www.missionfrontiers.org/issue/article/putting-it-to-the-test.

Wright, C. Thomas. 1998. "Contextual Evangelism Strategies." In *Missiology: An Introduction to the Foundations, History, and Strategies of World Missions*, edited by John Mark Terry, Ebbie Smith, and Justice Anderson, 450–66. Nashville: Broadman & Holman.

Wright, N. T. 1997. *For All God's Worth: True Worship and the Calling of the Church.* Grand Rapids: Eerdmans.

Würtz, Elizabeth. 2005. "Intercultural Communication on Web Sites: A Cross-Cultural Analysis of Web Sites from High-Context Cultures and Low-Context Cultures." *Journal of Computer-Mediated Communication* 11 (1): 274–99.

Yamawaki, Niwako. 2012. "Within-Culture Variations of Collectivism in Japan." *Journal of Cross-Cultural Psychology* 43 (8): 1191–204.

Yamazaki, Hideo. 2004. "East Meets West in Japanese Communities." *KM Review* 7 (2): 24–27.

Yip, Tai M. 1995. "Spiritual Mapping." *Evangelical Missions Quarterly* 31 (2): 166–70.

Yoder, Michael L., Michael H. Lee, Jonathan Ro, and Robert J. Priest. 2009. "Understanding Christian Identity in Terms of Bounded and Centered Set Theory in the Writings of Paul G. Hiebert." *Trinity Journal* 30 (Fall): 177–88.

Zahniser, A. H. Mathias. 1997. *Symbol and Ceremony.* Monrovia, CA: MARC.

Zdero, Rad. 2004. *The Global House Church Movement.* Pasadena, CA: William Carey Library.

———. 2005. "Launching House Church Movements." *Mission Frontiers* 27 (2): 16–19.

———. 2011. "The Apostolic Strategy of House Churches for Mission Today." *Evangelical Missions Quarterly* 47 (3): 346–53.

Zehner, Damaris. 2005. "Building Teams, Building Walls." *Evangelical Missions Quarterly* 41 (3): 362–69.

Zheng, X., and J. W. Berry. 1991. "Psychological Adaptation of Chinese Sojourners in Canada." *International Journal of Psychology* 26 (4): 451–70.

Zhu, Yanxia, and Deborah Valentine. 2001. "Using a Knowledge-Based Approach to Develop Student Intercultural Competence in Industry." *Business Communication Quarterly* 64 (3): 102–9.

Subject Index

Scripture Index